S0-ABO-399

Principles of Public Speaking

FIFTEENTH EDITION

Kathleen M. German
Miami University of Ohio

Bruce E. Gronbeck
The University of Iowa

Douglas Ehninger

Alan H. Monroe

PEARSON

Boston   New York   San Francisco
Mexico City   Montreal   Toronto   London   Madrid   Munich   Paris
Hong Kong   Singapore   Tokyo   Cape Town   Sydney

Executive Editor: *Karon Bowers*
Senior Developmental Editor: *Ellen Darion*
Associate Editor: *Shannon Morrow*
Series Editorial Assistant: *Jennifer Trebby*
Marketing Manager: *Mandee Eckersley*
Composition Buyer: *Linda Cox*
Manufacturing Buyer: *Megan Cochran*
Designer: *Ellen Pettengell*
Editorial-Production Administrator: *Karen Mason*
Editorial-Production Service: *Omegatype Typography, Inc.*
Photo Research: *Katharine S. Cook*
Cover Administrator: *Linda Knowles*
Cover Designer: *Suzanne Harbison*
Electronic Composition: *Omegatype Typography, Inc.*

Copyright © 2004, 2001 Pearson Education, Inc.

All rights reserved. No part of the material protected by this copyright notice may be reproduced or utilized in any form or by any means, electronic or mechanical, including photocopying, recording, or by any information storage and retrieval system, without the written permission from the copyright owner.

To obtain permission(s) to use material from this work, please submit a written request to Allyn and Bacon, Permissions Department, 75 Arlington Street, Boston, MA 02116 or fax your request to 617-848-7320.

Between the time Website information is gathered and then published, it is not unusual for some sites to have closed. Also, the transcription of URLs can result in unintended typographical errors. The publisher would appreciate notification where these errors occur so that they may be corrected in subsequent editions.

Library of Congress Cataloging-in-Publication Data

Principles of public speaking / Kathleen M. German . . . [et al.].—15th ed.
    p. cm.
   Includes bibliographical references and index.
   ISBN 0-205-38067-0
    1. Public speaking.   I. German, Kathleen M.

  PN4129.15P75   2004
  808.5'1—dc21

                                              2002038646

Printed in the United States of America

10 9 8 7 6 5 4 3 2 1 RRD-OH 08 07 06 05 04 03

See photo and permissions credits on page 316, which constitutes a continuation of the copyright page.

Brief Contents

Contents

Part 2	Planning and Preparing Your Speech

Part 3   Presenting Your Speech

Part 4   Types of Public Speaking

Boxed Features

**Speaking of . . .
Apprehension**

**Speaking of . . .
Ethics**

**Speaking of . . .
Skills**

Preface

A TRADITION OF EXCELLENCE

Principles of Public Speaking, Fifteenth Edition, presents the fundamental principles that have helped thousands of students gain the expertise and confidence to speak in public. It combines the latest research of scholars in rhetorical and communication theory with practical advice to students on how to speak effectively in a culturally diverse society. It retains the core concepts that have been its trademark from its inception (e.g., Monroe's Motivated Sequence), while it also adapts electronic resources and technology to public speaking. Three keynote statements describe the basic approach of the book:

1. This textbook gets you on your feet quickly. Although you will need a communication vocabulary to prepare and critique speeches, you must also put concepts into practice early. Chapter 2, "Getting Started," will get you on your feet and speaking to your classmates. Later chapters will develop ideas in more detail to help you increase your expertise as a public speaker and a critical listener.

2. This textbook focuses on communication in your college life but also includes examples from the worlds of work, politics, and social activism. We recognize that your college environment probably commands your immediate attention, but we're sensitive to the fact that you're preparing for a lifetime of public participation. Therefore, we have incorporated applications and examples from both the college world and the world beyond.

3. This textbook challenges you technically, intellectually, and morally. Throughout your life, you will be expected to know how to accomplish goals (technical skills), how to analyze situations and propose courses of action (intellectual skills), and how to lead your social and professional lives in trustworthy ways (moral development). This book challenges you not only to develop your skills and thought processes through public speaking and critical listening but also to understand your responsibilities as a speaker and a listener.

THE PLAN OF THE BOOK

Principles of Public Speaking, Fifteenth Edition, is organized into four parts, reflecting the four major emphases of most contemporary courses in public speaking. Part 1, "Public Speaking and Critical Listening," provides you with *an orientation to the communication process.* Here you will encounter the conceptual underpinnings of communication theory; examine the public speaking skills that will enhance your success in school, at work, and in society; and learn how to adapt your ideas to the folks who make all the difference—the people in your audience. In Chapter 4, "Public Speaking and Cultural Life," you will consider the connection between culture and public speaking so that you will recognize the importance of attending to cultural differences. The chapters in Part I introduce important ways to think about speechmaking, even as you give your first classroom speeches. Numerous examples show you how the particular skills involved in public speaking apply to a variety of real-world contexts.

Part 2, "Planning and Preparing Your Speech," offers *a step-by-step approach to speech preparation.* You will learn how to confront and conquer your fears of public speaking by breaking down this complex task into its component parts: setting your purposes, articulating central ideas, finding and assessing supporting materials, organizing and outlining these materials, and building effective introductions and conclusions.

Building a speech is the first half of the speechmaking process. The other half is actually delivering your speech—putting your presentation into words, gestures, bodily actions, vocal patterns, and visual aids. That's what Part 3, "Presenting Your Speech," is all about. Every time you speak, you're communicating by way of four channels: language, sounds, movements, and visuals. The chapters in Part 3 will help you master how to send and control the message flowing through each channel.

There are many different kinds of speeches, each with its own demands and conventional rules. In Part 4, "Types of Public Speaking," you will learn about three broad categories of speeches: speeches to inform, speeches to persuade, and argumentative speeches. Studying the characteristics of each of these types of speeches will help you refine your speechmaking skills and learn how to adapt them to particular speaking occasions.

FEATURES OF THE BOOK

With each new edition we strive to keep the text up to date and lively by rewriting material, reorganizing sections, and refining the features that complement the presentation. Features in the Fifteenth Edition include the following:

1. New! This edition breaks away from traditional instruction and offers you a way to "teach outside the book."

▶ **VideoWorkshop.** This integrated system of learning guides and CD-ROM video footage engages students by showing examples of speakers in action. End-of-chapter exercises correlate with VideoWorkshop modules.

▶ **Expanded coverage of electronic and World Wide Web databases.** Chapter 6 in particular will guide you in using these technologies to find and assess supporting materials and evaluate the types and use of computer-generated visual aids.

▶ **Using the Web activities.** These exercises at the end of each chapter will familiarize you with how to use the Internet as a research tool.

▶ **Web Exploration icons tie the text to the Companion Website.**
The book's Website, www.ablongman.com/german15e, includes links to
additional electronic resources and interactive tools that are integrated
with core concepts presented in the book.

**2. New! Focus on orality as a central experience in contemporary so-
ciety.** Although digital resources play an important role in preparing to speak,
Principles of Public Speaking, Fifteenth Edition, is committed to showing student
speakers why oral, face-to-face communication constitutes the core of human relations and culture. Chapter 1 introduces the idea of orality, and the following chapters develop the mechanisms whereby speechmaking builds the bonds of
society.

3. Appreciation of diversity. Serious attention to the role of cultural practices reflects the fact that we live and interact in an increasingly diverse society.
Successful public speakers recognize the connections between culture and public speaking and are able to adjust their styles and presentations to their audience. Chapter 4, "Public Speaking and Cultural Life," focuses specifically on the
role of culture in communication.

4. Critical thinking emphasis. Critical thinking is an important part of
overall education, including speech instruction. We cover critical thinking
throughout the book and highlight the topic with special emphasis in Chapter 3,
"Critical Listening," and Chapter 14, "Argumentation and Critical Thinking."

5. Attention to ethics in public speaking. We discuss speech ethics in
the first chapter of the book and in a series of boxed features titled "Speaking
of . . . Ethics." These boxes examine the moral consequences of communicating
and help you explore your own thinking about ethical choices in speechmaking.
Box topics include "Considering Cultural Practices" in Chapter 4 and "Name-
Calling" in Chapter 14.

6. Focus on practical applications to speechmaking in society. Boxed
features entitled "Speaking of . . . Apprehension" and "Speaking of . . . Skills"
examine questions and fears of public speakers. These boxes describe speaking
situations in which you might find yourself and ask you to look beyond the
classroom to consider the role of public speaking in society. Box topics include
"First-Time Fears" in Chapter 1 and "Handling Hostile Audiences" in Chapter 5.

7. Sample outlines and speeches. Sample outlines and speeches demonstrate the application of speechmaking principles. Annotations on many of the
outlines and speeches alert you to the rhetorical principles being used.

8. Refining the central concepts developed by Monroe and Ehninger.
Alan Monroe (1903–1975) and Douglas Ehninger (1913–1979) worked with students and teachers to develop strategies for teaching public speaking to students
of varied backgrounds and talents. With this textbook, you are heir to the pedagogy they built:

▶ Monroe's motivated sequence, the greatest formula for putting together
a speech. Others have copied it, but none have topped it.
▶ A critical examination of the forms of supporting materials.
▶ Exploration of types of language use, including imagery.

- ▶ Exploration of various kinds of introductions, organizational patterns, and conclusions.
- ▶ Discussion of the factors of attention that help you capture and keep your listeners' interest.
- ▶ Focus on argumentation that teaches you how to build an argumentative speech and analyze the arguments of others.

Principles of Public Speaking has guided students for over half a century by setting the standard for education in the basic speech course. Commitment to this standard combined with coverage of the latest research in communication theory and recognition and understanding of contemporary issues and challenges make this textbook as useful today as it has been through all its editions.

RESOURCES FOR INSTRUCTORS

The ancillary program for *Principles of Public Speaking,* Fifteenth Edition, includes the following instructional supplements:

Print Resources

The Instructor's Manual. Written by Ferald Bryan of Northern Illinois University, this is an extensive guide to teaching the public speaking course. For each chapter, it includes an outline of key concepts, questions to check student comprehension and to encourage critical thinking, detailed descriptions of classroom activities, impromptu speaking exercises, and a bibliography for further reading.

Test Bank. Written by Cynthia Brown El of Macomb Community College, the test bank includes over 1,200 test items—true/false, multiple choice, short answer, and essay questions.

A Guide for New Public Speaking Teachers: Building toward Success, **Second Edition.** This guide, written by Calvin L. Troup of Duquesne University, covers such topics as preparing for the term, planning and structuring your course, evaluating speeches, utilizing the textbook, integrating technology into the classroom, dealing with challenges, and much more.

The *ESL Guide to Public Speaking.* Written by Debra Gonsher Vinik of Bronx Community College of the City of New York, this guide provides strategies and resources for instructors teaching in a bilingual or multilingual classroom. It also includes suggestions for further reading and a listing of related Websites.

Great Ideas for Teaching Speech (GIFTS), **Third Edition.** This book, written by Raymond Zeuschner of California Polytechnic State University, provides descriptions of and guidelines for assignments successfully used by experienced public speaking instructors in their classrooms.

Electronic Resources

Computerized Test Bank. The printed test questions also are available electronically through Allyn & Bacon's computerized testing system, TestGen EQ.

The fully networkable test-generating software is now available on a multi-platform CD-ROM. The user-friendly interface enables instructors to view, edit, and add questions; transfer questions to tests; and print tests in a variety of fonts. Search and sort features allow instructors to locate questions quickly and arrange them in a preferred order.

Allyn & Bacon's Contemporary and Classic Speeches DVD. Allyn & Bacon presents a collection of famous classic and contemporary speeches. This DVD includes over 120 minutes of video footage in an easy-to-use format. Each speech is accompanied by a biographical and historical summary that helps students understand the context and motivation behind each speech. This DVD is available free to professors and students when packaged with any new Allyn & Bacon text. Contact your A&B sales representative for additional details and ordering information.

VideoWorkshop for Public Speaking: A Course-Tailored Video Learning System (www.ablongman.com/videoworkshop). *VideoWorkshop for Public Speaking,* by Tasha Van Horn of Citrus College and Marilyn Reineck of Concordia University, St. Paul, is a new way to bring video into your course for maximized learning! This total teaching and learning system includes quality video footage on an easy-to-use CD-ROM, plus a Student Learning Guide and an Instructor's Teaching Guide with textbook-specific Correlation Grids. This program brings textbook concepts to life with ease and helps your students understand, analyze, and apply the objectives of the course. VideoWorkshop is available for your students as a value-pack option with this textbook.

The Allyn & Bacon Student Speeches Video Library. This video collection includes three two-hour American Forensic Association videos of award-winning student speeches and three videos with a range of student speeches delivered in the classroom. Contact your local Allyn & Bacon sales representative for ordering information. Some restrictions apply.

The Allyn & Bacon Communication Video Library. This collection of communication videos is produced by Films for the Humanities and Sciences. Contact your local Allyn & Bacon sales representative for ordering information. Some restrictions apply.

The Allyn & Bacon Public Speaking Video. This video includes excerpts of classic and contemporary speeches as well as student speeches to illustrate the public speaking process. One speech is delivered two times by the same person under different circumstances to illustrate the difference between effective and noneffective delivery based on appearance, nonverbal style, and verbal style. Some restrictions apply.

The Allyn & Bacon Public Speaking Key Topics Video Library. Adopters of Allyn & Bacon communication texts may receive one video from this series. Video topics include critiquing student speeches, addressing your audience, and speaker apprehension. Some restrictions apply.

The Allyn & Bacon Communication Studies Digital Media Archive, Version 2.0. This archive, available on CD-ROM, offers more than 200 still images, video excerpts, and PowerPoint™ slides that can be used to enliven classroom presentations.

The PowerPoint™ Package. This text-specific package, prepared by Dan Cavanaugh, consists of a collection of lecture outlines and graphic images keyed to every chapter in the text. It is available at www.ablongman.com/ppt.

The Allyn & Bacon Public Speaking Transparency Package. This package contains 100 public speaking transparencies created with PowerPoint™ software. These provide visual support for classroom lectures and discussion on a full range of course topics. An expanded version is available on the Web at www.ablongman.com/ppt.

CourseCompass for Public Speaking. CourseCompass, powered by Blackboard and hosted nationally, is Allyn & Bacon's own course management system. CourseCompass helps you manage all aspects of teaching your course. The public speaking course features preloaded content such as quiz questions, video clips, instructor's manuals, PowerPoint™ presentations, still images, course preparation and instruction materials, VideoWorkshop for Public Speaking, weblinks, and much more! This course provides an abundance of resources to help you effectively teach and manage your class in the CourseCompass environment. Go to www.coursecompass.com for more information. (Also available in Blackboard and WebCT.)

CourseCompass for Public Speaking, Professional Development Edition. This collection of helpful instructional materials features public speaking teaching strategies, resources, and video examples that you can access over the Internet using CourseCompass, our dynamic, interactive teaching and learning environment. For course coordinators working with adjuncts or teaching assistants, our CourseCompass for Public Speaking, Professional Development Edition, provides training materials to your instructors whether they're on campus or not. You can access our preloaded instructional materials, add your own materials, and make the resulting combination available to the other instructors for their own instructional development and for the continued benefit of their students. Go to www.coursecompass.com for more information.

RESOURCES FOR STUDENTS

Print Resources

Research Navigator for Speech Communication. Written by Terrence Doyle of Northern Virginia Community College, this free reference guide includes tips, resources, activities, and URLs to help students. Part one introduces students to the basics of the Internet and the World Wide Web. Part two includes over thirty Web activities that tie into the content of the text. Part three lists hundreds of web resources for speech communication. The guide also includes information on how to correctly cite research, and a guide to building an online glossary. In addition, the Research Navigator for Speech Communication booklet contains a student access code for the **Research Navigator** database, offering students free, unlimited access to a collection of more than 25,000 discipline-specific articles from top-tier academic publications and peer-reviewed journals, as well as popular news publications such as the *New York Times*.

The Speech Preparation Workbook. Written by Jennifer Dreyer and Gregory H. Patton of San Diego State University, the *Speech Preparation Workbook* takes students through the various stages of speech creation—from audience analysis to writing the speech—and provides guidelines, tips, and easy-to-fill-in pages.

Preparing Visual Aids for Presentations, **Second Edition.** This thirty-two-page booklet, written by Dan Cavanaugh, provides a host of ideas for using today's multimedia tools to improve presentations. It includes suggestions for how to plan a presentation, guidelines for designing visual aids, storyboarding, and a walkthrough that shows how to prepare a visual display using PowerPoint™.

Public Speaking in the Multicultural Environment, **Second Edition.** This two-chapter essay by Devorah A. Lieberman of Portland State University includes activities and helps students think about the effects that the diverse backgrounds of audience members can have, not just on how speeches are prepared and delivered but also on how those speeches are perceived.

Outlining Workbook. Written by Reeze L. Hanson and Sharon Condon of Haskell Indian Nations University, this workbook includes activities, exercises, and answers to help students develop and master the critical skill of outlining.

Electronic Resources

The Companion Website with Online Practice Tests. This site, prepared by Diana Murphy, can be accessed at www.ablongman.com/german15e. An online study guide and much more, this site is tied to the text and provides enriching chapter-by-chapter resources. The Companion Website contains online learning objectives, flashcards, and a fully expanded set of practice tests for each chapter.

The Allyn & Bacon Public Speaking Website. This site, prepared by Terrence Doyle of Northern Virginia Community College, is designed to help students use the Internet along with their public speaking textbook to learn about the process of public speaking and to prepare speeches. It can be accessed at www.ablongman.com/pubspeak.

Speechwriter Software, Version 1.1, Interactive. This Interactive Speechwriter Software by Martin R. Cox contains sample speeches, tutorials, self-test questions on key concepts, and templates for writing informative, persuasive, and motivated sequence speeches. This product is available for student purchase or available free when packaged with any new A&B text. Some restrictions apply.

Speech Writer's Workshop CD-ROM, Version 2.0. This exciting public speaking software includes a *Speech Handbook* with tips for researching and preparing speeches; a *Speech Workshop,* which guides students step-by-step through the speech writing process; a *Topics Dictionary,* which gives students hundreds of ideas for speeches; and the *Documentor* citation database, which helps students format bibliographic entries in either MLA or APA style. This product is available free when packaged with any new Allyn & Bacon text. Some restrictions apply.

VideoWorkshop for Public Speaking: A Course-Tailored Video Learning System (www.ablongman.com/videoworkshop). *VideoWorkshop for Public Speaking,* by Tasha Van Horn of Citrus College and Marilyn Reineck of Concordia University, St. Paul, is a new way to bring video into your course for maximized learning! This total teaching and learning system includes quality video footage on an easy-to-use CD-ROM, plus a Student Learning Guide with textbook-specific Correlation Grids. The result? A program that brings textbook concepts to life with ease and that helps you understand, analyze, and apply the objectives of the course.

Allyn & Bacon's Contemporary and Classic Speeches DVD. Allyn & Bacon presents a collection of famous classic and contemporary speeches. This DVD includes over 120 minutes of video footage in an easy-to-use format. Each speech is accompanied by a biographical and historical summary that helps you understand the context and motivation behind each speech.

Public Speaking Tutor (www.aw.com/tutorcenter). The Tutor Center (Access Code Required) provides students free, one-on-one, interactive tutoring from qualified public speaking instructors on all material in the text. The Tutor Center offers students help with understanding major communication principles as well as methods for study. In addition, students have the option to submit self-taped speeches for review and critique by Tutor Center instructors to help students prepare for and improve their speech assignments. Tutoring assistance is offered by phone, fax, Internet, and e-mail during Tutor Center hours. For more details and ordering information, please contact your Allyn & Bacon publisher's representative.

ACKNOWLEDGMENTS

We owe a great debt to instructors who took the time to review the previous editions and offer feedback and suggestions for the preparation of this edition:

- Lisa Abramson, Western Oregon University
- David Airne, University of Missouri–Columbia
- Robert Arend, Miramar College
- Eugenia E. Badger, University of Louisville
- Arlene Badura, Schoolcraft College
- George Bang, University of Cincinnati
- Charles Beadle, Valdosta State University
- Rita Bova, Columbus State Community College
- Marti Brodey, Montgomery College
- Michael Butterworth, College of Lake County
- Mina Casmir, Pepperdine University
- Rick Casper, Dawson Community College
- Dennis Fus, University of Nebraska–Omaha
- Fred Garbowitz, Grand Rapids Community College
- Carla Gesell-Streeter, Cincinnati State Technical and Community College
- Richard Harrison, Kilgore College
- Richard Katula, Northeastern University

▶ Michael Leal, Cameron University
▶ John Ludlum, Otterbein College
▶ Linda Gentry Martin, Florida Community College at Jacksonville
▶ Mary L. Mohan, SUNY Geneseo
▶ Barry Morris, State University of New York College–Cortland
▶ Rhonda Parker, University of San Francisco
▶ Renee Reeves, Rose State College
▶ Sam Walch, Pennsylvania State University, Main Campus

A special thank you is also due to the thousands of students and instructors who have used this textbook. Their support and suggestions over the years have helped to make *Principles of Public Speaking* comprehensive and enduring. In this way, this textbook belongs to all those who have shared it.

Kathleen M. German
Bruce E. Gronbeck

Chapter 1

Studying Public Speaking in Higher Education

"**WHY TAKE A SPEECH CLASS?** I've been speaking all of my life!"

"How in the world can you justify using expensive college and university resources on something as technique-oriented as public speaking?"

"Sure, the business school needs to require speaking. Accountants need all of the help they can get! But why require it of the rest of us?"

"Okay, maybe our international students profit from taking this class, but not somebody from Cleveland, Ohio!"

"If you want to take the easiest class at this school, sign up for public speaking!"

Teachers of public speaking have listened to these sorts of comments for all of their years in the classroom. The course is too easy, or it's too hard. It's too technique-oriented or too theory-oriented. It should be required, or it should be thrown out. Then the first speech must be delivered, and the comments change:

1

"What should I talk about?"

"How should I start my speech?"

"Why am I doing this? What do I want to achieve?"

"How should I stand? What do I do with my hands?"

"What if they can't understand my awkward English pronunciation?"

"What if someone asks a question I can't answer?"

"What if I forget what I want to say?"

Such questions take you into the details of public speaking. But answering them involves more than giving advice such as "Stand this way," "Hold your head that way," "Talk louder," or "Check your fly." What is involved, ultimately, is understanding that while public speaking is a **personal act,** it's also a **social act**—one involving other people who have their roles and expectations. Because public speaking is a social act, you are forced to think seriously about the culture within which you're speaking: its traditional rules for public talk, the usual ways of talking in specific situations (from a pulpit versus from a locker room bench), even relationships between males and females, whites and other-raced peoples, and rich and poor as they've developed in various regions of a country. Such rules, folkways, and relationships exist and can force you to think about more than your own sweaty palms and pounding chest. They also account for why public speaking is mandated as a course in higher education.

In this chapter, we'll explore the study of public speaking in colleges and universities, the functions of public speaking in the social-political contexts of a multicultural society, the basic elements making up the process of talking publicly, and important ethical questions that you must face even before you give your first speech.

STUDYING PUBLIC SPEAKING IN HIGHER EDUCATION

Before we plunge any farther into this book, you need to think a bit more about why you need training in public speaking and how you can learn to do it better.

The Need for Speech Training

As a student in a public speaking class, you're likely to feel a range of emotions: fear of what might happen to you in the middle of a speech, excitement at the prospect of learning how to better control yourself and your words in front of an audience, boredom when reading some of the chapters in this book, smugness when you find yourself saying, "I already know [or do] that!," or even anger at being asked to do something you would rather not do publicly.

While the prospect of speaking in public seems scary, exciting, boring, or whatever other emotion you experience when you're about to talk, learning to channel your perfectly natural feelings in positive directions to come across as poised, prepared, and even persuasive is one reason you're here. In addition, you're in this class because many people in higher education believe that public speaking is something that well-educated, community-oriented people must be

Studying communication helps you become a more shrewd consumer of messages.

able to do well. Preserving your own identity while creating a sense of community is a special challenge as the new century unfolds before us.

Actually, if you ask speech teachers why students need such training, you'll find no unanimity in their answers. Some will stress the **social imperative:** Speech skills are necessary for all social beings, and the federal government mandated speech training as long ago as 1964, in the Primary and Secondary Education Act. The ability to control various social events and confrontations and make them function smoothly also has been important to students of speech, as Kenneth Burke noted, because the public sphere is

> the Scramble, the Wrangle of the Market Place, the flurries and flare-ups of the Human Barnyard, the Give and Take, the wavering line of pressure and counterpressure, the Logomachy, the onus of leadership, the Wars of Nerves, the War. . . . Rhetoric is concerned with the state of Babel after the Fall . . . [in] the lugubrious regions of malice and the lie.[1]

Speech skills must be sharpened through study and practice, because otherwise, you could not participate with maximum effect in public events and, worse, could be victimized by unscrupulous others in the human barnyard.

You also learn about the technicalities of public speaking not only to be a better maker of messages but also to be a more sophisticated receiver of public talk. There is a **consumer imperative** to speech education. Roderick Hart has written that a student of speech must engage in both "reflective complaining" and "reflective compliments," that a student must become someone "who knows when and how to render an evaluation."[2] To understand how public communication works, you must have an understanding of basic processes and varied techniques, a vocabulary for talking about both, and some sense as to what kinds of standards can be used to make value judgments about speeches. A good course in public speaking teaches you as much about listening to as about making speeches.

Finally, behind any solid course in public speaking is an **intellectual imperative.** In fact, speech training is an important part of a liberal arts education. This has been so since Isocrates made it central to his training of the orator-statesmen of fourth-century B.C.E. Greece:

> For [the power to speak publicly] it is which has laid down laws concerning things just and unjust, and things honourable and base; and if it were not for these ordinances [i.e., of public speech] we should not be able to live with one another. It is by this also that we confuse the bad and extol the good. Through this we educate the ignorant and appraise the wise; for the power to speak well is taken as the surest index of a sound understanding, and discourse which is true and lawful and just is the outward image of a good and faithful soul.[3]

In this grand conception, the study of human speech is the study of the ethics, practical philosophy, and eloquent expressions of the human spirit. The greatest examples of public speaking endure well past the time and place they were given: Pericles' funeral oration in 427 B.C.E. over the dead of the Peloponnesian War; William the Conqueror's exhortation to his troops before the Battle of Hastings in 1066; Jacques-Bénigne Bossuet's sermons before the bodies of French kings and queens in the seventeenth century; William Pitt the Elder's thunderous orations on British cruelties and stupidities in the American colonies; Abraham Lincoln's Gettysburg Address in 1863, soon after Sojourner Truth's identification of black women's problems with those of white women in "Ain't I a Woman?"; Mahatma Gandhi's message of nonviolent resistance in India, inspiring Martin Luther King, Jr.'s "I have a dream" speech at the Washington Monument in 1963; Barbara Jordan's explanation of what "We the people" means from her seat on the House Judiciary Committee as it was about to impeach President Richard Nixon. In your time, just think about all of the calls for public civility that were issued in the 1990s from the socially conscious Miss Manners to the religiously motivated Ralph Reed, from William Bennett on the right to Senator Daniel Patrick Moynihan on the left.

You'll likely not be asked to comment eloquently on the human condition and ways of improving it generally, as did all of these people. But you must understand, clearly and unmistakably, that public speaking is about more than you and your problems. You take courses in public speaking to improve your self-confidence and sense of personal empowerment, of course, but also for social, self-protective, and intellectual reasons.

Sojourner Truth (Isabella Baumfree) found a moral basis for speaking in her opposition to slavery prior to the Civil War.

Ways to Learn More about Public Speaking

There are, naturally, many different ways to learn about public speaking. Your instructor probably won't have you pursue all of them, but some certainly will be part of his or her pedagogy. Consider the following:

1. *A speech classroom is a laboratory and hence an ideal place for trying new behaviors.* You should try to develop new skills in the assigned speeches. Tell a story in the conclusion, use PowerPoint or access the World Wide Web to make visual aids, or deliver a speech from in front of rather than behind a lectern. The speech classroom is a comparatively safe environment for experimentation.

2. *Practice new speech techniques on friends, in a variety of settings, and in the speech classroom.* Practicing public speaking is every bit as important as practicing music instruments, soccer formations, or on-the-job interactions. You can't just read about speaking and then do it well. Speaking skills develop through the hit-and-miss process of practice: in the privacy of your own room, in front of friends who

are willing to humor you, in other classes, and, of course, in your speech class-room. Get feedback wherever you can.

3. *Work on your speech consumer skills as well.* In your lifetime, you'll be ex-posed to thousands upon thousands of public messages in the form of speeches, classroom pitches, TV ads, and chat room exchanges. Practice in listening—try-ing to accurately comprehend and fairly evaluate what others say publicly—hones skills that are equally as important as speaking skills.

4. *Learn to criticize expertly the speeches of others.* You can use this book as a tool for analyzing speeches you find in print (e.g., with the *Speech Index*),[4] hear in per-son, or access electronically.

Through activities both inside and outside your speech classroom, speaking and analyzing the speeches of others, you will develop and hone the skills that will make you a more productive and successful member of society.

Orality in Social-Political Life

So, then, you might ask, why all the stress on public speaking, on oral commu-nication? You're literate, and so you can write a letter or even have a flyer printed and distributed from street corners. You live in the electronic age, and so you can use a cell phone to call someone, hoping to sell that person a product or an idea. Additionally, you can turn on your computer, participate in a news-group, mailing list, or chat room with folks who have the same interests that you do, or even send a message to your congressional representative via his or her e-mail address. And then there are radio and TV call-in programs, Minicams for making QuickTime movies that you can distribute electronically, fax machines, and on and on. So why in the world do presidents still give televised speeches, why do teachers still offer classroom lectures, why do business teams still make oral presentations, and why do lawyers duke it out with opening and closing courtroom speeches?

There's something essentially, engagingly, powerfully human about speaking publicly to others. That's it, period. As far back as anyone can trace tribal relationships, hu-man beings have built their relationships with others—from parents to politi-cians—through face-to-face talk. Speech flows directly out of your mouth and into the ears of others; your movements, vocal tones of sadness or excitement, bodily tensions and facial displays are directly accessible to those who watch and listen. That sort of person-to-person contact in public simply cannot be wholly reproduced on paper, through electronically boosted sound waves, or via video or digital pictures.

The centrality of **orality**—of direct, in-person, spoken connections between people—to human relationships cannot be denied. Edward Hall argued almost fifty years ago that the "biological roots" of "all culture" could be found in speech,[5] while more recently, Walter Ong urged us to remember that the "sounded word" is a tremendous source of "power and action."[6]

It is through sound that you act on others—calling them ("Hey you!"), sin-gling them out ("Come here, Eugenia!"), recognizing their group identity ("Re-member the Titans!" or the gladiators' "We who are about to die salute you!"). The ancients even practiced word magic, that is, they found supernatural power

Speaking of . . . Apprehension

First-Time Fears

When you get up to speak for the first time, if you haven't already, the biggest thing on your mind will most likely be stage fright. Some fears can be overwhelming, interrupting good ideas and stopping otherwise great talks dead in their tracks.

The key is to use your anxiety to energize your performance. Expect that you'll be anxious, but don't let it get the best of you. The rush of adrenaline that comes just before you get up to speak should be used to fuel your speech. Below are some tips to help you cope with stage fright.

1. Prepare ahead of time. Uncertainty about what you're going to say just adds to the anxiety. You don't need that.
2. Breathe slowly and deeply. You can't expect to support your voice and movement without oxygen.

3. Think about your ideas. Concentrate on what you're sharing with your listeners, not on how you're feeling.
4. Don't let your imagination run wild. A listener who yawns probably didn't get enough sleep last night. Make it your goal to keep that person awake during your speech.
5. Brace yourself for the natural physical symptoms of adrenaline. Expect damp palms, a dry throat, or your own peculiar symptoms.

Above all, give yourself a break. Don't expect perfection the first time you speak—or even the second. Speaking well sometimes takes years of practice. Give yourself a chance and take every opportunity to develop and polish your skills.

---

in oral incantations, as you'll remember from Shakespeare's witches in *Macbeth:* "Double, double toil and trouble;/Fire burn, and cauldron bubble." The power of naming was shown in the Bible in Genesis 2:20, where Adam named all of the animals in order to have dominion over them. Finally, speaking words calls up important events—their identities and the motivations that should flow from them. "Remember the . . . [Alamo, Maine, etc.]!" is a speaker's demand to recall from memory an event that provides a reason for listeners to act together in particular ways.

What is suggested by thinking about orality in the social world is this: Public speaking is a primary mechanism for bringing people together, for getting them to share perspectives and values, so that they can recognize who they are or can get something done. So, then, let's look at the basic parts of the process of public speaking.

BASIC ELEMENTS IN THE SPEECHMAKING PROCESS

Public speaking is an **interactive process.** That is, it is a transaction or exchange among people in public, rather than interpersonal, settings. Four basic elements of speaking work together to create the speech process—a speaker, a message, listeners, and the context. Let's consider each of these four basic elements:

Web Exploration

For more information on the four basic elements of public speaking go to www.ablongman.com/german15e

The **speaker** is the source of the message. As the primary communicator in the public speaking situation, the speaker brings an individual perspective, identity, and experiences to the communication transaction.

The **message** comprises both the factual content of the speech and the speaker's attitudes and values on the topic. The message is transmitted by selecting words and ideas then arranging them in a particular pattern.

The **listener** (someone who receives and interprets your message) is also a partner in the speech transaction. You may think of public speaking as communication flowing in only one direction from speaker to listener, but that is not an entirely accurate picture. Listeners bring prior knowledge, attitudes, and interests to the speech situation. They also provide verbal and nonverbal **feedback** such as frowns, laughter, yawns, or questions. Feedback refers to messages your listeners send to you before, during, and after your speech.

Speakers and listeners engage each other in a **context.** Some parts of the communication context are obvious, such as the physical setting in which the speech takes place. Other elements, however, are more subtle. The context of the speech also includes the social expectations and cultural rules that come into play when speakers and listeners interact.

To understand how the basic elements function in the communication process, consider a professor teaching an introductory class in, say, social work. As a speaker, that instructor must convey a sense of professionalism (he or she knows the subject matter and participates regularly in professional activities as either a caseworker in the field or a scholar at conventions) and pedagogical ex-

A careful listener can come out of lectures and discussion sessions with a clear, concrete set of notes.

pertise (he or she knows how to teach beginners, orally, in step-by-step fashion). Messages (lectures, discussions) are constructed in such a way that social work practice is clearly outlined, with factual information clearly distinguishable from opinion or judgment. A careful listener can come out of those lectures and discussion sessions with a clear, concrete set of notes. As that last point suggests, the listener—say, you—does have important roles here. You enter into a kind of contract with that professor: If he or she offers relevant material in clear and engaging ways, you agree to record it, question it, and use it to write tests or papers. You agree, at least during that class in that term, to absorb and use the material, at least within the classroom context. You also agree to give the teacher feedback—questions in class, responses to a course evaluation sheet, perhaps even face-to-face comments just as the professor agrees to read and fairly evaluate your social work and skills.

So professors and students generally have clearly defined communication roles, expectations about messages, and usually shared conceptions of what ought to be going on in classrooms. If both speaker and listener understand what's expected of them in a particular context, the public speaking interaction satisfies both parties.

ETHICAL RESPONSIBILITIES FOR SPEAKERS

Because public speaking is an interactive process, you have certain responsibilities to your listeners—and they to you. Each time you speak publicly, you are contributing to a process of community building and affecting the lives of others. The act of speaking therefore always involves making ethical choices. You must consider how you are looking, ethically, to your audience; that is the matter of **ethos.** And, you have to take into account the **moral frames** of your listeners if you want to convince them of anything.

Web Exploration

For additional coverage of the ethical dimensions of public speaking go to www.ablongman.com/german15e

Ethos in the Western World

We begin etymologically. The English word *ethics* is derived from the Greek word *ethos*. Actually, we still use that word, too, to mean something like credibility or reputation. It had a larger meaning, however, in ancient Greece. "Motives and aims, no matter how pure or how grandiose," argued Hannah Arendt, "are never unique; like psychological qualities, they are typical, characteristic of different types of persons."[7] To Aristotle, a person who had ethos demonstrated while speaking that he or she shared characteristics with others in the community, that is, had good sense, good will, and good morals.[8]

1. *Good sense.* To demonstrate to others that the person was talking from a position of experience and knowledge, of information tempered by personal experience. To talk knowledgably.
2. *Good will.* To communicate a sense for caring not only about himself or herself but, more important, about the audience members, their needs, their status, and their future. To talk caringly.
3. *Good morals.* To speak in the language of the beliefs and values of listeners, to share their visions, their fears, and their hopes. To talk morally in the broad sense of that term.

Ethos for the Greeks was thus an orientation to life that individuals shared with their community. What made individuals people with ethos was their public demonstration of knowing and understanding what their communities held as important, shared commitments and living out those commitments in public talk. Ethos was a multifaceted idea, reflecting what people know, care about, and use as guidelines for living.

That such an understanding of ethos is relevant to us today can be seen in public opinions about President Bill Clinton in the 1990s. In surveys about his personal morals, he tended to score very low; usually fewer than a quarter of the respondents believed that he was personally moral. Yet if those same people were asked who understood the country's needs and knew where to lead them, he was supported by 60 percent or more of the country; and if they were asked what politician cared about them, more than two-thirds of the respondents believed that he did. President Clinton demonstrated that the Greek standards for ethos could sustain a politician in office even if his personal life was questionable.[9]

The Moral Bases of Public Decision Making

We likewise must understand that the word *moral* comes from the Latin word *mores*, which referred to what most people believed to be important guidelines for shared values and activity. Stephen Carter calls civility, that is, the commitment to a civic life, "the sum of the many sacrifices we are called upon to make for the sake of living together. . . . We should make sacrifices for others not simply because doing so makes social life easier (although it does), but as a signal of respect for our fellow citizens, marking them as full equals, both before the law and before God."[10]

The idea of public morality or civility therefore encompasses both ethical commitments to community standards and etiquette, that is, observation of acceptable ways of treating others. To act in accordance with community beliefs and values, however, is to work with moral frames, shared values or ways of looking at and valuing the world. Two implications of understanding community beliefs and values as moral frames for handling even disagreement or differences are especially important to public speakers:

1. *To be successful, you must find some moral frame that you share with your listeners if you're going to convince them that you have their best interests at heart.* Donald Moon calls this the **skyhook principle.**[11] You often speak to people whose backgrounds differ from yours, who hold different—even what have been called incommensurate or absolutely opposed—values. How can you convince people who hold values that are in conflict with yours to do anything? Moon's answer is: Find a skyhook. Find a higher value, a higher appeal, that will transcend your differences. This is what Jesse Jackson did in 1988, for example, when he tried to convince people of all ethnic backgrounds to work together in aid of the poor. He sought to demonstrate that in spite of our ethnic, political-ideological, economic, or geographical differences, Americans as a country could survive and prosper only by overcoming those differences. "Survive" and "prosper"—stay alive, make progress—were moral or valuative frames that Jackson hoped were transcendent. "Keep hope alive!" he shouted. He hoped that skyhooks could lift people's vision above their ethnic clashes, ideological differences, economic disparities, and geographical dispersion.[12]

To Senator Ben Nighthorse Campbell of Colorado, the "Indian Way" places greater value on contributions to society than on ownership of material possessions.

2. Finding a shared moral frame, however, still demands that you be true to what you yourself believe. Jackson sacrificed none of his own deeply seated beliefs and values when he called for "common ground" and "common sense" in the 1988 speech to the National Democratic Party convention. His integrity was intact. You, too, should always be looking for moral frames that you share with your listeners—not ones that only they accept, but ones from which you both work. Then you'll be both true to yourself and interesting to your audience.

The moral bases for public speaking, therefore, are not merely ethical or religious tenets, though those can be a part of the moral bases for community. They are broader than that: They're all of the frames—social, psychological, legal, economic, scientific, philosophical, political, and religious—that human beings in a community generally understand and even largely (though not necessarily universally) accept and live by. In communities as diverse, as multicultural, as the United States, the search for workable moral frames will become one of your most important tasks as a public speaker when you set out to persuade people to change their minds or behaviors.

YOUR FIRST SPEECH

Now it's time to get you started—up on your feet and ready to converse with an audience in a classroom. Your first speech should follow a few simple guidelines.

Structuring the speech in three main parts works well—the introduction, the body, and the conclusion. Begin by stating your main or central idea clearly in your introduction. Doing so will help listeners follow your ideas through to the end of your speech. Likewise, your last few sentences should recapture the main idea of your speech to wrap it up and give it a sense of finality. Most speakers draw on their own knowledge as they develop their ideas. Notice how a beginning student, Delores Lopez, used her own experiences in her first speech assignment "Who Am I?" Delores explains why she is in a public speaking class:

> One word that describes my life is "change." Ever since I can remember, things around me have constantly changed. I'm forty-two years old and as I look back, I see lots of change.
>
> When I was a kid, a high school education was enough. My parents didn't go to college; no one in my family did. Although education was respected in my family, there wasn't enough money for us to go on to school. My dad was partially disabled in an industrial accident and we depended on my mom's job to support us. While I was in high school, I had a weekend job and after graduating, I found a full-time job to help support my younger brothers and sisters. At the time, I never considered going to college. It wouldn't have mattered if I had wanted to go. I didn't have the time or money. But things have changed. After I had my oldest son, my mom took care of him and I went back to work. Now he's seventeen and I want him to go to school—to have an opportunity I didn't have. I want his life to be different than mine has been.
>
> My life has changed too. The corporation where I work has been downsizing and looking for leadership within the ranks. My supervisor has encouraged me to go back to school. She thought I was smart enough to make it, and I know I can study hard. The company is even paying part of my tuition. In this economic climate I realize that to be without higher education is to be more disadvantaged than ever. Maybe those of you who don't have kids don't realize the financial pressures of raising kids.
>
> There is one skill that is in demand in my company. They're looking for leadership qualities in their employees—especially the ability to present oneself and communicate well with others. That's why I decided to take this class in public speaking. As you can see, there has been a lot of change in my life. Some of those changes have come from outside—my job, my family. But, I'm changing inside too. I am more confident about what I want in my life and I'm finding ways to meet my goals. I'm looking forward to working with all of you; I think we can learn from each other.

Notice how Delores's speech was divided into three main sections. In the introduction she mentioned the theme of change. She elaborated on that idea by tracing changes in her own life, building on what she knew best, her own experiences. Examples from her family supported and elaborated the theme. Delores answers the question "Who Am I?" by explaining how she has come to be in her public speaking class. The final sentences of the speech summarize the main theme of change. Of course, there's more to consider as you develop your skills in public speaking. Chapter 2 will give you additional advice to get you started.

Speaking of . . . Ethics

Ethics and Public Speaking

Occasionally, we'll include a boxed area devoted to "ethical moments"—ethical decisions that public speakers must make in preparing and delivering their talks. We hope that you'll take a moment to think about the problems presented and their solutions in your life. You might discuss some of these problems with others to get alternative perspectives.

Here are some typical ethical questions that you might face in the speeches you'll give this term:

1. You read a fascinating article about fund-raising ideas for organizations. Should you borrow these ideas and present them as your own at your next club meeting? Do you need to acknowledge everything you learn from others? Must you always cite sources?
2. An article says exactly what you intended to say about the use of tanning beds. Then you find a more recent article claiming that new research contradicts the first article. Should you ignore the new evidence?
3. An authority whom you wish to cite uses the words *perhaps, probably, likely,* and *often.* Should you strike these words from the quotation to make it sound more positive? After all, you're not tinkering with the ideas, only with the strength of assertion.

Ethical decisions such as these will confront you regularly, both in your speech classroom and throughout the rest of your life. Take a few moments now to consider such situations and to articulate your position. Identify your moral standards before you face ethical dilemmas on the platform.

ASSESSING YOUR PROGRESS

Chapter Summary

1. You need training in public speaking, even in higher education, because of its roles in developing your public identity and helping others work out problems in their communities.
2. There are social, consumer, and intellectual imperatives for studying public speaking.
3. Your speech classroom gives you a unique opportunity to practice your speaking skills on a live audience, get feedback from listeners, and become a more critical consumer of oral messages and a more expert critic of speech making generally.
4. Orality is central of social life and hence is relevant to your successes even in a print- and electronically oriented world.
5. Speaking is a transaction involving a speaker, listeners, and a message within a context.
6. Listeners attribute ethos, or credibility, to speakers on the basis of their perceptions of the speakers' good sense, good will, and good morals; in turn, speakers must learn to work within listeners' moral frames if they're to succeed.
7. Your first speech should have an introduction, body, and conclusion that develop a main or central idea.

Key Terms

consumer imperative (p. 4)   message (p. 8)
context (p. 8)   moral frames (p. 9)
ethics (p. 9)   orality (p. 6)
ethos (p. 9)   personal act (p. 2)
feedback (p. 8)   skyhook principle (p. 10)
intellectual imperative (p. 4)   social act (p. 2)
interactive process (p. 7)   social imperative (p. 3)
listener (p. 8)   speaker (p. 8)

Assessment Activities

1. Interview a representative of a local group that schedules public speeches or lectures, the director of the campus speakers' bureau, or someone in a position to discuss the speech skills that are characteristic of the best professional speakers. Bring a list of those skills to class and, in discussion, share the basic competencies of effective speakers that your resource person emphasized.

2. When you get into a discussion mode in some other class, quickly prepare a speechlike contribution, with an introduction, body, and conclusion. Keep it short—under a minute—but make sure that you articulate your main idea, then develop it, and then draw a conclusion. Come back to class ready to discuss how that felt: Did you feel more and better prepared for discussion? Did anyone pick up on your idea to agree with or oppose it? Did the conclusion make it easier for others to see the implications of what you were arguing? A "speech" is not always a formal event, the kind you associate with the president of the United States; it's also sometimes simply a well-structured impromptu response to others.

3. Make a list of your personal speaking abilities. (Your instructor may make this an assignment in a journal that you will maintain throughout the term.) What are your ethical limits when it comes to public speaking? How does your speaking reflect the variability or diversity in your audience's backgrounds? Assess your integrity as a speaker.

Using the Web

1. Go to http://www.uiowa.edu/~commstud/resources/index.html and look under "Rhetorical Studies, Theory and Practice." Examine some of the subdirectories, to see what kinds of materials are available. Build a short, one-minute speech (or a written report) on one of them, describing what you found and what sorts of uses could be made of it in class.

2. Access the National Speakers Association site: http://www.nsaspeakers.org. Access the page to discover more about opportunities available to professional speakers.

3. Individuals have made outstanding contributions to society through public speaking. Search the Internet for their biographies and texts of their speeches. You might look for such individuals as Elizabeth Cady Stanton, Red Cloud, George Washington Carver, Frederick Douglass, Emma Goldman, Stephen Douglas, Eleanor Roosevelt, Jesse Jackson, Bill Clinton, and

Ronald Reagan. A good place to start is the "Speeches and Speechmakers" directory under the Communication Resources index listed in 1 above.

 ## Using VideoWorkshop

Watch the speeches in Module 6, "Credibility." As you watch, concentrate on how students can gain competence and derive credibility as public speakers. Then answer Questions 1–9.

References

1. Kenneth Burke, *The Grammar of Motives and the Rhetoric of Motives* (orig. pub. 1945, 1950; Cleveland: Meridian Books, 1962), 547.

2. Roderick P. Hart, *Modern Rhetorical Criticism,* 2nd ed. (Boston: Allyn and Bacon, 1997), 34.

3. Isocrates, *Isocrates II* [including *Antidosis*], trans. George Norlin (Cambridge, MA: Harvard University Press, 1927), 327.

4. Roberta Briggs Sutton, ed., *Speech Index: An Index to 259 Collections of World Famous Orations and Speeches for Various Occasions,* 4th ed. Rev. & enl (Metuchen, NJ: Scarecrow Press, 1966); and Charity Mitchell, *Speech Index: An Index to Collections of World Famous Orations and Speeches for Various Occasions,* 4th ed. Suppl. 1966–1980 (Metuchen, NJ: Scarecrow Press, 1982). Also use Internet search engines to find various collections of speeches. Start at "Speeches and Speechmakers" at http://www.uiowa.edu/~commstud/resources/index.html.

5. Edward T. Hall, *The Silent Language* (orig. pub. 1959; New York: Fawcett World Library, 1966), 37.

6. Walter J. Ong, *Orality and Literacy: The Technologizing of the Word* (orig. pub. 1982; New York: Routledge, 1988), 31.

7. Hannah Arendt, *The Human Condition: A Study of the Central Dilemmas Facing Modern Man* (orig. pub. 1958; rpt. New York: Doubleday Anchor Books, 1959), 184–185.

8. Aristotle, *Rhetoric,* 1378a.

9. When you wish to follow trends in public opinion polls, a good place to go on the Web is http://www.PollingReport.com, which assembles multiple polls especially on political topics.

10. Stephen L. Carter, *Civility: Manners, Morals, and the Etiquette of Democracy* (New York: HarperPerennial, 1998), 11.

11. J. Donald Moon, *Constructing Community: Moral Pluralism and Tragic Conflicts* (Princeton, NJ: Princeton University Press, 1993), esp. 20–21.

12. See Jesse Jackson, "Common Ground and Common Sense," in *Diversity in Public Communication: A Reader,* edited by Christine Kelly, E. Anne Laffoon, and Raymie E. McKerrow (Dubuque, IA: Kendall/Hunt, 1994).

CHAPTER OUTLINE

Chapter 2

Getting Started

YOU LEARNED ABOUT YOUR ROLE as a public speaker in our society in Chapter 1. While there's a lot to discover about speechmaking, you can learn enough about the basics to begin speaking right away. As you prepare to speak, you'll probably ask questions like these:

► How do I choose a topic?

► How do I make ethical choices for the content of my speech?

► What will my listeners want to hear?

► Where do I find the material for my speech?

► What kind of notes should I make?

► What's the best way to practice delivering my speech?

By answering these questions now, you'll be well on your way to success. The key to effective speechmaking is planning. You can save time and effort by planning carefully.

There's no magic formula for speaking. However, if you follow the seven steps offered in this chapter—either as they are presented here or in another order that works for you—you'll be ready for your audience. By the end of this chapter, you'll have mastered the basic steps for delivering your first speeches.

SELECTING AND NARROWING YOUR SUBJECT

Web Exploration

For more on selecting a topic go to

www.ablongman.com/ german15e

The most difficult task for many speakers is to choose a subject. Sometimes the subject is chosen for you, but often you will choose your own topic for classroom speeches. Begin by asking yourself questions: What do you know something about? What are you interested in talking about? What topics will interest your listeners? Does the occasion or situation suggest a topic for discussion? It's important to answer these questions carefully. Your answers will help you select and narrow your subject. A well-chosen speech topic is the first step to a successful speech. Let's examine in more detail the processes of choosing and narrowing a topic.

Speaking of . . . Skills

Brainstorming to Generate Topics

Having trouble coming up with possible speech topics? Try this brainstorming exercise:

1. Get a large blank sheet of paper and a pencil.
2. On the left-hand side of the paper, write the letters of the alphabet in a column.
3. Then, as quickly as you can, write down single words beginning with each of the letters. Write down any word that comes to your mind. Repeat until you have the entire sheet filled. You might begin like this: A—apples, alphabet, alarm, alimony; B—bazaar, balsa, baboon, bassoon, balloon; C—comics, cologne, colors, confetti.
4. Next, consider each of the words as a key to potential topics. For example, *apples* might suggest apple pie recipes, Johnny Appleseed and other early American legends, pesticide controversies, fruit in our diets, farm and orchard subsidies, or government price controls of farm produce. This is just the beginning. From one key word, you can derive many possible speech topics.
5. Obviously, not all of these topics would be great speech topics, but this exercise gives you a creative and quick way to generate lots of ideas.

It's a good idea to begin selecting a topic by listing those subjects that you already know something about, choosing the ones you'd like to share with others, and thinking about ways you can relate them to your listeners. If the purpose of your first classroom speech is to inform your classmates about a subject, you might come up with the following list of things you know something about:

High school baseball (you played baseball)
Sharks (you did a science project on this subject)
Halloween (it's your favorite holiday and you love to make costumes)
The Internet (you like to surf)
Soap operas (you watch them)
Smoking (you quit two years ago)
Careers in accounting (you're considering them now)
Photography (you like taking amateur photos)
Skin cancer (you're worried about suntanning)

Next you need to consider the people who make up your audience. Which topics would interest them most? When you ask yourself this question, you realize that several topics, such as making Halloween costumes, careers in accounting, and photography, are mainly of interest to you. Members of your audience have made career choices, and they already have hobbies. Unless you can come up with ways to involve your listeners in your career or your hobbies, you should probably cross these topics off your list.

You should also think about your listeners' expectations. What do they already know, and what do they expect to learn? They may already know more than you do about the Internet and soap operas. You'll certainly need to eliminate these topics from your list unless you plan to do a lot of research. Now you have a narrower list of potential topics—those that will interest your audience and meet your listeners' expectations.

After some additional thought, you decide to inform your classmates about sharks because you've done a lot of research on this subject and know that you can arouse their interest. Once you've determined your general subject, you can generate subtopics, including the following:

The types of sharks
The life cycle of the shark
Endangered species of sharks
Shark habitats and habits
Famous shark stories
Sharks as a source of human food
Movies about sharks
Shark cartilage as a potential cure for cancer
Shark attacks
The historical evolution of the shark

From this list of subtopics, ask yourself additional questions to narrow the topic even further. How much time do I have to deliver this speech? What do my classmates already know about my topic? Can I group some of these ideas together? After you answer these questions, you may end up with an informative speech focusing on three topics that cluster around the characteristics of sharks:

The types of sharks
The life cycle of the shark
Shark attacks

As you can see from this example, you begin with a broad list of potential topics. Then you select those that reflect your knowledge, the expectations of your listeners, and the requirements of the occasion. Finally, you consider the possible subtopics and choose several that fit the time limits and go together naturally. This kind of systematic topic selection is the first step in successful speaking. The next step is to identify your speaking purposes and central idea.

DETERMINING YOUR PURPOSES AND CENTRAL IDEA

Web Exploration

To analyze general and specific purposes of your speech go to

www.ablongman.com/german15e

Once you know what you want to talk about, you need to ask yourself still more questions: Why do you wish to discuss this subject? Why might an audience want to listen to you? Is what you're discussing appropriate to the occasion? To answer these questions you must analyze the reasons for your speech. First, think about the **general purpose,** the primary reason you will speak in public. Next, consider your **specific purposes,** the concrete goals you wish to achieve in a particular speech. Finally, focus your thoughts on a central idea, the statement guiding the thoughts you wish to communicate.

General Purposes

If you examine most speeches, you'll identify one of three *general purposes:* to inform, to persuade, and to entertain. This chart summarizes the general purposes for speaking:

General Purpose	Audience Response Sought
To inform	Clear understanding
To persuade	Acceptance of ideas or behaviors
To entertain	Enjoyment and comprehension

Throughout this book, we will emphasize speeches to inform and speeches to persuade. These types of speeches dominate the speaking occasions you'll face in life.

Speaking to Inform   When you speak *to inform,* your general purpose is to help your listeners expand their knowledge—of an idea, a concept, or a process. This is the aim of scientists who gather at the International AIDS Conference to report their research results to colleagues, of presidential press secretaries who make public announcements, of job supervisors who explain the operation of new equipment, and of your professors in college classes.

To create understanding, you must change the level or quality of information possessed by your listeners. They should leave your speech knowing more than they did before they heard it. For example, you might inform your classmates about herbal medicine, photographic composition, laser surgery, Web page construction, tornadoes, Individual Retirement Accounts, anorexia nervosa, the Tet Offensive, or any number of topics. If you talk about laser surgery, for instance, assume that they may already have some knowledge. To increase their understanding, you will need to focus on innovative surgical techniques using lasers,

You should practice your speaking skills whenever the opportunity arises.

such as LASIK surgery. You might even speculate about how lasers will change standard surgical procedures in the future. By providing explanations, examples, statistics, and illustrations, you expand your listeners' knowledge. Your goal as an informative speaker is to impart both knowledge and overall understanding.

Speaking to Persuade   If you seek to influence listeners' beliefs and actions, then your purpose is *to persuade*. Celebrities sell us on the benefits of cars and shampoos; lawyers convince jurors to recommend the death penalty; activists exhort tenants to stand up to their landlords; politicians debate taxes.

As a persuasive speaker, you usually seek to influence the beliefs and attitudes of your listeners. You might want to convince them that John F. Kennedy was shot by several assassins, that education is the cornerstone of freedom, or that life exists after death. In these cases, you are attempting to alter beliefs or attitudes. Sometimes, however, you will want to persuade your listeners to act. You might want them to contribute money to the Humane Society, sign a petition against a landfill project, vote for a new tax levy, or boycott a local grocery store. In this type of persuasive speech, called a speech *to actuate*, you ask your listeners for specific actions. You might ask your classmates to quit watching television, cut back on caffeine consumption, donate blood, sign prenuptial agreements, start stock portfolios, or register to vote.

Speaking to Entertain   Sometimes a speaker's general purpose may be *to entertain*. The goal is to amuse and divert listeners so that they relax and enjoy themselves. After-dinner speeches, travel lectures, and even commencement addresses can be highly entertaining. Gatherings of friends and associates may provide the occasions for such speeches to entertain.

Humor is often used, although speeches to entertain are not simply comic monologues. While a lecture on the customs of another culture may entertain an audience with amusing anecdotes, a great deal of information can be presented. As you can see, the skills required are subtle and often difficult to master because they combine enjoyment with comprehension.

To inform, to persuade, and to entertain are the general purposes of speaking. By thinking about general purposes, you identify your overall speaking goal. The next step is to focus on the specific purposes of your speech.

Specific Purposes

Your *specific purpose* combines your general purpose for speaking with your topic. For example, if your topic is aircraft and your general purpose is to inform, then your specific purpose might be to inform your audience about the role of aircraft in military combat or to provide them with a history of aircraft design. If your general purpose is to persuade, then your specific purpose might be to persuade your listeners that safety regulations governing air travel ought to be changed. The specific purpose provides a focus for your speech by combining your general purpose with the topic of your speech.

While some specific purposes are public, some are private—known only to you. For example, you probably hope you'll make a good impression on an audience, although you're not likely to say that aloud. Some purposes are short-term; others are long-term. If you're speaking to members of a local organization on the importance of recycling, your short-term purpose might be to convince them to save their aluminum cans, while your long-term purpose could be to gather support for a citywide recycling program.

While you may have several private and public short-term and long-term specific purposes whenever you speak, you need to identify a dominant one. It is important to identify one dominant specific purpose to guide your speech preparation. A single specific purpose, one that you can articulate for an audience, focuses you on precisely what you want your audience to understand, believe, or do.

Suppose that you wanted to take on the challenge of getting more of your classmates to use electronic databases. Consider various ways of wording your specific purpose:

- ▶ "The purpose of my speech is to explain how electronic retrieval systems can put the resources of other libraries at your fingertips" (understanding).
- ▶ "The purpose of my speech is to show my listeners that computers are good for much more than playing games" (beliefs).
- ▶ "The purpose of my speech is to get my classmates to search electronic databases for their next speech" (action).

All these purposes involve electronic databases, yet each has a different specific focus, making it a different speech. Locking onto a specific purpose allows you to zero in on your primary target.

Central Ideas

Once you've settled on a specific purpose for your speech, you're ready to compose a sentence that expresses it. You need to capture the controlling thought of your speech to guide your development of it. This **central idea** (sometimes called a *thesis statement*) is a statement that captures the essence of the information or concept you wish to communicate to an audience, usually in a single sentence. For example, your central idea for a speech on diamonds might be: "The value of a diamond is largely determined by four factors: color, cut, clarity, and carat."

In a persuasive speech, the central idea phrases the belief, attitude, or action you want an audience to adopt. Your central idea for a persuasive speech on dieting might be: "Avoid fad diets because they create dangerous imbalances in essential nutrients and break down muscle tissue."

The precise phrasing of central ideas is very important because wording conveys the essence of your subject matter, setting up audience expectations. Examine Table 2.1 for examples of ways to word speech purposes. Then consider this example—assume that you've decided to give an informative speech on fixing a leaky faucet. You might phrase your central idea in one of three ways:

- ▶ "With only minimal mechanical skills, anyone can fix a leaky faucet."
- ▶ "With a few simple supplies, you can fix a leaky faucet for less than $10."
- ▶ "Fixing a leaky faucet yourself will give you a sense of accomplishment as well as free you from depending on plumbers for making home repairs."

Note that the phrasing of the central idea controls the emphasis of the speech. The first version stresses the individual audience member's ability to complete the task. Presumably, the speech would offer a step-by-step description of the repair process. The second version suggests a quite different speech, focused on securing

Web Exploration

For more examples of central ideas for your speech go to

www.ablongman.com/german15e

TABLE 2.1 *Speaking Purposes*

This table provides a guide to the relationships between the general purpose, specific purpose, and central idea of your speech.		
General Purpose	**Specific Purpose**	**Central Idea**
To help your listeners understand an idea, concept, or process (to inform)	To teach your listeners about the Federal Reserve Board	"The most important influence on interest rates in this country is the Federal Reserve Board."
To influence your listeners' actions (to actuate)	To get your listeners to walk to classes this week (short-term goal) To get your listeners to develop a fitness program (long-term goal)	"You should start a fitness program today to improve the quality of your life."
To influence your listeners' thoughts (to persuade)	To increase your listeners' appreciation of the role of pure scientific research	"Basic scientific research is the foundation for discoveries in medicine, agriculture, business, and everyday life."

the inexpensive supplies. In contrast, the third version concentrates on benefits to the listener.

The process of selecting your subject, determining your general and specific purposes, and phrasing your central idea is the process of narrowing. When you put it all together, here is the result for an informative speech:

SUBJECT: Plumbing repair

GENERAL PURPOSE: To inform

SPECIFIC PURPOSE: To explain how you can fix a leaky faucet.

CENTRAL IDEA: Most leaky faucets require a new washer that you can install in less than an hour for about $2.00.

Work on your general and specific purposes before constructing your speech. Your speaking purposes clarify your relationship to your audience. They also guide your search for speech materials.

ANALYZING THE AUDIENCE AND OCCASION

Communication is a two-way street. That means you need to consider your listeners when you are preparing to speak. It's tempting to focus only on yourself—your goals, your fears, and your own interests. However, if you want to speak so that you reach others, then you must construct the speech from your listeners' viewpoint.

Responsible speakers regularly ask questions such as "How would I feel about this topic if I were in their place?" or "How can I adapt this material to their interests and habits, especially if their experiences or understandings are different from mine?" Putting yourself in your listeners' shoes is what researchers call **audience orientation,** an ability to understand the listener's point of view. Being audience-oriented will push you to construct speeches from the receiving end of the communication process, investigating aspects of the audience's demographic and psychological background that are relevant to your speech. Chapter 5 takes up the topic of audience orientation in detail.

For now, you should find out how much your listeners already know about your subject so that you can adjust to their level of understanding. You should also discover their attitudes toward your subject. If they are apathetic, you must create interest; if they are hostile or favorable, you must adapt what you say. In a public speaking class, this type of investigation is easy enough to conduct—start asking questions. After all, your whole purpose in speaking is to connect with your listeners!

It is also important to consider the occasion on which you're speaking. The occasion is what brings people together; consequently, it often determines listeners' expectations. Do they expect to hear a comic monologue? Does the situation demand a serious approach such as a lecture? Will your listeners be tired, wide awake, or distracted by outside noises?

In addition to answering these questions, you should consider the nature and purpose of the occasion. Is this a voluntary or captive audience? How many people will attend? Will the speech be delivered indoors or outdoors? Will the audience be sitting or standing? Will there be other speakers? Will you need to make special arrangements for equipment such as a public address system or an overhead projector?

Throughout the process of developing your speech, consider your listeners and the occasion. Your listeners' expectations and the reasons they have gathered to hear you will influence your choice of topic and the focus of your speech. As you examine the remaining steps in the process of speech development, remember that your ultimate goal is to communicate with your listeners.

GATHERING YOUR SPEECH MATERIAL

Once you have considered the subject and purpose of your speech and analyzed the audience and occasion, you'll be ready to gather the materials for your speech. Ordinarily, you'll start by assembling what you already know about the subject and deciding which ideas you want to include. You'll probably find that what you already know is not enough. You'll need to supplement what you know with additional information—facts, illustrations, stories, and examples. You can gather some of this material from newspapers, magazines, books, government documents, or radio and television programs. You can acquire other information through interviews and conversations with people who know something about the subject that you do not know. And more and more information is becoming available through electronic databases and the World Wide Web.

As you search for materials, if you plan to deal with a current question of public interest, you should consult such sources as the "The Week in Review" section of the *Sunday New York Times, U.S. News and World Report, The Wall Street Journal, Harper's,* and *The Observer.* Many magazines of general interest can be accessed via electronic database searches and the Internet; numerous encyclopedias, yearbooks, government reports, almanacs, and other reference materials can be found in your college library. This important topic—locating supporting materials—will be covered in detail in Chapter 6.

MAKING AN OUTLINE

Early in your preparation, make a rough list of the points you wish to include in your speech. As you gather information on your topic, you will begin to see a pattern emerging from clusters of information. From these clusters, you can develop a final order for the principal points you wish to present, together with the subordinate ideas that will explain or prove these points. Flesh out your ideas with supporting materials such as examples, statistics, and quotations.

Remember our speech topic on sharks from the beginning of this chapter? Well, after gathering information on sharks, we're ready to develop an outline. We started with several potential topic areas: the types of sharks, the life cycle of the shark, and shark attacks. Our research revealed amazing amounts of information on each of theme topics—too much for a short speech. So we've narrowed our speech topic to shark attacks. Our outline for an informative speech might look like the outline on the next page.

Shark Attacks[1]

I. Many of us fear shark attacks.
   A. News stories draw attention to these events.
   B. Films such as *Jaws* sensationalize the threat.

II. The realities of shark-human contact are quite different from media portrayals.
   A. More frequent opportunities for shark-human interactions increase the number of attacks.
      1. More intense use of marine waters for recreation increases the contact between people and sharks.
      2. However, the percentage of attacks remains extremely low—approximately 2 percent worldwide.
      3. Sharks have more to fear from humans than vice versa.
         a. There are fewer than 100 shark attacks worldwide per year with only 25–30 fatalities.
         b. Fishermen kill between 30 million and 75 million sharks each year.
         c. Eighty shark species are threatened with extinction.
   B. The risk of shark attack is minimal.
      1. On average, more people are killed by bee stings in the United States than are killed by sharks worldwide.
      2. Annually, thousands more people are harmed by rat bites, squirrel bites, and even bites by fellow humans than by shark attacks.
      3. Your own home is a more dangerous place than the ocean in terms of serious and fatal injuries you're likely to sustain.
      4. Even driving to the beach is fifty times more likely to be fatal than swimming or surfing.

III. Education and technology can maximize water safety.
   A. Educated surfers and swimmers are smart about using the ocean water.
      1. They avoid waters where dangerous sharks are known to be common.
      2. They avoid deep channels or waters that suddenly become deep.
      3. They avoid swimming and surfing at dusk and dawn when sharks usually feed.
      4. They avoid swimming and surfing where people are fishing or cleaning fish.
      5. They swim and surf in groups where lifeguards are on duty; safety exists in numbers.
      6. They leave watches and reflective jewelry on the beach.
      7. They stay out of the water if they have open wounds or during menstrual periods.
   B. Technological developments hold promise for making human-shark interactions safer.
      1. Some companies claim to have developed effective chemical shark repellents.
      2. The Protective Oceanic Device, or POD, uses an electrical field to discourage aggressive sharks.
      3. Shark cages protect divers who must work underwater.
      4. At crowded beaches that are known to attract sharks, metal mesh shark nets safeguard swimmers.

IV. Humans become prey to sharks mostly by accident.
   A. The threat from sharks is exaggerated.
   B. Education and technological developments can aid in preventing shark attacks.
   C. Taking realistic steps to prevent shark attacks will protect humans and sharks alike.

In this outline, we've followed several themes in a topical pattern of organization. When you deliver the speech, you will use linking statements or transitions to guide your listeners. You might say, "Many of our fears of sharks are exaggerated by television and films. Let's examine the facts," or "Now that we've seen the realities of shark attacks, let's look at steps that can help prevent them," or "Here are four technological developments that offer protection for divers and others who must work in the shark's ocean habitat."

In Chapter 7, you'll find a number of additional organizational patterns for arranging the ideas in a speech. There, too, you'll find the form for a complete outline. For now, remember two simple but important rules: (1) Arrange your ideas in a sequence that is clear to your listeners and (2) make sure that each point is directly related to your specific purpose. If you follow these rules, your speech should be coherent.

PRACTICING ALOUD

When you have completed your outline, you're ready to practice your speech (see Figure 2.1). Even though you might feel silly talking to yourself, practice aloud to refine the ideas and phrasing of your speech and to work on delivery skills.

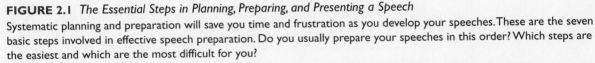

FIGURE 2.1 *The Essential Steps in Planning, Preparing, and Presenting a Speech*
Systematic planning and preparation will save you time and frustration as you develop your speeches. These are the seven basic steps involved in effective speech preparation. Do you usually prepare your speeches in this order? Which steps are the easiest and which are the most difficult for you?

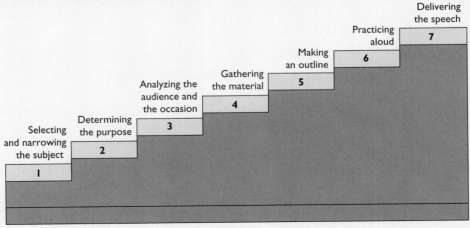

Many people practice alone before delivering their first speech to an audience.

Give practice a chance. It can mean the difference between an adequate effort and an outstanding speech. Repeatedly read through the outline until you've made all the changes that seem useful and until you can express each idea clearly and smoothly. Then write out a notecard with brief cues for each of your main ideas. Next, try to talk through the speech by looking at your notecards. As you practice aloud, you might inadvertently leave out some points; that's okay. Practice until all of the ideas come out in their proper order and the words flow easily. Talk at a normal rate, and don't mumble. Finally, if possible, get a friend to listen to your speech, give you direct feedback, and help you practice making eye contact with a real person.

DEVELOPING CONFIDENT DELIVERY

Now you're ready to present your speech. Even if you've prepared fully, you still might be asking, "How can I deal with my nervousness? If I'm anxious, how can I convey a sense of self-confidence to my listeners?" If you have thought about some strategies for coping with anxiety, you'll be ready to deal with it. Although there's no foolproof program for developing self-confidence, there are some practical ways to communicate confidently:

1. *Realize that tension and nervousness are normal.* They can even benefit you. Remember that tension can provide you with energy. As adrenaline pours into

Speaking of . . . Skills

Practicing Your Speech

If you've ever learned to play the piano or drive a car with a standard transmission, you know that you can't master it all at once. You must practice to improve. The same principle can be applied to improving your public speaking skills. Practice repeated over time will result in more improvement than a single practice session. In addition, remember these guidelines:

1. Keep practice sessions brief. It's better to practice your speech for a few minutes at a time over the course of several days than to go through it repeatedly for two hours the day before it's due.
2. Practice in different settings. Deliver your speech as you walk to classes, in front of your friends, or in an empty classroom. This kind of varied practice encourages flexibility.
3. After you start your speech, finish it without stopping to correct errors or to restart it. You aren't going to deliver your speech exactly the same way every time you give it. Expect some changes in your speech delivery and phrasing.

your bloodstream, you experience a physical charge that increases alertness. A baseball pitcher who's not pumped up before a big game may find that his fastball has no zip. Similarly, a speaker who's not pumped up may come across as dull and lifeless. Practice speaking often so that you learn how you react to stress and develop strategies for coping with it.[2]

2. *Focus on your ideas.* Think about what you want to communicate to your listeners. When you speak, you want their minds to be focused on your ideas, not on the way you're presenting them. Speech anxiety arises in part because of self-centeredness; sometimes you're more concerned with your personal appearance and performance than with your topic. One means of creating confidence is to select topics that you are interested in and know a lot about. By doing this, you make the situation topic-centered rather than self-centered. Have you ever wondered why you can talk at length with friends about your favorite hobby, sports, or political interests without feeling anxious? The fact that you're talking about a subject that interests you may be part of the answer.

3. *Look at your listeners.* Americans tend to mistrust anyone who doesn't look them in the eye. If you look at your notes rather than at your listeners, they may get the impression that you don't care about them or that you aren't interested in their reactions to your message. Eye contact with members of your audience will signal your eagerness to communicate with them. In addition, you can watch your listeners' faces for feedback and make minor adjustments as you speak. If you notice looks of puzzlement, for example, you'll certainly want to adjust by further explaining your ideas.

Speaking of . . . Apprehension

State and Trait Apprehension

Research distinguishes between two kinds of speech anxiety: state apprehension and trait apprehension. **State apprehension** refers to the anxiety you feel in particular settings or situations. For example, perhaps you can talk easily with friends but are uncomfortable when being interviewed for a job. This sort of apprehension is also known as *stage fright,* because it's the fear of performing that leads to your worries about failure or embarrassment.

Stage fright has physiological manifestations that vary from one person to another. You can probably list your own symptoms—clammy hands, weak knees, dry mouth, and a trembling or even cracking voice. Its psychological manifestations include mental blocks (forgetting what you're going to say), vocal hesitation, and nonfluency.

While some aspects of nervousness are characteristic of the situation, others are a part of your own personality. This kind of apprehension, called **trait apprehension,** refers to your level of anxiety as you face any communication situation. A high level of anxiety leads some people to withdraw from situations that require interpersonal or public communication with others.

4. *Remember to breathe.* Although this seems like unnecessary advice, research shows that stress can interfere with your breathing. To counter the effects of stress, breathe deeply using your diaphragm. Your chest should expand, pushing down and out against your waistband. An adequate supply of oxygen will help calm your anxiety and support your vocal apparatus as you speak, so remember to breathe!

5. *Relax your body.* Realize that you are being seen as well as heard and that your body can communicate confidence. In addition, bodily movements and changes in facial expression can help clarify and reinforce your ideas. You might smile as you refer to humorous events or step toward your listeners as you take them into your confidence. Keep hands free at your sides so that you can gesture easily. As you say, "On the other hand," you might raise one hand to reinforce your statement. As you speak, your body uses up the excess adrenaline it generates. The very act of talking aloud reduces fear.

6. *Speak in public as often as you can.* Public speaking experience will not eliminate your fears, but it will help you to cope. Speaking frequently in front of your classmates is a great way to practice coping with anxiety. Then, as you gain confidence and poise, you'll want to try speaking to different audiences and in different settings. So speak up in class discussions, join in conversations with friends, and contribute to public meetings. You might even decide to run for office!

There are no shortcuts to developing speaking confidence. For most of us, gaining self-confidence results from experience and from understanding the process of communication. The uneasy feeling in the pit of your stomach may always be there, but it need not paralyze you. As you gain experience with each of the essential steps—from selecting a subject to practicing the speech—your self-confidence as a speaker will grow.

ASSESSING YOUR PROGRESS

Chapter Summary

1. Select and narrow your subject, making it appropriate to you and your listeners.
2. Determine your general and specific purposes, then word the central idea to guide your development of the key ideas.
3. Analyze your audience and the occasion to discover what you might say and how you might say it.
4. Gather your material, beginning with what you already know and supplementing it with additional research.
5. Arrange and outline your points to package your ideas clearly and coherently.
6. Practice your speech aloud, working from outlines and then notecards, first alone and then with an audience.
7. Recognize that self-confidence can be developed by understanding the communication process and through public speaking experience.

Key Terms

audience orientation (p. 24)
central idea (p. 23)
general purpose (p. 20)

specific purposes (p. 20)
state apprehension (p. 30)
trait apprehension (p. 30)

Assessment Activities

1. Go to the library or log onto the Internet and read several popular magazines and newspapers from the week that you were born. Sort out the events of that week and write a clear central idea for a brief informative speech. Organize your ideas and use some illustrations or perhaps some expert testimony from the sources you examined. Follow the rest of the steps suggested in this chapter for developing a speech; then deliver it to your classmates. After the speech, ask for feedback. Was the central idea clear? Did your listeners follow the structure of the speech easily? Did your delivery convey confidence?
2. Rewrite each of the following statements, making it into a clear and concise central idea for a speech to inform:
   a. "Today I would like to try to get you to see the way in which the body can communicate a whole lot of information."
   b. "The topic for my speech has to do with the high taxes people have to pay."
   c. "A college education might be a really important thing for some people, so my talk is on college education."
   Be ready to present your central ideas in a class discussion.
3. For each of the following statements, write a central idea for a persuasive speech that incorporates the three ideas. Compare your phrasing of the central ideas with those of your classmates.
   a. Many prison facilities are inadequate.

   b. Low rates of pay result in frequent job turnover in prisons.
   c. Prison employees need on-the-job training.
4. To learn brainstorming, you must practice it. Form groups, appoint a
   recorder to jot down all ideas, then practice brainstorming with the questions listed below. Don't evaluate or editorialize until the brainstorming
   session has stopped. The goal is to list as many ideas as possible. To evaluate the success of the brainstorming session, compare the number of ideas
   generated.
   a. How can an egg be packaged so that it will not break when dropped from
      the top of a twenty-foot ladder?
   b. What can we do with all the waste from excess product packaging clog-
      ging our landfills?
   c. What adjustments would our society have to make if there were three
      sexes instead of two?
   d. Imagine that aliens have been spotted hovering over our cities in space-
      craft. How can we communicate with them?
   e. You are a scientist who has just discovered how to double a person's IQ.
      Should you share your discovery?

Using the Web

1. There are many places to find excellent examples of speeches on the
   Internet. You might locate the home page for the History Channel: Great
   Speeches, Douglass: Archives of American Public Address, and Columbia
   University's Inaugural Addresses of the Presidents of the United States.
2. Having trouble finding a speech topic? Visit reputable media sites on the Internet like CNN, ABC, CBS, NBC, or PBS. You can also find regional newspapers on the Internet. These sources will give you an idea about what's
   current. Use your search engine to locate the Internet Public Library or Electronic Newsstand. Browse through thousands of publications from all over
   the world. These should give you some good ideas for speeches.

Using Video Workshop

Watch the speeches in Module 4, "Topic Selection." As you watch,
think about the ways that meaningful speech topics can be generated. Then answer Questions 1–9.

References

   1. Materials for this speech outline were obtained from the Websites for the
PBS *NOVA* program featuring shark attacks, the U.S. Office of Naval Research,
the American Institute of Biological Sciences, the Florida Museum of Natural History, and the International Shark Attack File.

2. Michael Neer, "Reducing Situational Anxiety and Avoidance Behavior Associated with Classroom Apprehension," *Southern Communication Journal,* 56 (1990): 49–61; John Gorhis and Mike Allen, "Meta-Analysis of the Relationship Between Communication Apprehension and Cognitive Performance," *Communication Education,* 41 (1992): 68–76; James McCroskey, "Oral Communication Apprehension: A Summary of Current Theory and Research," *Human Communication Research,* 4 (1977): 78–96.

Chapter 3

Critical Listening

IN YOUR DAILY LIFE, you spend more time listening than you do reading, writing, or speaking. Listening accounts for over 40 percent of your communicative time.[1] You might assume that you're a good listener from all that practice, but you really don't know until you discover that you've missed something important. The fact is, you've probably never had any training in listening, especially for situations such as class lectures in which you're expected to acquire technical or abstract materials primarily through listening.

Conversations, classroom lectures, group meetings, and electronic media expose you to an amazing amount of information every day. If you are to make the best use of all that information, you must hone your listening skills.

Both speaker and listener are active partners in the communication process. As a speaker, you reach out to your audience; and in turn, as a listener, you respond. Listening is a central part of the communication process.

After a more detailed introduction to the idea of listening, this chapter will focus on practical listening techniques that you can use in almost any listening situation. We'll finish by suggesting how you can put new listening skills to work in your classes.

HEARING AND LISTENING

Hearing is the first step in the listening process. To listen to a message, you first must hear it. **Hearing** is the physiological process of receiving sound waves. Sound waves travel through the air and set up vibrations on the eardrum; these vibrations, in turn, are transmitted to the brain. Hearing is affected by the laws of physics and the neurophysiology of the body. Any number of factors can interfere with hearing—distracting noises, sounds that are too soft, or hearing loss. Some of these conditions can be improved. The speaker can change speaking volume, and audience members can move to better seats to facilitate hearing. Listeners cannot provide feedback to the speaker if their hearing is blocked.

Listening, on the other hand, involves thinking. After sound waves are translated into nerve impulses by the middle ear and the auditory nerve, they're sent to the brain for interpretation. This process of interpretation—registering impulses, assigning them to meaningful contexts, and evaluating them—constitutes listening. **Listening** is the thinking process whereby people generate meaning from sounds.

Web Exploration

To test your listening skills go to

www.ablongman.com/ german15e

BARRIERS TO GOOD LISTENING

Listening is easy to define but hard to practice. You've probably developed some barriers to good listening. You'll have to recognize and remove them if you're going to become a better listener. At one time or another, most of us experience these five barriers to good listening:

1. *Passive listening.* Many of us are just plain lazy listeners, tuning in and out as our attention dictates. As a result, we often miss important facts and ideas. Because we are partners in the communication transaction, we need to become active listeners, identifying our purposes for listening, taking notes, and evaluating the ideas in the message.

2. *Drifting thoughts.* You can comprehend many more words per minute than someone can utter; you probably can process about 400 words per minute, while most speakers produce only about 125 to 175 words per minute. As a result, you may fill the time lag with other thoughts. Your **internal perceptual field** is the world of your own thoughts. While someone is speaking, you may

Speakers receive several types of feedback. Immediate feedback occurs during the speech. Delayed feedback happens after the communication transaction.

be remembering a television show you saw last night or planning the menu for supper or thinking about a topic for your next term paper.

3. *Physical distractions.* Sometimes your attention is diverted by elements outside your own thoughts. Your **external perceptual field** is those things in your physical environment such as the buzz of overhead lights, the sun's glare off your teacher's glasses, or a banging radiator that can distract you. Our attention can be sidetracked by physical interference so that we hear and process only part of a spoken message.

4. *Trigger words.* We often bring our emotions into the speech setting. Memories of past events or strong feelings can be triggered by a word or a reference. Many people spend time mentally debating with speakers and remain stuck on one idea while the speaker moves ahead to others. For example, some listeners become hostile when they hear a speaker refer to a secretary as "my girl." They may spend several minutes fuming and miss the next part of the speaker's message.

5. *Self-fulfilling prophecies.* Preset ideas can get in the way of good listening. If you've heard that Professor Rogers is a dull lecturer, you probably enter the class expecting to be bored. Sometimes previous encounters with a speaker can color your expectations.

Like most people, you probably have predispositions about topics and people. If you let these predispositions get in the way of careful listening, you're likely to miss important parts of speeches. It is important to overcome these barriers to become an active listener and a better participant in the communication transaction. Here are some suggestions for developing your listening skills.

PRACTICAL LISTENING TECHNIQUES

While hearing is a natural physiological process for most people, listening is another matter. You've got to work hard to listen well. The good news, though, is that you can train yourself to listen better. You can begin to practice better listening habits in three ways: (1) determine your purposes for listening, (2) develop techniques that help you comprehend speeches, and (3) design questions that help you evaluate or assess speeches on criteria that matter to you.

Know Your Purposes

The first thing good listeners must do is figure out why they're listening. This is not as obvious as it seems, because, if you think about it, you engage in many different kinds of listening. On any given day, you may listen intently to your instructors in order to learn new concepts, you may listen to your favorite music to relax, and you may listen attentively to be sure that a car salesperson isn't skipping over essential features of the dealer's guarantee.

Researchers have identified five kinds of listening that reflect purposes you may have when communicating with others:[2] appreciative, discriminative, empathic, comprehension, and critical.

Appreciative listening focuses on something other than the primary message. Some listeners enjoy seeing a famous speaker. Others relish a good speech, a classic movie, or a brilliant performance. On these occasions, you listen primarily to entertain yourself.

Discriminative listening requires listeners to draw conclusions from the way a message is presented rather than from what is said. In discriminative listening, people seek to understand the meaning behind the message. You're interested in what the speaker really thinks, believes, or feels. You're engaging in discriminative listening when you draw conclusions about how angry your parents are with you, based not on what they say but on how they say it. You draw inferences from the presentation of the message rather than from the message itself.

Empathic or therapeutic listening is intended to provide emotional support for the speaker. Although it is more typical of interpersonal than public communication, empathic listening does occur in public speaking situations, for example, when you hear an athlete apologize for unprofessional behavior, a religious convert describe a soul-saving experience, or a classmate reveal a personal problem to illustrate a speech. In each case, your role is supportive.

Listening for comprehension occurs when you want to gain additional information or insights from the speaker. You are probably most familiar with this form of listening because you've relied heavily on it for your education. When you listen to a radio newscast, to a classroom lecture on the principal strategies in an advertising campaign, or to an elections official explaining new registration procedures, you're listening to understand—to comprehend information, ideas, and processes.

Critical listening is the most difficult kind of listening because it requires you to both interpret and evaluate the message. It demands that you go beyond understanding the message to interpreting it and evaluating its strengths and weaknesses. You'll practice this sort of listening in class. And as a careful consumer, you'll also use critical listening to evaluate television commercials, political campaign speeches, advice from talk show guests, or arguments offered by salespeople. When you are listening critically, you decide whether to accept or reject ideas and whether to act on the message.

You may have many different purposes for listening, and that's why the first question you ought to ask yourself is "What's my purpose in listening?" Do you expect to gain information and insight to make a decision? Or are you listening to enjoy yourself, to understand the feelings of another human being, to assess someone's state of mind, or to test ideas? Knowing why you're listening will help you listen more efficiently and effectively. In the rest of this chapter, we'll focus on listening for comprehension and critical listening because those are the kinds of listening you use primarily in a public speaking situation.

Speaking of . . . Skills

Good Note Taking and Active Listening

One of the easiest ways to practice your listening skills while in college is to work on note taking. As you become a better note taker, you'll also become a better listener. Here are some tips for improving your note-taking skills.

1. *Get organized.* Develop a note-taking system such as a loose-leaf notebook so that you can add, rearrange, or remove notes. Use separate notebooks for different subjects to avoid confusion.
2. *Review your notes regularly.* This will prepare you to ask questions while the lecture or readings are still fresh in your mind and will help to keep you oriented to the class. Research shows that students who review their notes achieve significantly more.
3. *Leave a 2- to 3-inch blank margin.* Later, you can add facts, clarification, reactions, and other alterations after comparing your notes with other students' or after doing related reading. Such critical commentary is an important stage in merging the material in the notes with your own thoughts.
4. *Write more.* Making a conscious effort to record more ideas and more words related to a speech or lecture will help you to remember the important ideas, structure, and supporting evidence. Research shows that most students don't take enough notes.

The problem is compounded with long messages; students take even fewer notes as the speech or lecture continues.

5. *Develop a note-taking scheme.* Consider using abbreviations such as the ampersand (&) for *and*, *btwn* and *w/o* for *between* and *without* or specialized notations like *mgt* and *ac-ctg* for *management* and *accounting*. Color-code your notes or use highlighter pens to remind yourself of the most important parts of the material.

By taking these steps, you can become an active listener who's engaging in a two-way communication channel.

See: Kenneth A. Kiewra, "Note-taking and Review: The Research and Its Implications," *Instructional Science*, 16 (1987): 233–249.

Listening for Comprehension

Listening for comprehension is the kind of listening you usually do in class lectures. Fully comprehending what's being said requires that you understand the three essential aspects of speech content: *ideas, structure,* and *supporting materials.* You've got to understand clearly what ideas you're being asked to accept, how they're related to each other, and what facts and opinions underlie them. Asking three questions will help you comprehend a message:

1. *What are the main ideas of the speech?* Determine the central idea of the speech and look for the statements that help develop it. These main ideas should serve as the foundation on which the speaker builds the speech. The next time you listen to a soap commercial, listen for the main ideas: Are you encouraged to buy it because of its cleaning power, smell, sex appeal, or gentleness to your skin? Before you decide to buy a new brand of soap, you ought to know something about its characteristics. Now transfer this listening behavior to a speech. Always know what ideas you're being sold.

2. *How are the main ideas arranged?* Once you've identified the main ideas, you should figure out the relationships between them. In other words, identify the structure of ideas and then examine it. If a speaker is explaining affirmative action laws, which ideas are highlighted? Does the explanation seem reasonable? Is the speaker limited only to one perspective? Who is defined as the victim? Does the speaker express sympathy for one point of view over another?

3. *What kinds of materials support the main ideas?* Consider the timeliness, quality, and content of the supporting materials. Are facts and opinions derived from sources too old to be relevant to current problems? Is the speaker quoting recognized authorities on the subject? Ask yourself whether the materials clarify, amplify, and strengthen the main ideas of the speech. For example, if a speaker claims that the murders at Columbine High School in Littleton, Colorado, in 1999 show that school violence is a growing national problem, ask yourself several questions: How many episodes of school violence occurred during the entire year? Over the past decade, have incidents of school violence increased or decreased? Is this example typical of the kinds of violence in schools?

Listening well has been a human (and canine) concern for a long, long time.

Web Exploration
For more analysis of the RRA technique go to
www.ablongman.com/
german15e

In other words, to comprehend the content, make sure you know what ideas, relationships, and evidence you're being asked to accept. To be an active listener, you should constantly employ the **RRA technique:** *review, relate,* and *anticipate.*

Take a few seconds to *review* what the speaker has said. Mentally summarize key ideas each time the speaker initiates a new topic for consideration.

Relate the message to what you already know. Consider how you could use the information in the future.

Anticipate what the speaker might say next. Use this anticipation to focus on the content of the message.

By reviewing, relating, and anticipating, you can keep your attention centered on the message. Using the RRA technique keeps you actively engaged in the listening process.

Critical Listening

Once you've figured out why you're listening, how the ideas are arranged, and what supporting materials are being presented, you're in a position to form some opinions. You, after all, are the reason the speech is being given, so you're the one who must decide whether the speaker's ideas are worth accepting. Making such a judgment is a good way to protect yourself from inflated claims, dated information, and unethical speakers. Completely assessing a speech could include asking yourself about the situation, the speaker, and the message. The following questions will help you listen critically:

1. *How is the situation affecting this speech and my reception of it?* What is the reason for the speech? Is the speaker expected to deal with particular themes or subjects? Am I in sympathy with this speech occasion? Speeches in churches, basketball arenas, and Rotary Clubs are very different from one another, and you must adjust your evaluation criteria to each situation.

2. *How is the physical environment affecting the speaker and my listening?* Is the room too hot or too cold? Too big or too small? What other distractions exist? The physical environment can have an important impact on your listening. In uncomfortable environments, you might have to compensate: lean forward, move up, or concentrate more closely.

3. *What do I know about the speaker?* The reputation of this person may influence you, so think about it. Are you being unduly deferential or hypercritical of the speaker just because of his or her reputation? Do you think the speaker will be fair and honest because he or she represents your interests or is similar to you? Don't let your assumptions about the speaker get in the way of critical listening.

4. *How believable do I find the speaker?* Are there things about the speaker's actions, demeanor, and words that seem either pleasing or suspicious? Does the speaker use adequate and compelling supporting material to reinforce the message? Try to figure out why you're reacting positively or negatively and then ask yourself whether it's reasonable for you to believe this speaker.

5. *Is the speaker adequately prepared?* Imprecise remarks, repetitions, backtracking, vague or missing numbers, and the lack of solid testimony are all signs of a poorly prepared speaker. For example, a speaker who is talking about how audiences influence TV programming decisions should discuss, among other things, the networks' use of focus groups. If the speaker doesn't discuss this, you'll know that he or she hasn't gotten very far into the topic. Similarly, if the speaker can't clearly explain the different rating systems, you should question the reliability of other information in the speech.

6. *What's the speaker's attitude toward the audience?* How is the audience being treated: cordially or condescendingly, as individuals or as a general group, as inferiors or as equals? Answering these questions will help you not only to assess your experience but also to form some questions for the speaker after the speech.

7. *How solid are the ideas being presented?* We've been stressing this point throughout the chapter because it's crucial for you to assess the ideas in terms of your own knowledge and experience. Just one warning: You could be mistaken yourself, so don't automatically dismiss new ideas. But listen more carefully to ideas that are new and different or seem strange, making sure that you understand them and that they're well supported.

8. *Are the ideas well structured?* Are important concepts missing? For example, anyone who talks about the branches of the federal government but then ignores the Supreme Court has an incomplete set of ideas. Are logical links apparent? The comparisons must be fair; the cause-and-effect links clear and logical; and the proposals for correcting social wrongs both feasible and practical. Structural relationships between ideas are what give them their solidity and coherence as a package.

9. *Is sufficient evidence offered?* The world is filled with slipshod reasoning and flawed evidence. Bad reasoning and a refusal to test the available evidence, after all, led the American high command to believe that Pearl Harbor was an im-

Speaking of . . . Ethics

Deliberately Misguiding Listeners

Some advertisers, politicians, sales representatives, and even friends have learned how to misguide their listeners without actually lying. They hope, of course, that you'll draw the conclusions they want you to on the basis of distracting or misdirective statements. You can recognize these situations by thinking and listening critically. Here are some things to listen for:

1. *Percentages rather than absolute numbers.* You're told that women's salaries went up 50 percent more than men's last year. Should you cheer? Maybe not. Even if women got a 3 percent raise when men got 2 percent, there's such a differential in their salaries that the actual dollar amount of women's and men's raises was probably about the same.
2. *Characteristics of the sample.* Beware when the manufacturer tells you that "Four out of five of the dentists surveyed preferred the ingredients in Smiles-Aglow toothpaste." How big was the sample? Were the dentists surveyed working in Smiles-Aglow labs or were they in private dental practice? You need to know more about them to know whether this claim is solid.
3. *Hasty generalization.* The neighbor who tells you that "Most folks on this block are against the widening of our street" may have talked to everyone, although that's not likely. He probably means "most folks I know on this block"—and then you'd better find out how many that it is. Press him for details before you accept or reject his judgment.

Are speakers lying when they use these distracting or misguiding techniques? Are they acting unethically? Where does ethical responsibility lie—with the speaker or with the audience?

Source: Andrew Wolvin and Carolyn Coakley, *Listening,* 5th ed. (Dubuque, IA: Brown and Benchmark, 1995), pp. 3–11 and chaps. 4–8.

pregnable port in 1941. Listen for evidence; write down the key parts of the evidence so you can mull it over, asking yourself if it's good enough to use as a basis for changing your mind. Be demanding; adopt a "show me" attitude. Insist on adequate evidence and logical reasons when a speaker asks you to make crucial decisions.

You might not ask all of these questions every time you hear a speech, because your listening purposes vary considerably from occasion to occasion. However, you will want to ask yourself most of these critical listening questions before you make important decisions such as whom to vote for, whether to take the job offer, or if you should make a major purchase. To practice critical listening, you can begin now in your classes.

DEVELOPING SKILLS FOR CRITICAL LISTENING

Your speech classroom is set up to teach skills that you can use for the rest of your life. Listening is one of the skills you'll need to survive in your career, your

TABLE 3.1 *Speech Evaluation Form*

Use this form to focus your listening skills.

The Speaker	The Speech as a Whole
☐ Confident?	Audience's expectations met?
☐ Enthusiastic about the topic?	
☐ Well prepared?	
☐ Use of notes and lectern unobtrusive?	

The Speaker
☐ Confident?
☐ Enthusiastic about the topic?
☐ Well prepared?
☐ Use of notes and lectern unobtrusive?

The Speech as a Whole
Audience's expectations met?
_____
_____
_____
_____
_____
_____
_____
_____
_____

The Message
☐ Sufficiently narrowed topic?
☐ Clear general purpose?
☐ Sharply focused specific purpose?
☐ Well-phrased central idea?
☐ Ample support from varied, trustworthy sources?
☐ Introduced adequately?
☐ Concluded effectively?
☐ Major points clear, balanced?

Strengths of the speech?
_____
_____
_____
_____
_____
_____
_____
_____

The Channel
☐ Voice varied for emphasis?
☐ Conversational style of delivery
☐ Appropriate rate of delivery?
☐ Nondistracting body movement?
☐ Gestures used effectively?
☐ Face expressive?
☐ Language unambiguous, concrete?
☐ Language vivid, forcible?

Possible improvements?
_____
_____
_____
_____
_____
_____
_____
_____

The Audience
☐ All listeners addressed?
☐ Ideas adapted to audience segments?
☐ Attitudes toward speaker and subject acknowledged?
☐ Supporting materials tailored to the audience?

Questions for the speaker?
_____
_____
_____
_____
_____
_____
_____
_____

community, and your social life. You'll have to listen to understand your employer's explanation of a new computer system, to make reasonable decisions between two political candidates who offer different views of health care reform, and to follow a neighbor's instructions as she tells you how to rewire a light fixture. The ability to listen can help you make money, be a good citizen, and keep you from frying your fingers on a 110-volt circuit!

Your classes are excellent settings for practicing new listening skills and refining old ones. Use the Speech Evaluation Form in Table 3.1 as a checklist when listening to speeches. It will challenge your listening skills. During this term, we also suggest that you improve your listening in the following ways:

1. *Practice critiquing the speeches of other students.* Practice note-taking techniques; ask questions of the speaker; take part in post-speech discussions. You can learn as much from listening well as from speaking yourself.

2. *Listen critically to discussions, lectures, and student-teacher interactions in your other classes.* You're surrounded with public communication worth analyzing when you're in school. You can easily spot effective and ineffective speech techniques in those classes.

3. *Listen critically to speakers outside of class.* Attend public lectures, city council meetings, religious rallies, or political caucuses. Watch replays of presidential or congressional speeches on C-SPAN. You'll be amazed by the range of talent, techniques, and styles exhibited in your community every week.

4. *Examine the supporting materials, arguments, and language used in newspapers and magazines.* Refine your critical listening skills by practicing critical reading. Together, they represent the skills of critical thinking you need to survive in this world. Critical thinking is the process of consciously examining the content and logic of messages to determine their bases in the world of ideas and to assess their rationality. **Critical thinking** is the backbone of evaluation. It's what happens when you actively listen and read others' messages.

Overall, then, listening makes public speaking a reciprocal activity. Listeners seek to meet their diverse needs, ranging from personal enjoyment to crucial decision making, through specialized listening skills designed for each listening purpose. When both speakers and listeners work at making the speech transaction succeed, public speaking reaches its full potential as a partnership in communication.

ASSESSING YOUR PROGRESS

Chapter Summary

1. Both the speaker and the listener are critical participants in the communication transaction.

2. Hearing is a physiological process; listening is a psychological process by which people seek to comprehend and evaluate sounds.
3. There are five purposes for listening: appreciative listening, discriminative listening, empathic (therapeutic) listening, listening for comprehension, and critical listening.
4. To improve your listening skills sort out the essential aspects of speech content: ideas, structure, and supporting materials.
5. The RRA technique—review, relate, and anticipate—can help you listen more efficiently.
6. To improve your speech evaluation skills, practice assessing the situation, the speaker, and the message.

Key Terms

appreciative listening (p. 38)
critical listening (p. 39)
critical thinking (p. 45)
discriminative listening (p. 38)
empathic or therapeutic
   listening (p. 38)

external perceptual field (p. 37)
hearing (p. 36)
internal perceptual field (p. 36)
listening (p. 36)
listening for comprehension (p. 39)
RRA technique (p. 41)

Assessment Activities

1. Conduct a class discussion on a controversial topic such as doctor-assisted suicide, multiculturalism and political correctness, the rights of smokers, or health care reform. Establish the rule that before anyone can speak, he or she first must summarize to the satisfaction of the previous speaker what that person said. What conclusions can you draw about people's ability to listen and provide feedback? How do good listening and feedback reduce the amount and intensity of disagreement?
2. Keep a listening log. For two or three days, record your oral communication interactions noting (a) to whom you were speaking, (b) what were your listening purposes, and (c) how effectively you listened. After completing the log, do a self-assessment: What are your strengths and weaknesses as a listener? What changes would make you a better listener?

Using the Web

1. Locate the Website of the International Listening Association (http://www.listen.org). You'll discover numerous listening tests and exercises for improving your listening skills in public speaking and interpersonal situations.
2. Visit a chat room and observe the listening skills of individuals who are participating in the discussion. Can you identify barriers to good communication? How did these barriers affect other participants? Suggest some ways to overcome these barriers.

Using VideoWorkshop

Watch the speeches in Module 2, "Listening." As you watch, think about the ways in which speakers can identify, learn, and improve on critical listening skills. Then answer Questions 1–10.

References

1. Steven Rhodes, "What the Communication Journals Tell Us about Teaching Listening," *Central States Speech Journal,* 36 (1985): 24–32.

2. Andrew Wolvin and Carolyn Coakley, *Listening,* 5th ed. (Dubuque, IA: Brown and Benchmark, 1995).

Chapter 4

Public Speaking and Cultural Life

T ITS SIMPLEST, a **culture** is a social group's system of meanings. We can think of culture as the sorts of meanings that a given people attaches to persons, places, ideas, rituals, things, routines, and communication behavior. You've been taught since you were an infant who is powerful or not (people), how to act at home and in public buildings (places), what's true and false about the things you encounter in the world (ideas), how to greet family and strangers (routines), and the most effective—and ineffective—ways to get favors from your teacher or your boss (communication behavior). Your culture thus is made up of pieces of social knowledge that represent how you've been taught to think and act successfully within the world of human beings.

All of this is true for everyone else as well. We've all been taught about people, places, rituals, ideas, and the rest. Unfortunately, the meanings for those entities that you've been given may not be the same as the meanings someone else has learned; your experiences are different from those of others. This happens not only on an individual basis, but also on a group basis. In some important ways, men and women have been given different social educations. So have whites and Hispanics, poor and rich folk, and people who hear and those who cannot. All of our differences in psychological, social, political, economic, and behavioral—which is to say cultural—education can cause speakers some serious problems.

> Tricia was distraught. "I can't go out there!" She was a delegate from the Speech Communication Student Association about to speak at a gathering of the campus African American, Hispanic, and international students' associations for working together to make the city council reconsider a rezoning decision that would wipe out two blocks of student apartments and student-oriented stores. "Here I am, a white speech major born in Iowa, a state that's 94 percent white. And there they are, from Chicago and New York, even from foreign countries totally different from mine. They'll resent me. What do we have in common?" "That's the question you must answer," replied her best friend, Grant. "What do you have in common? You're all students here, you all live in or next to the neighborhood about to be destroyed, you all enjoy gathering at those stores and shops on Tripp Street—you have a lot in common!" "Well, I guess we do, but . . . " "But nothing!" said Grant. "Quit emphasizing your differences. Sure you have them, but think of what you share and how your differences will become a collective strength in front of the city council. You'll be part of a broad spectrum of students confronting city councilors who think of this only as a neighborhood with funny-smelling food. That's what to talk about."

Training in public speaking is in part a matter of learning about the cultural expectations of one's audience. Speakers must learn what those expectations are in order to be seen as socially competent and conceptually relevant to others. Speakers who want to affect audiences must learn to be exceptionally good at phrasing ideas and engaging the feelings of others within the communication traditions of their listeners' cultural traditions.

Learning about the cultural practices and expectations of one's listeners is easier said than done, however. There is a tension between one's self and society, between the individual and the collectivity, especially in the United States, where children have been taught to maximize their potentials and to be their own persons. On the one hand, you are you, a unique individual with your own life experiences and your own thoughts about the world. On the other hand, you always are marked by social categories. You are an individual, yes, but you also are reminded regularly that you're gay, of Polish descent, twenty-something, an Episcopalian, a junior in college who works as a sales clerk, and so on. You are an individual, but part of your self-identity—and certainly a major part of others' perception of you—is socially and culturally determined.[1]

In a world where identities are both individually and collectively diverse, you must answer some difficult questions as you prepare to talk publicly:

> ▶ Can you respect individual differences and cultural diversity while attempting to get a group of people to think alike and work together?

The ability to communicate across gender, racial, and class lines is an essential skill for all members of diverse communities.

▶ Can you recognize the diversity of your audience's experiences, even their ideological schisms, while you nonetheless attempt to enact a public image that is credible?

▶ Can you be true to yourself and your commitments while adapting to others?

▶ Can you successfully negotiate the differences between what audiences expect of you and what you expect of yourself?

These are not easy questions to answer, and you don't think of them every time you rise to say a few words. When you face audiences as different from you as Tricia felt her audience was from her, however, you'll want to follow her friend Grant's advice and look for the common ground—the shared beliefs, attitudes, values, goals, and desires that turn a group of listeners into a people who are unified in thought and action.[2]

In this chapter, we discuss relationships between public speaking and cultural life by first examining the components of culture—especially oral culture—more specifically. Then, we review some strategies that you can use to unify and direct your listeners' thoughts and actions, even when they come from diverse cultural backgrounds.

UNDERSTANDING CULTURAL PROCESSES

We've defined culture generally. Before you can think about strategies for responding to key points of cultural diversity in your speeches, however, you'll want to think more about how it affects your everyday life.

Orality and Cultural Life

We talked briefly about orality or **oral culture** in Chapter 1. Now it is time to think about that idea more concretely. Earlier, we noted that your relationships with others are built primarily via face-to-face talk. Direct, in-person, spoken connections between people generate the essence of what it is to be human. Standing up in front of others—to recite a Christmas piece, to declare one's maturity in a Jewish community, to demonstrate that you know how to read or spell in school, or to pledge allegiance to your sorority or fraternity family—is traditionally, in all societies, a way of manifesting and marking your membership in communities. Oral performance is simply the most fundamental of methods for bonding the individual to the group.

What makes face-to-face, oral communication so important to groups? Media theorist Walter Ong has identified a series of characteristics of the "sounded word,"[3] and his list includes the following items, among others:

1. Speech tends to be **integrative:** In speech, you often draw together ideas or stereotypes held by the group, attaching them to people and events. Such aggregating or integrating of cultural beliefs and specific subject matters leads to oral formulas (not just "the student" but "the bright student," not just "the warrior" but "the brave warrior"). References in oral speech to "workable" or "practical" plans, "glorious" dawns and "star-lit" skies, and the like come off as clichés in written language, but are used regularly in oral language because of their familiarity and shared use across groups. Speech thus integrates members of a society by identifying their personal characteristics as they are valued by others and by recollecting reactions-to-the-world that are shared across peoples. Speeches, therefore, not only are about something, a *policy,* but they simultaneously are reassembling a group, a *polity.*

2. Speech tends to be **redundant:** You often repeat yourself in public speaking, saying the same thing in more than one way. Notice that the last sentence could have ended at the comma, for the point was presumably clear. In speech, however, the second half likely would have been added, giving listeners a chance to catch the point again in case it wasn't clear in its first phrasing. That's oral language: redundant or repetitious, with backlooping to help people keep up with the flow of the conversation.

3. Speech tends to be **traditionalist:** A group's traditional beliefs and values usually are reflected in public oral language. Sayings such as "It's six of one and half a dozen of another," "That's the way the ball bounces," "A bird in the hand is worth two in the bush," and "Better safe than sorry" capture traditional beliefs for many Westerners: There's no difference between two alternatives, there are things you can't control in life, don't risk what you already have for something that could go wrong, and take the sure alternative. Such sayings live in oral culture and so tend to appear in speeches. Not all such sayings are conservative—"Let your reach exceed your grasp" urges you to take chances—though most are, probably because they have arisen out of situations in which the group or society is reining in individualism. "Strike while the iron is hot" also suggests that immediate action is valued over a wait-and-see attitude. So in reality, traditionalist epithets or aphorisms can be either

conservative or more radical in the West, for that's the way Western culture is: contradictory in its view of group safety and individual initiative. Oral communication draws on both kinds of sayings, which so often mark speech making.

4. Speech tends to be **concrete.** You might write, "Relationships between blacks and whites in America are complex," but in a speech, you're more likely to be effective if you get specific: "Two-thirds of our undergraduates of all ethnicities live within nine blocks of campus, side by side in the same student apartments. While blacks and whites in the state of Iowa tend to be separated, in Iowa City the university draws them together, standing in the same lines at John's Grocery, drinking beer at the Sports Column and coffee at the Java House, listening to live music side by side on the Ped Mall. Sharing not only classrooms but life situations means that blacks and whites in Iowa City cannot ignore each other." Here, the concrete references to particular places in the neighboring environment help listeners visualize ideas—an important feature in oral communication, in which one cannot reread something that wasn't grasped immediately.

5. Speech is **agonistically toned.**[4] That is Ong's phrase. It suggests that when people gather together to make decisions publicly by speech, things get a little heated. It's as though public speaking is taking the place of ancient rituals of combat. One can disengage when writing, building complex, philosophically structured bases for one's ideas. Not so in speech. It's immediate. The disagreements usually occur between people who are present to each other and in front of the group that's making a decision. So public speakers often become aggressive when a group is going to decide an issue. Speech is personal, flowing out of your mouth and body; it's you who performs it. Writing can be circulated when you're not there and so is more distanced. Speech is immediate, personal—and therein lies its feistiness and yet its power.

6. Speech is **participatory.** The audience likewise is personally involved. It's there, part of the environment. They're often addressed directly, even personally. So you might say, "How many of you have plans to stop at the Bloodmobile at the Student Union today? How many? How about you, Jill—are you going? Jake? Lisa? Maurice?" You cannot make someone else read something, but you have a very good chance of making them listen—of making them participate in public interaction.

7. Speech is **situational.** It occurs in the here and now. You can read a newspaper in the bathroom or tonight after supper; you might read a book a chapter at a time before you go to sleep. But speaking happens right here, right now. At its best, a public speech deals with issues that are visible in the immediate situation, in the actual lives of listeners who are there. If listeners don't know that, you've got to convince them that such is the case: "So how many of you have stopped for a drink at a fountain in one of the university buildings today? How many times do you figure that you stop at a drinking fountain during a week? Three? Four? Twice a day? Even if you take a drink only three times a week, you have about a 1-in-20 chance of ingesting enough lead to make you sick. For, you see . . . ." Here, the speaker tries to make a water-quality speech

relevant to the particular context within which listeners find themselves—as students living in a college campus environment.

So oral culture tends to be dominated publicly by speech communication that is integrative, redundant, traditionalist, concrete, agonistically toned, participatory, and situational. All of these characteristics suggest that the public speaker relies on group (cultural) resources when putting a speech together. This is not to say that knowledge of one's topic, care in phrasing one's own position on that topic, technical information, and awareness of how speeches usually are put together in a particular society are not important. Of course they are. It is to say, however, that the use of public, oral channels for communication within some group or society demands care in approaching the act of talking itself. Relationships between individuals and groups maintained in oral settings also tend to require knowledge of oral language traditions of the kind we've been reviewing.

The Challenges of Speaking in a Multicultural Society

Earlier, we raised this question: Can you respect individual difference and cultural diversity while attempting to get a group of people to think alike and work together? We think that you can. But it's hard work. As we've just noted, you have to know at least something about other people's oral language traditions: how they talk to each other, beliefs and values that are important because of their upbringing and families, ways in which they signal disagreement or agreement, how they respond to each other (i.e., their participatory practices), and how they talk in different situations—perhaps one way in families and another in public settings such as church or a governmental office.

If you think about all of the different American **co-cultures** (those, such as the culture of womanhood versus the culture of manhood, that coexist in a society as relatively complete ways of life) and **subcultures** (smaller groups of people such as bikers or particular religious groups that define their lifestyles at least in part by how they're different from the dominant culture), you can scare yourself, as Tricia did. Cultural differences can terrify a speaker who's not familiar with them. As you think about the black, Hispanic, gay/lesbian/transgendered, and women's empowerment movements of the 1960s and 1970s, the growing emphasis on cultural diversity in the 1980s, and passage of the Americans with Disabilities Act in 1991, you realize that you've got to be very careful when trying to respect cultural orientations of audience members even in a simple speech. **Multiculturalism**—the recognition that a country such as the United States possesses not a unified culture, but one with several subcultures and powerful co-cultures that interpenetrate yet are separate from one another—is a fact of life.[5]

To reiterate, your cultural life is both acquired and later negotiated face-to-face. In a multicultural society that means that you must work particularly hard at accessing listeners' cultural traditions that are likely to affect how they react to your speeches and at negotiating important differences between your beliefs, attitudes, values, and usual ways of behaving and theirs. To inform, entertain, and persuade others through public speaking, you have to be able to span the gap between your cultural orientations and theirs. How can you accomplish those tasks?

STRATEGIES FOR IDENTIFYING AND NEGOTIATING CULTURAL DIFFERENCES

One of any speaker's primary jobs is to acknowledge relevant cultural experiences or expectations affecting listeners' reception of a message, even while calling for unified thought and action. Relevance is an important concept here. If you're giving a speech on how to fillet fish, for example, your audience's racial background probably is irrelevant, but if you're talking about federal programs for low-income housing, race likely becomes a relevant issue. If you're discussing police profiling, race is central. So how can you recognize cultural difference or diversity while seeking to get people to work together? You might have to understand the difference between your personal speaking style and those known and understood by your audiences (see Table 4.1). Consider the following strategies the best speakers have used regularly over the last few years.

Recognizing Diversity

When cultural differences between and among audience members are likely to come to people's minds when you're speaking, you should probably recognize them. Even in their differences, after all, members of a group must learn to think and act together. A famous example of this challenge in recent years was the

TABLE 4.1 *What's Your Conversational Style?*

There are cultural preferences for varied conversational styles. Researchers have identified four dimensions that govern these preferences. Which of the following is more comfortable for you?	
Direct/Indirect	1. "Can I borrow your pen?" (direct) 2. "I didn't bring a pen to class today." (indirect)
Elaborate/Succinct	1. "Your eyes have a blue tone that picks up the color in your blouse." (elaborate) 2. "You look good in blue." (succinct)
Personal/Contextual	1. "I think it's your fault." (personal) 2. "The time limits for the meeting won't allow for further discussion." (contextual)
Instrumental/Affective	1. "When I finish my homework, I'll be able to watch television." (instrumental) 2. "I hate Mondays!" (affective)

For additional information, see: William Gudykunst and Stella Ting-Toomey, *Culture and Interpersonal Communication* (Newbury Park, CA: Sage, 1988), pp. 99–116.

Million Man March on Washington organized by Minister Louis Farrakhan of the Black Muslim Nation in the fall of 1995. In fact, nearly one million people came, including many non-Muslims. Minister Farrakhan had to recognize his listeners' diverse backgrounds so that all, not just Black Muslims, would respond to his message. First, he read from a speech given by a white slaveholder in 1712 who advocated using fear, distrust, and envy to fracture the slave community. Then he noted:

> And so, as a consequence, we as a people now have been fractured, divided and destroyed, filled with fear, distrust and envy. Therefore, because of fear, envy and distrust of one another, many of us as leaders, teachers, educators, pastors and persons are still under the control mechanism of our former slave masters and their children.
>
> And now, in spite of all that division, in spite of all that divisiveness, we responded to a call and look at what is present here today. We have here those brothers with means and those who have no means. Those who are light and those who are dark. Those who are educated, those who are uneducated. Those who are business people, those who don't know anything about business. Those who are young, those who are old. Those who are scientific, those who know nothing of science. Those who are religious and those who are irreligious. Those who are Christian, those who are Muslim, those who are Baptist, those who are Methodist, those who are Episcopalian, those of traditional African religion. We've got them all here today.[6]

Minister Farrakhan's reputation as a black militant almost demanded that he include a message of reconciliation between and among the various branches of

When addressing the Million Man March in Washington, D.C., Louis Farrakhan had to demonstrate the breadth of his vision and to overcome both racial and religious divisions in his immediate and televisual audience.

African American culture. If the Million Man March was to succeed, he had to argue that African Americans, regardless of cultural diversity, had to commit themselves to common goals: "Black man, you don't have to bash white people, all we gotta do is go back home and turn our communities into productive places. All we gotta do is go back home and make our communities a decent and safe place to live."[7] In this case, the speaker recognized diversity but stated his goals in terms of the actions of individuals, not groups. Thus, diversity didn't turn into the kind of divisiveness advocated by the slaveholder of 1712.

Inventorying the diversity of cultures in one's audience is a technique that you can quickly learn to use. For example, in a speech on why students in your school's Study Abroad Program should consider going to school in Malta, you might say,

> Malta has earned its reputation as "The Crossroads of the Mediterranean," and for that reason, it can provide a wonderful social and educational experience for all of you. Those of you who want to learn in English will find classes taught in your mother tongue; those with ears for foreign languages will discover a score of them spoken in apartment complexes and restaurants. Churchgoers can find Catholic, Protestant, and Islamic houses of worship. White Eurocentric people and Black Afrocentric people work and play together on Malta. You can take side trips to nearby sites reflecting a variety of cultural experiences: You can eat scampi in Italy, couscous in Morocco, goulash in Croatia, tapas in Spain, or lamb in Sicily. Your palate—and your mind—will be opened to a dozen cultures on Malta, allowing all of you to find a niche for comfortable living in a foreign land.

Even if the topic doesn't seem inherently multicultural, you'll want to be sensitive to diversity all of the time. For example, if you plan to mention dating in a speech on teenage urban lifestyles, think about whether you can assume that everyone in your audience practices only heterosexual relationships. When talking about the hyper-growth of city government, don't unnecessarily gender the employees by calling managers "he" and secretaries "she."

Negotiating Multicultural Values

Because audiences often form into groups on the basis of the diverse characteristics of the individuals composing them, it's likely that different segments see the world in different ways, using some of the same words as others but meaning quite different things. This is because people's **value orientations**—their habitual ways of thinking about positive and negative grounds for human thought and action—tend to become materialized in highly idiosyncratic ways. Consider, for example, how the phrase *family values* was talked about in the 1990s. Everyone supports family values, but varied value orientations—we can call them liberal, middle-of-the-road, and conservative ideologies—lie underneath different people's use of that label (see Table 4.2)

These, of course, are simplified versions of people's political positions, but when most people argue about a governmental policy toward family values, they deal in such simplifications. That *family values* can mean such different things to people shouldn't be surprising, because the issue is a strongly divisive one in American society today. The differences are so great that you can't ignore

Web Exploration
For links to other readings on diversity go to
www.ablongman.com/german15e

TABLE 4.2 *The Diversity of "Family Values"*

Conservative Ideology	• America is in moral decline and must return to older family values.
	• We've become a permissive society characterized by divorce, illegitimacy, juvenile crime, and spoiled children.
	• We must bolster the traditional, two-parent, heterosexual family as the best environment for children and eliminate governmental (including school) interference with the family's operations.
Liberal Ideology	• America has to give parents more aid in raising their children.
	• Everyone, not just parents, has a stake in making sure that children are cared for, supported, and raised to be good citizens.
	• Because financial resources are so varied in this country and so many families are troubled, government at the local, state, and national levels must help parents with child care, health care, paid parental leave when children are infants, and other forms of financial assistance.
	• It is better to help all forms of family—single- and dual-parent, traditional and nontraditional—with their children than to deal with juveniles in prisons later.
Middle-of-the-Road Ideology	• Raising children should primarily be a matter of parental responsibility but with governmental safety nets in place.
	• Parents must be made more responsible for the growth and actions of their children yet should have help available in the form of family planning agencies, subsidized adoption and abortion services, and sex education in the schools.
	• If parents fail or abuse their children, the state should rescue children from such situations; but if not, parents should be made to take responsibility for their children's care, feeding, and nurture.

them when talking about this topic, either. Rather, you're better advised to recognize the differences and define the phrase *family values* carefully, so that your listeners know exactly what you're talking about. Even then, you may well want to negotiate among the varied definitions. You might have to say, "All right, then, on what do we agree? How far can we go together in helping parents raise their children?" It was precisely this kind of thinking that got liberals, conservatives, and middle-of-the-roaders together in 1993 to form a coalition in Congress. That coalition passed the Family and Medical Leave Act in the name of both fostering traditional families (by requiring businesses to pay a parent who stayed at home with an infant) and recognizing a child's needs (by guaranteeing him or her parental support in the earliest stages of social life). The middle-of-the-roaders saw this act as a perfect example of family-business-government coop-eration and so were equally supportive.

The tricky part of negotiating across value differences is to make sure that negotiations don't turn into erasure. Differences need not—and usually should not—be ignored or hidden. The best negotiators recognize them, but also assert that they should not stand in the way of cooperation. So when Elizabeth Bird, director of the Human Rights Campaign and herself a lesbian, asked the anti-gay Christian Coalition to open a dialogue on family values and lifestyles, she rec-ognized differences but sought a shared commitment to treat those differences respectfully:

> We are, all of us and those we represent, human beings. As Americans, you will have your political candidates; we will have ours. But we could, both of us, ask that our candidates speak the truth to establish their right to leadership, rather than abuse the truth in the interest of one evening's headline. We may work for differ-ent outcomes in the elections, but we can engage in an ethic of basic respect and decency.[8]

Accepting Multiple Paths to Goals

A still more difficult challenge often is to convince people that there are many ways to reach a shared goal. Thus, for example, some colleges and universities al-low students to meet a foreign-language requirement in varied ways, such as a demonstration of skills (oral or written test), life experiences (having grown up in a household that spoke the language), and in-class instruction (taking enough

Latino/a speaking styles often must combine characteristics learned in their local communities with those needed for talking to broader multicultural audiences.

classes to become proficient). Likewise, smoking cessation programs often allow smokers to try different approaches to quitting, such as hypnosis, psychotherapy, a patch or nicotine gum, group therapy, and cold-turkey regimes.

Suppose you're in a situation, however, in which people tend to say, as some parents do to their children, "There's only one way to do this: the right way!" In such situations, how can speakers create a sense of tolerance and acceptance of multiple paths leading to common goals? Metaphors and allegories (see Chapter 9) are useful ways of letting people see the utility of allowing multiple paths to shared goals. In his speech at the Atlanta Exposition in 1894, black social activist Booker T. Washington used the metaphor of the hand, whereby individual ethnic groups (i.e., the fingers) were depicted as attached to and a part of the same social system (i.e., the hand). In urging the U.S. Forest Service to hire a more culturally diverse workforce, Native American Henri Mann Morton used the metaphors of a former chieftain to argue that multiple paths can lead to the same goal:

> Finally, I would like to leave you with the words of one of our Cheyenne philosophers, High Chief, who said:
>
> > In this land there are many horses—red, white, black, and yellow. Yet, it is all one horse.
> > There are also birds of every color, red, white, black, and yellow. Yet, it is all one bird. So it is with all living things.
> > In this land where once there were only Indians, there are different races, red, white, black, and yellow. Yet, it is all one people.
> > It is good and right.
>
> High Chief was a wise man. He knew that cultural uniquenesses have a strength of their own. At the same time he recognized our common humanity.
>
> You, too, know this, as indicated by your powerful theme of "Strength through Cultural Diversity."[9]

The metaphor of colors—even Jesse Jackson's political group of the 1980s was called the Rainbow Coalition—is useful. It suggests how differences can be focused into a whole, just as the color spectrum is blended together to make "light." Historical examples also are useful, such as pointing to the success of multinational forces in times of war (the Allies of World War II or the Kosovo campaign), interpersonal and group efforts in times of disaster (people-to-people medical programs in Honduras), and the overcoming of differences in times of celebration (the building of the multiracial South African Olympic team for the first time in 1996). Teaching people to accept multiple paths or cooperative arrangements to shared goals is a technique that you must learn to use almost daily in your speech if you're going to successfully get past those matters that divide listeners into distrustful groups.

Working through the Lifestyle Choices of Others

An old saying recommends, "When in Rome, do as the Romans do." Often, you do. You might eat with chopsticks and a flat-bottomed spoon when in a Thai restaurant, kiss Romanians on both cheeks when greeting them, or take a siesta after lunch in Mexico. Urging people to accommodate to the lifestyles of other cultures is something you'll need to do on occasion, particularly if that's the only way to come together and if coming together is important to you.

A classic Western story of accommodation, of surrender to another's lifestyle, comes from the Book of Ruth in the Bible. Ruth, a Moabite, had been married to Mahlon, an Israelite from Judah. Mahlon and his brother died, so their mother Naomi decided to return from Moab to Judah. Ruth pleaded with Naomi to take her to Judah. Naomi kept thinking of reasons for Ruth not to move to what, for her, would be a foreign land. Ruth finally gave a short speech:

> Entreat me not to leave you or to return from following you; for where you go I will go, and where you lodge I will lodge; your people shall be my people, and your God, my God; where you die I will die, and there will I be buried. May the Lord so do to me and more also if even death parts me from you.[10]

Speaking of . . . Skills

Rhetorical Framing

For the last twenty years, cognitive psychologists have done research on **rhetorical framing**—the variety of conceptual borders that can be put on factually equivalent messages. The idea that human beings come to perceive, comprehend, and ultimately evaluate aspects of the world through cognitive frames is an essentially rhetorical notion. It demands that speakers be highly sensitive to how they tell their audiences to look at the world. You should practice using three kinds of cognitive frames for messages you're delivering to listeners:

1. *Metaphorical frames.* Herbert Simons argues that much political discussion depends on metaphors used as frames for policies. William Benoit, for example, compared the use of bridge metaphors employed by Bill Clinton and Bob Dole in their 1996 acceptance speeches, finding Clinton able to make his "bridge to the twenty-first century" metaphor a powerful tool for conceptualizing his agenda, with Dole not taking enough time to develop his bridge metaphor well enough to do him any good.

2. *Narrative frames.* The work done through the 1990s by Stanford communication researcher Shanto Iyengar has focused on story forms in the news. A recent study is one done by Jay Rosen of New York University and Princeton Survey Research Associates of story forms on the front pages of the *New York Times, Washington Post,* and *Los Angeles Times* and four regional papers (*Atlanta Constitution, Idaho Statesman, Rocky Mountain News,* and *Minneapolis Star-Tribune*) during January–February 1999. He found that only 16 percent of the stories were straight news accounts of the who-what-when-where-why-how variety. Most (30 percent) were combative stories of conflict, winners, and losers; 12 percent were explanatory stories about larger trends or historical contexts; 8 percent dealt with public or political policy; and the rest of the stories were written in various minor narrative forms. In a study of the last two weeks of the 2000 election campaign, Cristina Alsina, Philip Davies, and Bruce

Gronbeck found that over 60 percent of the stories in the *New York Times* and *Washington Post* dealt with candidate personalities and activities, not with the issues or policy stands they were taking.

3. *Valuative Frames.* Issues can be framed by values—by looking at them ethically, economically, socially, aesthetically, and the like. Gronbeck found that local news broadcasts tended to emphasize dominant community values when reporting the news. Jerusha Detweiler, Brian Bedell, Peter Salovey, Emily Pronin, and Alexander Rothman discovered that arguments featuring positive values ("gain-frames") were more persuasive that those featuring negative values ("loss-frames").

A good way, then, to think about your tasks as a public communicator is to start first by thinking about the sorts of rhetorical frames that will most likely be attractive and understandable to your listeners who have different cultural backgrounds.[11]

The Book of Ruth records: "And when Naomi saw that she was determined to go with her, she said no more."[12] Furthermore, Ruth's actions led her future husband, Boaz, to notice her accommodation:

All that you have done for your mother-in-law since the death of your husband has been fully told me, and how you left your father and mother and your native land and came to a people that you did not know before. The Lord recompense you for what you have done, and a full reward be given you by the lord, the God of Israel, under whose wings you have come to take refuge![13]

Here, we see an extraordinary effort at persuasion built around a full surrender to the lifestyle of others. In offering to engage in a series of acts reflective of another's lifestyle—living (lodging) with Naomi, dwelling among her people, worshipping her deity, and being buried with her—Ruth was able to enter into a complete and (apparently) mutually satisfying relationship with Naomi and all of Israel. Indeed, as a result of these promises, Ruth became the great-grandmother of the most famous of Israel's kings, David. Obviously, such a strategy of accommodation can have great personal consequences; one's own lifestyle may well be sacrificed. That very sense of personal sacrifice, perhaps, is why it's such a powerful approach to the transcendence of difference: If you're willing to give up part of your own identity, you are demanding to be taken with utmost seriousness.

Hence, in urging your classmates to pressure Congress to pass a more aggressive policy on protecting gay rights in governmentally funded charity programs, you might say,

Now, for many, perhaps even most, people in this class, the issue of gay rights in government-subsidized faith-based charities seems irrelevant. You're not gay, right? And you don't plan on working for the Salvation Army, do you? You say, "Why worry?" Well, there are plenty of reasons to worry. If charitable organizations can dictate the sexual lifestyle of their employees with the endorsement of the federal government, then such government tolerance for exceptions to anti-discrimination laws in the states can expand. If faith-based charities drive out gay employees with Washington's blessing, then they're weakening civil rights in this country as well as closing employment doors to about 10 percent of our population. If Washington allowed exceptions to antidiscrimination laws in areas of welfare, why not do it as well for companies that bid on federal construction contracts or serve as vendors to the American military? And if your sexual orientation can be dictated, how about dress codes, mandatory overtime, and the work week? Even those of you who are straight, therefore, have to deal with important social and legal questions flowing from the Salvation Army's request for exceptions to government policy.

In this kind of argument, you work through a lifestyle difference that most members of the audience do not experience, yet you do it in a way that asks them to see how it's relevant to their own.

Self-Identity in the Face of Difference

Most of the time, you probably won't be willing to surrender your self-identity—your own life experiences and culture. This creates a quandary: How can you be true to yourself while managing to work effectively with others?

One technique is to recognize your similarities with others even while maintaining your own identity. This is what President Lyndon Johnson did in 1965 when urging Congress to pass civil rights legislation: "There is no Negro problem. There is no Southern problem. There is no Northern problem. There is only an American problem. And we are met here tonight as Americans—not as Democrats or Republicans—we are met here as Americans to solve that problem."[14] Johnson was searching for a transcendent identity with which, he hoped, all in his audience could associate.

Identity also can become a complicated issue when speakers see themselves as having multiple identities that sometimes seem to conflict. Speaking to the 1996 Republican National Convention, Mary Fisher had a potential identity problem. She had AIDS and was speaking as an AIDS advocate, yet she was speaking to an audience in which the more conservative members especially wanted little to do with AIDS patients or with federal programs for help. Fisher phrased the potential identity problem early in the speech: "I mean to live, and to die, as a Republican. But I also live, and will die, in the AIDS community—a community hungry for the evidence of [political] leadership and desperate for hope." To make use of that distinction and to overcome it, Fisher chose to strip away the conservative political culture of her listeners to demand their action: "The question is not political. It's a human question, sharpened by suffering and death, and it demands a moral response." Thus, she could argue, by the end of her speech, that political action should be undertaken not for ideological reasons but for social and cultural ones. Hugging a 12-year-old African American girl named Heidia, who had been born with AIDS, Fisher concluded her speech as follows:

> The day may come when AIDS will have its way with me, when I can no longer
> lift my sons to see the future or bend down to kiss away the pain. At that moment
> Max and Zack will become the community's children more than my own, and we

will be judged not through the eyes of politics but through the eyes of children. I may lose my own battle with AIDS, but if you would embrace moral courage tonight and embrace my children when I'm gone, then you and Heidia and I would together have won a greater battle, because we would have achieved integrity.[15]

To find ways of affirming your own self, your own ethos, while also recognizing and complementing your listeners' sense of self is a search that you'll continue throughout your lifetime when you speak publicly. Finding ways of achieving unity in the midst of social diversity is a central challenge to all who would inform and persuade others. You'll often find yourself saying such things as these:

- ▶ "Now I'm not a farmer myself—I teach school right here at this college. But I live in the country and see everywhere the struggles of the subsistence farmer. I know something about the hours you put in trying to survive on marginal land. I know you're anxious about how you'll educate your kids when you need a new tractor so you can rent more land. I know how you struggle to feed your family between your trips to market your cattle. You're facing the struggles of every low-income occupation in this country."

- ▶ "I'm not from the East Coast and seldom visit, yet I can understand that the stereotyping that makes us laugh at such sitcoms as *Everybody Loves Raymond* and *Will and Grace* is unsettling. Sure, comedy should help make us aware of our stereotypes by calling attention to them, but the question is: Can that backfire? Might the behavior of Raymond's dominating parents or the outrageous performance of sexual orientation just reinforce our stereotypes about New Yorkers? Especially lower/middle-class New Yorkers and those with alternative lifestyles?"

- ▶ "Okay, so college athletes not only get a free ride through school, but many also gain enough notoriety to gain a leg up on job hunting when they're done. But have you ever stopped to think about what they pay in time, stress, and physical problems for that glory? I never did until last fall, when I became the roommate of football player."

One final point: Just as you'll often maintain your own identity in the face of different others, so also will you want to urge others to act from a conviction that their own cultural identities provide the grounds for action. Karl Marx began his treatise on the proletarian revolution with the call, "Workers of the world, unite!" That very first sentence signaled his argument that workers, as a class, had to take control of their own destinies because the upper (bourgeois) classes certainly weren't serving their interests. The phrases "Sisterhood is powerful" and "Black power" likewise were rallying cries in the 1960s for groups to recognize their own ability to influence their social, economic, and political relationships with others. So, occasionally, you will affirm not only your own but also others' identities as the bases of thought and action.

Speaking of . . . Ethics

Adapting to Moral Codes

The stated theme of this chapter is simple: You must learn to adapt your ways of talking to the cultural orientations of your listeners to achieve your goals as a speaker. What, however, are the moral limits of that requirement?

1. Must you use profanity if talking about opponents of your position just because members of your audience do?
2. Is it ethical to play to the fears a Jewish audience might have of Arabs in a speech on the evils of population control?
3. When talking to an audience of Indians about birth and population control, must you confront the practice in some of the poorer parts of India of aborting female fetuses just because of the cost of dowries?

4. What sorts of appeals to motivation and hard work should you use when talking to an audience of people whose unemployment rate has been about 40 percent for the last fifteen years?
5. What if you want to talk about a subject that is taboo (i.e., unspoken) in your family? Suppose one or both of your parents drink too heavily: How can you talk about it constructively? Or can you?

Set up some discussions in class in which you tackle these and similar problems that members of your group have encountered. Moral judgments become even more difficult to render when the participants have significantly different cultural backgrounds.

This is not to say that you'll always accept the lifestyle choices of others. There will be times when you'll find it important to confront the socially dangerous or personally destructive behaviors of, for example, a drug addict or an alcoholic. There may be lifestyle choices that others have made that don't appeal to you, and you may find it impossible to accept appeals for cultural consistency. Sometimes appeals to male bonding or sisterhood, to your whiteness or brownness, to your youth or status as an elderly person get nowhere. Some questions will transcend cultural practices in your mind, and you'll be forced to face them, such as what happens when most Americans are confronted by white supremacists. Even then, however, it's vitally important to understand all you can about others' cultures so that you can select confrontational strategies that have a chance of actually moving listeners to change their life patterns.

Throughout much of this book, you'll find us returning to questions of cultural life, multiculturalism, and the search for social unity. We do not approach what are essentially the cross-cultural dimensions of social life for political reasons. Although multiculturalism assuredly has strong political dimensions, our focus is cultural, not political. If you don't understand that speakers must adapt to their listeners' cultural moorings, you'll have great difficulty speaking to any but your own close circle. Social life—and hence public communication—is rooted in cultural practices.[16] Thus, it becomes your job to understand and to adapt your public speaking strategies to those practices.

ASSESSING YOUR PROGRESS

Chapter Summary

1. Culture is a social group's system of meanings.
2. Given cultural differences between and among people, a central question every speaker must answer is this: Can you respect individual differences and cultural diversity while nonetheless attempting to get a group of people to think alike and work together?
3. Orally based and negotiated culture operates in face-to-face encounters. Connections between people constructed by public speaking tends to be integrative, redundant, traditionalist, concrete, agonistically toned, participatory, and situational.
4. In a multicultural society, speakers must work particularly hard to recognize the varied cultural language or speaking traditions of audience members even while seeking to inform, entertain, and persuade them.
5. At least five primary strategies for communicating with multicultural audiences are available to public speakers: (1) recognizing diversity while calling for unity, (2) negotiating among diverse values, (3) accepting multiple paths to shared goals, (4) working through the lifestyle choices of others, and (5) maintaining self-identity in the face of cultural differences.

Key Terms

agonistically toned (p. 53)	participatory (p. 53)
co-cultures (p. 54)	redundant (p. 52)
concrete (p. 53)	rhetorical framing (p. 61)
culture (p. 49)	situational (p. 53)
integrative (p. 52)	subcultures (p. 54)
multiculturalism (p. 54)	traditionalist (p. 52)
oral culture (p. 52)	value orientations (p. 57)

Assessment Activities

1. Do a demographic profile of your speech classroom: Have everyone anonymously record their sex, age, family economic status, religious background, place of birth or home state, and ethnic background. Your instructor will tabulate the results and then distribute them to everyone. Write down the central idea or claim for your next speech, and ask yourself in what ways should the cultural backgrounds of your listeners as seen in the demographic profile affect how you handle this idea or claim. Turn it in for your instructor's comments.
2. Take one of the following topics and, by yourself or in class discussion, identify three or more value orientations that might be held by ideologically liberal, conservative, and middle-of-the-road people. Then suggest at least two shared goals that you think might be acceptable to most people in all three groups. Work with one of the following topics:
   a. Undocumented (illegal) aliens
   b. Legalization of same-sex marriages

 c. Federal subsidies to faith-based charities

 d. Tuition as the basic method for financing higher education

 e. Federal funding of stem-cell-based medical research

 ## Using the Web

1. Go to your school's Website. How does it mark or signal important aspects of your school's culture? Pictures of students with varied demographic characteristics? Activities for students with varied interests? Varied living situations for students staying on and off campus? Historical accounts of how the school has changed culturally over time? If you were to compare your class with what your school's Website tells you, how might that comparison direct you to frame a speech, say, recruiting high school seniors to come to your school next year?

2. Go to the home page of the intellectual journal *Cultural Analysis*. Use this page to explore the current and some past pages of this journal. For example, read Regina Bendix's article on "The Pleasures of the Ear" in Volume 1 (it's in a PDF file, so you'll need the program Acrobat Reader to do this). Or go to another article that interests you. What, if anything, does looking at articles in this journal suggest that you can do when analyzing an audience culturally?

3. Go to http://www.flash.net/~pieper/index.html. This takes you to the home page of Brave News World, a Website devoted to cultural analysis of serious and not-so-serious issues. Here, you can look at an interesting piece on Middle Eastern cultures, or you can go the archive and find Chris Pieper's "Don't Vote for a Speechwriter," an essay on the role of speechwriters in preparing presidential campaign statements (in this case, for George W. Bush in 2000). The site might cause you to think more about humor and irony as you negotiate differences between yourself and people who are culturally different from you.

 ## Using Video Workshop

Watch the speeches in Module 1, "Ethics." As you watch, concentrate on how public speakers can demonstrate a sensitivity to audience diversity. Then answer Questions 1–11.

References

 1. To explore the role of social categories of human beings is to begin dealing with the "consequences of differences and divergences, boundaries and borders," in the words of Angie McRobbie, *Postmodernism and Popular Culture* (New York: Routledge, 1994), 6. Differences and divergences should not be thought of as tools for shattering societies, as so often happens when scholars begin thinking about "the postmodern," but rather as a phenomenon that enriches your life experience and provides you with interesting challenges when you're trying to alter other people's worlds in positive ways.

 2. What is here called *common ground* is termed *radical categories* by cognitive scientist George Lakoff. A radical category is a variation on some central model.

So in one of his examples, the category "mother" can have different radicals or variations in interpretation: "(1) The birth model: the mother is one who gives birth. (2) The genetic model: the mother is the female from whom you get half your genetic traits. (3) The nurturance model: your mother is the person who raises and nurtures you. And (4) the marriage model: your mother is the wife of your father" (*Moral Politics: What Conservatives Know That Liberals Don't* [Chicago: University of Chicago Press, 1966], 8). Radical categories thus represent different ways of looking at a particular phenomenon or idea. As such, the term will be useful to us when we talk about rhetorical framing later in this chapter.

3. Walter J. Ong, *Orality and Literacy: The Technologizing of the Word* (1982; rpt. New York: Routledge, 1995), 31. "Sounded word" is used in the first heading of ch. 3 of this book, "Some Psychodynamics of Orality" (pp. 31–77), which is devoted to considering a wide range of characteristics of orality. We'll examine only some of those characteristics here.

4. Ibid., p. 43.

5. For a discussion of co-cultures, see the introduction and essays in Alberto González, Marsha Houston, and Victoria Chen, eds., *Our Voices: Essays on Culture Ethnicity and Communication*, 2nd ed. (Los Angeles: Roxbury Press, 1996). How these ideas play out publicly is explored in Clint C. Wilson II and Félix Gutiérrez, *Race, Multiculturalism, and the Media*, 2nd ed. (Thousand Oaks, CA: Sage, 1995).

6. From "Transcript from Minister Louis Farrakhan's Remarks at the Million Man March," 17 October 1995, p. 4, available at CNN's Website, http://cnn.com/US/9510/megamarch/10-16/transcript/index.html.

7. Ibid, p. 15.

8. Reprinted in *In Our Own Words: Extraordinary Speakers of the American Century,* edited by Robert Torricelli and Andrew Carroll (New York: Kodanska International, 1999), p. 419, from a speech given at the Hilton Hotel in Washington, DC, September 1995.

9. Henri Mann Morton, "Strength through Cultural Diversity," keynote address at the Northwest's Colville and Okanogan National Forest conference on cultural diversity, 23 March 1989, reprinted in Bruce E. Gronbeck et al., *Principles and Types of Speech Communication*, 12th ed. (New York: Longman, 1994), 327.

10. Ruth I:16–17, *Holy Bible,* Revised Standard Version.

11. Cristina Alsina, Philip E. Davies, and Bruce E. Gronbeck, "Preference Poll Stories in the Last Two Weeks of Campaign 2000: Uses of the Massed Opinions of Numbered Citizens," *American Behavioral Scientist,* 44 (2001): 2288–2305. William L. Benoit "Framing through Temporal Metaphor: The 'Bridges' of Bob Dole and Bill Clinton in Their 1996 Acceptance Addresses," *Communication Studies,* 52 (2001): 70–84. Jerusha B. Detweiler, Brian T. Bedell, Peter Salovey, Emily Pronin, and Alexander J. Rothman, "Message Framing and Sunscreen Use: Gain-Framed Messages Motivate Beach-Goers," *Health Psychology,* 18 (1999): 189–196. Shanto Iyengar, *Is Anyone Responsible? How Television Frames Political Issues* (Chicago: University of Chicago Press, 1991). Shanto Iyengar and Richard Reeves, eds., *Do the Media Govern? Politicians, Voters, and Reporters in America* (Thousand Oaks, CA: Sage, 1997). Jay Rosen and Princeton Survey Research Associates, "Framing the News: The Triggers, Frames, and Messages in Newspaper Coverage," in http://www.journalism.org/framing/html. Herbert W. Simons with

Joanne Morreale and Bruce Gronbeck, *Persuasion in Society* (Thousand Oaks, CA: Sage, 2001).

12. Ruth 1:18, *Holy Bible,* Revised Standard Version.

13. Ibid., Ruth 2:11–12.

14. President Lyndon Baines Johnson, "We Shall Overcome," delivered to a joint session of Congress, 15 March 1965, reprinted in Theodore Windt, ed., *Presidential Rhetoric 1961 to the Present* (Dubuque, IA: Kendall/Hunt, 1994), 67.

15. Mary Fisher, address to the Republican National Convention, 12 August 1996, transcription done from the C-SPAN broadcast of the address.

16. See ch. 8 on social criticism in Malcolm O. Sillars and Bruce E. Gronbeck, *Communication Criticism: Rhetoric, Social Codes, Cultural Studies* (Prospect Heights, IL: Waveland Press, 2001).

THE BUSHWICK &
POLICE BRUTALITY SAY:
STOP

Killing Innocent People

Violent Cops Must

Diallo
Louima

Chapter 5

Understanding Your Audience

E VERY TIME A SALESPERSON gets ready to call on a client, every time a lawyer prepares to address a jury, every time a teacher plans a lecture, and every time you get ready to give a speech, audience analysis comes into play. Successful salespeople, lawyers, teachers, and speakers know that effective public speaking is audience-centered. You improve your chances of getting the desired response by tailoring your communication to your listeners—whether a client, a jury, a classroom, or an audience. People understand things in terms of their own experiences. To be most effective, you must analyze your listeners and select experiences that are common to them.

As you know by now, you need to interact with the people you are addressing. Because of the richness and diversity of the American population, you can't assume that everyone thinks and acts exactly as you do. Think about your listeners as you select your speech topic, establish your purpose, and narrow your subject. Each of the remaining steps in speech preparation—selecting supporting materials, arranging the sequence of ideas, and developing introductions and conclusions—also requires that you keep your audience in mind. Your effectiveness as a speaker depends on how you adapt to your audience.

Obviously, you can't address your speech to each person individually. But you can identify common features among your listeners. Think of your audience as an onion. You peel away one layer and find others. The most effective way to understand your audience may be to peel away as many layers as possible. Identifying those layers or characteristics is the key to audience analysis. Once you have determined the primary features of your listeners, you can begin to adapt your ideas to them. This chapter discusses the demographic and psychological features of listeners, how to find out about your audience, and how to use what you learn. Let's first turn to demographic analysis.

ANALYZING YOUR AUDIENCE DEMOGRAPHICALLY

Web Exploration
For more demographic analysis, go to
www.ablongman.com/
german15e

Demographic analysis is the study of observable characteristics in groups of people. In any audience, you will notice traits that group members share. You should determine your listeners' general age, gender, education, group membership, and cultural and ethnic background. Let's examine each of these factors individually.

Age

Are your listeners primarily young, middle-aged, or older? Does one age group seem to dominate a mixed audience? Is there a special relationship between age groups—parents and their children, for instance? Are your listeners your peers, or are you much younger or older?

Watch a nursery school teacher talk to preschool children, and you'll see how age gaps of twenty years or more can be overcome. Nursery school teachers know that they must adapt to their young listeners or risk chaos. They adapt partly by simplifying their vocabulary and shortening their sentences. If you've ever read a story to a child, you know another secret to engaging youngsters. You can command their attention through animation. If you talk like a wizard or a teapot or a mouse, you can see children's eyes widen. The point is this: Even if your listeners are very different from you, you can still engage them by recognizing what captures their attention. In this way, you are using audience analysis to make your message more effective.

Gender

Is your audience predominantly male or female, or is the group made up of both genders? Do your listeners maintain traditional gender roles, or do they assume different roles? Ted chose date rape as the topic for a classroom speech. He was concerned about the lack of information about date rape on his campus and wanted to provide his classmates with the facts. But two things bothered Ted. First, one of his friends asked him why he was giving a speech on this topic. To the friend, it seemed that date rape was an inappropriate topic for a male speaker. Ted was surprised at his friend's reaction but also wondered whether others in his class would have the same thought. In addition, Ted realized that both men and women were members of his class. He wondered how he could interest everyone in the subject.

After some thought, Ted decided to handle the problem of gender by convincing his listeners that date rape is not an issue that affects just women. Everyone should be concerned. To reveal the extent of the problem, Ted planned to present statistics showing the rising number of date rapes. Ted would tell his listeners that he hadn't realized the extent of the problem until a good friend confided that she'd been raped by another student who offered to walk her back to her apartment after a party. By using a personal example, he tackled the stereotype of the rapist as an unknown midnight assailant lurking in a dark alley. In this way, Ted was able to convince his classmates that date rape affected both men and women. Because he was legitimately concerned about the problem and engaged everyone in his audience, Ted stimulated their concern about date rape. Ted's awareness of gender as a demographic variable allowed him to deal with his audience effectively.

Education

How much do your listeners already know about your subject? Does their experience allow them to learn about this subject easily and quickly? Obviously, people who have worked with a computer word-processing program, for example, will learn its new features more quickly than people who have not.

Knowing the educational background of your audience can guide you in your choice of language, kinds of supporting material, and organizational pattern. Assume that you are addressing the faculty senate as a student advocate of expanded student parking on campus. This audience will demand strong support for your arguments. You can express complex arguments in technical language. The general educational level of your listeners requires that you adapt your ideas and their development. However, when you are invited to speak to a local citizens' group about the proposal for expanded student parking, you will have to broaden your language, supporting material, and organization for a more diverse audience.

Group Membership

Do your listeners belong to groups that represent special attitudes or identifiable values? Are they part of a formal organization such as a church, chamber of commerce, or scouting group, or have they spontaneously come together? Can you pick out common traditions or practices within the organization? What is the cultural climate of the organization?

In some ways, Americans are joiners. We form churches, fan clubs, support groups, hobby organizations, chat rooms—the list seems endless. You can find a group to join for almost any purpose. We come together to share common experiences, to solidify common values, and to express feelings. Often, group members share demographic characteristics. For example, doctors, lawyers, and dentists join professional societies based on occupational similarities. Consumer advocacy groups and support groups are united by purpose. Members of labor unions hold jobs and economic welfare in common. Homeowners' groups share geographic features. Political parties and religious groups attract people who share common values. Tee ball clubs, high school reunions, and associations of retired persons unite people who are similar in age. Groups share similar interests and goals that can be identified readily. Identifying these common interests is an important element of assessing your audience, as the following example illustrates.

The city council in Abby's hometown wanted to build an incinerator for disposal of solid waste to save money. Abby was against the incinerator project, and after voicing her opinions at a backyard barbecue, she found herself representing a grassroots group of local homeowners. Abby attended the next city council meeting to express the views of the neighborhood. She told the city council that more money could be saved by recycling household plastics, selling aluminum cans, and mulching grass clippings. Those simple steps would reduce the waste significantly and make a new incinerator unnecessary. Abby's clinching argument was to remind council members that several of them were up for reelection. Her arguments hit a nerve; the incinerator project was canceled. As members of a group, the city council was dependent on homeowners' approval for their jobs.

Cultural and Ethnic Background

Are members of your audience predominantly from particular cultural groups? Do your listeners share a special heritage? Can you identify common origins among listeners? More and more, the United States is becoming a multiracial, multicultural society. Currently, over 25 percent of all Americans identify themselves as multiracial, and that number is expected to grow rapidly in the next ten years. Many Americans celebrate their roots in other countries or cultures, and those strong cultural heritages may bear on your speech-making experience. It is important to recognize the cultural and ethnic diversity of your listeners, as the following example shows.

Ed, a student in mass communication, was invited to talk about American media to a group of visiting students sponsored by the Japanese Youth Exchange Program. He realized that some of his examples would be familiar to his listeners. Many Japanese are avid sports fans, follow *The Simpsons,* and have fan clubs for American celebrities. The Japanese also enjoy their own programs. Considering this, Ed decided to investigate Japanese television more fully. He found many examples of high-quality programs. After reading some particularly interesting research on Japanese soap operas, Ed discovered *Oshin,* the daily serial drama that was rated high among television programs in Japan. He read about the series, which dramatizes the life of an early-twentieth-century heroine. The struggle of new ideas with traditional values is featured in most episodes, and Ed realized how conflict characterizes both Japanese and American soap operas. This recognition of the similarity in television programming gave Ed an idea for his speech. He decided to focus on conflict in soap opera programming and to use both American and Japanese programs as examples. The speech was a hit. Like Ed, you should recognize when the background of your audience influences the speech topic and its development.

Using Demographic Information

The importance of demographic analysis does not lie in simply recognizing the variables present in an audience. This is just the first step. The key is to decide which of these demographic factors will affect your listeners' reception of your message. In other words, you must shape your message with your audience in mind.

Sometimes several factors may affect your message. For example, if you've been asked to talk to a local kindergarten class about your baseball card collection, you must take age and education into consideration. You should adapt to your young listeners by using simplified concepts—talking about the number of hits rather than ERAs. You should also keep your talk brief to accommodate shorter attention spans. And, most importantly, you should involve children by using visual aids. Bring several cards for them to hold and examine.

If you were to talk about your baseball card collection to a group of local business owners, on the other hand, your message would be very different. The age and education of your listeners would still influence your message development, but since those demographic factors would be different, your message should be adapted to the changes. Since your listeners are older and better educated, they can understand more complex ideas. For example, you might focus on the investment potential of baseball card collections. As owners of businesses, their group membership suggests that they would be interested in the commercial aspects of your collection.

Demographic analysis helps you adapt your message to your listeners more effectively. Demographic analysis can assist you in understanding your listeners by pinpointing the factors that are common among them. You can better select and develop your key ideas if you know who is listening to your speech.

ANALYZING YOUR AUDIENCE PSYCHOLOGICALLY

Careful psychological analysis of your audience may provide clues about how they think. This is especially important when your general speaking purpose is to inform or to persuade. Before you can hope to add understanding, alter their thoughts, or prompt actions, you need to know what ideas your listeners already hold.

To analyze your audience psychologically, you can use **psychological profiling.** That is, you identify what your listeners already think and feel, much as you would discover their demographic characteristics. Beliefs, attitudes, and values are the key concepts in discussing the psychology of listeners. After we have examined each of these concepts, we'll discuss ways in which you can use them to tailor your message to your listeners.

Beliefs

The first task of psychological profiling is understanding your audience's beliefs. **Beliefs** are convictions about what is true or false. They arise in many ways—from firsthand experiences, from public opinion, from supporting evidence, from authorities, or even from blind faith. For example, you might believe that calculus is a difficult course on the basis of your own experience. At the same time, you might also believe that calculus is important for your career because of what your parents and high school teachers have told you. Each of these beliefs is supported by different kinds of external evidence. Each belief can be held with a different degree of conviction. Let's explore each of these characteristics of beliefs.

Beliefs are supported by varying degrees of external evidence. When you say, 'Research has proven that infant blue whales gain an average of ten pounds per day," you're very sure of that belief because you know that marine biologists have proven it. You hold this belief with certainty because you have hard evidence to support it. Other beliefs might not have strong external evidence to support them. As a speaker, you can indicate to your listeners the kind of evidence you have chosen to support your claims. You might say, "Marine biologists agree that . . ." to convey the strength of your facts. Or you can indicate that your beliefs are based on personal observations by saying, "In my opinion. . . ."[1]

Beliefs are also held with varying degrees of conviction. Some of your beliefs might be right, and others might be wrong. History is filled with examples of beliefs that later turned out to be wrong. In any case, as a speaker, you must understand the strength with which your audience holds its beliefs so that you can adapt your message accordingly. For example, if your speech topic is the importance of taking a foreign language while in college but you know that your audience believes foreign languages to be useless, you will need to construct your message with your audience's beliefs in mind. Another audience might consider foreign languages to be critical for a liberal education. Your message for this audience would be quite different.

Once you have investigated your audience's beliefs, how can you use this information? You need to determine which beliefs will help you and which are obstacles to be overcome. Imagine that you are explaining facets of Malay culture to a North American audience. Since most of your listeners probably don't believe in *hantu,* the malicious spirits that take the form of beasts or old men in Malay culture, you will have to make a special effort to help them understand this difference in culture. Until your listeners appreciate the importance of spirits in Malay culture, they will have difficulty comprehending it. Or suppose that you are opposed to granting rights to gay personnel in the military. You want to convince your classmates to accept your point of view. Consider what your listeners believe to be true. If they accept that gays already serve in the military and have served with distinction, then you may have to convince them that the presence of gays is disruptive. On the other hand, if they think that the number of gays in the armed forces is negligible or that gay personnel do not make good soldiers, your job is much easier. Thus, determining what your audience believes and how strongly their beliefs are held will help you focus your ideas.

Attitudes

The second goal of psychological profiling is to identify audience attitudes. **Attitudes** are tendencies to respond positively or negatively to people, objects, or ideas. Attitudes express our individual preferences and feelings such as "I like my public speaking class," "Classical music is better than rap music," and "Prague is a beautiful city." In other words, they are emotionally weighted. Attitudes often summarize our personal reactions to our beliefs about the world (see Table 5.1).

Attitudes often influence our behavior. One dramatic example of the strength of attitudes occurred when the Coca-Cola Corporation introduced "New Coke," a refigured formula, with disastrous results. Although extensive blind taste tests indicated that people preferred New Coke's flavor, consumers reacted negatively because of their loyalty to the classic formula. Their attitudes

Powerful attitudes often come into play in our everyday lives.

TABLE 5.1 *Beliefs and Attitudes*

Beliefs and attitudes are psychological constructs held by individuals or by groups.	
Beliefs	**Attitudes**
Seat belts save lives.	Fastening my seat belt takes too much time.
Vegetables contain important minerals and vitamins.	Broccoli tastes good.
My grandparents came from Mexico City.	I love my grandfather.

Web Exploration

For examples of highly opinionated editorials go to www.ablongman.com/ german15e

influenced their purchasing behavior, and the corporation wisely "reintroduced" Coca-Cola Classic.

As a speaker, you should consider the dominant attitudes of your listeners. Audiences may have attitudes toward you, your speech subject, and your speech purpose. Your listeners may think you know a lot about your topic, and they may be interested in learning more. This is an ideal situation. However, if they think you're not very credible and they resist learning more, you must deal with their attitudes. For example, if a speaker tells you that you can earn extra money in your spare time by selling magazine subscriptions, you may have several reactions. The thought of extra income from a part-time job is enticing. At the same time, you suspect that it might be a scam, and you feel uncomfortable because you don't know the speaker well. These attitudes toward the speech topic, purpose, and speaker will undoubtedly influence your final decision about selling subscriptions.

Values

The third component of psychological profiling is understanding audience values. **Values** are the basic concepts organizing one's orientation to life. They underlie an individual's particular attitudes and beliefs. For many Americans, life, freedom, family, and honesty are basic values. These are deeply ingrained and enduring; as a result, they are very resistant to change. Imagine trying to convince a friend to renounce American citizenship. No matter how noble your cause, you will probably meet powerful resistance because you are attacking fundamental values.

Values are more basic than beliefs or attitudes. They serve as the foundations from which beliefs and attitudes may spring (see Figure 5.1). For example, a person may hold the value "Human life is sacred." That value can be expressed in multiple attitudes: "Abortion is wrong" or "Mercy killing is immoral." That value may also be expressed in beliefs such as "A fetus should be treated as a human being," "Most Americans are opposed to abortion rights legislation," or "Religious authority ought to be respected on questions of morality."

Values, then, underlie an individual's particular attitudes and beliefs. Former Representative Barbara Jordan, the first African American woman to give the keynote address at the Democratic National Convention, identified basic values

Values serve to motivate people to action. Political change is often based on shared value orientations.

that her audience shared. Among them, she listed "equality for all and privileges for none."[2] Her speech is highly regarded because she highlighted common ground—shared values that organized and influenced the beliefs and attitudes of her listeners.

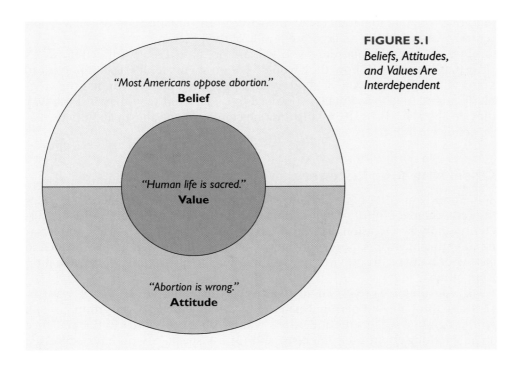

FIGURE 5.1
Beliefs, Attitudes, and Values Are Interdependent

"Most Americans oppose abortion."
Belief

"Human life is sacred."
Value

"Abortion is wrong."
Attitude

DISCOVERING DEMOGRAPHIC AND PSYCHOLOGICAL FACTORS

Now that you understand which demographic and psychological factors are important to consider in developing a speech, you should think about how you're going to discover this information. You may already know the answer: You can ask your listeners for their opinions, and you can observe them and draw inferences from your observations.

Surveying Your Listeners

Often the best source of information about your audience is your listeners themselves. Ask them. You may not have the services of a professional pollster, but you can conduct informal interviews with members of the group or develop a more formal survey to assess their beliefs, attitudes, and values.

Suppose you are concerned about the rapidly rising number of sexually transmitted diseases among local teenagers. As the parent of a teenager, you are convinced that every effort should be made in the schools to halt this trend, including making condoms available to all students. If you intend to convince the school board to take action on this issue, you need to know how the members of the board currently feel about the issue. Your plan is clear: You talk to the members of the board individually and find out.

However, you may also have to convince the local Parent-Teacher Association to support your plan. This presents an entirely different problem since there are thousands of parents in your school district. Even if you spent hours on the phone, you still probably couldn't interview every parent in the district. Your alternative is to talk to parents who are active in the organization or call a representative sample to get an accurate profile of their views.

In each case, the questions you will ask are basic. You want action, so it's clear that you will ask how they would vote on the issue. It's also important to know whether they'll vote at all, so you will need to find out whether they regularly attend meetings. Finally, you need to understand why they feel the way they do about the issue. By asking this question, you'll be able to identify the basic points of conflict.

Observing Your Listeners

Sometimes you don't have direct access to members of your audience. If this is the case, then you must rely on indirect observation and inference for your audience analysis. Occasionally you'll have public statements, earlier conversations, voting behaviors, purchasing decisions, and other information on which to base your analysis. At other times, you will have to rely on indirect information from others.

If you aren't closely tied to the group you will address, you'll want to (1) think through your personal experiences with members of the group, (2) talk with program chairpersons and others who can tell you who is in the audience and something about their interests, and (3) ask speakers who have addressed this or similar audiences what you can expect. Keep in mind that these strategies provide limited information. You can supplement this information by attending a few meetings of the group yourself or reading the constitution of or other literature about the group. Don't forget to check the Internet. Many groups maintain home pages, and you can gain information from them. In combination, these observations will help you adjust your speech to your listeners.

Finally, you can consult published sources that provide demographic and survey information on broad segments of our society. Opinion polls, market surveys, political profiles, and demographic shifts are all available in your library or on the Internet in sources such as *Statistical Abstract of the United States, Survey of Current Business, Business Conditions Digest, Bureau of Labor Statistics News, Statistics of Income Bulletin,* and *Facts on File.*

Using Your Psychological Profile

After you have developed a profile of your audience's beliefs, attitudes, and values, how can you use this information? Understanding your audience's beliefs, attitudes, and values will help you make decisions about three aspects of your speech: your ideas, your supporting materials, and your phrasing. Your psychological profile can help you do the following:

1. *Frame your ideas.* For example, if your listeners believe that childhood is a critical time of development, you can move from this belief to recruit volunteers for a day care co-op. If they value family life, you can touch on this theme to solidify their commitment. On the other hand, if your listeners are apathetic about childhood development, you must establish the critical nature of the early years of child development before you can hope to persuade them to support a co-op.

2. *Choose your supporting materials.* If your audience analysis shows that your listeners consider statistics to be reliable, you should use scientific studies or numerical data in your speech. On the other hand, if your audience believes in the divine inspiration of the Bible, you can cite biblical testimony to sway them.

3. *Phrase your ideas.* You can choose your words to reflect the intensity of your audience's convictions. If your listeners are ready to picket a local video rental store, then your language should show the urgency of immediate action. Demand action now. On the other hand, if they are reluctant to take up placards, then you should use less forceful words.

USING AUDIENCE ANALYSIS IN SPEECH PREPARATION

Audience analysis helps you search for clues to the way your listeners think and act. Identifying the demographic and psychological characteristics of your listeners is an important step toward good communication. Using these characteristics helps you discover what might affect the audience's acceptance of your ideas. Consider how audience analysis helps you prepare to speak through audience targeting and audience segmentation.

As you consider your reasons for speaking, you need to determine what you can realistically expect to accomplish with your particular audience in the time you have available. Analysis of your audience helps you develop your speaking purposes, your goals, and the appeals you will use.

Developing Your Purposes

Suppose you have a part-time job with your college's Career Planning and Placement Office; you know enough about its operations and have enough personal interest in it to want to speak about career planning and placement to a variety of listeners. What you've discovered about different audiences should help you determine appropriate, specific purposes for each. If you were to talk to a group of incoming students, for example, you would know that they probably:

- ▶ Know little about the functions of a career planning and placement office (have few beliefs in this area).
- ▶ Are predisposed to look favorably on career planning and placement (have a positive attitude toward the subject).
- ▶ Are more concerned with such short-term issues as getting an adviser, registering, and learning about basic degree requirements than they are with long-range matters such as finding jobs (are motivated by practical values).
- ▶ See you as an authoritative speaker and consequently are willing to listen to you (have a positive attitude toward the speaker).

Given these audience considerations, you would probably provide basic rather than detailed information about career planning and placement. You might phrase your specific purpose as follows: "To brief incoming students on the range of services offered by the Career Planning and Placement Office." This orientation will include a brief description of each service and a general appeal to your audience to use these services to make some curricular decisions.

If you spoke to a group of graduating college seniors on the same subject, you would address your listeners differently. You would discover that they:

- ▶ Are familiar with the Career Planning and Placement Office through personal use or through roommates and friends who have used it (have beliefs that are based on personal experience).
- ▶ Have strong positive feelings about career planning and placement because they are hoping to use such services to find jobs when they graduate (have a positive attitude toward the subject).
- ▶ Tend to think education has prepared them to "earn a decent living" (have a practical perspective on the topic).
- ▶ May view you as an unqualified speaker on this subject, especially if you aren't a senior or aren't a full-time employee of the office (have a negative attitude toward the speaker).

Given these factors, you should offer more specific details in some areas. Because your listeners are probably aware that they will soon need career placement help, you might describe the special features of the office rather than simply outlining its general duties. You could reassure them that the office successfully places many students and point out that the process is more successful when students allow ample time for résumé development, job searching, and interviewing. You could demonstrate your expertise by talking about career possibilities across a variety of fields—especially if you know what fields are represented in the group you are addressing. You might phrase your specific purpose as follows: "To inform graduating seniors about ways in which the office can help students find employment and about specific types of information and assistance that the office provides to students." Audience analysis will help you shape your specific purposes and determine which are most appropriate to your listeners.

Developing Your Goals

As you develop your speaking goals, it is important to consider both the demographic and psychological dimensions of your listeners. Demographic and psychological factors affect what your listeners will comprehend as well as how they will interpret your message.

Demographic factors such as age, gender, education, group membership, and cultural and ethnic background will help you understand your listeners' familiarity with your topic, motivation to listen, and ability to understand your message. If your goal is to explain the new tax laws, your message will take a very different form for part-time teenage workers than for senior citizens. Imagine the same informative speech for an audience of tax accountants. As you can see, the demographic nature of your audience is critical as you think about the complexity of the information you will share as well as the ways in which your listeners will probably use that information.

You can use the psychological factors that you discover through audience analysis to understand how your listeners will probably interpret your message. Your listeners' beliefs, attitudes, and values can be important clues to how they will perceive what you say. For example, in speaking to a local Parent-Teacher Association about a new after-school program of foreign language and culture instruction, you're addressing an audience of school administrators, teachers, and parents. Each of these groups has varying beliefs, attitudes, and values that will affect their perception of the program. School administrators may believe that cost is prohibitive, while teachers may think the program will enhance the current curriculum, and parents may want to know how the program will affect their children. Probably most audience members value education. As you think about how you will present your information, you should consider framing it within the broad value of education while at the same time addressing the practical problems of cost and implementation.

Be realistic about the degree of change you can expect from your listeners. How intensely can you motivate an audience to react to a topic? If your listeners are strongly opposed to downtown renovation, a single speech—no matter how eloquent—will probably not reverse their opinions. One attempt may only neutralize some of their objections. This is a more realistic goal for a single speech than completely reversing opinions.

How much action can you expect after your speech? If your prespeech analysis indicates that your listeners strongly support after-school programs, you

may be able to recruit many of them to work long hours lobbying and participating in telephone marathons. However, if they only moderately support such
programs, you might ask for a small monetary donation rather than an actual
time commitment. Audience analysis should help you set realistic communication goals.

Developing Your Appeals

So far, we've focused on how audience analysis helps you to target your audience as a group. Keep in mind that no matter how close together people are
seated in the room, they are still individuals. Sometimes you can approach each
listener individually. However, such communication is time-consuming and in-
efficient when you're dealing with matters of broad public concern.

Using an approach called **audience segmentation** you can divide your listeners into a series of subgroups or "target populations." A typical college audience, for example, might be segmented by academic standing (incoming students
through seniors), by academic major (art through zoology), by classroom performance (A+ to F), or even by extracurricular activity (ROTC, SADD, Young Republicans, Pi Kappa Delta). You can direct main ideas to each of these subgroups.

Suppose you were to give a speech to members of a local community club,
urging them to fund a scholarship. Through audience analysis, you discover that
the club is composed of social service personnel, educators, and business people.
By thinking of the club as segmented into these subgroups, you are in a position
to offer each subgroup some reasons to support your proposal. For example, you
might appeal to social service workers by saying, "The social-team concept means
educating others who will contribute to the improvement of the community."
For the educators in your audience, you could state, "By denying education to
capable students, we neglect to tap into one of the most important resources of
our community—young people." Finally, for business people, you might declare,
"Well-educated citizens contribute more to the financial resources of the community as investors, property owners, and heads of households."

Speaking of . . . Skills

Handling Hostile Audiences

How do you gain a positive response from people who disagree with you? While it is un-
reasonable to expect to convert every member of a hostile audience, you can improve
your chances of getting them to listen with the following strategies:

1. *Establish good will.* Let them know you are concerned about the issues or problems
   you're discussing.
2. *Start with areas of agreement.* Develop some common ground before you launch into
   controversial territory.
3. *Offer principles of judgment.* Determine the basis on which you and your listeners can
   evaluate ideas.

4. *Develop positive credibility.* If your listeners respect you, they are less likely to reject your ideas.
5. *Use experts and supporting material to which your audience will respond.* Choose your supporting material with your audience in mind.
6. *Disarm your listeners with humor.* Mutual laughter establishes positive rapport.
7. *Use a multisided presentation.* Recognize more than one perspective on the issues.

Above all, be realistic when addressing a hostile audience. Remember that the more strongly an audience opposes your position, the less change you can reasonably expect to occur.

For more information, see: Herbert Simons, *Persuasion* (New York: Random House, 1986), pp. 150–160.

You can see how each statement is directed to segments of your audience. These main ideas implicitly refer to the commitment of social services to helping people from all strata of life, to educators' beliefs and attitudes that youth are a national resource, and to business leaders' commitment to financial responsibility and success.

Understanding your audience is a key step in speech preparation. To become a competent speaker, you must make many decisions about your topic, specific purposes, and phrasing for central ideas and main ideas. Demographic and psychological analyses of audience members will help you make these decisions. If you learn all you can about your listeners and use relevant information to plan your speech, you'll improve your chances for success.

A SAMPLE AUDIENCE ANALYSIS

In this chapter, we have surveyed various factors that you will consider as you analyze your audience and occasion. If you work systematically, these choices will become clearer. Suppose you want your local city council to adopt a program in which drug addicts can exchange used hypodermic needles for clean ones. You think such a program will help prevent the spread of AIDS (acquired immunodeficiency syndrome) among drug addicts. You might prepare the following analysis of your audience as you plan your speech:

I. *General Description of the Audience:* The city council comprises 15 members elected to office by local districts. The city manager and mayor also attend council meetings. Citizens sometimes attend and speak at council meetings.

II. *Demographic Analysis*
   A. *Age:* Most of the council members are between 45 and 65.
   B. *Gender:* The council is composed of 12 men and 3 women. The mayor and city manager are men.
   C. *Education:* All but four of the council members have finished high school; several completed B.A. degrees in various fields, including political science, pharmacy, nursing, home

economics, and accounting. Two health professionals on the council are familiar with disease history and control.

   D. *Group Membership:* All listeners are politically active and registered voters. Although they do not necessarily share party affiliation, they all value participation in the democratic process.

   E. *Cultural and Ethnic Background:* Ethnic background is mixed, but predominantly African American, European, and Hispanic.

III. *Psychological Profile*

   A. *Factual Beliefs:* Anyone who contracts AIDS will die of it. In spite of promising new research, there is no cure for AIDS.

   B. *Opinions:* Most consider AIDS to be a problem associated with particular groups, including homosexual males, hemophiliacs, and intravenous drug users.

   C. *Attitudes:* Members of the council probably were surprised by the recent news of the AIDS death of a prominent community resident. They probably do not consider themselves likely victims.

   D. *Values:* They are committed to the democratic process and take pride in political involvement at the community and state levels. They see themselves as common people— "the heart of America"—fulfilling the American dream. Council members often point to community progress in civil rights issues, general educational reforms, and high voter turnout during elections.

   With this prespeech audience analysis completed, you have a better idea of how to frame your speech. From your analysis you conclude that the council may initially resist your needle exchange proposal because they think that AIDS affects only a small number of people who engage in high-risk behaviors. They may believe that most citizens are not at risk. Realizing this, you can choose among several approaches:

   1. Stress the listeners' commitment to the welfare of the community and their belief in the rights of citizens, even members of minority groups. Encourage their feelings of pride in previous civic accomplishments and challenge them to face the AIDS crisis.

   2. Make it clear that the needle exchange program is not simply a moral issue. Stress the practical importance of treating disease, regardless of moral issues. Use projections of future infection rates to emphasize that everyone's health may be affected if AIDS is allowed, through ignorance or neglect, to spread unchecked.

   3. Identify other communities that have used needle exchange programs with success. Overcome audience apathy and hostility by encouraging members to discuss the disease further.

   4. Ask the council to sponsor an open forum for continued attention to the issue, rather than demanding immediate commitments or political action.

   5. Praise the group's excellent record in community projects. Stress the farsightedness of the council on other difficult issues. Aim the bulk of the speech at gaining approval for open-minded discussions.

Speaking of . . . Ethics

Using Audience Analysis Ethically

Marketers can often determine the underlying emotions and values that drive consumer choices using a process called "psychographics." This ability to understand consumer behavior based on demographic and psychological profiling gives marketers an impressive tool. It also gives rise to some ethical concerns. Consider the following uses of audience analysis:

1. Research suggests that many people who suffer from alcoholism feel deep social inadequacy and alienation. Advertisers often associate alcohol with social situations such as parties. Is this attempt to target alcoholics by tapping their need for companionship an ethical use of audience analysis?
2. Some fixed beliefs are **stereotypes,** the perception that all individuals in a group are the same. Is

it appropriate for speakers to use stereotypes? For example, a speaker might say, "We all know the rich cheat on their taxes. Let's raise the tax rates in the higher income brackets to compensate" or "You can't trust him—he's a politician!"

3. Should advertisers of security devices such as pepper sprays, alarm systems, and handguns play on women's fears of rape and assault?
4. Tobacco companies target young people by offering inducements to purchase cigarettes, such as free gifts. Is this ethical?

For more information on psychographics, see: Rebecca Piirto, *Beyond Mind Games: The Marketing Power of Psychographics* (Ithaca, NY: American Demographics Books, 1991).

As you can see, when you understand your listeners it's much easier to tailor a specific message for them. You are more likely to develop an effective speech when you first consider the demographic and psychological characteristics of your listeners.

ASSESSING YOUR PROGRESS

Chapter Summary

1. Public speaking is audience-centered.
2. The primary goal of audience analysis is to discover the demographic and psychological characteristics of your listeners that are relevant to your speech purposes and ideas.
3. Demographic analysis is the study of audience characteristics such as age, gender, education, group membership, and cultural and ethnic backgrounds.
4. Psychological profiling seeks to identify the beliefs, attitudes, and values of audience members.
5. Beliefs are convictions about what is true or false.
6. Attitudes are tendencies to respond positively or negatively to people, objects, or ideas.
7. Values are basic concepts organizing one's orientation to life.
8. Audience segmentation allows you to identify audience subgroups for more effective selection of main ideas.

Key Terms

attitudes (p. 77)   psychological profiling (p. 75)
audience segmentation (p. 84)   stereotypes (p. 87)
beliefs (p. 76)   values (p. 78)
demographic analysis (p. 72)

Assessment Activities

1. Choose the text of a speech from this textbook, from the VideoWorkshop, from *Vital Speeches of the Day* (or another anthology of speeches), or from a newspaper, such as the *New York Times*. Identify statements of fact and opinion in the speech. Determine the speaker's attitudes and values from statements in the speech. Develop a profile of the audience and assess the effectiveness of the speech for this group of listeners.

2. Gather some magazine advertisements and bring them to class. As a class or in groups, share your advertisements. Speculate about the audiences for which they were intended. To what attitudes are the advertisers trying to appeal? Are they trying to create beliefs? What tactics do they use? How effective do you think these tactics are?

3. Imagine that you are the chief speechwriter for each of the individuals listed below. Decide which audience subgroups you will need to address. What values, attitudes, and beliefs are they likely to hold? What can you say in your speech to engage their attention and support?

   a. The president of the United States, addressing the nation on prime-time television concerning the latest international diplomatic development.

   b. The president of your student government, welcoming first-year students to campus at the beginning of the academic year.

   c. A defense lawyer, conducting closing arguments in a murder trial.

   d. A ninth-grade teacher, cautioning a class about the use of illegal drugs.

🌐 Using the Web

1. Locate a home page for an organization. What insight does the page give you into the nature of the organization? From the material provided, determine who is likely to belong to the group. Speculate about age, gender, education, and cultural or ethnic background. What attitudes, beliefs, and values do you think members of this organization might hold in common? Explain your conclusions.

2. Make a list of your primary interests and hobbies. Search the Internet for clubs, chat rooms, and resource groups for each of the items on your list. Compare your results with other class members.

Using VideoWorkshop

Watch the speeches in Module 3, "Audience Analysis." As you watch, concentrate on the ways that a careful analysis of audience can impact the success of a speech. Then answer Questions 1–11.

References

1. For more discussion, see: David L. Bender (ed.), *American Values* (San Diego, CA: Greenhaven Press, 1989); Milton M. Rokeach, *Beliefs, Attitudes, and Values: A Theory of Organization and Change* (San Francisco: Jossey-Bass, 1968); and Rokeach, *The Nature of Human Values* (New York: Collier-Macmillan, Free Press, 1973).

2. See Wayne Thompson, "Barbara Jordan's Keynote Address: Fulfilling Dual and Conflicting Purposes," *Central States Speech Journal,* 30 (1979): 272–277.

Chapter 6

Finding and Using Supporting Materials

THE TWENTIETH CENTURY, called by many the Communications Century, has generated the miracles of information technology: the telegraph, the telephone, film, television, the computer chip, satellites, fax machines, electronic mail, cell phones, and digital sound and video reproduction. You have at your disposal staggering amounts of information that can be accessed more easily than ever before. As you put your speeches together, you will need to find and sort through this information, choosing the supporting material that works best for your speech.

This chapter explores the challenge of finding and assembling the materials relevant to your speeches, your audiences, and the speech occasion. Your challenge, ultimately, is to turn information into knowledge—to transform streams of facts into something your listeners can use in their daily lives. Devoting careful thought to how you will organize your search for supporting materials and then how you will put those materials to use will make your preparation time more productive. First we will examine the sources of supporting materials, and then well suggest some ways of using these materials.

DETERMINING THE KINDS OF SUPPORTING MATERIALS YOU'LL NEED

To guide your choice of supporting materials, you need to consider your main topic, your audience, and the ideas you intend to discuss. Thinking about these elements should help you decide what kind of supporting materials you will need. Consider the following critical questions to guide the selection of supporting materials before you begin your search process.

1. *What support does your topic require?* Specific topics require certain sorts of supporting materials. It's obvious that you wouldn't use the same kind of supporting material to describe your experience biking in Maui as you would to report your international relation club's financial status. The rational requirements of your speech topic should suggest the appropriate forms of supporting material.

2. *What does your audience need to know?* No matter what forms of support you choose, merely citing the findings of research is clearly not enough. You also need to think about what your audience already knows and what they need to know. Your search for supporting materials should reflect your listeners' needs.

If you give a speech on skin cancer, your audience is probably most interested in knowing their chances of getting it. They may be unaware that certain practices, such as the use of tanning beds, increase the risk of getting skin cancer, and they probably don't know about the latest treatment methods. These are certainly things you will want to find out as you search for supporting material on this topic.

3. *Which form of support will be most effective for your topic?* Different forms of supporting material accomplish different results. Explanations, comparisons, and statistics will help you develop the topic so your listeners can better understand it. Examples and testimony will lend interest to the topic. In an introduction to a speech on fire alarms, you might use an example of a local house fire to stimulate audience interest and then, in the body of the speech, use statistics to establish the importance of installing fire alarms.

4. *How objective is your supporting material?* To read and think critically, you must be able to distinguish among sources of information. One way to differentiate is to distinguish between what historians call **primary sources** (eyewitness/firsthand accounts) and **secondary sources** (accounts based on other sources of information). The diary of a woman who survived the terrorist attack on the World Trade Center would be a primary source; a *Washington Post* story about the event would be a secondary source. Obviously, each type of supporting material reflects a different perspective on the events of September 11, 2001.

Speaking of . . . Skills

How Much Is Enough?

Have you ever found yourself wondering, "How much supporting material should I use in my speech?" While there's no absolute rule governing the number or kind of supporting materials, you need enough support to establish your points. This varies according to the quality and kind of supporting materials. Here are some guidelines:

1. *Complex or abstract ideas are enhanced by concrete supporting materials such as visual aids and specific examples.* A graph or example from daily life would clarify a speech on chaos theory.
2. *Controversial points require a lot of authoritative evidence.* This means that a speech for raising income taxes would benefit from statistics, budget trend information, and well-respected testimony.
3. *Speakers with low credibility need more supporting material than speakers with high credibility.* If you plan to speak on educational reform for the next century but your only experience has been as a student, you should use a lot of supporting material.
4. *If your topic is abstract or distant from your listeners' experiences, use concrete supporting material to establish identification with listeners.* A speech on life in a space station doesn't come alive until you insert specific details and concrete examples.
5. *If your audience's attention or comprehension is low, use more examples.* Enliven a speech on accounting procedures with a story or a specific instance.

This initial thinking about your topic (a) helps you decide what supporting materials your topic requires, (b) guides your selection of supporting materials in light of your audience demands, (c) determines which forms of supporting material are most effective for your topic, and (d) indicates what supporting material will be most objective.

SOURCES OF SUPPORTING MATERIALS

So where do you find the materials you'll need for your speeches? You'll find those materials exactly where you find all ideas in this world: in electronic networks and storage technologies, in print, in interaction with others with special knowledge, and in information-gathering instruments you construct.

The Electronic World

You've seen the ads: AT&T promising you access to information from anywhere, the Pentium IV chip bringing you sounds and images from every imaginable source, and your own college or university promising to link you internationally with other institutions of learning and with new ideas. But how? To survive, you must learn to search electronically with a click of a mouse.

The Electronic Card Catalog   Your college or university electronic card catalog should be your first stop. It will provide a wide array of library holdings and
electronic databases for you to consider. Suppose you want to do a speech on the
financing of home health care for the terminally ill through hospice organizations. If you enter "death" to begin your search, you'll put up several thousand
hits—far, far too many. If you enter "hospice," you'll still get an overwhelming
number of items. But if you narrow your search further by entering "hospice
costs," you'll get a manageable number of sources to examine further.

Learning to narrow through precise specification of topic or through subcat-
egorization will make your searches less frustrating. Most search sites offer you
Boolean searches, in which you use such words as *and, or,* and *not* to control the
subject matter. So "medieval *or* architecture" gets you all references with either
word; "medieval *and* architecture" pulls up references to all works with both
words in them; and "medieval *and* architecture *not* England" will highlight
medieval architecture everywhere except England. Knowing authors, titles, and
the like will help even more. Take time to look at the pamphlet or online help
menu to make sure that you can use your local electronic catalog with maximum
efficiency.

Finally, find out what databases you can access through your library system.
ERIC (Educational Resources Information Center) will help you locate scholarly
papers in the humanities; MEDLINE will get you into psychosocial and physiological studies of disease and associated medical problems; Lexis-Nexis will give
you access to a staggering number of public and commercial information
sources—news, politics, economic matters, polling, and the like in newspapers,
magazines, organizational newsletters, and other data sources.

CD-ROM Searches   Check the holdings of your local library. Many offer on
CD-ROMs sources such as the *New York Times Index, The Oxford English Dictionary,
The Modern Language Association Indexes, Encyclopaedia Britannica,* perhaps even the
Table of Contents to Communication Journals, which will include as databases all articles published in National Communication Association journals since 1990. As
more and more databases become available on CD-ROM (or online), you'll be
able to link electronically with the actual articles you want.

Web Exploration
To practice using different
types of URLs go to
www.ablongman.com/
german15e

Speech Research on the Web   Every time you tune into a sports broadcast,
news hour, or even prime-time television show, you're told that you can use a
"www" command to get to its home page: ESPNET's sports scores for the day,
CNN International's informational background on big stories, *USA Today* online,
or National Public Radio's discussion group. Among the endless choices, here is
a sample of useful sites for speech resources:

Subject	Site
Genealogy	http://www.genealogy.org/~ngs
Health (disease control)	http://www.cdc.gov/cdc.htm
Health (advice)	http://www.drkoop.com
Electronic newspapers	http://www.enews.com
USA Today	http://www.usatoday.com
City networks	http://www.city.net

Maps	http://www.mapquest.com
Links to people	http://www.bigfoot.com
Sports	http://www.wwcd.com/hp/sports.html
White House	http://www.whitehouse.gov
House of Representatives	http://www.house.gov
U.S. Senate	http://www.senate.gov
Subject guide to the WWW	http://gateway.lib.uiowa.edu/index.htm

On the Internet, you'll discover utterly amazing places: the places where the Aryan (white power) women hang out, individuals' home pages paying homage to Marilyn Monroe or Nostradamus, full texts of song lyrics, places where you can watch the election returns live from many countries, sites with sound bites and video clips, and, of course, sites where you can shop for John Deere tractors or find parts for your 1950 9N Ford tractors. Because almost anyone can put up a site on the Web for modest cost, you must learn to evaluate sites for quality of

Computerized database searches can yield vast information rapidly and efficiently.

information and importance of opinion. Here are some of the tests outlined by Esther Grassian of the UCLA College Library:[1]

Content and Evaluation

1. How complete and accurate are the information and the links provided by this source?
2. How good is this site vis-à-vis other sites or print sources? (A librarian can help you answer this question.)
3. What are the dates on the site and its materials?
4. How comprehensive is it? Is the site builder interested only in certain aspects of a topic (e.g., the Arab side of the Arab-Israeli conflict)? Does it attempt to cover everything available—and if so, how? Are evaluations of links to other sources provided?

Sources and Dates

1. Who produced the site? Why? What authority or knowledge does the producer have? Is there a sponsoring organization that has a vested interest in what results from people using the site?
2. Is there an evident bias in the materials that you find?
3. When was the site set up and when was it last revised? How up-to-date is it?
4. Is it easy to contact the producer with questions?

Structure

1. Does the site follow good graphics principles? Is the use of art purposive or just decorative?
2. Do the icons clearly represent what is intended?
3. Does the text follow basic tenets of good grammar, spelling, and composition?
4. Are links provided to Web subject-trees in directories—lists of Web sources arranged by subject?
5. How usable is the site? Can you get through it in a reasonable time?

Web Exploration

For more on Internet content evaluation go to www.ablongman.com/german15e

Search Help   You need to be able to use **search engines** to help you through the maze of material available electronically. A search engine is an online database that allows you to explore broad subjects and find specific information by being directed to a source. They come with different virtues: *Large databases* include Google, Yahoo!, All the Web, AltaVista, HotBot, Excite, InfoSeek, and Lycos. *Advanced search features* allow you to search in special ways; for example, Ask Jeeves asks you questions in natural language, Simpli.com has pull-down menus to help you focus, and both InfoSeek and AltaVista help you refine questions. *Annotated directories* such as the Britannica Internet Guide, LookSmart, Snap.com, and the Mining Company tell you how to get into the search process. Included among *business directories* are Livelink Pinstripe, Dow Jones Business Directory, SearchZ, and Northern Light Industry Search. A nice online guide to search engines, *Guide to Meta-Search Engines* by Jian Liu, will help you even further as you make your way through these and other tools.[2] See Table 6.1 for advice on which search engines to use for which approaches to information finding and retrieving.

TABLE 6.1 *Internet Search Engines*

Information Needed	Characteristics of the Search Engine
Overview of topic	Yahoo! organizes information in "trees" from general to specific topics. Google is the largest, fast search engine.
Relevant hits only	Excite has excellent summaries, and you can ask for "more documents like this one."
Review of what's available on the Internet	MetaCrawler works across engines; Inference Find searches engines, merges the results, and removes redundancies.
Pinpoint research	AltaVista is massive yet has a fast indexer of full texts; MSN and Ask Jeeves work well on subcategories.
Common words	HotBot is fast and powerful, and ranks results as well as other options for searches; Excite, Yahoo!, and Lycos are tailored to less-experienced searchers.
Have a date	HotBot Super Search limits by date.
Scientific information	AltaVista has the best rating among general engines.
Proper names	AltaVista and InfoSeek are sensitive to capital letters; HotBot can search names in regular or reversed order (Sam Jones; Jones, Sam).
Images, sounds, media types (Java, VRML), extensions (e.g., .gif)	Try Lycos Media, HotBot Super Search, Yahoo! Computers and Internet, Google Image Search, and American Memory.
E-mail discussion groups	LISZT is a directory of mailing lists and those who run them.
Quotations	Go to The Quotations Page; Bartlett; Land of Quotes.

Information taken from material prepared by Debbie Abilock (1996), updated June 13, 1998, at http://nuevaschool.org/~debbie/library/research/adviceengine.html and Jennifer Tanaka, "The Perfect Search," *Newsweek*, September 27, 1999, pp. 71–72. See also commentary by Danny Sullivan at SearchEngineWatch.com.

The Print World

While the nature of libraries is changing rapidly in our electronic world, libraries are still repositories for useful print sources. Generally speaking, there are more controls on print than electronic sources, making print resources valuable sources of information. The trick for using traditional print competently is to look for different kinds and qualities of information in different places.

Newspapers   Newspapers are obviously a useful source of information about events of current interest. Your school or city library undoubtedly keeps on file copies of one or two highly reliable papers, such as the *New York Times, The Observer,* the *Wall Street Journal,* or the *Christian Science Monitor,* as well as the leading newspapers of your state or region. Through the *New York Times Index,* you can locate the paper's accounts of people and events from 1913 to the present. Another useful and well-indexed source of information on current happenings is *Facts on File,* issued weekly since 1940. Almost all major newspapers will run their own Websites as well, and Lexis-Nexis gives you electronic access to more than 200 major and local newspapers.

Magazines   The average university library subscribes to hundreds of magazines and journals. Some, such as *Time, Newsweek,* and *U.S. News & World Report,* summarize weekly events. *The Atlantic* and *Harper's* are representative of monthly publications that cover a wide range of subjects of both passing and lasting importance. *The Nation, Vital Speeches of the Day, Fortune, Washington Monthly,* and *The New Republic,* among other magazines, contain comment on current political, social, and economic questions. More specialized magazines include *Popular Science, Scientific American, Ebony, Sports Illustrated, Field and Stream, Ms., Better Homes and Gardens, Rolling Stone, Byte, Today's Health, National Geographic,* and *The Smithsonian.*

Indexes are available for most publications; a reference librarian can show you how to use them.

Yearbooks and Encyclopedias   The most reliable source of comprehensive data is the *Statistical Abstracts of the United States,* which covers a wide variety of subjects ranging from weather records and birthrates to steel production and election results. Information on Academy Award winners, world records in various areas, and the "bests" and "worsts" of almost anything can be found in the *World Almanac, The People's Almanac, The Guinness Book of World Records, The Book of Lists,* and *Information Please.* Encyclopedias, such as the *Encyclopaedia Britannica* and *Encyclopedia Americana,* attempt to cover the entire field of human knowledge and are valuable chiefly as initial reference sources or for background reading. (Check for electronic versions of all of these.)

Documents and Reports   Various government agencies—state, national, and international—as well as many independent organizations publish reports on special subjects. Many state universities publish reports on issues related to agriculture, business, government, engineering, and scientific experimentation. Such endowed groups as the Carnegie, Rockefeller, and Ford Foundations and such special interest groups as the Foreign Policy Association, the Brookings Institution, the League of Women Voters, Common Cause, and the U.S. Chamber of Commerce also publish reports and pamphlets. Though by no means a complete list, *The Vertical File Index* serves as a guide to some of these materials.

Books   Most subjects suitable for a speech have been written about in books. Generally, you will find authoritative books in your school library and more popularized treatments in your city's public library. You can access your library's holdings via computer.

Biographies   The *Dictionary of National Biography,* the *Dictionary of American Biography, Who's Who, Who's Who in America, Current Biography,* and more specialized works organized by field contain biographical sketches especially useful in locating facts about famous people and in documenting the qualifications of authorities whose testimony you may quote.

Speaking of . . . Skills

Conducting an Interview

You need to observe these general guidelines in planning an informational interview:

1. *Decide on your specific purpose.* What do you hope to learn from the interview? Can the person you are interviewing provide precise information from a unique perspective? Determine what you would like to glean from the interview and communicate that purpose directly to the person you plan to interview.

2. *Structure the interview in advance.* Plan your questions in advance so that you have a clear idea of *what* to ask *when*. The interview may not follow your list exactly, so you'll need to remain flexible and free to deviate from your interview plan to clarify or elaborate on a previous response. Begin the interview by setting limits on what will be covered during the session. End the interview by recapping the main ideas and expressing your appreciation.

3. *Remember that interviews are interactive processes.* Adept interviewers should be good listeners. You should listen carefully to what is said and accurately interpret the significance of those comments. There is a definite pattern of "turn taking" in interviews that allows plenty of opportunity to clarify remarks and opinions.

4. *A good interviewer builds a sense of mutual respect and trust.* Feelings of trust and respect are created by revealing your own motivation, by getting the person to talk, and by expressing sympathy and understanding. Good communication skills and a well-thought-out set of questions build rapport in interview situations. You should always follow up the interview with a note or letter expressing your appreciation for the person's shared time and expertise.

The Face-to-Face World

When looking for material, many of us forget the easiest and most logical way to start: by asking questions. The goal of an **informational interview** is to obtain answers to specific questions. In interviewing someone, you seek answers that can be woven into the text of your speech. Interviews increase your understanding of a topic so that you will avoid misinforming your audience, drawing incorrect inferences from information, and convoluting technical ideas. Your interviewee may be a content expert or someone who has had personal experience with the issues you wish to discuss. If you're addressing the topic of black holes, who is better qualified to help you than an astronomer? If you're explaining the construction of a concrete boat, you might contact a local civil engineer for assistance. If you wish to discuss anorexia nervosa, you might interview a person who has suffered through the disorder. Interviews can provide compelling illustrations of human experiences. (See the box above.)

FORMS OF SUPPORTING MATERIALS

After you've located your supporting materials, you need to choose among them. The supporting materials that are used to clarify, amplify, or strengthen your ideas fall into four categories: (1) comparisons and contrasts, (2) examples, (3) statistics, and (4) testimony (see Figure 6.1).

Comparisons and Contrasts

Comparisons and contrasts are useful verbal devices to clarify ideas—to make them distinctive and focused. Pointing out similarities and differences helps listeners comprehend your ideas and opinions.

Comparisons   **Comparisons** connect something already known or believed with ideas a speaker wishes to have understood or accepted. Comparisons, therefore, stress similarities; they create analogies. In the early hours of September 11, 2001, during the terrorist attacks on the World Trade Center and the Pentagon, many journalists and politicians compared the unfolding events to the 1941 attacks on Pearl Harbor. This comparison created an analogy between the terrorist attacks and the aerial bombing that precipitated the U.S. entry into World War II. Both were surprise attacks that resulted in tremendous loss of life.

Contrasts   **Contrasts** help to clarify complex situations and processes by focusing on differences. A speaker explaining professional football would want to contrast it with the more familiar rules governing interscholastic football. To clarify the severity of the 1999 drought in the East, the news networks contrasted average rainfall for normal summers with the current rainfall.

Contrasts can be used not only to clarify unfamiliar or complex problems, but also to strengthen the arguments that you wish to advance. A student speaker argued that regulations governing ocean vessels should be strictly enforced. Explaining the reasons, for the huge federal fine against Royal Caribbean

FIGURE 6.1 *The Forms of Supporting Materials*
The supporting materials used to clarify, amplify, or justify your central ideas or claims are comparison and contrast, examples, statistics, and testimony. What should you consider as you choose supporting material?

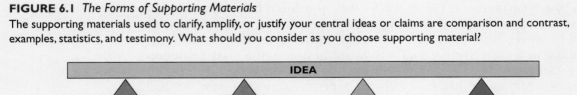
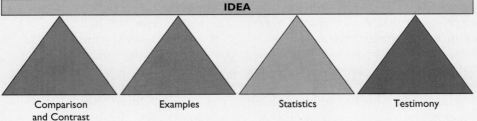

Speaking of . . . Skills

Choosing Supporting Materials

Recent research compared qualitative and quantitative supporting material. Qualitative supporting material includes examples, anecdotes, and analogies such as "a friend of mine was in a car crash, and a seat belt saved her." Quantitative supporting materials are statistical or numerical information such as "a recent investigation found that people are 50 percent more likely to be injured if they are not wearing a seat belt."

The research found that both qualitative and quantitative supporting material are equally effective in changing attitudes initially. However, qualitative supporting materials worked much better over time. There are two reasons that qualitative supporting materials strengthen long-term attitude change:

1. Qualitative supporting materials are more vivid, and the impact of vivid images is greater than that of numbers.
2. We can more easily remember qualitative supporting materials than numerical information.

See: Dean C. Kozoleas, "A Comparison of the Persuasive Effectiveness of Qualitative versus Quantitative Evidence," *Communication Quarterly,* 41 (1993): 40–50.

Cruise Lines in July 1999, she said, "While crew members wore 'Save the Whales' buttons, ships discharged hazardous chemicals into their ocean wakes." This speaker brought the issue of enforcement into sharp focus by stressing the contradictions in an actual instance. Contrasts can cut to the heart of issues quickly and dramatically.

In another case, H. Ross Perot spoke at the Reform Party Nominating Convention in 1996. He used this contrast to show why private enterprise works better than government: "In business, you can promote people based on their performance. In politics, you get promoted based on your acting ability."[3]

Perot's contrast is startling but serves as clear support for his central idea that a business leader should be the next president of the United States. Helping your listeners reason along with you by visualizing differences is an excellent strategy for getting them to accept your ideas.

Comparisons and Contrasts Used in Combination   You can use comparisons and contrasts together to double their impact on your audience. For example, a student speaker focused on the messages in cartoons. To help his listeners understand how cartoons provide commentary, he compared and contrasted *Rocky and Bullwinkle* with *Beavis and Butthead.* He said,

> Both cartoons have stirred up considerable public controversy. In the 1960s, some people boycotted *Rocky and Bullwinkle* just as some refuse to watch *Beavis and Butthead* today. There are major differences, however. *Rocky and Bullwinkle* episodes pitted the pair against Boris and Natasha, mimicking the Cold War conflict between the United States and the Soviet Union. *Beavis and Butthead,* on the other hand,

avoid political commentary while focusing on the struggle of the main characters with adolescence.

Whenever using comparisons and contrasts, try to make sure that at least one of the items is familiar to listeners. Comparing professional football and interscholastic football will make no sense to an Irish fan, who probably doesn't know anything about either one. You'd have to compare and contrast professional football and European rugby to clarify the game for her.

Examples

Examples can be powerful ways to involve an audience in your topic because they make abstract or general ideas easier to comprehend. Examples take various forms—they can illustrate concepts, conditions, or circumstances; they can narrate events; or they can be listed as undeveloped specific instances.

Types of Examples   **Hypothetical examples** are made up. **Factual examples** (or real examples) are recitations of events that actually happened or people, places, and things that actually exist. If you were giving a speech on why homeowners should move into apartments, you might narrate a "typical" homeowner's day: a leaky faucet to fix, a lawn to mow, real estate taxes to pay, and a neighbor's dog to chase out of the flower garden. Although not all of these events occurred in the same day, asking listeners to imagine what life would be like if they did would help you convey the carefree life of an apartment dweller. For many audiences, factual examples are more potent. Many speakers have been highly successful with this type of supporting material. For instance, actors Christopher Reeve and Michael J. Fox use their own life experiences to argue for increased research funding for medical conditions.

While some speakers glean examples from their own lives, others illustrate ideas with the lives of others. Former Minnesota Governor Jesse Ventura advocated extending rights to gay partners with this example: "I have two friends who have been together for forty-one years. If one of them becomes sick, the other one is not even allowed to be at the bedside. I don't believe government should be so hostile, so mean-spirited. . . . Love is bigger than government."[4] Notice how Ventura drew his conclusion immediately after the example. This helps listeners to grasp the point of the example, strengthening your argument.

Sometimes speakers use a list of specific instances. Their power comes from cumulative effect rather than vivid detail. You can use a single specific instance if you only need a quick example, for instance: "You're all familiar with the windows in this classroom, but you might not have noticed their actual construction. I want to talk about those windows—those double-glazed, low-emissivity, gas-filled windows—and how the use of such windows contributes to reduced energy consumption on campus and in your life."

More often, though, speakers pile up specific instances to help establish a point. In the famous passage in his declaration of war, President Franklin Delano Roosevelt listed the islands attacked by the Japanese Imperial forces. More recently, Mary Fisher spoke at the 1996 Republican National Convention about AIDS. She said to the delegates: "[T]he AIDS virus is not a political creature. It does not care whether you are Democrat or Republican, it does not ask whether

Web Exploration
For the full text of this speech go to
www.ablongman.com/
german15e

you are Black or White, male or female, gay or straight, young or old." She continued by adding details to the series of specific instances:

> Tonight, I represent an AIDS community whose members have been reluctantly drawn from every segment of American society. Though I am White, and a mother, I am one with a Black infant struggling with tubes in a Philadelphia hospital. Though I am female, and contracted this disease in marriage, and enjoy the warm support of my family, I am one with the lonely gay man sheltering a flickering candle from the cold wind of his family's rejection.[5]

With these accumulated instances, Fisher demonstrated to her listeners the impact of the disease on all Americans.

Choosing Examples   When selecting examples, whether hypothetical or factual, you should keep three considerations in mind:

1. *Is the example relevant?* If the connection is vague, it won't accomplish its goal. If your hypothetical story about a spring break road trip is fun to listen to but not related to your speech on saving the Florida Everglades, you're in trouble!

2. *Is it a fair example?* An audience can be quick to notice unusual circumstances in an illustration or story; exceptional cases are seldom convincing. Having parachutists landing in the Wal-Mart parking lot to change a flat tire in your story, for example, would stretch the credulity of your listeners.

3. *Is it vivid and impressive in detail?* Be sure your extended examples are pointed and visual. When a student argued for more humane treatment of slaughter animals, he described the procedures at a local auction barn, traced typical routes to processing plants, and detailed the handling of animals in the holding pens. This example was specific and detailed enough to convince listeners that there was cause for change.

Statistics

Statistics are numbers that show relationships between or among phenomena—relationships that can emphasize size or magnitude, describe subclasses or parts (segments), or establish trends. By reducing large masses of information into generalized categories, statistics clarify situations, substantiate potentially disputable central ideas, and make complex aspects of the world clear to your listeners.

Magnitudes   We often use statistics to describe a situation or to sketch its scope or seriousness; that is, its size or **magnitude.** The effect on listeners can be especially strong if one statistical description of the size of a problem is piled up on others. Notice how former U.S. Surgeon General Antonia Novello used multiple statistical descriptions of magnitude while urging citizens to think of violence as a community health problem:

> Violence is a legitimate public health concern. It is your challenge—and mine. My friends, it is no small problem that: homicidal violence is now the leading cause of death among our youth; and that, in fact, every 14 hours a child younger than 5 is murdered. Firearms are now involved in one in every four deaths among 15- to

24-year-olds. And it is no small problem that domestic violence—along with child abuse and the abuse of the elderly—is found in every community and one-fourth of all American families; and [among] up to six often-married couples. Domestic violence today is the second most common cause of injury to women overall, and the leading cause of injuries to women ages 15 to 44. It is more common than automobile accidents, muggings, and rapes combined.[6]

Not all uses of magnitudes, of course, need such piling up of instances. Simple, hard-hitting magnitudes sometimes work even better. For example, Brenda Theriault of the University of Maine, arguing that there is "very little nutritional value in a hamburger, chocolate shake, and fries," simply noted that "of the 1,123 calories in this meal, there are 15 calories of carbohydrates, 35 calories of protein, and 1,073 calories of fat."[7] These were all the numbers the listeners needed in order to understand the nutrition in a typical fast-food meal.

Segments   Statistics that are used to isolate the parts of a problem or to show aspects of a problem caused by separate factors, parts, or aspects are statistical **segments.** In discussing the sources of income for a college or university, for example, you would probably segment the income by percentages coming from tuition and fees, state and federal money, gifts and contributions, special fees such as tickets, and miscellaneous sources. Then you'd be in a position to talk reasonably about next year's proposed tuition hike. A student speaker used survey results in this fashion to show how people shop on the World Wide Web:

> In 1996, people spent a total of $518 million dollars on products and services they found via the Web. Computer products sales comprised 27 percent of this total and travel another 24.3 percent, making up over half of all Web sales. The remainder of the sales is divided almost equally among adult entertainment, general entertainment, food/drink, gifts/flowers, and apparel.[8] This year Web sales are expected to set new records.

As this example illustrates, the most important value of statistics doesn't lie in the numbers themselves but in how you interpret and use them. In using statistical data, always answer the question, "What do these numbers mean or demonstrate?" In this case, it's clear that computer products and travel dominate Website sales.

Trends   Statistics often are used to point out **trends,** or indicators that tell us about the past, the present, and the future. The comparison of statistical data across time allows you to say that a particular phenomenon is increasing or decreasing (see Table 6.2). If you were arguing for stricter controls on chewing tobacco, you might cite Federal Trade Commission statistics revealing that chewing tobacco sales have increased steadily. Over the ten-year period from 1985 to 1995, revenues grew by more than $100 million annually, exceeding $1.7 billion in 1995.[9] This upward trend suggests that something should be done to control smokeless tobacco. You could make your case even stronger by citing a corresponding upward trend in cancers of the lips, gums, and tongue.

Using Statistics   When you use statistics to indicate magnitude, to split phenomena into segments, or to describe trends, you can help your listeners by softening the numbers. Four strategies you can use are:

Web Exploration

For examples of how to use magnitudes, segments, and trends go to

www.ablongman.com/
german15e

TABLE 6.2 *Types of Statistics*

In a speech to inform, a speaker might use three types of statistics to describe students at Central University. What other forms of supporting material could complement these numbers?		
Magnitudes	**Segments**	**Trends**
"Three-fourths of all Central University students come from the state."	"Sixty percent of all Central University students major in business; 25 percent are humanities majors; the remaining 15 percent are in fine arts."	"Since 1975, enrollment at Central University has increased by 90 percent every five years."

1. *Translate difficult-to-comprehend numbers into more understandable terms.* In a speech on the mounting problem of solid waste, Carl Hall illustrated the immensity of 130 million tons of garbage by explaining that trucks loaded with that amount would extend from coast to coast three abreast.[10]

2. *Don't be afraid to round off complicated numbers.* "Nearly 400,000" is easier for listeners to comprehend than "396,456"; "just over 33 percent" or, better yet, "approximately one-third" is preferable to "33.4 percent."

3. *Use visual materials to clarify statistics whenever possible.* Use a computer-generated graph; hand out a photocopied sheet of numbers; prepare a chart in advance. Such aids will allow you to concentrate on explaining the significance

Compile complex information in a form that your listeners can easily understand.

of the numbers rather than on making sure the audience hears and remembers them.

4. *Use statistics fairly.* Arguing that professional women's salaries increased 12.4 percent last year may sound impressive to listeners until they realize that women are still paid less than men for equivalent work. In other words, provide fair contexts for your numerical data and comparisons.

Testimony   When you cite the opinions or conclusions of others, you're using **testimony.** Sometimes testimony merely adds weight or impressiveness to an idea, as when you quote Mahatma Gandhi or Mother Teresa. At other times, it lends credibility to an assertion, especially when it comes from expert witnesses. When Janice Payan addressed the Adelante Mujer Conference, she used testimony in another way. She cited her favorite poem as a source of inspiration for her listeners. She urged them to seek success as she quoted the poet: "I wish someone had taught me long ago, How to touch mountains."[11]

Testimony should relate to the ideas you are discussing and should strengthen them. When you use quotations in your speech, they should accomplish more than simply amplifying or illustrating an idea.

Testimony also should satisfy four more specific criteria:

1. *The person quoted should be qualified, by training and experience, to speak on the topic being discussed.* Athletes are more credible talking about sports equipment or exercise programs than they are endorsing breakfast food or local furniture stores.

2. *Whenever possible, the authority's statement should be based on firsthand knowledge.* A Florida farmer is not an authority on an Idaho drought unless he or she has personally observed the conditions. Veterinarians aren't usually experts on human diseases, and Hollywood stars may not know much about script writing.

3. *The judgment expressed shouldn't be unduly influenced by personal interest.* Asking a political opponent to comment on the current president's performance will likely yield a self-interested answer.

4. *Your listeners should perceive the person quoted to be an actual authority.* An archbishop may be accepted as an authority by a Roman Catholic audience but perhaps not by Protestant or Hindu listeners. When citing testimony, don't use big names simply because they're well known. The best testimony comes from subject-matter experts whose qualifications your listeners recognize.

Finally, always acknowledge the source of an idea or particular phrasing. Avoid plagiarism—claiming someone else's ideas, information, or phraseology as your own. Plagiarism is stealing. Give your source credit for the material, and give yourself credit for having taken the time to do the research.

FUNCTIONS OF SUPPORTING MATERIALS

As you choose supporting materials for your speech or as you listen to others speak, you should be conscious of the role of supporting material. While there is no absolute rule about how each kind of supporting material functions, there is general agreement about what supporting materials accomplish in your speech. Here are some guidelines for choosing your supporting materials:

1. *Complex and abstract ideas benefit from the use of specific information.* Use examples to clarify complex or abstract ideas. Compare the relationship of subatomic particles to balls on a billiard table, for instance. Such simplification is especially useful when your listeners have little background or knowledge about your topic or when the subject matter is complex. Examples also provide more vivid details and make ideas more immediate. Thus, they can stimulate your listeners' enthusiasm for complex or abstract material.

When your audience has only minimal knowledge of a concept, you should use comparisons, examples, and statistical magnitudes and trends to help you amplify the idea. These forms of support expand on your idea so that your audience can more easily comprehend and examine it.

2. *If your idea is controversial or if members of your audience are hostile, use supporting material such as statistics and testimony.* These forms of supporting material are generally regarded as highly rational and credible, so they work well with controversial topics or hostile listeners. If you are trying to get management to accept a union, for example, you will certainly need credible supporting material. When there is disagreement among experts on the issue, you will need an abundance of supporting material.

3. *Supporting materials can enhance your credibility as a speaker.* While your listeners may question your ability to understand the complex nature of the International Monetary Fund, they will respect authorities on the subject. They will also probably be reluctant to question supporting material such as statistical information. You should always use supporting materials when you are not an expert or when your status is lower than that of your listeners.

4. *Supporting materials provide audience members with ammunition for later discussions.* When you ask for a raise, you are more likely to get it by providing information about your job performance. Your supervisor can use this information in defending your raise to others. If you are asking your listeners to make sacrifices or to accept ideas that are unfamiliar to them, use plenty of supporting material. It provides the reassurance they need to take a risk and embrace a new thought.

5. *Generally, examples create human interest, while statistics provide reasonable proof.* Listeners tend to respond subjectively to narratives. On the other hand, their response to statistics is often more detached and objective. In a speech on street children in Brasilia, you would establish the significance of the problem by providing statistics. But you would involve your listeners by telling them about the danger and hunger suffered by Emilio, who lives on the streets.

A WORD ABOUT PLAGIARISM

Now that we've discussed locating and generating material for your speeches, we come to a major ethical issue: plagiarism. **Plagiarism** is defined as "the unacknowledged inclusion of someone else's words, ideas, or data as one's own."[12]

Web Exploration
For an example of how to use supporting materials go to
www.ablongman.com/german15e

Web Exploration
For further explanation of plagiarism go to
www.ablongman.com/german15e

In speech classes, students occasionally take material from a source they've read and present it as their own. Even if listeners have not read the article, it soon becomes apparent that something is wrong: The wording differs from the way the person usually talks, the style is more typical of written than spoken English, or the speech is a patchwork of eloquent and awkward phrasing. In addition, the organizational pattern of the speech may lack a well-formulated introduction or conclusion or be one not normally used by speakers. Often, too, the person who plagiarizes an article reads it aloud badly—another sign that something is wrong.

Plagiarism is not, however, simply undocumented verbatim quotation. It also includes (a) undocumented paraphrases of others' ideas and (b) undocumented use of others' main ideas. For example, you are guilty of plagiarism if you paraphrase a movie review from *Newsweek* without acknowledging that staff critic David Ansen had those insights or if you use economic predictions without giving credit to *Business Week.*

SAMPLE OUTLINE FOR AN INFORMATIVE SPEECH

In the outline, note how the speaker has combined verbal and visual material to establish and develop the central idea. In this speech, the supporting material is used to amplify the idea.

How We Breathe

The speaker establishes the comparison, an analogy, immediately upon starting the speech.

The speaker might point to parts of the body as they're mentioned—collarbone, shoulder bones, abdominal wall, diaphragm.

An explanation reveals the function of the muscles.

Demonstrative movements also would be appreciated by the audience: a lifting of the shoulders and chest cavity when talking about inhalation, a dropping of the rib cage and abdominal wall when describing exhalation.

I. The human breathing mechanism may be likened to a bellows, which expands to admit air and contracts to expel it.
   A. When we inhale, two things happen.
      1. Muscles attached to the collarbone and shoulder bones pull upward and slightly outward.
      2. Muscles in the abdominal wall relax, allowing the diaphragm—a sheet of muscle and tendon lying immediately below the lungs—to fall.
   B. This permits the spongy, porous lungs to expand.
      1. A vacuum is created.
      2. Air rushes in.
   C. When we exhale, two things happen.
      1. Gravity causes the rib cage to move downward.
      2. Muscles in the abdominal wall contract, squeezing the diaphragm upward.
   D. The space available to the lungs is thus reduced.
      1. The lungs are squeezed.
      2. Air is emitted.
   E. The similarity between the breathing mechanism and a bellows is represented in this diagram:
         [Show "How We Breathe" diagram.]

II. In summary, then, to remember how the human breathing mechanism works, think of a bellows.
   A. Just as increasing the size of the bellows bag allows air to rush in, so increasing the space available to the lungs allows them to admit air.
   B. Just as squeezing the bellows bag forces air out, so contracting the space the lungs can occupy forces air to be emitted.

The summary compares a bellows to how the lungs work.

SAMPLE OUTLINE FOR A PROBLEM-SOLUTION SPEECH

Study the following outline. Notice that a variety of supporting materials are used to strengthen each of the points in the speech. Although the proof of a single point may not require as many different supporting materials as are used in this outline, the variety of support shows how a number of different forms can be combined in a speech.

The Heartbreak of Childhood Obesity

I. Childhood obesity is an increasing problem in our society.
   A. Michelle is a typical American child—15 percent overweight.
   B. U.S. Department of Health and Human Services survey reveals a 54 percent increase in childhood obesity between 1963 and 1993.
   C. The prediction for the future is even more bleak.
   D. After defining the nature of obesity, let's examine the causes of obesity in children and investigate some solutions we can implement.

This speech starts with an illustration and trend statistics.

II. Obesity is defined as a positive energy balance.
   A. This means that more energy is conserved than expended.
   B. Over time, the excess energy is stored by the body in fat cells.
   C. Approximately 2500 extra calories become an extra pound of body weight.

An explanation clarifies what is meant by obesity.

III. There are three primary causes for childhood obesity.
   A. Some children inherit the tendency to acquire extra weight.
      1. Parents who are obese tend to have children who are also obese.
      2. Experiments with mice have located genetic triggers for overeating.
      3. The genetic predisposition to gain extra weight is a contributing factor in childhood obesity, according to experts.
   B. Eating style also contributes to obesity.
      1. Dr. Daniel A. Kirschenbaum, who specializes in childhood obesity, reports that obese children typically show a "high-density" eating style.
      2. A "high-density" eating style refers to both the quantity and frequency of eating among children.
      3. High-density eating is a behavior that contributes to obesity.
      4. Emotional stress may trigger high-density eating style.

The problem of obesity is developed as a three-part explanation.

To develop the problem, the speaker provides a comparison with lab mice, testimony of Dr. Kirschenbaum and Dr. Dietz, an explanation of high-density eating style, and magnitude statistics.

C. Television viewing is also a culprit among obese children.
  1. Dr. Steven Gortmaker of Harvard University says that many children watch over 30 hours of television weekly.
  2. Inactivity, including television watching, results in a positive energy balance and, over time, leads to obesity.
  3. In addition, Dr. William Dietz of Tufts University notes that children's eating habits are influenced by television commercials for food high in sugar and fat.

IV. You can control weight gain in children with four steps.
  A. Don't assume the child will grow out of it.
    1. If your family has a history of weight problems, be alert for them in your children.
    2. Four out of five children can be helped if the problem is dealt with immediately.
  B. Monitor mealtimes.
    1. To limit high-density eating style, do not permit between-meal snacks.
    2. Teaching children to consume food at a slower pace, according to Dr. William Johnson and Dr. Peter Stalonas, is also helpful.
    3. It is easier on the child if the entire family switches to a low-fat diet.
  C. Substitute other activities for television viewing.
    1. Over 50 percent of obesity problems in children could be controlled more effectively if parents simply turned off the television set.
    2. Encourage activity in the child.
      a. Enroll the child in athletic activities like swimming or soccer.
      b. Encourage walking to and from school; just a half hour of walking per day can correct a positive energy balance.
  D. Join a support group for the parents of obese children.
    1. Contact the World Service Office of Overeaters Anonymous.
    2. Speak to a representative of your local community service organization.

V. Now that you understand the causes of childhood obesity and some of the solutions, it's time to act.
  A. Think about the consequences if you don't act now.
    1. Obesity in childhood predisposes a person to a lifetime of medical and psychological trouble.
    2. Obesity contributes to 90 percent of the cases of Type II diabetes in later life; over half of the cases of cardiovascular disease; and immeasurable emotional distress.
  B. Remember Michelle? If her parents begin now, they can spare Michelle the bleak future faced by too many of our overweight American children.

In the solution section, the speaker uses magnitude statistics, explanations, testimony, segment statistics, and examples.

The conclusion to the speech offers segment statistics and testimony, plus a reference to the introductory illustration.

ASSESSING YOUR PROGRESS

Chapter Summary

1. Your search for supporting materials should be purposeful; you should attempt to assemble materials that are relevant to your speeches, your audiences, and the occasions on which you're speaking.

Speaking of . . . Ethics

What Is the Ethical Response?

1. You can't find exactly the right testimony from an expert to prove a point you want to make in a speech. Is it okay to make up a quotation to use if you know it will result in a better grade on your speech?

2. Should you rip out a page from a magazine in the library if it contradicts something you plan to say in your speech? If the page is missing, nobody will know about the contradiction.

3. If you are a spokesperson for a company, is it okay to suppress facts about the side effects of a new fat-free product? What if the side effects aren't fatal and the product will let thousands of people lose weight?

4. If you can sell more life insurance when you exaggerate the death benefits, should you do it? What if your job depends on increasing your monthly sales? Is it okay to distort facts to keep your job?

5. Should you post a message on the Internet that you know isn't supported by facts? What if it's just a joke?

6. Should you deliberately conceal the source of a fact because you know it's not credible? What about attributing the fact to another, more credible source?

2. To plan your search, you should consider (a) the rational requirements of the topic, (b) the audience demands, (c) the power to prove generally associated with various kinds of supporting materials, and (d) the objectivity of your sources.

3. In executing your searches, learn to access the electronic world, the print world, and the face-to-face world.

4. Supporting materials clarify, amplify, or strengthen the speaker's ideas.

5. Comparisons and contrasts point out similarities and differences between things.

6. Examples provide specific details about ideas or statements you want listeners to accept. They can be hypothetical or factual.

7. Statistics are numbers that show relationships between or among phenomena. Some emphasize size or magnitude; some describe subclasses or segments; and some establish trends or directions over time.

8. Testimony comes from the opinions or conclusions of credible persons.

9. Plagiarism is representing another's ideas or phrases as your own.

Key Terms

Assessment Activities

1. Select a major problem, incident, or celebration that has appeared in the news recently. Examine a story or article written about it in several of the following: the *New York Times, Christian Science Monitor, USA Today, Time, Newsweek, The New Republic,* and either the *Wall Street Journal* or *Business Week.* In a column from each source, note specifically what major facts, people, incidents, and examples or illustrations are included and what conclusions are drawn. Evaluate the differences among the sources you consulted. How are their differences related to their readership? What does this exercise teach you about the biases or viewpoints of sources?

2. Your instructor will divide your class into groups of two to four people, trying to make sure that at least one person in each group has access to the Internet. Look for the following material, recording the source with a careful citation of where the information was found:
   a. Weekly or daily summary of current national news
   b. Daily summary of stock market information
   c. Text of Bill Clinton's grand jury testimony of August 17, 1998
   d. A mission statement for the National Education Association
   e. Current status of California legislation on social services for illegal immigrants
   f. A list of CDs put out by John Pizzarelli
   g. Brief sketch of the Big Ten conference's basketball schedules
   h. At least three different definitions of the word *wit* and dates when those meanings came into use

3. Plan an interview of a celebrity or famous person. First, find out about the person by conducting a library search. Then develop your interview questions. You might consider interviewing a political leader such as Tony Blair, Jesse Ventura, or Nelson Mandela. Or you could choose a controversial social figure such as Dr. Jack Kevorkian, Howard Stern, or Camille Paglia. What questions will you ask? Why? What is the best method for recording answers during the interview?

4. Amplify each of the following statements with a comparison/contrast, an example, statistics, and testimony. Share your results with your classmates. Evaluate the effectiveness of each form of supporting material. Which support is most involving for listeners? Which is most convincing? Which establishes the scope of the idea?
   a. Abraham Lincoln was our greatest president.
   b. Most Americans consume too much processed sugar.
   c. May is the best month for vacationing.
   d. The combustion engine changed human life more than any other invention in history.
   e. Without practical experience, education is unfinished.

🌐 Using the Web

1. The federal government compiles data on hundreds of topics. Check the variety of statistical information you can obtain from government sources. Use your search engine to locate the GAO (Government Accounting Office)

reports or consult http://lib-www.ucr.edu/govpub/ for a database of federal, state, and local government resources that can be accessed by subject, keyword, or title.

2. Spice up your speeches with quotations from experts and celebrities. Search for specific people such as David Letterman, Maya Angelou, Groucho Marx, and Margaret Atwood. You can also search for compilations of quotations.

3. Archives for social science data are readily available online. Two excellent starting points are the Smithsonian Institution Research Information Website and the Interuniversity Consortium for Political and Social Research at the University of Michigan.

 ## Using VideoWorkshop

Watch the speeches in Module 5, "Research and Support." As you watch, take note of how to evaluate and use effective supporting materials. Then answer Questions 1–10.

References

1. Esther Grassian, "Thinking Critically about World Wide Web Resources," http://www.library.ucla.edu/libraries/college/instruct/web/critical.htm, 1997.

2. Found at http://www.indiana.edu/~librcsd/search/sla.html. Because IBM helped Indiana University puts its library online, it has become a most important research source.

3. H. Ross Perot, CNN Coverage of the Reform Party Nominating Convention, Long Beach, CA (11 August 1996).

4. Jesse Ventura with Jay Waler, Jessica Allen, and Bill Adler, *The Wit and Wisdom of Jesse 'the Body' ('the Mind') Ventura* (New York: Quill Books, 1999).

5. Mary Fisher, "A Whisper of AIDS," reprinted in *Women's Voices in Our Time,* edited by Victoria L. DeFrancisco and Marvin D. Jensen (Prospect Heights, IL: Waveland Press, 1994).

6. Antonia Novello, "Your Parents, Your Community—Without Caring There Is No Hope," *Vital Speeches of the Day,* 59 (15 July 1993): 591.

7. Brenda Theriault, "Fast Foods," Speech given at the University of Maine, Spring 1992.

8. John Simons, "The Web's Dirty Secret," *U.S. News & World Report,* 121 (19 August 1996): 51.

9. Federal Trade Commission, *1997 Smokeless Tobacco Report.* Available at: http://www.ftc.gov/bcp/reports/smokeless97.htm.

10. Carl Hall, "A Heap of Trouble," *Winning Orations,* 1977.

11. Janice Payan, "Opportunities for Hispanic Women: It's Up to Us," *Vital Speeches of the Day,* 56 (1 September 1990): 591.

12. Louisiana State University, "Academic Honesty and Dishonesty," adapted from LSU's Code of Student Conduct, 1981.

Chapter 7

Organizing and Outlining Your Speech

THINK OF THE LAST SHOPPING TRIP you made for groceries. How did you do it? Did you wander aimlessly around the store looking for something that you might need? If you shop this way, you probably get home and discover that you forgot something important. Giving a speech is somewhat like a shopping trip. If you don't plan and organize it, you're undoubtedly going to leave out something important. Like an efficient shopper, you can organize your speaking so that both you and your listener get the most out of it. We'll discuss how to choose the pattern of organization and outline your speech. Let's begin with developing a speech plan.

DEVELOPING YOUR SPEECH PLAN

Approaching your speech in an organized manner is important for several reasons. Just as you waste time wandering around a store if you don't have a shopping list, you appear to be confused if you give a disorganized speech. The result can be chaotic. There are five reasons to organize your speeches:

1. *Your listeners learn more from an organized speech because there is an obvious pattern for categorizing the new material you present.* When you arrange the information, it's easier for them to learn it. So good organization leads to better comprehension.

2. *An organized speech is easier for you to present.* The ideas fit together more logically, and even if you forget a phrase or two, the speech will still flow naturally because the ideas hold it together.

3. *You will appear more credible when you give an organized speech.* Your listeners will realize that you have prepared well and will be more likely to accept your expertise.

4. *Some evidence suggests that well-organized speeches are more persuasive.* You can see why—if listeners trust your preparation and don't have to strain to understand the ideas, they are more likely to be impressed by your message.

5. *Good organization lowers the frustration level for everyone—you and your listeners.* This is reason enough to practice developing clear and effective organization in your speaking.

Developing Your Central Idea

The first step in planning your organization is determining your central idea. As you may recall from Chapter 2, your central idea is a statement of your speech goal, developed when you blend your general purpose to inform or to persuade with your topic.

Phrasing a central idea is especially critical, because the focus you select limits the scope of your speech and controls your relationship with your audience. Your central idea determines the way you develop your whole talk—your main points, the information you include, the organization you follow, and the ways you link your points. For example, each of the following central ideas expresses a different focus and relationship with listeners:

> "You can conserve energy by recycling aluminum cans, walking to classes, and using lower-wattage light bulbs at home."
> "The development of the computer chip began thirty years ago and continues today."
> "If our city builds a new parking garage, it will dangerously strain city finances."

These three central ideas establish very different parameters for developing a speech. The first offers three tangible actions a listener can take to save energy. The scope of the speech is limited to practical solutions. It also establishes listener involvement and responsibility in implementing the solution. The second topic, on the other hand, suggests an historical perspective that provides information and less directly involves the audience. Finally, the speaker who proposes the third topic is preparing to develop an argument.

In each case, the phrasing of the central idea determines how the topic will be approached and what will be the role of the listener. This, in turn, should help you determine which organizational pattern is best for your speech.

Choosing Your Organizational Plan

To help you further, here are some clear general guidelines for organizing your speech. After you have identified your central idea, ask these questions to determine what you're looking for in an organizational pattern:

1. *What structure is best suited to the ideas in my speech?* Your speech topic may offer natural groupings among ideas that will be easy for your listeners to recognize. For example, if your speech traces the Battle of Gettysburg day by day, it is probably organized by time. If, on the other hand, you are detailing the causes, symptoms, and cures for Lyme disease, your ideas fall into a causal pattern. And, a speech on the layout of your campus is clearly spatial. You should consider the natural pattern suggested by the ideas of your speech as you think about organizing your speech.

2. *What structure is best adapted to my audience's needs?* Keep your listeners in mind—what they know, expect, and need. If your listeners have never heard of bioremediation, then you need to develop your speech on this topic in a very different way than if they are environmental scientists. You can't ignore your listeners' need to process information efficiently. That means beginning with what they already know.

3. *How can I make the speech move steadily forward toward a satisfying finish?* Listeners need a sense of forward motion—of moving through a series of main points toward a clear destination. Backtracking slows down the momentum of the speech, giving it a stop-and-start progression rather than a smooth forward flow. You'll also enhance the sense of forward motion with forecasts, as well as transitions and physical movement to indicate progression.

Once you've planned your central idea and answered basic questions about the plan of your speech, you're ready to choose the type of arrangement. Often, your topic will determine the type of organization needed. Some topics require chronological order, while other topics can be organized in topical, spatial, or causal patterns. However, the needs of your audience may require a special pattern of organization adapted to them. We will discuss first some speech-centered types of organization. Then we'll consider some audience-centered patterns of organization.

SPEECH-CENTERED PATTERNS OF ORGANIZATION

As we use the term here, **organization** is the order or sequence of ideas in a pattern that suggests their relationship to each other. There are four general

Web Exploration
To further analyze different types of organization go to www.ablongman.com/ german15e

categories of organization for speeches that arise from the demands of the topic: chronological, spatial, causal, and topical.

Chronological Patterns

Chronological patterns arrange ideas in a time sequence. When using a chronological sequence, you might relate events in the order they occurred or describe a process as it should be completed. You begin at one point in time and move forward or backward to some concluding point. For example, you might describe how to prepare an elegant cinnamon pear tart beginning with preparation of the crust and ending with baking instructions. The results wouldn't be the same if you presented the instructions in another order.

Where you begin and end will depend on your central idea. Suppose you wanted to trace the evolution of modern flight. You could start in 1903 with the Wright brothers or from Russia's launching of *Sputnik* in 1957. The beginning of the chronology depends on your goal. Are you trying to tell the whole story of aviation or the more specific story of space flight? Similarly, suppose you wanted to argue that children acquire vital language skills in the first months of their lives. You would need to begin tracing language acquisition even before the child's first vocalizations.

The following example traces the history of experts' advice to parents over the past century. Notice how time organizes the ideas in the speech:

  I. Early in the twentieth century, experts began to focus on childhood as an important period of individual development.
   A. In 1914, books advised mothers to thwart bad habits like thumb sucking by pinning an infant's sleeves to the bed.
   B. During the Great Depression of the 1930s, the federal government developed welfare plans to aid children.

 II. The baby boom years from 1940 to 1960 saw the rise of several models.
   A. Behaviorist models using stimulus-response training were popular.
   B. In 1946, pediatrician Dr. Benjamin Spock published one of the most popular manuals for raising children, offering an alternative to behaviorist models.
   C. In 1952, French psychologist Jean Piaget identified distinct stages in the intellectual maturation of children.

III. More recently, advice to parents focuses on nurturing children to strengthen their emotional development.
   A. In 1969, English psychiatrist Dr. John Bowlby proved that babies seek out specific adults for protection.
   B. In 1997, the Conference on Early Childhood Development and Learning drew attention to the crucial first years in a child's life.

Spatial Patterns

In **spatial patterns,** the major points of the speech are organized by their position, that is, their location or direction from each other. A speech on the movement of weather systems from the north to the south across the United States would fit such a pattern. If you conduct a tour of your campus or describe the constellations in the Southern Hemisphere, you would probably use a spatial pattern. Spatial patterns can trace ideas from east to west, from top to bottom, from left to right, or even from inside to outside. Consider how this example circles the globe:

I. Around the world, active volcanoes continue to shape the face of the earth.
   A. Begin in Mexico with the famous Popocatepetl (2002 eruption).
   B. Then move along the coast of North America to Mount St. Helens in the state of Washington (1991 eruption) before continuing northwest to the Cleveland volcano in Alaska (2001 eruption).
   C. Visit the island of Hawaii, where Kilauea is active (2001 eruption).
   D. Cross the Pacific to the Japanese islands, which feature a number of active volcanoes, including Miyake-Jima (2002 eruption) and Mount Asama (1991 eruption).
   E. Drop down to Mount Kerinci in Sumatra (1987 eruption) and White Island in New Zealand (2000 eruption).
   F. Head west to the Congo in Africa to Mount Nyiragongo (2002 eruption).
   G. Then go to Italy's Etna (2001 eruption), Iceland's Hekla (2000 eruption), and home again.[1]

Causal Patterns

Causal patterns of speech organization show a relationship between causes and effects. Causal patterns assume that one event results from or causes another. This pattern of organization gives listeners a sense of coherence because ideas are developed in relationship to each other. Causal patterns may move in two directions: (a) from present causes to future effects or (b) from present conditions to their apparent causes.

When using a *cause-effect pattern,* you might point to the increasing cost of attending college and then argue that one of the effects of increased costs is reduced enrollments among students from less privileged socioeconomic backgrounds. Or, using an *effect-cause pattern,* you could note that dropping college enrollments resulted, at least in part, from increasing costs. Compare the following two outlines:

I. Colleges and universities across the United States are raising tuition.

II. The effect of these tuition hikes is to change the socioeconomic profile among students.
   A. Middle-income students are squeezed by tuition increases.
   B. Financially disadvantaged students often must drop out.

I. The socioeconomic profile of American colleges and universities has changed.

II. Tuition increases have caused limited access to higher education.
   A. Middle-income students are not able to afford additional tuition increases.
   B. Financially disadvantaged students are forced to choose employment over education.

Notice that the first outline uses a cause-effect pattern; the second uses an effect-cause pattern. Adapt your speech to the situation by beginning with ideas that are better known to audience members; then proceed to the lesser-known facets of the problem. Use cause-effect if listeners are better acquainted with the cause; use effect-cause if the opposite is true.

Topical Patterns

Some speeches on familiar topics are best organized in terms of subject-matter divisions that are easily recognized. Sports strategy is divided into offense and defense; kinds of courts into municipal, county, state, and federal jurisdictions; and types of trees into deciduous and evergreen categories. When you use a **topical pattern** of organization, you list aspects of persons, places, things, or processes. Occasionally, a speaker tries to list all aspects of the topic. More often, however, a partial listing of the primary or most interesting aspects is sufficient. For example, suppose you wanted to give a speech to a general audience about stress. The following outline shows how you could organize the speech topically:

I. Symptoms of stress
    A. Physical symptoms
    B. Emotional symptoms

II. Types of stress inducers
    A. Physical stress
    B. Emotional stress

III. Methods of stress reduction
    A. Relaxation techniques
    B. Meditation
    C. Exercise

Topical patterns are among the most popular and easiest to use. If you plan to list only certain aspects of the topic, take care to explain your choices early in your speech. If you don't plan to talk about biofeedback as a means of reducing stress, you should tell your listeners. You might say, "I will focus on the three most common approaches to stress reduction and will present simple techniques that everyone can apply immediately."

The patterns of speech organization discussed so far—chronological, spatial, causal, and topical—are determined principally by the subject matter. While these patterns do not ignore the audience, it's the subject that usually suggests the pattern of organization.

AUDIENCE-CENTERED PATTERNS OF ORGANIZATION

At times, audience-oriented patterns of organization will more effectively arrange your material. These patterns often work well because they're based on the listeners' needs. You can ask several questions to determine whether an audience-oriented pattern of organization will work for you:

▶ Can I introduce a new idea by comparing it to something my listeners already know?

► How would a person approach this idea for the first time?
► What are common, recurring questions about this topic?
► Am I presenting a solution to a problem?
► Can I eliminate all but one alternative solution to a question or problem?

If you've answered "yes" to any of these questions, you might consider organizing your speech based on your listener's needs.

We'll examine five audience-centered patterns of organization: familiarity-acceptance order, inquiry order, question-answer order, problem-solution order, and elimination order.

Familiarity-Acceptance Order

Familiarity-acceptance order begins with what the audience knows or believes (the familiar) and moves on to new or challenging ideas (the unfamiliar). In an informative speech on quarks, you can begin with what the audience already knows about molecules and then introduce the new information on the subatomic particles called quarks.

Familiarity-acceptance order is very well suited to persuasive speeches, especially if your listeners are skeptical or hostile. You can begin your speech by acknowledging values or ideas that are accepted by your listeners and then proceed to more controversial issues. When your reasoning is valid and your conclusions are sound, your listeners will have difficulty rejecting your claim without denying the underlying facts or values that they already accept.

Here are the main points from a persuasive speech outline using familiarity-acceptance order:

I. How many of us here are married or plan on getting married sometime in the future?

II. Marriage is an important social institution because it publicly expresses the love and commitment of two people for each other.

III. Same-sex marriages should be allowed.
   A. Public recognition would encourage acceptance of same-sex partnerships.
   B. Homosexuals would be allowed to participate in employee benefit plans now reserved for heterosexual married partners.
   C. Legal sanctions involving spouses, such as property inheritance and hospital visitation, would become inclusive.

Even if you don't agree with the conclusions of this speaker, it is more difficult to reject the central idea of the speech because the speaker began with something you probably accept and then moved to the more controversial part of the speech.

Inquiry Order

Inquiry order provides a step-by-step explanation of how you acquired information or reached a conclusion. Often, scientists use this pattern as they carefully describe their research procedures in order to demonstrate the reliability of their findings. Similarly, if you want to persuade your neighbors to plant a new variety of oak tree, you could recount how you studied the varieties that seemed to be dying in your neighborhood, investigated possible choices, and searched for new varieties until the kind you now advocate emerged as the best.

Inquiry order has a double advantage. First, it displays relevant facts and alternatives for the audience. Second, it enables listeners to judge for themselves the worth of the information or policy being presented as it unfolds.

Question-Answer Order

Question-answer order raises and answers listeners' questions. First, you must determine which questions are most likely to arise in your listeners' minds. Then you need to develop your speech to answer each key question in a way that favors your conclusion. For example, when you buy a new car, you want to know about its principal features, the available options, its gas mileage, and its cost. When first learning about a new bond issue, listeners wonder how it will affect their taxes or government services. By structuring your speech to address these questions, you can maintain audience interest and involvement.

Problem-Solution Order

When you advocate changes in action or thought, your main points may fall naturally into a **problem-solution order.** First, you establish the existence of the problem. If your listeners are already aware of the problem, you can remind them of the primary issues. For example, if your listeners walk or ride bicycles to classes, they'll be unaware that there aren't enough parking spaces on campus; but if they drive automobiles, they'll be quite familiar with the parking shortage. You also need to depict the problem in a way that will help your listeners perceive it in the same way that you do. For example, your listeners may tolerate the parking shortage as a simple inconvenience of college life. You will need to show them that there is no reason to accept a parking shortage.

Once you've established that a problem exists, you must propose a solution to it. Your solution should be workable and practical. It would be silly to suggest that a multimillion-dollar parking complex be built if financing isn't available or if the parking complex is too small. However, a car-pooling or busing system would be less expensive and limit the number of cars on campus.

Elimination Order

When your CD player doesn't work, you probably systematically search for what's wrong: Are the batteries fresh? Is the lock switch off? Is the CD player programmed correctly? Just so, with **elimination order,** you first survey all the available solutions and courses of action that can reasonably be pursued. Then, proceeding systematically, you eliminate each of the possibilities until only one remains.

Elimination order is well suited to persuasive speeches. If you want student government to bring a special performer to campus, you might show that all other suggested entertainers are booked up, too expensive, or lack widespread appeal. In this way, you lead the members of student government to agree with the choice you advocate.

To use elimination order effectively, you first must make an inclusive survey of options. If you overlook obvious choices, your listeners won't be convinced by your analysis. Second, you must make the options mutually exclusive; otherwise, your listeners may choose more than one. Consider this example in which the speaker makes only one alternative seem the best:

I. Three options have been proposed.
   A. Jeep Grand Cherokee is a mid-priced vehicle.
   B. Ford Explorer is more expensive than the Jeep.
   C. Isuzu Trooper is least expensive of the three options.

II. The first two options should be eliminated.
   A. The Jeep Grand Cherokee is so popular that you get less for your money than you do with the others.
   B. The Ford Explorer is the newest of the three and, feature for feature, the most expensive.

III. The Isuzu Trooper is therefore the best way to go.
   A. It has the same features as the others for less money.
   B. It's been around long enough to have a solid history of customer care and good repair.

Of course, the elimination order works best if listeners agree with the criteria you've suggested for judgment. If cost is no object, the Grand Cherokee or Explorer still will be considered. Or someone might object that while the Explorer is a comparatively new model, Ford Motor Company has a long history in the United States. Study your listeners to make sure the criteria for elimination are acceptable to them.

OUTLINING YOUR SPEECH

Once you have determined the type of organization you will use to arrange your ideas, you should record the ideas in an outline. Outlining is an important tool for a speaker for two reasons:

1. *Testing.* A rough outline allows you to see your ideas. When you outline a speech, you can discover which ideas you've overemphasized to the exclusion or underdevelopment of others. Your outline is a testing device.

2. *Guiding.* When you're actually delivering a speech, a speaking outline is the preferred form of notes for many, perhaps even most, speakers. A good speaking outline shows you where you've been, where you are, and where you want to get before you sit down. You even can include in your speaking outline special directions to yourself ("show map here"; "emphasize this idea").

To profit from both the testing and guiding aspects of outlines, you must learn to build complete, solid structures. Two types of outlines are most helpful for speakers. You can benefit from a rough outline as you plan your speech. And you need to develop a speaking outline to help you present your speech. So we'll discuss some strategies for developing the rough outline (a testing device) and a speaking outline (a guiding device).

Types of Outlines

You should develop your outline, as well as the speech it represents, gradually through a series of stages. Your outline will become increasingly complex as the ideas in your speech evolve and as you move the speech closer to its final form. But then, once you're ready to speak, the outline becomes simplified again. For the purposes of the public speaker, the rough outline and the speaking outlines are most important because they govern the discovery of ideas and the presentation of them. So we'll concentrate on these.

Developing a Rough Outline A **rough outline** establishes the topic of your speech, clarifies your purpose, and identifies a reasonable number of subtopics. Suppose your instructor has assigned an informative speech on a subject that interests you. You decide to talk about drunk driving because a close friend was recently injured by an intoxicated driver. Your broad topic area, then, is drunk driving.

In the six to eight minutes you have to speak, you obviously can't cover such a broad topic adequately. After considering your audience and your time limit,

As you construct the rough outline of your speech after research, you should identify a reasonable number of ideas and arrange them in a way that will be clear to your listeners.

you decide to focus your presentation on two organizations, Mothers Against Drunk Driving (MADD) and Students Against Driving Drunk (SADD).

As you think about narrowing your topic further, you jot down some possible ideas. You continue to narrow your list until your final ideas include the following:

Founders of MADD and SADD
Accomplishments of the two organizations
Reasons the organizations were deemed necessary
Goals of MADD and SADD
Action steps taken by MADD and SADD
Ways in which your listeners can get involved

Then help your listeners follow your thinking by clustering similar ideas. Experiment with several possible clusters before you decide on the best way to arrange your ideas.

Your next step is to consider the best pattern of organization for these topics. A chronological pattern would enable you to organize the history of MADD and SADD, but it would not allow you to discuss ways your listeners could help. Either cause-effect or effect-cause would work well if your primary purpose were to persuade. However, this is an informative speech, and you don't want to talk about the organizations only as the causes of reducing alcohol-related accidents.

In considering the audience-centered patterns, you decide that an inquiry order might work. You discard it, however, when you realize that you don't know enough about audience members' questions to use this organizational pattern effectively. After examining the alternatives, you finally settle on a topical pattern. A topical pattern allows you to present three clusters of information:

1. Background of MADD and SADD: information about the founders, why the organizations were founded
2. Description of MADD and SADD: goals, steps in action plans, results
3. Local work of MADD and SADD: the ways in which parents work with their teenagers and with local media to accomplish MADD and SADD goals

As you subdivide your three clusters of information, you develop the following rough outline:

I. Background of MADD and SADD
   A. Information about the founders
   B. Reasons the organizations were founded

II. Description of the organizations
   A. Their goals
   B. The action steps they take
   C. Their accomplishments so far

III. Applications of their work on a local level
   A. "Project Graduation"
   B. Parent-student contracts
   C. Local public service announcements

A rough outline identifies your topic, provides a reasonable number of subtopics, and reveals a method for organizing and developing your speech.

Notice that you've arranged both the main points and subpoints topically. A word of warning: You should make sure that the speech doesn't turn into a "string of beads" that fails to differentiate between one topic and the next. With topical outlines, always figure out a way to make the topics cohere, hold together. Doing so will help you develop effective transitions as you practice your speech.

The next step in preparing an outline is phrasing your main headings as precisely as possible. Then you can begin to develop each heading by adding subordinate ideas. As you develop your outline, you'll begin to see what kinds of information and supporting materials you need to find.

Developing a Speaking Outline   Your rough outline would be too detailed to use when you're actually delivering a speech; you'd probably be tempted to read to your listeners. If you did that, you'd lose your conversational tone. Therefore, you need to compress your rough outline into a more useful form. A **speaking outline** uses key words or phrases to jog your memory when you deliver your speech. It is a short, practical form to use while delivering your speech (see Figure 7.1). The actual method you use to create your speaking outline will depend on your personal preference; some people like to work with small pieces of paper, others with notecards. Whatever your choice, however, your speaking

FIGURE 7.1
Sample Speaking Outline (on Notecards)

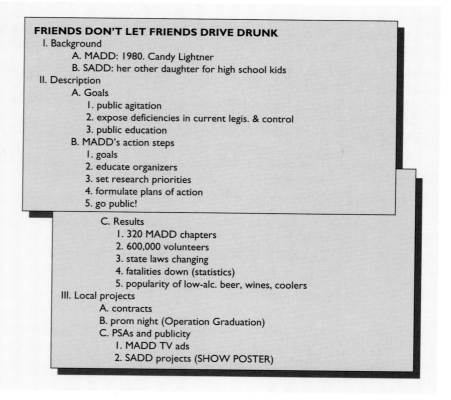

FRIENDS DON'T LET FRIENDS DRIVE DRUNK
I. Background
    A. MADD: 1980. Candy Lightner
    B. SADD: her other daughter for high school kids
II. Description
    A. Goals
        1. public agitation
        2. expose deficiencies in current legis. & control
        3. public education
    B. MADD's action steps
        1. goals
        2. educate organizers
        3. set research priorities
        4. formulate plans of action
        5. go public!

    C. Results
        1. 320 MADD chapters
        2. 600,000 volunteers
        3. state laws changing
        4. fatalities down (statistics)
        5. popularity of low-alc. beer, wines, coolers
III. Local projects
    A. contracts
    B. prom night (Operation Graduation)
    C. PSAs and publicity
        1. MADD TV ads
        2. SADD projects (SHOW POSTER)

outline should be unobtrusive. Large notebook pages will distract your listeners from what you have to say. There are five things to keep in mind as you prepare your speaking outline:

1. *Note most points with only a key word or phrase.* A word or two should be enough to trigger your memory, especially if you've practiced the speech adequately.
2. *Write out fully the ideas that must be stated precisely.* You don't want to make mistakes with people's names or statistical information or exact quotations.
3. *Include directions for delivery such as "SHOW POSTER."*
4. *Find methods of emphasis that will easily catch your eye, show the relationship of ideas, and jog your memory during your speech delivery.* You might use capital letters, white spaces, underlining, indentation, dashes, and highlighting with colored markers to emphasize important ideas.
5. *Use your speaking outline during your practice sessions so that you are familiar with it when you give your speech.*

Guidelines for Preparing Outlines

The amount of detail that you include in an outline will depend on your subject, on the speaking situation, and on your previous experience in speech preparation. New subject matter, unique speaking contexts, and limited prior speaking experience all indicate the need for a detailed outline. Your instructor may even require a full-sentence outline to help you develop the content of your speech. Under any circumstances, a good outline should meet these basic requirements:

1. *Each unit in the outline should contain one main idea.* If two or three ideas merge under one subpoint, your audience will lose direction and become confused. Suppose you are outlining a speech advocating the use of U.S. military personnel to bolster airport security. You should include the following subpoint: "Also current airport security is lax, and placing military personnel in airports would cost less than hiring civilians to screen passengers and baggage." Notice that this point combines two separate ideas about current security and costs. It would be more effective to separate the ideas and develop them as individual points. You could do it this way:

Web Exploration
To view some sample outlines go to
www.ablongman.com/german15e

A. Current airport security is lax.
B. Placing armed military personnel in airports would cost less than hiring civilians to screen passengers and baggage.

2. *Less important ideas in the outline should be subordinate to more important ones.* Subordinate ideas are indented in an outline, and they are marked with subordinate symbols. Doing a good job with subordination helps you know what to emphasize when you're speaking. Proper subordination lets the main arguments stand out and the evidence clearly relate to those arguments. Consider the following example:

I. The cost of medical care has skyrocketed.
   A. Hospital charges are high.
      1. A private room may cost more than $1,500 a day.
      2. X-rays and laboratory tests are expensive.

Speaking of . . . Skills

Memory and Organization

Research on organization and memory has shown that taking some specific outlining steps will help you and your listeners remember what you're talking about:

1. *The magic numbers.* In a classic study, psychologist George Miller concluded that there is a limit to the number of items a person can easily recall—seven, plus or minus two. More recent research has suggested that a more manageable number of items is five, plus or minus two. Limit the number of points you make to from three to seven (preferably in the three-to-five range).

2. *Chunking.* But what if you want to include a lot more information? The answer: "Chunk it." Divide the information into chunks or groups. Listeners are much more likely to remember five chunks of information than seventeen separate points.

3. *Map your movement.* As we've suggested throughout this chapter, mapping your ideas helps your listeners follow your speech. Listeners can't read your speaking outline so you have to give them a verbal map of your ideas. You can signal your most important ideas ("I have three main points.") and subordinate ideas ("There are two advantages of my first argument."). Letting an audience see, by means of your language, the coordinated or equal relationships among your main ideas will help keep listeners from getting lost.

4. *Mnemonics.* Mnemonics help you remember ideas. When you learned "Thirty days hath September, April, June, and November . . . ," you learned an easily recalled ditty that in turn helped you remember which months had thirty days and which had thirty-one. Speakers, too, can sometimes find a mnemonic to help listeners remember: for example, the three Rs of conserving resources ("recycle," "reduce," and "reuse") or the ABC sequence ("airwaves," "breathing," "compression") for cardio-pulmonary resuscitation taught in CPR classes.

For Further Reading: G. Mandler, "Organization and Memory," in *Human Memory: Basic Principles,* edited by Gordon Bower (New York: Academic Press, 1977), 310–354. See also Mandler's articles in C. R. Puff, ed., *Memory Organization and Structure* (New York: Academic Press, 1979), 303–319. G. A. Miller, "The Magic Number Seven, Plus or Minus Two: Some Limits on Our Capacity for Processing Information," *Psychological Review,* 63 (1956): 81–97.

    B. Doctors' charges constantly go up.
       1. Complicated operations cost thousands.
       2. Office calls usually cost between $55 and $100.
    C. Drugs are expensive.
       1. Most new antibiotics cost $7 to $20 per dose.
       2. The cost of nonprescription drugs has mounted.

   3. *Phrase your main points effectively.* You can help your listeners understand your message better if you are concise, choose vivid language, and use parallel structure.

▶ Be concise. State your main points as briefly as you can without distorting their meaning. Crisp, clear, straightforward statements are easier to grasp than rambling, vague, complex declarations. Say, "Get regular exercise," not "Regular and repetitive exertion, considering age and physical conditioning, lends itself to improved physiological functioning."

▶ Use vivid language. Whenever possible, state your main points in evocative words and phrases. Drab, colorless statements are easily forgotten; punchy lines grab attention. Phrase your main points so they'll appeal directly to the concerns of your listeners. Instead of saying, "We should take immediate action to reduce the costs of higher education," say, "Cut tuition now!"

▶ Use parallel structure. In a speech, your listeners have only one chance to catch what you're saying; parallelism in sentence structure helps them do so. The repetition of a key phrase aids the listener in remembering this series: "Cope with cold and flu season by washing your hands, getting enough sleep, and taking vitamin C. Wash your hands to destroy the viruses. Get enough sleep to reduce physical stress. Take vitamin C to fortify your body." Notice in this series that the most important phrases are repeated. Such parallelism will help your listeners remember the major ideas in your speech.

ASSESSING YOUR PROGRESS

Chapter Summary

1. An organized speech is (a) easier for listeners to comprehend, (b) easier to present, (c) perceived as more credible, (d) often more persuasive, and (e) lowers both speaker and listener frustration.
2. A well-developed central idea helps determine the best organizational pattern for a speech.
3. Organization is the sequence of ideas in a pattern that suggests their relationship to each other.
4. Four speech-centered types of organization are chronological, spatial, causal (effect-cause and cause-effect), and topical.
5. Audience-centered organizational patterns include familiarity-acceptance, inquiry, question-answer, problem-solution, and elimination order.
6. Speakers use outlines for testing their ideas and guiding their oral presentation of those ideas.
7. Rough outlines test ideas; speaking outlines guide ideas.
8. Guidelines for outlining include (a) each unit should contain only one idea; (b) less important ideas should be subordinate to more important ones; (c) main ideas should be phrased effectively.
9. When phrasing main points, be concise, use vivid language, and use parallel structure.

Key Terms

causal patterns (p. 119)
chronological patterns (p. 118)

elimination order (p. 122)
familiarity-acceptance order (p. 121)

inquiry order (p. 121)   rough outline (p. 124)
organization (p. 117)   spatial patterns (p. 118)
problem-solution order (p. 122)   speaking outline (p. 126)
question-answer order (p. 122)   topical pattern (p. 120)

Assessment Activities

1. For each of the following topics, suggest two ways in which materials might be organized. Consider which organizational pattern would be more effective:
   a. Directions for driving in snow.
   b. The evolution of digital imaging.
   c. A rationale for including women in combat.
   d. The effect that the influx of tourists from the West will have on Russia.
   e. A description of the proposed route for a highway bypass.
2. Bring a short magazine or newspaper article and a photocopy of it to class. Cut the photocopy into separate paragraphs or sentences. Ask a classmate to assemble the separated paragraphs or sentences into a coherent story. Compare your classmate's results to the original article.
3. For a speech entitled "The Investigator as a Resource," discussing why a lawyer may want to hire a private investigator on a case-by-case basis, rearrange the following points and subpoints in proper outline form:
   a. Investigative services can save the lawyer time.
   b. Investigative reports indicate areas the lawyer should concentrate on to build a case.
   c. It is advantageous for a lawyer to employ an investigator on a case-by-case basis.
   d. The investigator performs two basic services.
   e. Known witnesses must be interviewed and other witnesses identified.
   f. The investigator examines reports from the FBI and other governmental and private agencies and evaluates them for reliability and to determine what must be done.
   g. The investigator examines, collects, preserves, and analyzes physical evidence.
   h. The investigator compiles information in an effort to reconstruct an incident.
   i. Lawyers may need detective assistance only occasionally, on especially critical cases.
   j. Investigative reports can be used in out-of-court settlements.

Using the Web

1. Many online tutorials are available to help you develop outlining skills. You might do a general search under the key word "outlining." Or check out sites maintained by colleges and universities, such as Purdue University (http://owl.english.purdue.edu).
2. Visit two sites on the Internet that cover similar information but organize it differently. For example, you could visit two college Websites, two automo-

tive Websites, two newspaper Websites, and so on. How did each Website organize its information? Which organizational pattern did each site use? Was one site more visual than the other? Was one clearer and easier to use? Why? Was information quickly obtained or did you have to hunt for data?

Using VideoWorkshop

Watch the speeches in Module 7, "Organization and Outlines." As you watch, pay particular attention to patterns and outlines that will help you structure ideas into a speech. Then answer Questions 1–13.

References

1. The data in this outline were taken from the University of North Dakota–Grand Forks Website: http://volcano.und.nodak.edu/vw.html.

Chapter 8

Beginning and Ending Your Speech

JUST AS AEROBICS INSTRUCTORS begin with warm-ups and end with cool-downs, so must you systematically prepare your audience to encounter new ideas and then take them back to their own worlds at the end of your speech. Your success in getting a listener's attention is partly due to how well you frame your speech ideas with a powerful introduction and a strong conclusion. Well-prepared introductions and conclusions also allow you to develop a relationship between you as a thinking, acting human being and your listeners as fellow human beings. Furthermore, the introduction and conclusion signal clearly when your speech starts and ends to prevent confusion among your listeners.

Introductions and conclusions are not trivial aspects of public speaking. Introductions form first impressions that can affect your listeners' perceptions of the remainder of the speech. Conclusions give you one last opportunity to reinforce your main ideas, leave a lasting impression, and cement your relationship with your listeners. In fact, people most often remember what they first hear or see (the **primacy effect**) and what they most recently have seen or heard (the **recency effect**). That is why introductions and conclusions require special effort when you prepare your speeches.

In this chapter, we review ways to capture and sustain listeners' attention, examine the purposes of introductions and conclusions, and suggest various strategies for beginning and ending speeches.

Web Exploration

For some examples of how the factors of attention can be utilized go to

www.ablongman.com/
german15e

CAPTURING AND HOLDING ATTENTION

When you connect to a favorite Website, you can block out the rest of the world. Sometimes you can pay attention so completely that it seems like only minutes instead of hours have passed. **Attention** is the ability to focus on one element in a given perceptual field. When attention is secured, competing elements in the perceptual field fade and, for all practical purposes, cease to exist. That explains why everything else disappears when you are hooked up to a Website.

How can you capture and hold the attention of your listeners as effectively when giving a speech? Your ideas can be accompanied by nine appeals that have high attention value. These factors of attention can be used anywhere in your speech. You can exploit them in your introduction or conclusion, or at any important point in mid-speech. The **factors of attention** are activity, reality, proximity, familiarity, novelty, suspense, conflict, humor, and the vital (see Figure 8.1).

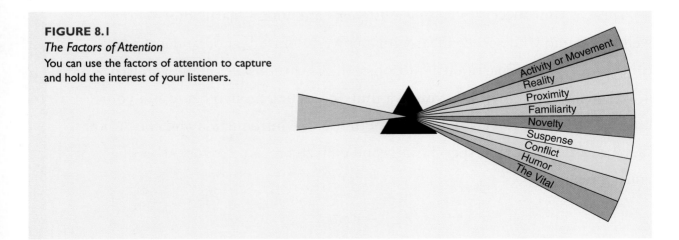

FIGURE 8.1
The Factors of Attention
You can use the factors of attention to capture and hold the interest of your listeners.

Activity

Suppose you've got two TV sets side by side. On one set, two journalists seated at a table discuss U.S. foreign policy options in the Middle East while on the other, you're seeing fiery Arab and Israeli stump speakers getting crowds to go wild. Which set are you likely to watch? You, too, can create a sense of activity by seeking to do the following:

> *Choose active verbs. Raced, tore, shot through, slammed, ripped, slashed, catapulted, flew, flashed*—most of these are simple verbs, but they depict activity.
> *Select dynamic stories.* Use illustrations that depict action, that tell fast-moving stories. Propel your story forward, and your audience will stay with you.
> *Use short segments.* Keep your speech moving; it will seem to drag if one point is expanded while other points are skimmed over.

Reality

The earliest words you learned were names for tangible objects such as *mommy, cookie,* and *toy.* The ability to abstract—to generalize—is one of the marks of human intelligence, but don't lose your audience by becoming too abstract. Refer to specific events, people, and places. For example, when we referred to "tangible objects," an abstract phrase, we gave you three real examples: *mommy, cookie,* and *toy.* Concrete words have more force than general references.

Proximity

Proximity means "nearness"; we usually notice things that closely surround us. A direct reference to a person in the audience, a nearby object or place, an incident that has just occurred, or the immediate occasion helps you to command attention. The following introduction uses proximity to engage the listeners:

> Do you realize how much beer is available within three blocks of this classroom? Think about it—the Airport, Gene's, the Green Bottle, Tippler's, the Sports Page, Deadhead's, Bo Madison's, the Irish Tradition, Mondora's, the Lynn Street Café, the Underground, Mac's, the Taco Grande, Vince's, the Piazza, Gin Alley. And that doesn't include every restaurant that serves beer and wine with meals. Should we start wondering what our zoning laws are encouraging, especially involving potential damage to our bodies and our minds?

Familiarity

References to the familiar are attention-sustaining, especially in the face of new or strange ideas. The familiar is comfortable. People drive the same route to work, children sing the same songs over and over, and you've probably watched your favorite movie more than once. Stories about Cap Anson, Shoeless Joe Jackson, Babe Ruth, Dizzy Dean, and Joe DiMaggio get repeated on occasions when cultural memories of baseball, as America's great sport, are invoked. How many times have you heard speakers repeat Martin Luther King, Jr.'s famous phrase "I have a dream"? We like the reassurance that such familiarity provides.

Novelty

Novel happenings, dramatic incidents, or unusual developments attract attention. Look at the tabloid newspaper headlines next time you're in the grocery checkout line: "Grandmother Gives Birth to Quadruplets," "Madonna to Marry Alien from Mars," "Elvis Sighted at County Fair." These bizarre stories catch our attention. References to size and contrast work well to create novelty.

When using novelty, blending the familiar and the novel, the old and the new, often yields the best results. Otherwise you risk stretching the credulity of your listeners, as do those supermarket tabloids. To stimulate interest in the evolving nature of the self-defense plea in criminal courts, you might cite recent highly publicized trials in which alleged victims claim self-defense in response to years of physical or mental abuse. Citing specific cases, such as the Menendez brothers' murder of their parents, provokes interest through novelty.

Suspense

Much of the appeal in mystery stories arises because we don't know how they will end. Films such as *Unbreakable* and *The Sixth Sense* have enough unusual twists to hold audiences spellbound. You, too, can use uncertainty in your speeches by pointing to puzzling relationships or unpredictable forces. Introduce suspense into the stories you tell, building up to a surprising climax. Hint that you'll divulge valuable information later: "Stay with me through this speech, because by the end you'll learn how to cut your book bill in half every semester."

Conflict

Controversy grabs attention. Soap operas are fraught with love, hate, violence, passion, and power struggles. Conflict, like suspense, suggests uncertainty; like activity, it's dynamic. The next time you hear the news, listen for conflict. Newscasters often portray shipwreck survivors as "battling nature." Sportscasters describe athletes as "overcoming adversity." And even weather forecasters talk about "fighting off Arctic blasts of frigid air." The concept of struggle brings the sense of urgency to the day's events.

In your speeches, you can create conflict among ideas, such as the competing theories about the aggressiveness of young boys: Are males genetically programmed to be aggressive, or are they made that way by environmental influences such as media violence? Put these competing theories in conflict with each other to reveal their differences. When your ideas are cast as pugilists, they become dramatic and engaging.

Humor

Listeners usually pay attention when they're enjoying themselves. Humor can unite you and your audience by relaxing everyone and providing a change of pace. When using humor to capture and hold attention, remember to stick close to your central idea by choosing humor that is relevant. Be sure to use only humorous stories that are in good taste and so avoid offending members of your audience. Comedian Bill Cosby met both of these requirements when he poked fun at a University of South Carolina graduating class. In his commencement speech, Cosby reminded his listeners:

> All across the United States of America, people are graduating. And they are hearing so many guest speakers tell them that they are going forth. As a parent I am concerned as to whether or not you know where "Forth" is. Let me put it to you this way: We have paved a road—the one to the house was already paved. "Forth" is not back home.[1]

The Vital

The phrase *the vital* was coined by Alan Monroe, the original author of this textbook, to reflect our tendency to be concerned with things that immediately benefit us. We pay attention to matters that affect our health, reputation, property, or employment. When a speaker says, "Students who take internships while in college find jobs after graduation three times as fast as those who don't," you're likely to pay attention—getting a job is vital to you. Appealing to *the vital*, therefore, is a matter of personalizing the speech for a particular audience—making it as relevant to their concrete circumstances as possible.

There are nine different ways to stimulate attention: activity, reality, proximity, familiarity, novelty, suspense, conflict, humor, and the vital. Use these attention-getters to grab and maintain your listeners' attention throughout your speech. They give your speech sparkle and spunk, they reach out to your listeners, and they help your listeners follow and remember your speech.

BEGINNING YOUR SPEECH

The beginning of a speech must gain the listeners' attention, secure good will and respect for the speaker, and prepare the audience for the main ideas of the speech. As was noted already, you can use the factors of attention to engage your listeners during the beginning moments of your speech. But attention is not enough. You must also secure good will and respect as well as prepare your listeners for the main ideas that follow your introduction. In many situations, your own reputation or the chairperson's introduction will help to generate good will.

You can also refer to your own experience with the topic to boost your credibility. You gain additional respect from your listeners when you share your background research with them.

However, there may be times when your audience is opposed to you or your topic. In these instances, it's important to deal with opposition openly so that you will receive a fair hearing. By commenting on the differences between your views and those of your listeners, you can let them know that you're aware of disagreements but are seeking areas of consensus. And when confronted by indifference, distrust, or skepticism, you must take steps early in the speech to change these attitudes so that your position will be received openly. Even if your listeners don't agree, you can often secure their respect for your honesty and integrity by dealing directly with them.

Finally, you can prepare your listeners for your speech by stating your purpose early. Let them engage the subject matter clearly and openly. Audiences that are forced to guess the purpose of a speech soon lose interest. A preview of your ideas and speech structure will help your audience follow along.

An introduction that secures your audience's attention and good will and prepares them to listen lays a solid foundation for acceptance of the central idea of your speech. You can establish attention by presenting your ideas in ways that create interest. We will examine a number of established means for tailoring your introduction to achieve the best results.

Referring to the Subject or Occasion

If your audience already has a vital interest in your subject, you need only to state that subject before presenting your first main point: "I'm glad to see how many of you came to learn more about finding summer internships. As the poster around campus indicated, I'm here tonight to talk about how you let people in your hometown know about this college's requirements for an acceptable summer internship relationship between a local business and student spending that summer back home."

President George W. Bush began his statement to the nation after the September 11, 2001, attacks on the World Trade Center and Pentagon by referring directly to the occasion:

> Today, our fellow citizens, our way of life, our very freedom came under attack in a series of deliberate and deadly terrorist acts. The victims were in airplanes, or in their offices; secretaries, businessmen and women, military and federal workers; moms and dads, friends and neighbors. Thousands of lives were suddenly ended by evil, despicable acts of terror. The pictures of airplanes flying into buildings, fires burning, huge structures collapsing, have filled us with disbelief, terrible sadness, and a quiet, unyielding anger. These acts of mass murder were intended to frighten our nation into chaos and retreat. But they have failed; our country is strong.[2]

Notice how President Bush moves from recognition of the events, the victims, and the media images to the American reaction in just a few sentences.

Using a Personal Reference or Greeting

At times, a warm, personal greeting from a speaker or the remembrance of a previous visit to an audience or scene should be made even more important. This often is the case when someone representing an organization or political unit in a visit to another organization or political unit is going to speak. Official ties are one thing, but if they can be personalized, then the audience may be even more open to developing a relationship with the speaker.

On December 27, 2001, Mayor Rudolph Giuliani left office. In the introduction to his farewell, he said, "People ask where I get my energy. Well, it's really simple. It comes from you. It comes from here. What I mean by that is that my strength and energy comes entirely from the people of the City of New York. And it comes from a place like this, St. Paul's Chapel."[3] Giuliani reminded his listeners of their common bonds and the significance their location. The brevity and forthrightness of his introduction struck exactly the right note on this occasion. Some audiences aren't tied so directly to you. In these cases, you'll need to discuss what brought you and your listeners together to establish this connection.

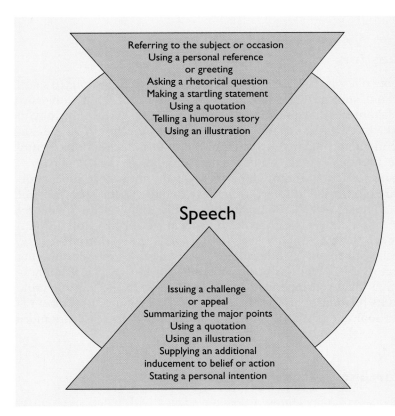

Referring to the subject or occasion
Using a personal reference or greeting
Asking a rhetorical question
Making a startling statement
Using a quotation
Telling a humorous story
Using an illustration

Speech

Issuing a challenge or appeal
Summarizing the major points
Using a quotation
Using an illustration
Supplying an additional inducement to belief or action
Stating a personal intention

FIGURE 8.2
Types of Introductions and Conclusions
You can choose among different types of introductions and conclusions for your speeches. As you choose your introduction, ask yourself whether it orients your audience to your purposes and ideas. When choosing a conclusion, ask whether it summarizes your ideas and achieves closure.

The way a personal reference introduction can be used to gain the attention of a hostile or skeptical audience is illustrated by a speech presented by Anson Mount, manager of public affairs for *Playboy,* to the Christian Life Commission of the Southern Baptist Convention:

> I am sure we are all aware of the seeming incongruity of a representative of *Playboy* magazine speaking to an assemblage of representatives of the Southern Baptist Convention. I was intrigued by the invitation when it came last fall, though I was not surprised. I am grateful for your genuine and warm hospitality, and I am flattered (though again not surprised) by the implication that I would have something to say that could have meaning to you people. Both *Playboy* and the Baptists have indeed been considering many of the same issues and ethical problems; and even if we have not arrived at the same conclusions, I am impressed and gratified by your openness and willingness to listen to our views.[4]

If a personal reference is sincere and appropriate, it will establish good will as well as gain attention. Avoid extravagant, emotional statements, however, because listeners are quick to sense a lack of genuineness. At the other extreme, avoid apologizing. Don't say, "I don't know why I was picked to talk when others could have done it so much better" or "Unaccustomed as I am to public speaking. . . ." Apologetic beginnings suggest that your audience needn't waste time listening. Be cordial, sincere, and modest, but establish your authority and maintain control of the situation.

Asking a Question

Another way to open a speech is to ask a question or series of questions to spark thinking about your subject. For example, Nicholas Fynn of Ohio University opened a speech about free-burning of timberland by saying, "How many of you in this room have visited a national park at one point in your life? Well, the majority of you are in good company."[5] Such a question introduces a topic gently and, with its direct reference to the audience, tends to engage the listeners.

Rhetorical questions, that is, those for which you do not expect direct audience response, are often used to forecast the development of the speech. After thanking the Charlotte, North Carolina, business community for the invitation to address them about the euro, the new European monetary unit (EMU), Lawrence Summers, the U.S. Deputy Secretary of the Treasury, introduced the body of his speech with rhetorical questions: "Three questions arise in thinking about EMU: what its effect will be on the economies of Europe; what implications the euro might have for the dollar; and how EMU will affect Europe's role in the world and its relations with the United States."[6] Such questions most often are used with topical organizations, when other types of forecasts are more difficult to use.

Making a Startling Statement

On certain occasions, you may choose to open a speech with what is known as the *shock technique,* making a startling statement of fact or opinion. This approach is especially useful when listeners are distracted, apathetic, or smug. It rivets their attention on your topic. For example, the executive director of the American Association of Retired Persons (AARP), after asking some rhetorical questions about health care, caught his listeners' attention with a series startling statements:

> Given what we're spending on health care, we should have the best system in the world. But the reality is that we don't. Thirty-seven million Americans have no health insurance protection whatsoever, and millions more are underinsured. We are twentieth—that's right, twentieth—among the nations of the world in infant mortality. The death rate for our black newborn children rivals that of Third World countries. And poor children in America, like their brothers and sisters in Third World nations, receive neither immunizations nor basic dental care.
>
> Those statistics give us a sense of the scope of the problem. What they don't adequately portray is the human factor—the pain and the suffering. While terminally ill patients may have their lives extended in intensive care units—at tremendous cost—middle-age minority women die of preventable and treatable cancer, hypertension and diabetes.[7]

Avoid overusing the shock technique. It can backfire if your listeners become angry when you threaten or disgust them.

Using a Quotation

A quotation may be an excellent means of introducing a speech, because it can prod listeners to think about something important and it often captures an appropriate emotional tone. A student in a public speaking class opened her informative speech by saying,

> One of my favorite movies is *Braveheart.* I've seen it so many times, I think I have it memorized. Maybe you remember one point in the movie where Mel Gibson's character William Wallace says, "Every man dies. Not every man truly lives." The historical William Wallace has lived, in myth and legend, for hundreds of years. In my speech today, I'd like to investigate his life as history records it. Who was William Wallace the man? What are the facts about his life and death? Let's begin with the historical record.

Quotations can be used to capture the theme of a speech. Harlan Cleveland, president of the World Academy of Art and Science, opened a speech to business executives concerned with human services in this manner:

> From my very first moments at Silver Bay [home of the conference], I found your company wonderfully congenial. Truth usually comes in small paradoxical packages, and one of them greeted me at our opening session. Our experience together, said Adrienne Riley, would be "very intense and totally relaxed." On both counts, her paradox quickly became true.
>
> I was especially glad to encounter in our program folder a quote from Mary Parker Follett, one of my favorite authors in my one-time field of public

administration: "All polishing is done by friction," she wrote long ago. "The music of the violin we get by friction. We left the savage style when we discovered fire by friction. So we talk of the friction of mind on mind as a good thing."

That's a hard sell to young students. I used to tell graduate students in public administration that the executive's task is not to get staff members to agree with each other. That's much too easy. The hard thing, the important thing. . . .[8]

We need not finish his thought—you can. The quotation from Follett set a theme—friction—that obviously now would become the theme of a speech on how to create an imaginative business organization. Quotations are more than decoration; they can set the mood and direct the flow of thought in positive directions.

Telling a Humorous Story

You can begin a speech by telling a funny story or relating a humorous experience. When doing so, however, observe the following three rules of communication:

1. Be sure that the story is at least amusing, if not funny; test it out on others before you actually deliver the speech. Be sure that you practice sufficiently so you can present the story naturally. And use the story to make a point instead of making it the center of your remarks. In other words, brevity is crucial.

2. Be sure that the story is relevant to your speech; if its subject matter or punch line is not directly related to you, your topic, or at least your next couple of sentences, the story will appear to be a mere gimmick.

3. Be sure that your story is in good taste; in a public gathering, an off-color or doubtful story violates accepted standards of social behavior and can undermine an audience's respect for you. You should avoid sexual, racist, antireligious, ageist, homophobic, and sexist humor.

CEO Heather Roulston Ettinger observed all three of these rules when she talked to the Akron Community Foundation:

Let me begin with a story that I think sets the tone for the change that is going to occur over the next few decades. Last summer, Buffalo Bills quarterback, Doug Flutie, was watching the final game of the Women's World Cup soccer match on TV with his 12-year-old soccer-playing daughter, Alexa. During the soccer match between the USA and China teams, the hugely successful advertisement for Gatorade featuring Michael Jordan and Mia Hamm came on. As most of you well know, Michael Jordan, formerly of NBA fame, is the most influential athlete of the last century. Mia Hamm was the star forward of the USA National team. You might remember the theme to this was "Anything you can do I can do better." As Doug Flutie tells the story, when the ad came on, Alexa asked, "Dad, who's the guy with Mia?"[9]

Ettinger went on to discuss the paradigm change that the story reveals about female role models in our society.

Using an Illustration

A real-life incident, a passage from a novel or short story, or a hypothetical illustration can also get a speech off to a good start. An illustration should be not only interesting to the audience but also relevant to your central idea. Deanna Sellnow, then a student at North Dakota State University, used this technique to introduce a speech on private credit-reporting bureaus:

> John Pontier, of Boise, Idaho, was turned down for insurance because a reporting agency informed the company that he and his wife were addicted to narcotics, and his Taco Bell franchise had been closed down by the health board when dog food had been found mixed in with the tacos. There was only one small problem. The information was made up. His wife was a practicing Mormon who didn't touch a drink, much less drugs, and the restaurant had never been cited for a health violation.[10]

The existence of a problem with private credit-reporting bureaus is clear from this introduction. If the illustration is humorous instead of serious, the effect is different but the introduction can be equally useful, as was the case when the chancellor of California State University, Charles Reed, opened the body of a lecture in this manner:

> As I mentioned, I want to talk today about a K–12 education continuum. But I first want to share with you a story about education as a lifelong continuum.
>
> When the renowned Justice Oliver Wendell Holmes Jr. was hospitalized at age 92, he received a visit from President Franklin D. Roosevelt. The president was surprised to see Justice Holmes reading a Greek primer.
>
> "What are you doing?" President Roosevelt asked him.
>
> "I am reading," replied Justice Holmes.
>
> "I can see that," said the president. "But why a Greek primer?"
>
> The justice looked at him and said, "Why, to improve my mind, of course."
>
> This story serves as a good illustration of the fact that the education of the human mind never stops. It does not stop at grade 8, grade 12, or after four years of college.[11]

Completing Your Introduction

You can use one of the approaches that we've discussed alone, or you can combine two or more. You might open with a startling illustration or a humorous reference to the occasion, for example. No matter what type of introduction you use, you should have three purposes in mind: arousing the attention of your listeners, winning their good will and respect, and setting a tone and direction for the substance of your talk. Your introduction should be relevant to the purpose of your speech and should lead smoothly into the first of the major ideas that you

Web Exploration
For an overview of the different types of introductions go to
www.ablongman.com/
german15e

wish to present; that is, your introduction should be an integral part of the speech.

Your introduction should also forecast the speech's development by means of a preview. The preview establishes your listeners' confidence in your organization, thus enhancing your credibility. It creates listener receptivity by providing a structure for you and your listeners to follow during the speech. Here are some examples of types of previews:

1. *Announce the organizational pattern.* You might say, "I'll develop the effects of the problem of spousal abuse and then examine its causes" (causal pattern). "In demonstrating how to check basic problems with your computer, I'll consider three topics. I'll be talking about the hard drive, the ancillary drive systems, and the word processing program" (topical order).

Speaking of . . . Skills

How Long Should It Be?

According to a classic study, the average speaker spends about 10 percent of the total speech on the introduction and 5 percent on the conclusion. The introduction may increase to 13 percent in speeches that are designed to stimulate or inspire, such as sermons, dedications, or memorials. In practical terms, this means that you will probably take one minute to introduce a ten-minute speech and thirty seconds to conclude it.

Can you think of circumstances in which you'd spend more time introducing or concluding your remarks? Less time?

For the original study, see: N. Edd Miller, "Speech Introductions and Conclusions," *Quarterly Journal of Speech*, 32 (1946): 181–183.

2. *Use mnemonic devices.* Acronyms aid memory; for example, "I'm going to discuss the ABCs of jogging: Always wear good shoes. Baby your feet. Call a podiatrist if problems develop."

3. *Employ alliteration.* Rely on sound similarities to create interest. For example: "My advice for finding someone to marry? Use the three As—availability, attitude, and *amour.*"

4. *Use repetition.* Reinforce your message by repeating the main phrases. You can say, "We need to examine how a lack of extensive night street lights creates a problem on campus, a problem on nearby streets, a problem on downtown streets, and, ultimately, even a problem on the seemingly quiet, wooded streets of suburbia."

When effective, your introductory remarks will both establish a common ground of interest and understanding and provide a structure to guide your audience toward the conclusion that you intend to reach.

ENDING YOUR SPEECH

Just as the introduction to your speech accomplishes specific purposes, so too does the conclusion. An effective conclusion does two things well: (1) it rounds off the message of the speech, letting listeners understand one more time the importance and significance of what you're saying, and (2) it completes the relationship you've constructed between you and them. If your speech has one dominant idea, you should restate it in a clear and forceful manner. If your speech is more complex, you may summarize the key points, or you may spell out the action or belief that these points suggest. And always say something that signals, even if indirectly, the end for now of your relationship.

In addition to reinforcing the central idea, your conclusion should leave the audience in the proper mood. If you want your listeners to express vigorous enthusiasm, stimulate that feeling with your closing words. Decide whether the response you seek is a mood of seriousness or good humor, of warm sympathy or utter disgust, of thoughtfulness or action. Then end your speech in a way that will create that mood.

Finally, a good ending should convey a sense of completeness and finality. Listeners grow restless and annoyed when they think the speech is finished, only to hear the speaker ramble on. Tie the threads of thought together so that the pattern of your speech is brought clearly to completion.

Speakers employ many strategies to convey a sense of closure to their speeches. We will examine the conclusion techniques that are used regularly.

Issuing a Challenge

You may conclude your speech by issuing a challenge to your listeners, requesting support or action, or reminding them of their responsibilities. That challenge can be as simple as the one used by Kofi Annan when addressing the U.N. Security Council on promoting peace in the new millennium: "This is the core challenge of the Security Council and the United Nations as a whole in the next century: to unite behind the principle that massive and systematic violations of human rights conducted against an entire people cannot be allowed to stand."[12] At other times, especially when aiming to create a mood of inspiration and determination, the challenge is expanded, as Harvard research associate Peter Gibbon did when talking to journalists about the need to become more self-critical:

> In the Age of Information, journalists and citizens face the same challenges. We need to study the past so as not to become arrogant, to remember the good so as not to become cynical, and to recognize America's strengths so as not to dwell on her weaknesses. We need to be honest and realistic without losing our capacity for admiration—and to be able to embrace complexity without losing our faith in the heroic.[13]

Notice Gibbon's use of parallel structure—to study, to remember, to recognize, and then "to be honest . . . without" and "to be able to embrace . . . without." Such attention to style elevates the challenge, giving it a seriousness that makes it harder for listeners to avoid it.

Summarizing the Major Points or Ideas

In an informative speech, a summary allows the audience to pull together the main strands of information and to evaluate the significance of the speech. In a persuasive speech, a summary gives you a final opportunity to present, in brief form, the major points of your argument. For example, a student presented this summary of an informative speech on tornadoes:

> You've seen the swirling funnel clouds on the six o'clock news. They hit sometimes without much warning, leaving in their paths death and destruction. Now you should understand the formation of funnel clouds, the classification of tornadoes on the Fujita scale, and the high cost of tornadoes worldwide in lives and property. Once you understand the savage fury of tornadoes, you can better appreciate them. Tornadoes are one of nature's temper tantrums.

If the student's purpose had been to persuade listeners to take certain precautions during a tornado alert, the summary of the speech might have sounded like this:

> The devastation left in the path of a tornado can be tremendous. To prevent you and your loved ones from becoming statistics on the six o'clock news, remember what I told you this afternoon. Seek shelter in basements, ditches, or other low areas. Stay away from glass and electric lines. And remember the lesson of the Xenia, Ohio, disaster. Tornadoes often hit in clusters. Be sure the coast is clear before you leave your shelter. Don't be a statistic.

In each case, summarizing the main ideas of the speech gives the speaker another opportunity to reinforce the message. Information can be reiterated in the summary of an informative speech, or the major arguments or actions can be strengthened in the summary of a persuasive speech.

Using a Quotation

You can cite others' words to capture the spirit of your ideas in the conclusion of your speech. Quotations are often used to end speeches. Quoted prose, if the author is credible, may gather additional support for your central idea. So in a speech on the need to reformulate this country's system of managed care, Howard Veit said, "I believe all the dynamics are in place for this transformation [of care systems] to take place. Dwight Eisenhower once said, 'Neither a wise man nor a brave man lies down on the tracks of history to wait for the train of the future to run over him.' Well, the train is coming. Fortunately, you have a choice about how you'll react."[14]

Poetry, too, may distill the essence of your message in uplifting language. Bishop Leontine Kelly concluded her speech celebrating the diversity of human talents with the words of a well-known Christian hymn: "How firm a foundation ye saints of the Lord, Is laid for your faith in God's excellent word."[15] The recognition of these familiar words probably inspired members of her audience.

Using an Illustration

Illustrations engage your listeners emotionally. If you use a concluding illustration, it can set the tone and direction of your final words. Your illustration should be both inclusive and conclusive—inclusive of the main focus or thrust of your speech and conclusive in tone and impact. Capturing the message and the way a speaker wanted an audience to feel about the message is nicely illustrated in American Medical Association president Nancy Dickey's description of a new AMA plan for health reform:

> There is an old painting that hangs in many medical museums that depicts this relationship [between patient and doctor] better than any words I can offer here. Perhaps some of you have even seen it. It shows a physician at a child's bedside. The physician is pensive, maybe even a bit prayerful. The child's parents are all but faded into the background. And there sits the physician—with none of today's tools or technologies to call upon—but nonetheless clearly connected to his patient.
>
> I want to be sure, that as we craft this new health system, that I am again allowed—even encouraged—to connect in that way to my patients . . . to listen, to hear, and to respond to their concerns.
>
> Yes, I want to keep all of the glories of modern medicine and technology, but I also want to combine them with the caring of a human heart. And I believe that working together, this imaginative, intellectual, and committed country can do that—if we put our minds to it, and give it the proper priority. I look forward to your help.[16]

Supplying an Additional Inducement to Belief or Action

Sometimes you may conclude a speech by quickly reviewing the principal ideas presented in the body and then supplying one or more additional reasons for endorsing the belief or taking the proposed action. So, in a student speech, Michael Twitchell spoke at length about the devastating effects of depression. After proposing numerous reasons for people to get involved in the battle, he offered in the conclusion to his speech an additional inducement:

> Why should you really care? Why is it important? The depressed person may be someone you know—it could be you. If you know what is happening, you can always help. I wish I had known what depression was in March of 1978. You see, when I said David Twitchell could be my father, I was making a statement of fact. David is my father. I am his son. My family wasn't saved; perhaps now yours can be.[17]

Web Exploration
For an overview of the different types of conclusions go to
www.ablongman.com/german15e

Stating a Personal Intention

Stating your own intention to adopt the action or attitude you recommend in your speech is particularly effective when your prestige with the audience is high or when you have presented a concrete proposal requiring immediate action. By professing your intention to take immediate action, you and your ideas gain credibility. In the following example, a speaker sets himself up as a model for the actions he wants his listeners to take:

> Today I have illustrated how important healthy blood is to human survival and how blood banks work to ensure the possibility and availability of blood for each of us. It is not a coincidence that I speak on this vital topic on the same day that the local Red Cross Bloodmobile is visiting campus. I want to urge each of you to ensure your future and mine by stopping at the Student Center today or tomorrow to make your donation. The few minutes that it takes may add up to a lifetime for a person in need. To illustrate how firmly I believe in this opportunity to help, I'm going to the Student Center to give my donation as soon as this class is over. I invite any of you who feel this strongly to join me.

Speakers sometimes indicate their personal intentions to take action. This is especially effective when the speaker is highly regarded by listeners or when immediate actions are urged.

Regardless of the means you choose for closing your speech, remember that your conclusion should focus the attention of your listeners on the central theme you've developed. In addition, a good conclusion should be consistent with the mood or tenor of your speech and should convey a sense of completeness and finality.

SAMPLE OUTLINE FOR AN INTRODUCTION AND CONCLUSION

An introduction and conclusion for a classroom speech on Mothers Against Drunk Driving (MADD) and Students Against Driving Drunk (SADD) might take the following form. Notice that the speaker uses suspense in combination with startling statements to lead the audience into the subject. The conclusion combines a summary with a final illustration and a statement of personal intention.

Friends Don't Let Friends Drive Drunk

Introduction

I. Many of you have seen the "Black Gash"—the Vietnam War Memorial in Washington, D.C.
   A. It contains the names of more than 40,000 Americans who gave their lives in Southeast Asia between 1961 and 1973.
   B. We averaged over 3000 war dead a year during that painful period.

II. Today, another enemy stalks Americans.
   A. The enemy kills, not 3000, but over 20,000 citizens every 12 months.
   B. The enemy is not hiding in jungles but can be found in every community in the country.
   C. The enemy kills, not with bayonets and bullets, but with bottles and bumpers.

III. Two organizations are trying to contain and finally destroy the killer.
   A. Every TV station in this town carries a public service ad that says "Friends Don't Let Friends Drive Drunk."
   B. In response to the menace of the drunk driver, two national organizations—Mothers Against Drunk Driving and Students Against Driving Drunk—have been formed and are working even in this community to make the streets safe for you and me.
   C. [Central idea] MADD and SADD are achieving their goals with your help.
   D. To help you understand what these familiar organizations do, first I'll tell you something about the founders of MADD and SADD; then, I'll describe their operations; finally, I'll mention some of the ways community members get involved with them.

   [Body]

Conclusion

I. Today, I've talked briefly about the Lightners and their goals for MADD and SADD, their organizational techniques, and ways in which you can get involved.

II. The work of MADD and SADD volunteers—even on our campus, where I'm sure you've seen their posters in the Student Center—is being carried out to keep you alive.
    A. You may not think you need to be involved; but remember: After midnight, one in every five or fewer drivers on the road is probably drunk. You could be involved whether you want to be or not.
    B. That certainly was the case with Julie Smeiser, a member of our sophomore class, who just last Friday was hit by a drunk driver when going home for the weekend.

III. If people don't take action, we could build a new "Black Gash"—this time for victims of drunks—every two years, and soon fill Washington, D.C., with monuments to needless suffering.
    A. Such monuments would be grim reminders of our unwillingness to respond to enemies at home with the same intensity with which we attacked enemies abroad.
    B. A better response would be to support actively groups such as MADD and SADD, who are attacking the enemy on several fronts at once in a war on motorized murder.

IV. If you're interested in learning more about SADD and MADD, stop by Room 324 in the Student Center tonight at 7:30 to hear the president of the local chapter of SADD talk about this year's activities. I'll be there; please join me.

Speaking of . . . Ethics

Revealing Responsible Intentions

Consider this scenario: You are planning a speech in which you hope to persuade your listeners to donate money to your political caucus. Should you reveal your intention in your introduction?

While we generally are unaffected by the awareness that persuasion is intended, we strongly react to deception. Research suggests the worst effect on listeners will occur if you disguise your intent but it is discovered as you speak.

Other factors such as your listeners' initial attitudes also influence how they will respond to your intention. If your listeners are highly involved or strongly committed to an opposing view, they will be less inclined to listen to you if they know your goal is to persuade.

In every case, avoid the appearance of direct manipulation. You should say, "Let's investigate the options together," rather than "Today I'm going to persuade you to. . . ." Most of us like to think that we have free choice.

For further information, see: Richard Petty and John Cacioppo, "Effects of Forewarning, Cognitive Responding, and Resistance to Persuasion," *Journal of Personality and Social Psychology,* 35 (1970): 645–655.

ASSESSING YOUR PROGRESS

Chapter Summary

1. You can capture and sustain your listeners' attention by using one or more of the nine factors of attention: activity, reality, proximity, familiarity, novelty, suspense, conflict, humor, and the vital.
2. Introductions should seize attention, secure good will, and prepare an audience for what you will be saying.
3. Types of introductions include referring to the subject or occasion, using a personal reference or greeting, asking a rhetorical question, making a startling statement of fact or opinion, using a quotation, telling a humorous story, and using an illustration.
4. In concluding your speech, you should attempt to focus the thoughts of your audience on your central theme, maintain the tenor of your speech, close off (or extend) the relationship built between speaker and listeners, and convey a sense of finality.
5. Techniques for ending a speech include issuing a challenge or appeal, summarizing the major points or ideas, using a quotation, using an illustration, supplying an additional inducement to belief or action, and stating a personal intention.

Key Terms

attention (p. 134)
factors of attention (p. 134)

primacy effect (p. 134)
recency effect (p. 134)

Assessment Activities

1. You've been asked to speak on a controversial issue. Assume that the setting for three versions of the speech will include three different occasions: a classroom at your school, where audience members are mixed in their support; a favorable ("pro") audience, highly sympathetic to you and your position; and an unfavorable ("anti") audience, hostile to you and your position. Write three introductions, one for each setting. Include a brief paragraph explaining your rhetorical strategies. Either turn these in or read them aloud as parts of a class discussion.
2. Consult the Internet or an almanac to find out what famous events occurred on this date in history. Then write an introduction for an informative speech to your classmates referring to the occasion. Ask your listeners if you secured their interest.
3. Participate in a chain of introductions and conclusions. One student will begin by suggesting a topic for a speech. A second student will suggest an appropriate introduction and conclusion and justify those choices. A third student will challenge those selections and propose alternative introductions and/or conclusions. Continue this discussion until everyone has participated. Which examples were most effective? Determine why they were effective.

Using the Web

1. Locate a database that includes a collection of speeches such as the Top 100 American Speeches of the 20th Century (http://www.americanrhetoric.com/top100speeches.htm). Identify the types of introductory and concluding strategies used by each speaker. Evaluate the effectiveness of these strategies.

 Using Video Workshop

Watch the speeches in Module 7, "Organization and Outlines." As you watch, think about what makes up an effective introduction and conclusion to a speech. Then answer Questions 1–13.

References

1. Bill Cosby, "University of South Carolina Commencement Address," 1990, unpublished manuscript available from the author.

2. President Bush's statement can be found at http://www.yale.edu/lawweb/avalon/sept11/presstate001.htm.

3. Mayor Giuliani's "Farewell Address" can be found at http://www.nyc.gov/html/rwg/html/200lb/farewell.html.

4. Anson Mount, Manager of Public Affairs for *Playboy* magazine, from a speech presented to the Christian Life Commission, in *Contemporary American Speeches,* 5th ed., edited by Wil A. Linkugel et al. (Dubuque, IA: Kendall/Hunt, 1982).

5. Nicholas Fynn, "The Free Burn Fallacy," *Winning Orations 1989.* Reprinted by permission of Larry Schnoor, Executive Secretary, Interstate Oratorical Association, Mankato, MN.

6. Lawrence H. Summers, "Transatlantic Implications of the Euro," *Vital Speeches of the Day,* 65 (15 January 1999).

7. Horace B. Deets, "Health Care for a Caring America: We Must Develop a Better System," *Vital Speeches of the Day,* 55 (1 August 1989).

8. Harlan Cleveland, "Imagination and Creativity," *Vital Speeches of the Day,* 65 (1 February 1999).

9. Heather Roulston Ettinger's address "Shattering the Glass Floor" can be found at http://www.votd.com/etting.htm.

10. Deanna Sellnow, "Have You Checked Lately?" *Winning Orations.* Reprinted by permission of Larry Schnoor, Executive Secretary, Interstate Oratorical Association, Mankato, MN.

11. Charles B. Reed, "Collaborating for Excellence: Building a Seamless K–12 System for California," *Vital Speeches of the Day,* 65 (1 June 1999).

12. Kofi Annan, "Relevance of the U.N. Security Council: Promoting International Peace in the Next Century," *Vital Speeches of the Day,* 65 (15 June 1999).

13. Peter H. Gibbon, "The End of Admiration: The Media and the Loss of Heroes," *Vital Speeches of the Day,* 65 (15 June 1999).

14. Howard Veit, "The Next Generation of Managed Care: The Age of Consumerism," *Vital Speeches of the Day,* 65 (15 April 1999).

15. Bishop Leontine Kelly, "Celebrating the Diversity of Our Gifts," reprinted in *Women's Voices in Our Time,* edited by Victoria L. DeFrancisco and Marvin D. Jensen (Prospect Heights, IL: Waveland Press, 1994), 115.

16. Nancy W. Dickey, "Health Care for the New Millennium: The AMA Plan for Health System Reform," *Vital Speeches of the Day,* 65 (15 April 1999).

17. Michael A. Twitchell, "The Flood Gates of the Mind," *Winning Orations.* Reprinted by permission of Larry Schnoor, Executive Secretary, Interstate Oratorical Association, Mankato, MN.

Chapter 9

Wording Your Speech

LANGUAGE FUNCTIONS ON MULTIPLE LEVELS. It is a referential, relational, and symbolic medium of communication. As language refers to things, it is *referential*. When you label or name things such as "dog," "tree," or "cupcake," you are employing the referential nature of language. As you probably realize, young children learn the power of language as a referential tool early.

Language also has *relational powers*; it suggests associations between people. "Give me that cupcake" not only points to the cupcake, but also indicates that one person has the power or authority to command another person. Some groups even use their own special languages that exclude others. Technical language is used most often by professionals. Slang doesn't sound right when

Getting someone to see your point of view often depends on strategic rhetorical decisions.

spoken by an outsider. It might sound odd, for example, to hear your grand-mother say, "He's a hottie!"

And language is *symbolic*, by which we mean that it can be disconnected from the concrete world. We can talk about unreal things such as unicorns and gremlins or abstract constructs such as democracy and love. Whole empires of thought can be constructed out of language. When you speak, it's not enough to know the words; you must also understand how language reflects human relationships and shared senses of reality—your culture and thinking.

In essence, we've been talking about the fundamental quality of orality that exists in our use of language. In the next three chapters, we'll turn our attention to the encoding of messages. **Encoding** occurs when you put ideas into words and actions. Encoding includes your choice of language, use of visual aids, and even bodily and vocal behaviors. In this chapter, we'll focus on selecting your speaking style, creating a speaking atmosphere, and using language strategically.

SELECTING YOUR STYLE

Generally, spoken language is uncomplicated; it has to be, since we use it every day—at the grocery store, over the back fence, around the supper table, and in the street. Usually, public speakers adopt the conversational quality of everyday language because listeners prefer it. Most of the time when you speak, you will choose this oral style.

Oral style is informal, similar to conversation. Occasionally, spoken language assumes a more complicated and formal style. This type of language more closely resembles written work and naturally is referred to as **written style.** It usually indicates a formal occasion or weighty topic. Consider the following examples of written and oral style:

Written Style	Oral Style
Remit the requested amount forthwith.	Pay your bill.
Will you be having anything else?	Whutkinahgitcha?
To avoid injury, keep hands away from the cutting surface.	Don't touch the blade!
Contact a service representative to register your dissatisfaction with the product.	Call to complain.

If you write out your whole speech before giving it, the result is likely to be stilted and stiff. It might sound more like an essay than a speech. For example, consider the following introduction:

> I am most pleased that you could come this morning. I would like to use this opportunity to discuss with you a subject of inestimable importance to us all: the impact of inflationary spirals on students enrolled in institutions of higher education.

Translated into an oral style, a speaker would say,

> Thanks for coming. I'd like to talk today about a problem for all of us: the rising cost of going to college.

Speaking of . . . Skills

Oral versus Written Style

How do you instantly recognize that a speaker has written out a speech? Inherently it sounds as though it's been written. The speaker uses written rather than oral style. Here are some ways in which oral style differs from written style:

1. The average sentence is shorter in oral communication.
2. You use fewer different words when you speak.
3. You also use a larger number of short words such as *it* and *the*. In fact, fifty simple words constitute almost half of your speaking vocabulary.
4. You refer to people more often with words like *I, you, me, our,* and *us.*
5. You use more qualifying words such as *much, many, a lot,* and *most.*
6. Your language choices are more informal, and you use more contractions.

Notice how much more natural the second version sounds. The first is wordy—filled with prepositional phrases, complex words, and formal sentences. The second contains shorter sentences and simpler vocabulary, and it addresses the audience directly.

For most speech occasions, you should cultivate an oral style. On rare, highly ceremonial occasions, you may decide to read from a prepared text. However, even then, you should strive for an oral style.[1] There are four qualities that will help you to develop a clear and effective oral style. Let's consider accuracy, simplicity, restatement, and coherence.

Accuracy

Careful word choice is an essential ingredient to effectively transmitting your meaning to an audience. Oral language is usually concrete and specific. If you tell a hardware store clerk, "I broke the doohickey on my whachamicallit, and I need a thingamajig to fix it," you'd better have the whachamicallit in your hand, or the clerk won't understand. When you speak, your goal is precision. You should leave no doubt about your meaning.

Since words are symbols that represent concepts or objects, your listeners may attach a meaning to your words that's quite different from the one you intended. This misinterpretation becomes more likely as your words become more abstract. Democracy, for example, doesn't mean the same thing to a citizen in the suburbs as it does to a citizen in the ghetto. Democracy will have different meanings for Americans who belong to the Moral Majority than it will from those who belong to the American Socialist Party.

Students of general semantics, the study of words or symbols and their relationships to reality, warn us that many errors in thinking and communication arise from treating words as if they were actual conditions, processes, or objects. Words are not fixed and timeless in meaning, nor does everyone use them in exactly the same way.

To avoid vagueness, choose words that express the exact shade of meaning you wish to communicate. You might say that an object shines, but the object might also *glow, glitter, glisten, flare, gleam, glare, blaze, shimmer, glimmer, flicker, sparkle, flash*, and *beam*. Each word allows you to describe the object more precisely.

Simplicity

"Speak," said Abraham Lincoln, "so that the most lowly can understand you, and the rest will have no difficulty." Because electronic media reach audiences and cultures more varied than Lincoln could have imagined, you have even more reason to follow his advice today. Say *learn* rather than *ascertain, try* rather than *endeavor, use* rather than *utilize, help* rather than *facilitate*. Don't use a longer or less familiar word when a simple one is just as clear. Evangelist Billy Sunday illustrated the effectiveness of familiar words in this example:

If a man were to take a piece of meat and smell it and look disgusted, and his little boy were to say, "What's the matter with it, Pop?" and he were to say, "It is undergoing a process of decomposition in the formation of new chemical compounds," the boy would be all in. But if the father were to say, "It's rotten," then the boy would understand and hold his nose. "Rotten" is a good Anglo-Saxon word, and you do not have to go to the dictionary to find out what it means.[2]

Simplicity doesn't mean *simplistic*. If you talk down to your audience, they will be insulted. Instead, speak directly using words that convey precise, concrete meanings.

Restatement

If accuracy and simplicity were your only criteria as a speaker, your messages might resemble a famous World War II bulletin: "Sighted sub, sank same." But because words literally disappear into the atmosphere as soon as they're spoken, you don't have the writer's advantage when transmitting ideas to others. Instead, you must rely heavily on restatement.

Restatement is the repetition of words, phrases, and ideas so as to clarify and reinforce them. The key here is not simply to repeat yourself, but to rephrase in order to advance listeners' understanding or acceptance of an idea. Advertisers frequently depend on restatement to reinforce their point. For example, the jingle for a typical laundry soap might make the point this way: "Suds gets your clothes clean. Suds removes dirt, stains, and odors. Suds tackles the toughest cleaning jobs your kids bring home."

Restating an idea from a number of perspectives usually involves listing its components or redefining the basic concept. You can see this principle of reiteration at work in this speech that a student gave on urban sprawl:

If you're like most Americans, your dream home is somewhere in the suburbs—plenty of fresh air, close to your job and schools, all on a wooded lot. But more and more of us are discovering that we're the victims of urban sprawl, the unplanned growth of housing developments that contribute to air pollution, traffic congestion, and visual blight. If you live in Las Vegas, your view of the mountains will be obscured by smog. If you live in Atlanta, you'll experience the longest average commute of any city in the country. And if you make Akron or Austin or Denver your home, population density increases yearly. The effects of urban sprawl can be seen across our nation. Every day, many Americans drive between 20 and 30 miles to work, more than 50 acres of farmland and woods are plowed under, and many of our cities can't meet federal clean air standards.[3]

This student speaker realized that her audience probably was uncertain about the meaning of the phrase "urban sprawl." She listed three effects of unchecked urban growth: air pollution, traffic congestion, and visual blight. Then she restated them in several ways so that her listeners could easily understand the focus of her speech.

Restatement can help your listeners remember your ideas more readily. However, be careful of mindless repetition; too many restatements, especially of simple ideas, can be boring.

Coherence

Just as you must use restatement because your audience doesn't have the luxury of reviewing the points, you must also signal where you're at in your speech because your listeners aren't able to perceive punctuation marks that might help them distinguish one idea from another as you speak. To be understood, oral communication requires **coherence,** or the logical connection of ideas. To achieve coherence, you should use forecasts or previews, summaries, and signposts.

Forecasts or *previews* precede the development of the body of the speech, usually forming part of the introduction. They provide clues to the overall speech structure. Previews are especially helpful in outlining the major topics of the speech. Consider the following examples:

> Today I am going to talk about three aspects of family life: trust, love, and commitment.

> There are four major elements in developing a winning résumé. We'll look at establishing your strengths, forming a positive impression, including sufficient detail, and developing an edge.

> The history of the Vietnam War can be divided into two periods: the French involvement and the commitment of American troops.

Each of these forecasts provides a link between the introduction to the speech and the development of ideas in the body of the speech. The forecast shows the listener what to expect. In a sense, you are providing a road map when you signal your speech structure in a forecast.

A **summary** provides coherence in your speech by recapping ideas you've covered. You can summarize ideas at interim points before you move on to another topic, such as "Trust is an important ingredient in promoting a strong family life for the two reasons we just examined. It increases self-disclosure and promotes a sense of well-being. Now, let's examine a second element: love."

It is especially important to summarize your main ideas at the end of your speech. It is your last chance to remind listeners of your main topics and leave them with a final impression of your speech. A final summary usually forms part of the conclusion and often parallels the forecasts. For example, a final summary might look like this:

> Today we talked about what constitutes a strong family life. Experts agree that there are three things that all families need: trust, love, and commitment.

> When you sit down to apply for your first job, remember the four major elements in developing a winning résumé. Think about establishing your strengths, forming a positive impression, including sufficient detail, and developing an edge.

> The history of the Vietnam War has been divided into two periods: the French involvement and the commitment of American troops.

Notice that all three examples of final summaries parallel the forecast for the speech. They are direct and clear, and they remind the listener of the primary structure of the speech.

In addition to forecasts and summaries, you must use **signposts** or *transitions*—linking phrases that move an audience from one idea to another. Signposts or transitions are words or phrases—such as *first, next,* or *as a result*—that help listeners follow the movement of your ideas. Signposts such as "the history of this invention begins in . . . " also provide clues to the overall message structure. The following are useful signposts:

▶ In the first place . . . The second point is . . .
▶ In addition to . . . notice that . . .
▶ Now look at it from a different angle . . .
▶ You must keep these three things in mind in order to understand the importance of the fourth . . .
▶ What was the result? . . .
▶ Turning now to . . .

The preceding signposts are neutral; they tell an audience that another idea is coming but don't indicate whether it's similar, different, or more important. You can improve the coherence of your speeches by indicating the precise relationships among ideas. Those relationships include parallel/hierarchical, similar/different, and coordinate/subordinate relationships. Here are some examples:

Parallel: Not only . . . but also . . .
Hierarchical: More important than these . . .
Different: In contrast . . .
Similar: Similar to this . . .
Coordinated: One must consider X, Y, and Z . . .
Subordinated: On the next level is . . .

Forecasts, summaries, and signposts are important to your audience. Forecasts and summaries give listeners an overall sense of your entire message; if listeners can easily see the structure, they'll better understand and remember your speech. The signposts lead your listeners step by step through the speech, signaling specific relationships between and among ideas.

CREATING AN ATMOSPHERE

You cultivate the atmosphere of the speaking occasion largely through your speaking style. In an informative speech, you want to convey your enthusiasm about your topic to your listeners, encouraging them to think about the information you present. In a persuasive speech, you want to inspire your listeners to alter their thoughts or behaviors.

Sometimes the atmosphere of the occasion dictates what speaking style should be used. You don't expect a light, humorous speaking style during a funeral. Even so, sometimes a eulogist will tell a funny or amusing story about the deceased. Yet the overall tone of a speech at a funeral should be solemn. In contrast, a speech after a football victory, election win, or successful fund drive is seldom somber. Victory speeches are times for celebration and unity.

The speaking **atmosphere** is the mind-set or mental attitude that you attempt to create in your audience. A serious speaker urging graduating seniors to remember the most important things in life might say, "Rank your values and live by them." That same idea expressed by actor Alan Alda sounded more humorous:

> We live in a time that seems to be split about its values. In fact it seems to be schizophrenic.
>
> For instance, if you pick up a magazine like *Psychology Today,* you're liable to see an article like "White Collar Crime: It's More Widespread Than You Think." Then in the back of the magazine they'll print an advertisement that says, "We'll write your doctoral thesis for 25 bucks." You see how values are eroding? I mean, a doctoral thesis ought to go for at least a C-note.[4]

How do you generate an atmosphere or mood in your listeners? The answer depends on the speaking situation, your speech purpose, and your listeners' expectations. You can adjust the intensity of your speech and manage the appropriateness of your language to communicate a relationship with your listeners.

Intensity

You can communicate your feelings about ideas and objects through word choices. You can communicate your attitude toward your subject by choosing words that show how you feel. This, in turn, suggests how you expect your listeners to react to the subject. In one way, you are demonstrating their response through your language choices. For example, consider these attitudinally weighted terms:

Highly Positive	Relatively Neutral	Highly Negative
companion animal	dog	cur
defender of the innocent	lawyer	bloodsucker
wedded bliss	marriage	entrapment
holy warrior	soldier	terrorist

These terms are organized by their intensity, ranging from highly positive terms such as *defender of the innocent* and *holy warrior* to highly negative terms like *bloodsucker* and *terrorist*. Such terms gain their potency by tapping audiences' attitudes.

How intense should your language be? Communication scholar John Waite Bowers suggested a useful rule of thumb: Let your language be, roughly, one step more intense than the position or attitude held by your audience.[5] For example, if your audience is already committed to your negative position on tax reform, then you can choose intensely negative words, such as *regressive* and *stifling.* If your audience is uncommitted, you should opt for comparatively neutral words, such as *burdensome.* And if your listeners are in favor of tax changes, you can use still less negative words, such as *unfair,* to encourage them to keep an open mind and avoid having them tune you out. Intense language can generate intense reactions, but only if you match your word choices to your listeners' attitudes.

Appropriateness

Your language should be appropriate to the speech topic and situation. Solemn occasions call for restrained and dignified language; joyful occasions call for informal and lively word choices. The language used for a marriage ceremony wouldn't work at a pep rally and vice versa. Suit your language to the atmosphere of the occasion.

Informal Language Make sure that your language is appropriate to your audience. Before you use informal language, check to see who's listening. Informal language, including slang, quickly goes out of style. *Gee whiz, wow, good grief, hip, cool, far out, homeboy, awesome, radical, gnarly,* and *hottie* became popular at different times. *Far out* would sound silly in a speech to your peers, and *hottie* would sound ridiculous to an audience of senior citizens. As you work through your speech, consider your language choices as inherent elements in developing the tone of your speech.

Gender-Neutral Language Words can communicate values or attitudes to your listeners. As we suggested in the introduction to this chapter, they also suggest relationships between you and your audience. Gender-linked words, particularly nouns and pronouns, require special attention. **Gender-linked words** are those that directly or indirectly identify males or females—*policeman, washerwoman, poet,* and *poetess.* Pronouns such as *he* and *she* and adjectives such as *his* and *her* are obviously gender-linked words. **Gender-neutral words** do not directly or indirectly denote males or females—*chairperson, police officer,* or *firefighter.*

Since the 1960s and the advent of the women's movement, consciousness of gendered language has gradually surfaced. The question of whether language use affects culture and socialization still is being debated. However, as a speaker, you must be careful not to alienate your audience or to propagate stereotypes unconsciously through your use of language. In addition to avoiding most gender-linked words, you've got to handle two more problems:

1. *Inaccurately excluding members of one sex.* Some uses of gendered pronouns inaccurately reflect social-occupational conditions in the world: "A nurse sees her patients eight hours a day, but a doctor sees his for only ten minutes." Many women are doctors, just as many men are nurses. Most audience members are aware of this and may be displeased if they feel that you're stereotyping roles in the medical profession.

2. *Stereotyping male and female psychological or social characteristics.* "Real men never cry." "A woman's place is in the home." "The Marines are looking for a few good men." "Sugar 'n spice 'n everything nice—that's what little girls are made of." Falling back on these stereotypes gets speakers into trouble with listeners, both male and female. In these days of raised consciousness, audiences are insulted to hear such misinformed assertions. In addition, these stereotypes conceal the potential in individuals whose talents are not limited by their gender.

These problem areas demand your attention. A speaker who habitually uses sexist language is guilty of ignoring important speaking conventions that have taken shape over the past several decades. How can you avoid sexist language? Here are four easy ways:

1. *Speak in the plural.* Say "Bankers are often . . . They face . . . " This tactic is often sufficient to make your language gender-neutral.

2. *Say "he or she" when you must use a singular subject.* Say "A student majoring in business is required to sign up for an internship. He or she can . . . " This strategy works well as long as you don't overdo it. If you find yourself cluttering sentences with "he or she," switch to the plural.

3. *Remove gender inflections.* It's painless to say "firefighter" instead of "fireman," "chair" or "chairperson" instead of "chairman," and "tailor" instead of "seamstress." Gender inflections can usually be removed without affecting your speech.

4. *Use gender-specific pronouns for gender-specific processes, people, or activities.* It is acceptable to talk about a mother as *her* or a current or former president of the United States as *him.* Men do not naturally bear children, and a woman has not yet been elected to the White House.

Ultimately, the search for gender-neutral idioms is an affirmation of mutual respect and a recognition of equal worth and the essential dignity of individuals. Gender differences are important in many aspects of life, but when they dominate public talk, they're ideologically oppressive. Be gender neutral in public talk to remove barriers to effective communications.[6]

Selecting an appropriate style is a matter of assessing yourself, your audience, the situation or context, and your speaking purposes. A thorough assessment of these variables will help you select an appropriate style.

In summary, wording your speech demands careful thought about the clarity of your language use, the persuasive force lying behind words, and the overall sense of tone or style that results from choosing language with particular characteristics. In the world of international diplomacy, a wrong word can cause a breakdown in negotiations. In your world, it can produce confusion, misunderstanding, or even disgust. Take time to shape your oral language as carefully as you shape your ideas.

USING LANGUAGE STRATEGICALLY

Developing an effective oral speaking style is important. You will also, however, want to tap more directly into the powers of language—the powers to alter people's minds and move them to action. To accomplish those goals, you need to use oral language strategically. We will focus on three of the most common language strategies: definitions, imagery, and metaphor.

Definitions

Audience members need to understand the fundamental concepts of your speech. You can't expect them to understand your ideas if your language is unfamiliar. As a speaker, you have several options when working to define unfamiliar or difficult concepts.

You're most familiar with a **dictionary definition,** which categorizes an object or concept and specifies its characteristics: "An orange is a fruit (category) that is round, orange in color, and a member of the citrus family (characteristics)." Dictionary definitions sometimes help you learn unfamiliar words, but they don't help an audience very much. If you do use dictionary definitions, go to specialized dictionaries. You certainly wouldn't depend on *Webster's Third International Dictionary* to define foreclosure or liability for a presentation on real estate law. For this technical application, sources such as *Black's Law Dictionary* and *Guide to American Law* are more highly respected.

Occasionally, a word has so many meanings that you have to choose one. If that's the case, use a stipulative definition to orient your listeners to your subject matter. A **stipulative definition** designates the way a word will be used in a certain context. You might say, "By rich I mean, . . . " or you might use an expert's stipulative definition such as this one from former President Jimmy Carter:

> Who is rich? I'm not talking about bank accounts. . . . A rich person is someone with a home and a modicum of education and a chance for at least a job and who believes that if you make a decision that it'll have some effect at least in your own life, and who believes that the police and the judges are on your side. These are the rich people.[7]

You can further clarify a term or concept by telling your audience how you are not going to use the concept—by using a **negative definition.** So Chicago police Sergeant Bruce Talbot defined "gateway drug" in this manner:

> [F]or adolescents, cigarette smoking is a gateway drug to illicit drugs such as marijuana and crack cocaine. By gateway drug I do not mean just that cigarettes are the first drug young people encounter, alcohol is. But unlike alcohol, which is first experienced in a social ritual such as church or an important family event, cigarettes are the first drug minors buy themselves and use secretly outside the family and social institutions.[8]

Web Exploration

To compare dictionary definitions with stipulative and other types of definitions, go to www.ablongman.com/ german15e

Definitions help listeners grasp concepts. Contextual definitions are used to clarify specific contexts.

Defining negatively can clear away possible misconceptions. Using a negative definition along with a stipulative definition, as did Sergeant Talbot, allows you to treat a commonplace phenomenon in a different way.

Sometimes you can reinforce an idea by telling your listeners where a word came from. One way to do this is by using an etymological definition. An **etymological definition** is the derivation of a single word; an example of this would be tracing the word *communication* back to its Latin origins.

One of the best ways to define is by an exemplar definition, especially if the concept is unfamiliar or technical. **Exemplar definitions** are familiar examples. You might tell your listeners, "Each day, most of you stroll past the Old Capitol on your way to classes. That building is a perfect example of what I want to talk about today: Georgian architecture." Be careful to use in your definition only those examples that are familiar to your audience members.

A **contextual definition** tells listeners how a word is used in a specific situation. For example, a driving instructor tells her student, "You're going to learn defensive driving. That means you'll be watching out for the other guy. It's not enough just to know the rules of the road. You need to be a proactive driver—watching out for danger spots and other drivers who aren't as careful as you are."

Still another means of making technical or abstract notions easier to understand is the **analogical definition.** An analogy compares a process or event that is unknown with known ones, as in, "Hospitals and labs use cryogenic tanks, which work much like large thermos bottles, to freeze tissue samples, blood, and other organic matter." By referring to what is familiar, the analogical definition can make the unfamiliar much easier to grasp. But the speaker must be sure that the analogy fits.

The points here are simple but important: (1) You have many different kinds of definitions to choose from when working with unfamiliar or difficult concepts. (2) Select definitional strategies that make sense for your subject matter, your audience, and your purposes.

Imagery

People grasp their worlds through the senses of sight, smell, hearing, taste, and touch. To intensify listeners' experiences, you can appeal to these senses. You can stimulate your listeners' sense indirectly by using language to recall images that they have previously experienced. **Imagery** consists of sets of sensory impressions evoked in the imagination through language. The language of imagery is rooted in the particular sensation that it seeks to evoke:

► *Visual imagery* describes optical stimuli such as size, shape, color, and movement. You might use contrasts of light and dark, brilliant hues of paint, and foreground action to help your listeners appreciate your favorite artists.

► *Auditory imagery* creates impressions of sounds through description. You can help your listeners hear the screeching and crashing of a demolition derby or the soft stillness of a winter snowfall by choosing your language carefully.

► *Gustatory imagery* depicts sensations of taste. Mention the saltiness, sweetness, sourness, or spiciness of various foods. Remember textures as well. While demonstrating how to make popcorn, you might mention the crispness of the kernels, the oily sweetness of melted butter, and the grittiness of salt.

► *Olfactory imagery* helps your audience to smell the odors connected with the situation you describe. Smell is a powerful sense because it normally triggers a flood of associated images. Think about a carnival. Blended with the bustle and confusion is a collage of smells—Polish sausages with fried onions, diesel fumes, rancid grease, cotton candy, and freshly mown grass.

► *Tactile imagery* comes to us through physical contact with external objects. In particular, tactile imagery gives sensations of texture and shape, pressure, and heat or cold. Let your listeners feel the smooth, slimy, stickiness of modeling clay. Let them sense the weight of a heavy laundry bag, the pinch of jogging shoes, the blast of a winter wind on their faces.

► *Kinesthetic imagery* describes the sensations associated with muscle strain and neuromuscular movement. You can share the triumph of marathon racing by letting your listeners feel the muscle cramps, the constricted chest, the struggle for air, and the magical serenity of getting a second wind before gliding toward the finish line.

► *Organic imagery* focuses on internal feelings or sensations such as hunger, dizziness, and nausea. There are times when an experience is incomplete without the description of inner feelings. The sensation of giddiness as a mountain climber struggles through the rarefied air to reach the summit is one example. Another is the way the bottom seems to drop out of your stomach when an airplane tips sharply, then rights itself.

Different people respond to different kinds of imagery, so you should insert several types of imagery in your speeches. In the following example, note how the speaker combines various sensory appeals to arouse listener interest and reaction:

The strangler struck in Donora, Pennsylvania, in October of 1948. A thick fog billowed through the streets enveloping everything in thick sheets of dirty moisture and a greasy black coating. As Tuesday faded into Saturday, the fumes from the big steel mills shrouded the outlines of the landscape. One could barely see across the narrow streets. Traffic stopped. Men lost their way returning from the mills. Walking through the streets, even for a few moments, caused eyes to water and burn. The thick fumes grabbed at the throat and created a choking sensation. The air acquired a sickening bittersweet smell, nearly a taste. Death was in the air.[9]

Image-evoking language can re-create experiences for others.

In this example, college student Charles Schaillol uses vivid, descriptive phrases to affect the senses of his listeners—visual: "thick sheets of dirty moisture"; organic: "eyes to water and burn"; and olfactory, gustatory: "sickening bittersweet smell, nearly a taste."

To be effective, such illustrations must seem plausible. The language must convey a realistic impression that the situation described could happen. The speaker who describes the strangler that struck Donora offers a plausible account of the event. More important, he does so in a fashion that arouses feelings. His listeners wouldn't have shared the experience if he had simply said, "Air pollution was the cause of death in Donora."

Metaphor

Images created by appealing to the senses are often the result of metaphors. A **metaphor** is the comparison of two dissimilar things. Charles Schaillol's description of fog as "thick sheets of dirty moisture" is one example. Scholar Michael Osborn notes that the metaphor should "result in an intuitive flash of recognition that surprises or fascinates the hearer."[10] Furthermore, good metaphors extend our knowledge or increase our awareness of a person, object, or event. When they're fresh or vivid, they can be powerful aids in evoking feelings. For example, referring to a table's "legs" is a metaphor, but it's boring. It's much more interesting to say, "Balanced on four toothpicks, the antique table swayed under its heavy burden."

Metaphors drawn from everyday experiences provide wide audience appeal. In the following speech, Martin Luther King, Jr., relied on our experiences of light and darkness:

> With this faith in the future, with this determined struggle, we will be able to emerge from the bleak and desolate midnight of man's inhumanity to man, into the bright and glittering daybreak of freedom and justice.[11]

This basic light-dark metaphor allowed King to suggest (a) sharp contrasts between inhumanity and freedom and (b) the inevitability of social progress as "daybreak" follows "midnight." The metaphor communicated King's beliefs about justice and injustice and urged others to action. Words are not neutral pipelines for thought. Words not only reflect the world outside your mind, but also, as critic Kenneth Burke suggests, help shape our perceptions of people, events, and social contexts. Language has a potent effect on people's willingness to believe, to feel, and to act.

Web Exploration
To explore the use of metaphor in speeches, go to www.ablongman.com/german15e

SAMPLE SPEECH

William Faulkner (1897–1962) presented the following speech on December 10, 1950, as he accepted the Nobel Prize for literature. His listeners might have expected a speech filled with the kind of pessimism so characteristic of his novels. Instead, he greeted them with a stirring challenge to improve humankind.

Notice in particular Faulkner's use of language. Although known for the tortured sentences in his novels, he expresses his ideas clearly and simply in his speech. His style suggests a written speech, yet his use of organic imagery and powerful metaphors keeps the speech alive. The atmosphere is generally serious, befitting the occasion. You might expect a Nobel Prize winner to talk about himself, but Faulkner did just the opposite. He stressed his craft, writing, and the commitment necessary to practice that craft; this material emphasis led naturally to an essentially propositional rather than narrative form. More than fifty years ago, William Faulkner offered a speech that is as relevant today as it was in 1950.

Faulkner establishes a series of contrasts built around a "not this . . . but this" construction to deflect attention from himself to his work. The contrasts sharpen the points he'll make throughout the speech; it's the art, not the artist, that counts; creating art is extraordinarily hard work; we can't write out of fear but out of the need to elevate the soul and spirit of humanity.

He frames his whole speech as an address to young writers.

When he addresses the issue of the bomb and our fear of it, he attacks that fear immediately. First, he suggests the presence of the fear and then via restatement comes back to it in the next three sentences. Second, he continues the linguistic contrasts between fear and spirit, human heart in conflict, and the agony and the sweat.

Faulkner expands this central idea via a series of literal and metaphorical contrasts. Read these sentences aloud to capture the pounding rhythm that guides them. Body metaphors complete the paragraph.

Faulkner concludes with a flood of imagery: images are auditory, visual, tactile, and organic ("lifting his heart").

The restatement of vocabulary, the images, the affirmation of life, and, of course, the sheer presence of Faulkner himself combine to make this one of the two or three greatest Nobel Prize speeches ever given.

On Accepting the Nobel Prize for Literature
William Faulkner[12]

I feel that this award was not made to me as a man, but to my work—a life's work in the agony and sweat of the human spirit, not for glory and least of all for profit, but to create out of the materials of the human spirit something which did not exist before. So this award is only mine in trust. It will not be difficult to find a dedication for the money part of it commensurate with the purpose and significance of its origin. But I would like to do the same with the acclaim too, by using this moment as a pinnacle from which I might be listened to by the young men and women already dedicated to the same anguish and travail, among whom is already that one who will some day stand here where I am standing./1

Our tragedy today is a general and universal physical fear so long sustained by now that we can even bear it. There are no longer problems of the spirit. There is only the question: When will I be blown up? Because of this, the young man or woman writing today has forgotten the problems of the human heart in conflict with itself which alone can make good writing because only that is worth writing about, worth the agony and the sweat./2

He must learn them again. He must teach himself that the basest of all things is to be afraid; and, teaching himself that, forget it forever, leaving no room in his workshop for anything but the old verities and truths of the heart, the old universal truths lacking which any story is ephemeral and doomed—love and honor and pity and pride and compassion and sacrifice. Until he does so, he labors under a curse. He writes not of love but of lust, of defeats in which nobody loses anything of value, of victories without hope and, worst of all, without pity or compassion. His griefs grieve on no universal bones, leaving no scars. He writes not of the heart but of the glands./3

Until he relearns these things, he will write as though he stood among and watched the end of man. I decline to accept the end of man. It is easy enough to say that man is immortal simply because he will endure: that when the last ding-dong of doom has clanged and faded from the last worthless rock hanging tideless in the last red and drying evening, that even then there will still be one more sound: that of his puny inexhaustible voice, still talking. I refuse to accept this. I believe that man will not merely endure: he will prevail. He is immortal, not because he alone among creatures has an inexhaustible voice, but because he has a soul, a spirit capable of compassion and sacrifice and endurance. The poet's, the writer's, duty is to write about these things. It is his privilege to help man endure by lifting his heart, by reminding him of the courage and honor and hope and pride and compassion and pity and sacrifice which have been the glory of his past. The poet's voice need not merely be the record of man, it can be one of the props, the pillars to help him endure and prevail./4

Speaking of . . . Ethics

Doublespeak

You can probably identify hundreds of words or phrases that are used to disguise facts. The Reagan and Clinton administrations didn't want to raise taxes but pursued *revenue enhancement* through *user fees.* People below the poverty line are *fiscal underachievers.* Nuclear weapons are labeled *radiation enhancement devices* and *peacekeepers.* And the 1984 invasion of Grenada was officially a *predawn vertical insertion.* Some language usage makes the unpleasant seem good and the positive appear negative. Language can shield us from the reality it represents.

Such name-calling is by no means limited to politicians. Advertisers market *new and improved* products. We're tantalized with *real faux pearls* and *genuine imitation leather.* Advertisers exploit our health consciousness with *low-cholesterol* and *high-fiber* ingredients. Take a few moments to think about the following uses of language:

1. Suppose that you notice biased language in an article you're reading to research a speech topic. Should you cite the article as supporting material in your speech?

2. You genuinely believe in your recommendations for solving the problems you outline in a speech, and you want to convince your listeners to sign a petition for change. Is it fair to use scare tactics or to tell them that they've got only one day left to act when in fact there's more time?

3. Should you ever use racy, obscene, or questionable language during a speech? Does it affect the relationship you establish with your listeners?

4. Is it ever fair to call people who aren't present crooks or attach similar labels to them?

5. Do you think language can obscure our understanding of reality? Under what circumstances do you think this happens? Should anything be done to make language more honest? What can you do to accomplish this?

ASSESSING YOUR PROGRESS

Chapter Summary

1. Language functions on referential, relational, and symbolic levels.
2. Encoding occurs when you put ideas into words and actions.
3. Successful speeches generally follow oral style that is typical of conversations.
4. You can cultivate oral style through accurate word choice, simple phrasing, restatement, and the coherent connection of ideas.
5. The intensity and appropriateness of language can be altered to contribute to the atmosphere created for your audience.
6. Rhetorical strategies are word and phrase choices intended to control the impact of the speech. Three of the most common rhetorical strategies are definition, imagery, and metaphor.
7. Speakers can define unfamiliar or difficult concepts in many ways including dictionary, stipulative, negative, etymological, contextual, and analogical definitions.
8. Imagery consists of word pictures that intensify listeners' experiences by engaging their senses. There are seven types of images: visual, auditory, gustatory, olfactory, tactile, kinesthetic, and organic sensations.
9. Metaphor is the comparison of two dissimilar things.

Key Terms

analogical definition (p. 167)
atmosphere (p. 162)
coherence (p. 160)
contextual definition (p. 166)
dictionary definition (p. 165)
encoding (p. 156)
etymological definition (p. 166)
exemplar definitions (p. 166)
forecasts (p. 160)
gender-linked words (p. 163)

gender-neutral words (p. 163)
imagery (p. 167)
metaphor (p. 169)
negative definition (p. 165)
oral style (p. 157)
restatement (p. 159)
signposts (p. 161)
stipulative definition (p. 165)
summary (p. 160)
written style (p. 157)

Assessment Activities

1. Find a complicated message (e.g., an insurance policy, an agreement for a credit card, income tax instructions, or a difficult passage from a book). Rewrite it in simple yet accurate language. Bring copies of both messages to class, and present them to your classmates. Which was more effective? Why?

2. Designate one member of your class to record the results, and then brainstorm for a list of terms. How intense is each term? For more neutral terms, think of highly positive and highly negative counterparts. For highly positive and highly negative terms, find a more neutral term. What value orientations do these terms reveal? What impact are such terms likely to have on listeners?

3. Choose one of the items listed below and describe it, using imagery to create an involving portrait for your listeners. How many kinds of imagery did you use? Which was most effective for your listeners?

A scene from your favorite movie
Your favorite cologne
A tropical plant
A breakfast food
A roller coaster ride
A complicated machine
The oldest building on campus
A walk through the park

Using the Web

1. Do an Internet search with the general term *dictionary.* What results did you find? Compare the kinds of general dictionaries available online. Next, refine your search by looking for medical, legal, architecture, slang, engineering, and philosophy dictionaries. What other specialized dictionaries can you find online?

2. Multiple resources for writers and speakers are available online. Check out handbooks for writers and speakers. If you're looking for another word to capture your thought, try searching for a thesaurus.

3. Are you confused about bias-free language? For answers to questions about how to avoid using language that excludes others, check the guidelines at http://www.pnl.gov/ag/usage/bias.html.

Using VideoWorkshop

Watch the speeches in Module 8, "Language." As you watch, concentrate on how to identify and generate an effective language style. Then answer Questions 1–12.

References

1. For a summary of several technical studies distinguishing between oral and written styles and for a discussion of sixteen characteristics of oral style, see John F. Wilson and Carroll C. Arnold, *Public Speaking as a Liberal Art,* 5th ed. (Boston: Allyn and Bacon, 1983), 227–229.

2. Quoted in John R. Pelsma, *Essentials of Speech* (New York: Crowell, Collier, and Macmillan, 1934), 193.

3. Information for this example was taken from an article by Daniel Pedersen, Vern E. Smith, and Jerry Adler, "Sprawling, Sprawling," *Newsweek,* (19 July 1999), pp. 23–27.

4. Alan Alda, "A Reel Doctor's Advice to Some Real Doctors," in Stephen E. Lucas, *The Art of Public Speaking* (New York: Random House, 1983), 364.

5. John Waite Bowers, "Language and Argument," in *Perspectives on Argumentation,* edited by G. R. Miller and T. R. Nilsen (Glenview, IL: Scott, Foresman, 1966), 168–172.

6. There are many studies of gender and communication. For overviews, see Barbara Bate, *Communication and the Sexes* (New York: Harper & Row, 1987); Judith C. Pearson, *Gender and Communication* (Dubuque, IA: Wm. C. Brown, 1985); and Lea P. Stewart, Pamela J. Cooper, and Sheryl A. Friedly, *Communication between the Sexes: Sex Differences and Sex-Role Stereotypes* (Scottsdale, AZ: Gorsuch Scaribrick, 1986).

7. James E. Carter, "Excellence Comes from a Repository That Doesn't Change," *Vital Speeches of the Day,* 59 (1 July 1993), 548.

8. Bruce Talbot, "Statement," Hearings before Senate Committee on Commerce, Science, and Transportation, *Tobacco Product Education and Health Promotion Act of 1991, S. 1088,* 14 November 1991, 102nd Congress (Washington, DC: U.S. Government Printing Office, 1991), 77.

9. From Charles Schaillol, "The Strangler," *Winning Orations.* Reprinted by permission of Larry Schnoor, Executive Secretary, Interstate Oratorical Association, Concordia College, Moorhead, MN. Published by the Interstate Oratorical Association.

10. Michael Osborn, *Orientations to Rhetorical Style* (Chicago: Science Research Associates, 1976), 10.

11. From Martin Luther King, Jr., "Love, Law and Civil Disobedience" (Martin Luther King, Jr., 1963). Reprinted by arrangement with the Estate of Martin Luther King Jr., c/o Writers House as agent for the proprietor New York, NY. Copyright 1961 Dr. Martin Luther King Jr., copyright renewed 1989 Coretta Scott King.

12. William Faulkner, "On Accepting the Nobel Prize for Literature," *The Faulkner Reader* (New York: Random House, 1954).

Chapter 10

Delivering Your Speech

IF YOU'RE STRUGGLING with the physical aspects of delivering your speeches, you're in good company. Many famous speakers have had to overcome severe delivery problems before becoming effective speakers. Abraham Lincoln suffered from extreme speech fright; Eleanor Roosevelt was awkward and clumsy; John F. Kennedy had a strong dialect and repetitive gestures; Helen Keller was blind and deaf. These speakers realized that success depends not only on careful planning before the speech but also on effective presentation. They each worked hard to develop the oral delivery skills that heightened the impact of their ideas.

You must be aware that you communicate with your entire body—your face, your gestures, your voice, and your posture. Your voice and bodily movements help to transmit your feelings and attitudes about yourself, your audience, and your topic. You might see speakers who approach the lectern dragging their feet and fussing with their notes. Their attitudes are abundantly clear even before they utter their first words. Unwittingly, these speakers establish audience predispositions that work against them. Even if their ideas are important, those ideas are overshadowed by distracting nonverbal communication.

If you've heard a recording or seen a video of Martin Luther King, Jr., giving his "I Have a Dream" speech, you can appreciate the dramatic difference between hearing him speak and merely reading a copy of the speech. The same is true of Jesse Jackson, Camille Paglia, Rush Limbaugh, Colin Powell, Ann Richards, and Susan Molinari. Oral presentation can add fire to the message. Orality's great strength—its edge—comes from the personal presence established by your voice and your physical presence.

Your speech will gain strength and vitality if it's presented well. To help you achieve this objective, we'll discuss three important aspects of presentation: selecting the method of presentation, using your voice to communicate, and using your body to communicate.

SELECTING THE METHOD OF PRESENTATION

How should you present your speech? Your choice will be based on several criteria, including the type of speaking occasion, the purpose of your speech, your audience analysis, and your own strengths and weaknesses as a speaker. Attention to these considerations will help you decide whether your method of presentation should be extemporaneous, impromptu, read from a manuscript, or memorized.

The Extemporaneous Speech

Most speeches that you'll deliver will be extemporaneous. An **extemporaneous speech** is one that is prepared in advance and presented from abbreviated notes. Most of the advice in this textbook pertains to extemporaneous speaking. Extemporaneous speeches are nearly as polished as memorized ones, but they are more vigorous, flexible, and spontaneous.

Before giving an extemporaneous speech, you must plan and prepare a detailed outline and speaking notecards. Then, working from the notecards, you practice the speech aloud, using your own words to communicate the ideas. Your expressions differ somewhat each time you deliver the speech. Your notes, however, regulate the order of ideas. With this approach, you gain control of the material and also preserve your spontaneity of expression. Good preparation is the key to extemporaneous speaking. Otherwise, your speech may resemble an

Speaking of . . . Apprehension

Impromptu Speaking

You'll probably be called on many times during your life to express your opinion, volunteer information, or contribute to a discussion. In these largely impromptu speaking situations, you can hone your impromptu speaking skills. As general preparation, consider these suggestions:

- Pay close attention to the discussion or the question being asked.
- Jot down a few notes to remind yourself of the key points being made.
- Relax by taking a few deep breaths and by making a conscious effort to think about the ideas rather than your feelings of apprehension.
- Channel your emotional energy into enthusiasm for your ideas.

The most critical part of an impromptu speech is its organization. Your listeners will be impressed by or- ganized thoughts because it will appear to them that you have prepared your comments. Organization increases your credibility. It also provides cues for you as you present your ideas. Most impromptu speeches can be organized using the following pattern:

1. *Point step.* Tell your listeners your main point.
2. *Reason step.* State a reason why your point is worth considering.
3. *Support step.* Provide an example, comparison, quotation, statistic, or story to support your reason.
4. *Restatement step.* Summarize by restating your main point.

To practice this plan for impromptu speaking, have someone ask you a question. Repeat the question, and then answer it using the four steps. As with many other skills, you will respond more effectively in an impromptu manner if you practice. So get started!

impromptu speech; in fact, the terms *impromptu* and *extemporaneous* are often confused.

The Impromptu Speech

An **impromptu speech** is delivered on the spur of the moment, with minimal preparation. The ability to speak off the cuff is useful in an emergency, but impromptu speeches can produce unpredictable outcomes. Whenever possible, you should carefully prepare and practice your speeches.

In an impromptu speech, you must rely entirely on previous knowledge and skill. You might be asked in the middle of a sorority meeting, for example, to give a progress report on your pledge committee. Or you might be called on in class to summarize the ideas in a paper you turned in last week. Or your professor might ask you to comment on the reading assignment.

For best results when speaking on an impromptu basis, try to focus on a single idea, carefully relating all details connected to that idea. If you relay the main theme for the annual March of Dimes fund drive or the central thesis of your paper, you'll be more likely to stay on track. Sticking with a single idea will keep you from rambling incoherently. See the box above for more suggestions.

The Manuscript Speech

A **manuscript speech** is written out beforehand and then read from a manuscript or TelePrompTer. By using TelePrompTers, speakers can appear to be looking at their listeners while they're really reading their manuscripts projected onto clear sheets of Plexiglas. When extremely careful wording is required, the manuscript speech is appropriate. When the president addresses Congress, for example, a slip of the tongue could misdirect domestic or foreign policies. Many radio and television speeches are read from manuscripts because of the strict time limits imposed by broadcasting schedules.

The Memorized Speech

On rare occasions, you might write out your speech and commit it to memory. When notecards or a TelePrompTer cannot be used, it may be acceptable for you to give a **memorized speech.** When making a toast at your parents' twenty-fifth wedding anniversary, for example, you probably wouldn't want to speak from notecards. Some speakers, such as comedians, deliver their remarks from memory to free their hands to mimic the movements of the character they are playing.

Speakers who use memorized presentations are usually most effective when they write their speeches to sound like informal and conversational speech rather than formal, written essays. Remember that with a memorized speech, you'll have difficulty responding to audience feedback. Since the words of the speech are predetermined, you can't easily adjust them as the speech progresses.

While you may use all four types of speech presentation for different occasions during your lifetime, extemporaneous speaking is the most important. Extemporaneous speaking displays your enthusiasm for speaking and the sincerity of your ideas. To develop your skills as an extemporaneous speaker, you will need to learn to use both your voice and your body to communicate with your listeners.

USING YOUR VOICE TO COMMUNICATE

Web Exploration
For some examples of vocal exercises, go to
www.ablongman.com/
german15e

Your voice is an instrument that helps convey the meaning of language. Since preliterate times, when all cultures were oral, voice has been the primary connector between people. Sounds flow among people, integrating them, creating a sense of identification, of community.[1] Although you have been speaking for years, you have probably not tapped the full potential of your voice—its power to connect you with others. You'll need to take time to practice in order to achieve your vocal potential, just as you would to master any instrument. The suggestions in this section will help you to get started.

You communicate your enthusiasm to your listeners through your voice. By learning about the characteristics of vocal quality, you can make your ideas more interesting. Listen to a stock market reporter rattle off the daily industrial averages. Every word might be intelligible, but the reporter's vocal expression may be so repetitive and monotonous that the ideas seem unexciting. Then listen to Al Michaels doing a play-by-play of a football game or Dick Vitale covering a basketball game. The excitement of their broadcasts depends largely on their voices.

Our society prizes one essential vocal quality above all others—a sense of **conversationality.**[2] The conversational speaker creates a sense of two-way, interpersonal relationship, even when behind a lectern. The best hosts of afternoon talk shows or evening newscasts speak as though they're engaging each listener in a personal conversation. Speakers who've developed a conversational quality— Oprah Winfrey, Peter Jennings, Barbara Walters, and Jay Leno, for example— have recognized that they're talking with, not at, an audience.

The Effective Speaking Voice

Successful speakers use their voices to shape their ideas and emotionally color their messages. A flexible speaking voice possesses intelligibility, variety, and understandable stress patterns.

Intelligibility   **Intelligibility** refers to the ease with which a listener can understand what you're saying. It depends on volume, rate, enunciation, and pronunciation. Most of the time, slurred enunciation, a rapid speaking rate, or soft volume is acceptable because you know the people you're talking with and because you're probably only three to five feet from them. In public speaking, however, you may be addressing people you don't know, often from twenty-five feet or more away. When speaking in public, you have to work on making yourself intelligible:

1. *Adjust your volume.* Probably the most important single factor in intelligibility is how loudly you speak. **Volume**—how loudly or softly you speak—is related to the distance between you and your listeners and the amount of noise that is present. You must realize that your own voice sounds louder to you than it does to your listeners. Obviously, if you're speaking in an auditorium filled with several hundred people, you need to project your voice by increasing your volume. However, you shouldn't forget that a corresponding reduction in volume is required when your listeners are only a few feet away. The amount of surrounding noise with which you must compete also has an effect on your volume. (See Figure 10.1.) Increase your volume to counter a distraction.

2. *Control your rate.* **Rate** is the number of words spoken per minute. In animated conversation, you may jabber along at 200 to 250 words per minute. This rate is typical of people raised in the northern, midwestern, or western United States. As words tumble out of your mouth in informal conversations, they're usually intelligible because they don't have to travel far. In large auditoriums or outdoors, though, rapid delivery can impede intelligibility. Echoes sometimes

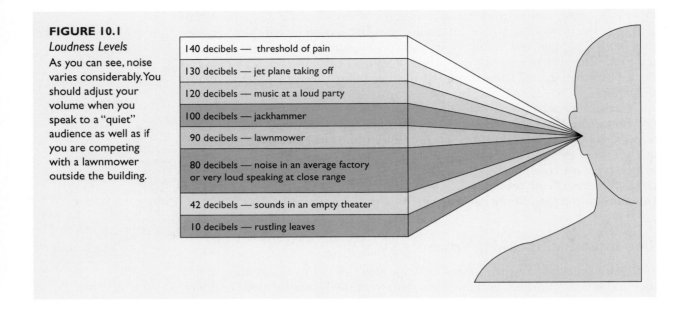

FIGURE 10.1

Loudness Levels

As you can see, noise varies considerably. You should adjust your volume when you speak to a "quiet" audience as well as if you are competing with a lawnmower outside the building.

140 decibels — threshold of pain

130 decibels — jet plane taking off

120 decibels — music at a loud party

100 decibels — jackhammer

90 decibels — lawnmower

80 decibels — noise in an average factory or very loud speaking at close range

42 decibels — sounds in an empty theater

10 decibels — rustling leaves

distort or destroy sounds in rooms; ventilation fans interfere with sound. Outdoors, words seem to vanish into the open air. When addressing larger audiences, cut your rate by a third or more. Obviously, you don't go around timing your speaking rate, but you can remind yourself of potential rate problems as you prepare to speak. Get feedback from your instructors and classmates regarding your speaking rate.

3. *Enunciate clearly.* **Enunciation** refers to the crispness and precision with which you form words. Good enunciation is the clear and distinct utterance of syllables and words. Most of us are "lip lazy" in normal conversation. We slur sounds, drop syllables, and skip over the beginnings and endings of words. This laziness might not inhibit communication between friends, but it can seriously undermine a speaker's intelligibility.

When speaking publicly, force yourself to say "going" instead of "go-in," "just" instead of "jist," and "government" instead of "guvment." You will need to open your mouth wider and force your lips and tongue to form the consonants firmly. If you're having trouble enunciating clearly, ask your instructor for some exercises to improve your performance. (See "Speaking of . . . Skills: Vocal Exercises.")

4. *Meet standards of pronunciation.* To be intelligible, you must meet audience expectations regarding acceptable pronunciation. Any peculiarity of pronunciation is sure to be noticed by some listeners. For example, the "t" in "often" is silent although some speakers pronounce it. Your different pronunciation can distract your listeners and undermine your credibility as a speaker.

Speaking of . . . Skills

Vocal Exercises

If you are concerned about improving your vocal control, these exercises can be helpful. Here's a sample of what you can do:

1. *Breath control.* Say the entire alphabet, using only one breath. As you practice, try saying it more and more slowly so as to improve your control of exhalation.

2. *Control of pitch.* Sing "low, low, low, low," dropping one note of the musical scale each time you sing the word until you reach the lowest tone you can produce. Then sing your way back up the scale. Now sing "high, high, high, high," going up the scale to the highest note you can reach. Sing your way back down. Go up and down, trying to sense the notes you're most comfortable with—your so-called optimum pitch. Give most of your speeches around your optimum pitch.

3. *Articulatory control.* Pronounce each of the following word groups, making sure that each word can be distinguished from the others. Have someone check your accuracy: jest, gist, just; thin, think, thing; roost, roosts, ghost, ghosts; began, begun, begin; wish, which, witch; affect, effect; twin, twain, twine. Or try the following tongue twisters:

The sixth sick sheik's sixth sheep's sick.

Three gray geese in the green grass grazing; gray were the geese and green was the grazing.

Barry, the baby bunny's born by the blue box beating rubber baby buggy bumpers.

A **dialect** is language use—including vocabulary, grammar, and pronunciation—unique to a particular group or region. Your pronunciation and grammatical or syntactical arrangement of words determine your dialect. You may have a foreign accent, a southern or northern dialect, a Vietnamese pitch pattern, a New England twang, or a Hispanic trill. A clash of dialects can result in confusion and frustration for both speaker and listener. Audiences can make negative judgments about the speaker's credibility—that is, the speaker's education, reliability, responsibility, and capacity for leadership—based solely on dialect.[3] Researchers call these judgments *vocal stereotypes*.[4] Wary of vocal stereotypes, many news anchors have adopted a midwestern American dialect, a manner of speaking that is widely accepted across the country. Many speakers become bilingual, using their own dialects when facing local audiences but switching to midwestern American when addressing more varied audiences. When you speak, you'll have to decide whether you should use the grammar, vocabulary, and vocal patterns of middle America.

Web Exploration

To learn more about different dialects, go to www.ablongman.com/german15e

Variety   As you move from conversations with friends to the larger arena of public speaking, you may discover that listeners accuse you of monotony of pitch or rate. When speaking in a large public setting, you should compensate for the greater distance that sounds have to travel by varying certain characteristics of your voice. Variety is produced by changes in rate, pitch, stress, and pauses.

1. *Vary your rate.* Earlier, we discussed the rate at which we normally speak. Alter your speaking rate to match your ideas. Slow down to emphasize your own thoughtfulness or quicken the pace when your ideas are emotionally charged. Observe, for example, how Larry King varies his speaking rate from caller to caller or how an evangelist changes pace regularly. A varied rate keeps an audience's attention riveted to the speech.

2. *Change your pitch.* **Pitch** is the frequency of sound waves in a particular sound. Three aspects of pitch—level, range, and variation—are relevant to effective vocal communication. Your everyday pitch level—whether it is habitually in the soprano, alto, tenor, baritone, or bass range—is adequate for most of your daily communication needs.

The key to successful control of pitch depends on understanding the importance of *pitch variation.* As a general rule, use higher pitches to communicate excitement and lower pitches to create a sense of control or solemnity. Adjust the pitch to fit the emotion.

Stress   A third aspect of vocal behavior is stress. **Stress** is the way in which sounds, syllables, and words are accented. Without vocal stress, you would sound like a computer. Vocal stress is achieved in two ways: through vocal emphasis and through the judicious use of pauses.

Use Vocal Emphasis.   **Emphasis** is the way in which you accent or attack words. You create emphasis principally through increased volume, changes in pitch, or variations in rate. Emphasis can affect the meanings of your sentences. Notice how the meaning of "Jane's taking Tom out for pizza tonight" varies with changes in word emphasis:

- ▶ "JANE's taking Tom out for pizza tonight." (Jane, not Alyshia or Shani, is taking Tom out.)
- ▶ "Jane's taking TOM out for pizza tonight." (She's not taking out Olan or Christopher.)
- ▶ "Jane's taking Tom OUT for pizza tonight." (They're not staying home as usual.)
- ▶ "Jane's taking Tom out for PIZZA tonight." (They're not having hamburgers or tacos.)
- ▶ "Jane's taking Tom out for pizza TONIGHT." (They're going out tonight, not tomorrow or next weekend.)

A lack of vocal stress not only gives the impression that you are bored but also causes misunderstandings of your meaning. Changes in rate can also be used to add emphasis. Relatively simple changes can emphasize where you are in an outline: "My s-e-c-o-n-d point is. . . ." Several changes in rate can indicate the relationship among ideas. Consider the following example:

We are a country faced with [moderate rate] . . . financial deficits, racial tensions, an energy crunch, a crisis of morality, environmental depletion, government waste [fast rate], . . . and - a - stif - ling - na - tion - al - debt [slow rate].

The ideas pick up speed through the accelerating list of problems but then come to an emphatic halt with the speaker's main concern, the national debt. Such variations in rate emphasize for an audience what is and what isn't especially important to the speech. If you want to emphasize the many demands on their time faced by parents, you could relate a list of daily activities at increasingly rapid rate. By the end of the list, your listeners would probably feel some of the stress facing parents.

Use Helpful Pauses. Pauses are the intervals of silence between or within words, phrases, or sentences. When placed immediately before a key idea or before the climax of a story, they can create suspense: "And the winner is [pause]!" When placed after a major point, pauses can add emphasis, as in: "And who on this campus earns more than the president of the university? The football coach [pause]!" Inserted at the proper moment, a dramatic pause can express feelings more forcefully than words. Clearly, silence can be a highly effective communicative tool if used sparingly and if not embarrassingly prolonged. Too many pauses and those that seem artificial will make you appear to be manipulative or overrehearsed.

Sometimes speakers fill silences in their discourse with sounds: um, ah, er, well-uh, you know, and other meaningless fillers. Undoubtedly, you've heard speakers say, "Today, ah, er, I would like, you know, to speak to you, um, about a pressing, well-uh, like, a pressing problem facing this, uh, campus." Such vocal intrusions convey feelings of hesitancy and a lack of confidence. You can make a concerted effort to remove these intrusions from your speech by being completely familiar with your notecards and the ideas of your speech. Practice your speech until the sentences flow naturally.

On the other hand, don't be afraid of silences. Pauses allow you to stress important ideas, such as the punch line in a story or argument. Pauses also intensify the involvement of listeners in emotional situations, such as when Cokie Roberts or Dr. Phil pauses for reflection during an interview.

Practicing Vocal Control

Your vocal qualities are of prime importance in determining the impression you make on an audience. While you can't completely control your vocal qualities, you can be alert to their effects on your listeners. Keep your repertoire of vocal qualities in mind as you decide how to express key ideas for an audience.

Don't assume that you'll be able to master all of the vocal skills we have described in one day. Take your time to review and digest the ideas presented. Above all, practice aloud. Record yourself on tape and then listen to the way you're conveying ideas. Ask your instructor to provide exercises designed to make your vocal instrument more flexible. When you're able to control your voice and make it respond to your desires, you'll have a great deal more control over your effect on listeners. Before any vocal skill can sound natural and be effective with listeners, it must become so automatic that it will work with little conscious effort. Once your voice responds flexibly in the enlarged context of public speaking, you'll be able to achieve the sense of conversationality that is so highly valued in our society.

USING YOUR BODY TO COMMUNICATE

Just as your voice can add dimension to your message, your physical behavior carries messages through the visual channel. You can use both your voice and your body to create a better understanding of your presentation. To help you explore the ways of enhancing your use of the visual channel, we'll examine the speaker's physical behavior.

Dimensions of Nonverbal Communication

While some use the phrase *nonverbal communication* to refer to all aspects of interpersonal interaction that are nonlinguistic, we'll focus the discussion here on physical behavior in communication settings. In recent years, research has reemphasized the important role of physical behavior in effective oral communication.[5] Basically, three generalizations about nonverbal communication should guide your speechmaking:

1. *Speakers disclose their emotional states through their nonverbal behaviors.* Your listeners read your feelings toward yourself, your topic, and your audience from your facial expressions. Consider the contrast between a speaker who walks briskly to the front of the room, head held high, and one who shuffles, head bowed and arms hanging limply. Communication scholar Dale G. Leathers summarized a good deal of research on nonverbal communication processes: "Feelings and emotions are more accurately exchanged by nonverbal than verbal means. . . . The nonverbal portion of communication conveys meanings and intentions that are relatively free from deception, distortion, and confusion."[6]

2. *The speaker's nonverbal cues enrich the message that comes through words.* You can use physical movement to reinforce the ideas of your speech. The words "We must do either this or that" can be illustrated with appropriate arm-and-hand gestures. Taking a few steps to one side tells an audience that you're moving from one argument to another. A smile enhances your comment on how happy you are to be there, just as a solemn face reinforces the dignity of a wedding.

3. *Nonverbal messages form a reciprocal interaction between speaker and listener.* Listeners frown, smile, shift nervously in their seats, and engage in many types of nonverbal behavior. The physical presence of listeners and the natural tendency of human beings to mirror each other when they're close together mean that nonverbal behavior is a social bonding mechanism.

For this chapter, we'll concentrate on the speaker's control of physical behavior in four areas: proxemics, movement and stance, facial expressions, and gestures.

Proxemics   **Proxemics** is the use of space by human beings. Two components of proxemics, physical arrangement and distance, are especially relevant to public speakers. Physical arrangements include the layout of the room in which you're speaking, the presence or absence of a lectern, the seating plan, the location of chalkboards and similar aids, and any physical barriers between you and your audience. Distance refers to the extent or degree of separation between you and your audience.[7]

Both of these components affect the message you communicate publicly. Typical speaking situations involve a speaker facing a seated audience. Objects in the physical space—the lectern, a table, several flags—tend to set the speaker apart from the listeners. This setting apart is both physical and psychological. Literally as well as figuratively, objects can stand in the way of open communication. If you're trying to create a more informal atmosphere, you should reduce the physical barriers in the setting. You might stand beside or in front of the lectern instead of behind it. In very informal settings, you might even sit on the front edge of a table while talking.

So what influences your use of physical space?

1. *The formality of the occasion.* The more solemn or formal the occasion, the more barriers will be used; on highly formal occasions, speakers may even speak from an elevated platform or stage.

2. *The nature of the material.* Extensive quoted material or statistical evidence may require you to use a lectern; the use of visual aids often demands such equipment as an easel, computer-aided projection equipment, a VCR, or an overhead projector.

3. *Your personal preference.* You may feel more at ease speaking from behind rather than in front of the lectern.

Elizabeth Dole used physical space in an unusual way in her speech to the 1996 Republican National Convention. Normally, convention-goers are separated from speakers by the raised stage. But Dole chose to move down among her listeners, captivating them and television audiences. Dole told her audience, "Tradition is that speakers at National Republican Conventions remain at this imposing podium. I'd like to break with tradition for two reasons. I'm going to be speaking to friends and secondly I am going to be speaking about the man I love. Just a lot more comfortable for me to do that down here with you."[8] Her explanation of her use of physical space addresses the three factors we've just discussed.

The distance component of proxemics adds a second set of considerations. In most situations, you'll be talking at what anthropologist Edward T. Hall has termed a "public distance"—twelve feet or more from your listeners.[9] (See Figure 10.2.) To communicate with people at that distance, you obviously can't rely on your normal speaking voice or subtle changes in posture or movement. Instead, you must compensate for the distance by using larger gestures, broader shifts of your body, and increased vocal energy. By contrast, you should lower your vocal volume and restrict the breadth of your gestures when addressing a few individuals at a closer distance. If you don't, you'll probably notice them backing away from you.

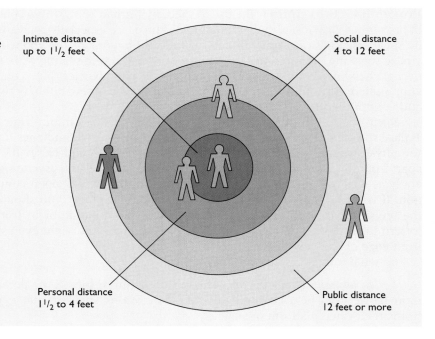

FIGURE 10.2

Classification of Interhuman Distance
Anthropologist Edward T. Hall has identified typical distances for various human interactions. Typically, public speaking occurs within social distance and public distance.

Intimate distance up to 1 1/2 feet

Social distance 4 to 12 feet

Personal distance 1 1/2 to 4 feet

Public distance 12 feet or more

Movement and Stance   The ways you move and stand provide a second set of bodily cues for your audience. **Movement** includes physical shifts from place to place; **posture** refers to the relative relaxation or rigidity and vertical position of the body. Movements and posture can communicate ideas about yourself to an audience. The speaker who stands stiffly and erectly may, without uttering a word, be saying, "This is a formal occasion" or "I'm tense, even afraid, of this audience." The speaker who leans forward, physically reaching out to the audience, often is saying silently, "I'm interested in you. I want you to understand and accept my ideas." The speaker who sits casually on the front edge of a table and assumes a relaxed posture may suggest informality and readiness to engage in a dialogue with listeners.

Movements and postural adjustments regulate communication. As a public speaker, you can, for instance, move from one end of a table to the other to indicate a change in topic; or you can accomplish the same purpose by changing your posture. At other times, you can move toward your audience when making an especially important point. In each case, you're using your body to reinforce transitions in your subject or to emphasize a matter of special concern.

But keep in mind that your posture and movements can also work against you. Aimless and continuous pacing is distracting. Nervous bouncing or swaying makes listeners seasick, and an excessively erect stance increases tension in listeners. Your movements should be purposeful and enhance the meaning of your words. Stance and movement can help your communicative effort and produce the impressions of self-assurance and control that you want to exhibit.

Movement and stance can communicate ideas about you to others around you.

Facial Expressions When you speak, your facial expressions function in a number of ways. First, they express your feelings. What researchers Paul Ekman and Wallace V. Friesen call "affect displays" are communicated to an audience through the face. **Affect displays** are facial signals of emotion that an audience perceives when scanning your face to see how you feel about yourself and how you feel about them.[10]

Second, facial changes provide listeners with cues that help them to interpret the contents of your message. Are you being ironic or satirical? Are you sure of your conclusions? Is this a harsh or pleasant message? Researchers tell us that a high percentage of the information conveyed in a typical message is communicated nonverbally. Psychologist Albert Mehrabian has devised a formula to account for the emotional impact of the different components of a speaker's message. Words, he says, contribute 7 percent, vocal elements 38 percent, and facial expression 55 percent.[11] From this formula, you can see how important the dimensions of delivery are in communication, particularly your voice and facial expressions. In fact, some Internet users have devised a set of symbols called *emoticons* such as LOL, meaning "laugh out loud," to give expression to their computer messages.

Third, the "display" elements of your face—your eyes, especially—establish a visual bond between you and your listeners. Our culture values eye contact. The speaker who looks people square in the eye is likely to be perceived as earnest, sincere, forthright, and self-assured. In other words, regular eye contact with your listeners helps to establish your credibility. Speakers who look at the floor, who read from notes, or who deliver speeches to the back wall sever the visual bond with their audiences and lose credibility.

Of course, you can't control your face completely, which is probably why listeners search it so carefully for clues to your feelings. You can, however, make sure that your facial messages don't contradict your verbal ones. When you're uttering angry words, your face should be communicating anger; when you're pleading with your listeners, your eyes should be engaging them intently. In short, let your face mirror your feelings. That's one of the reasons it's there!

Gestures   **Gestures** are purposeful movements of the head, shoulders, arms, hands, and other areas of the body that support and illustrate the ideas you're expressing. Fidgeting with your clothing and notecards and playing with your hair aren't purposeful gestures. They distract from the ideas you're communicating. The effective public speaker commonly uses three kinds of purposeful gestures:

Many of the gestures we use can have culturally defined meanings. These are called conventional gestures.

Descriptive gestures depict size, shape, or location.

1. *Conventional gestures* are physical movements that are symbols with specific meanings assigned by custom or convention, such as the circle formed by placing the thumb on the index finger to signal "Okay." These gestures condense ideas; they are shorthand expressions of things or ideas that would require many words to describe fully. A speaker can use the raised-hand "stop" gesture to interrupt listeners who are drawing premature conclusions or the "thumbs up" sign when congratulating them for jobs well done. Since culture determines the meanings of conventional gestures, you should understand how your audience views the gestures you'll use. Misunderstandings can be embarrassing or disastrous.

2. *Descriptive gestures* are physical movements that describe the idea to be communicated. Speakers often depict the size, shape, or location of an object by movements of the hands and arms; that is, they draw pictures for listeners. You might demonstrate the size of a box by drawing it in the air with a finger or raise an arm to show someone's height.

3. *Indicators* are movements of the hands, arms, or other parts of the body that express feelings. Speakers throw up their arms when disgusted, pound the lectern when angry, shrug their shoulders when puzzled, or point a threatening finger when issuing a warning. Such gestures communicate emotions to your

listeners and encourage similar responses in them. Your facial expressions and other body cues usually reinforce such gestures.[12]

You can improve your gestures through practice. As you practice, you'll obtain better results by keeping in mind that relaxation, vigor and definiteness, and proper timing affect the effectiveness of gestures.

1. *If your muscles are tense, your movements will be stiff and your gestures awkward.* You should make a conscious effort to relax your muscles before you start to speak. You might warm up by taking a few steps, shrugging your shoulders, flexing your muscles, or breathing deeply.

2. *Good gestures are natural and animated.* They communicate the dynamism associated with speaker credibility. You should put enough force into your gestures to show your conviction and enthusiasm. Avoid exaggerated or repetitive gestures such as pounding the table or chopping the air to emphasize minor ideas in your speech. Vary the nature of your gestures as the ideas in your speech demand.

3. *Timing is crucial to effective gestures.* The *stroke* of a gesture—that is, the shake of a fist or the movement of a finger—should fall on or slightly before the point the gesture emphasizes. Just try making a gesture after the word or phrase it was intended to reinforce has already been spoken. It appears ridiculous. Practice making gestures until they're habitual, and then use them spontaneously as the impulse arises.

Adapting Nonverbal Behavior to Your Presentations

You can gain more effective control of your physical behavior by learning how to orchestrate your gestures and other movements. You can make some conscious decisions about how you will use your body together with the other channels of communication to communicate effectively.

1. *Signal your relationship with your audience through proxemics.* If you're comfortable behind a lectern, use it; however, keep in mind that it's a potential barrier between you and your listeners. If you want your whole body to be visible to the audience but you feel the need to have your notes at eye level, stand beside the lectern and arrange your notecards on it. If you want to relax your body, sit behind a table or desk; but compensate for the resulting loss of action by increasing your volume. If you feel relaxed and want to be open to your audience, stand in front of a table or desk. Learn to use the space around you while speaking publicly.

Consider your listeners' needs as well. The farther you are from them, the more important it is for them to have a clear view of you, the harder you must work to project your words, and the broader your physical movements must be. The speaker who crouches behind a lectern in an auditorium of 300 people soon loses their interest. Think of large lecture classes you've attended or outdoor rallies you've witnessed. Recall the delivery patterns that worked effectively in such situations. Put them to work for you.

Speaking of . . . Apprehension

Breath Control

You can adapt some of the breathing techniques from yoga and meditation to help you control the physical stress that inhibits movement and vocal quality. Here's a simple but effective exercise to try:

1. Breathe in slowly, counting to 6 (one one thousand, two one thousand, etc.).

2. Hold your breath for a count of 3.

3. Exhale slowly counting to 6.

Repeat this exercise before you practice your speech. Then use it again to prepare for the delivery of your speech.

2. *Adapt the physical setting to your communicative needs.* If you're going to use visual aids—such as a chalkboard, flipchart, or working model—remove the tables, chairs, and other objects that might obstruct your audience's view. Increase intimacy by arranging chairs in a small circle, or stress formality by using a lectern.

3. *Adapt your gestures and movement to the size of the audience.* Keeping in mind what Hall noted about public distance in communication, you should realize that subtle changes of facial expression or small hand movements can't be seen clearly in large rooms or auditoriums. Although many auditoriums have a raised platform and a slanted floor to make you more visible, you should adjust to the distance between yourself and your audience by making your movements and gestures larger.

4. *Establish eye contact with your audience, looking specific individuals in the eye.* Your head should not be in constant motion, scanning the audience with rhythmic, nonstop machine-gun movement. Rather, take all your listeners into your field of vision periodically; establish firm visual bonds with individuals occasionally. Such bonds enhance your credibility and keep your auditors' attention riveted to you.

Some speakers identify three audience members—one to the left, one in the middle, and one to the right—and make sure they regularly move from one to the other of them. For those who don't have trouble moving from side to side, another technique is to do the same thing from front to back, especially if the audience isn't too big. Making sure that you are achieving even momentary eye contact with specific listeners in different parts of the audience creates the visual bonding that you want.

5. *Use your body to communicate your feelings.* When you're angry, don't be afraid to gesture vigorously. When you're expressing tenderness, let that message come across your relaxed face. In other words, when you communicate publicly, use the same emotional indicators as you do when you talk to individuals on a one-to-one basis.

6. *Regulate the pace of your presentation with bodily movement.* Shift your weight as your speech moves from one idea to another. Move more when you're speaking more rapidly. Reduce bodily action and gestures accordingly when you're slowing down to emphasize particular ideas.

7. *Finally, use your full repertoire of gestures.* You probably do this in everyday conversation without even thinking about it; re-create that behavior when addressing an audience. Physical readiness is the key. Keep your hands and arms free and loose so that you can call them into action easily, quickly, and naturally. Let your hands rest comfortably at your sides, relaxed but ready. Then, as you unfold the ideas of your speech, use descriptive gestures to indicate size, shape, or relationships, making sure the movements are large enough to be seen in the back row. Use conventional gestures also to give visual dimension to your spoken ideas. Keep in mind that there is no right number of gestures to use. However, as you practice, think of the kinds of body movements and gestures that complement your message and purpose.

Selecting the appropriate method of presentation and using your voice and body productively will enhance your chances of gaining support for your ideas. Practice is the key to the effective use of these nonverbal elements. Through practice, you'll have an opportunity to see how your voice and body complement or detract from your ideas. The more you prepare and practice, the more confident you'll feel about presenting the speech and the more comfortable you'll be. Remember that the nonverbal channel of communication creates meaning for your audience.

ASSESSING YOUR PROGRESS

Chapter Summary

1. Every speaker should effectively use both body and voice to convey meaning.
2. Choose an appropriate method of presentation—extemporaneous, impromptu, manuscript, or memorized.
3. Several factors will determine your choice of presentation method: the type of speaking occasion, the seriousness and purpose of your speech, your audience analysis, and your own strengths and weaknesses as a speaker.
4. A flexible speaking voice has intelligibility, variety, and understandable stress patterns.
5. Volume, rate, enunciation, and pronunciation interact to affect intelligibility.
6. Different standards of pronunciation create regional differences known as dialects.
7. Changes in rate, pitch, and stress and pauses create variety in presentation and help eliminate monotonous delivery.
8. Three generalizations about nonverbal communication are significant: (a) speakers reveal and reflect their emotional states through their non-verbal behaviors; (b) nonverbal cues enrich or elaborate the speaker's mes-

sage; and (c) nonverbal messages form an interaction between speaker and listener.

9. Speakers can use proxemics or space to create physical and psychological intimacy or distance. A speaker's movement and posture regulate communication.

10. Facial expressions communicate feelings, provide important cues to meaning, establish a visual bond with listeners, and establish speaker credibility.

11. Relaxed, definite, and properly timed gestures can enhance the meaning of a message.

12. Speakers commonly use conventional gestures, descriptive gestures, and indicators.

Key Terms

affect displays (p. 187)
conversationality (p. 179)
dialect (p. 181)
emphasis (p. 182)
enunciation (p. 180)
extemporaneous speech (p. 176)
gestures (p. 188)
impromptu speech (p. 177)
intelligibility (p. 179)

manuscript speech (p. 178)
memorized speech (p. 178)
movement (p. 186)
pitch (p. 182)
posture (p. 186)
proxemics (p. 185)
rate (p. 179)
stress (p. 182)
volume (p. 179)

Assessment Activities

1. Divide the class into teams and play charades. A game of charades will help you focus on the nonverbal elements of communication. Identify conventional gestures, facial expressions, and movements that clarify messages during the game.

2. Form small task groups. Appoint a member of the group to record ideas and then think of as many situations as possible in which each of the four methods of presentation would be used. Choose a reporter to convey the group's examples to the class. How many of the situations do you think you will encounter? Which situations are tied to success in a career?

3. Choose a selection from a poetry anthology and practice reading it aloud. As you read, vary your volume, rate, pitch and emphasis, and use pauses. Practice reading the poem in several ways to heighten different emotions or to emphasize different interpretations. Record your reading of the poem on tape and play it back to evaluate it, or ask a friend to listen and offer suggestions.

Using the Web

1. You can download software that will allow you to take advantage of sound-supported Internet sites. Use your browser to locate the Real Audio Website to get you started.

2. Many Websites as well as encyclopedias and other resources now accompany speech texts with segments of audio and video. Locate a famous speech such as Martin Luther King Jr.'s "I Have a Dream" speech or John F. Kennedy's inaugural address. View the video and listen to the words of these speakers.

Using VideoWorkshop

Watch the speeches in Module 9, "Delivery." As you watch, concentrate on the various methods of verbal and nonverbal communication in speech delivery discussed. Then answer Questions 1–10.

References

1. For a fascinating discussion of oral speech's communal powers—of its "psychodynamics"—see ch. 3 of Walter J. Ong, *Orality and Literacy: The Technologizing of the Word* (London: Methuen, 1982).

2. Thomas Frentz, "Rhetorical Conversation, Time, and Moral Action," *Quarterly Journal of Speech,* 71 (1985): 1–18.

3. Mark Knapp, *Essentials of Nonverbal Communication* (New York: Holt, Rinehart and Winston, 1980).

4. Klaus R. Scherer, H. London, and Garret Wolf, "The Voice of Competence: Paralinguistic Cues and Audience Evaluation," *Journal of Research in Personality,* 7 (1973): 31–44; Jitendra Thakerer and Howard Giles, "They Are—So They Spoke: Noncontent Speech Stereotypes," *Language and Communication,* 1 (1981): 255–261; Peter A. Andersen, Myron W. Lustig, and Janis F. Andersen, "Regional Patterns of Communication in the United States: A Theoretical Perspective," *Communication Monographs,* 54 (1987): 128–144.

5. Much of the foundational research is summarized in Mark L. Knapp and Judith Hall, *Nonverbal Communication in Human Interaction,* 3rd ed. (New York: Holt, Rinehart & Winston, 1982).

6. Dale G. Leathers, *Nonverbal Communication Systems* (Boston: Allyn and Bacon, 1975), 4–5.

7. For further discussion, see Leathers, 52–59.

8. Elizabeth Dole, "This Is a Defining Moment in Our Nation's History: Speech to the 1996 Republican National Convention," http://gos.sbc.edu/d/dole.html.

9. Hall divides interhuman communication distances into four segments: *intimate distance,* up to 1½ feet apart; *personal distance,* 1½ to 4 feet; *social distance,* 4 to 12 feet; and *public distance,* 12 feet or more. With these distinctions, he has carefully noted how people's eye contact, tone of voice, and ability to touch and observe change from one distance to another. See Edward T. Hall, *The Hidden Dimension* (New York: Doubleday, 1969), ch. 10.

10. Paul Ekman, *Emotion in the Human Face,* 2nd ed. (Cambridge: Cambridge University Press, 1982).

11. Albert Mehrabian, *Silent Messages* (Belmont, CA: Wadsworth, 1972); Robert Rivlin and Karen Gravelle, *Deciphering the Senses: The Expanding World of Human Perception* (New York: Simon and Schuster, 1984), 98. Such numbers, of course, are only formulaic estimates and are important only as proportions of each other.

12. For a complete system of classifying gestures, see Paul Ekman and Wallace V. Friesen, "Hand Movements," *Journal of Communication,* 22 (1972): 360.

Chapter 11

Using Visual Aids

TELEVISION MONITORS AND large-screen projections, film, videotape, videodiscs, CD-ROM, streaming video and related digital technologies, overhead and data projectors, billboards, sidewalk posters—images from an amazing range of sources dominate our everyday world.[1] From the time that you participated in "show-and-tell" in elementary school, you've used visual aids in your communication efforts. As you learn to speak in front of an audience, you'll continue to make use of visual aids as an essential part of the speech transaction. For these reasons, it's important for you to learn more about visual aids.

Research on visual media, learning, and attitude change has given us a lot of information about the impact of visual aids on audiences.[2] In this chapter, we'll combine what we've learned from social-scientific research with your needs as a speaker. First, we'll focus on the functions of visual aids; then we'll examine the various types of visual aids and explore ways to use them effectively.

THE FUNCTIONS OF VISUAL AIDS

Visual aids are illustrative and persuasive materials that rely primarily on sight. Visual materials enhance your presentation in two ways: (1) They aid listener comprehension and memory, and (2) they add persuasive impact to your message.

Comprehension and Memory

Web Exploration
To analyze research on the impacts of visual aids on audiences, go to
www.ablongman.com/german15e

Remember the old saying "A picture is worth a thousand words"? This saying contains a great deal of truth. We understand ideas better and remember them longer if we see them as well as hear them. Research has demonstrated that bar graphs are especially effective at making statistical information more accessible to listeners. Charts and human interest visuals, such as photographs, have proven to help listeners process and retain data.[3] Even simple pictures have significant effects on children's recall and comprehension during storytelling.[4] Visuals can be immensely valuable if your purpose is to inform or teach an audience. Visuals make information easier to understand, retain, and recall.

Persuasion

In addition to enhancing comprehension and memory, visuals can heighten the persuasive impact of your ideas because they engage listeners actively in the communicative exchange. Lawyers, for example, aware of the dramatic persuasive effects of visuals, often include visual evidence such as photographs of injuries or diagrams of crime scenes in their cases to sway the opinions of juries. Some lawyers even have experimented with the use of video technology to create dramatic portrayals of events to influence jury decisions; for example, by showing the dangerous traffic flow of an intersection in a vehicular homicide case. Legal presentations, business presentations, the ways in which architects offer a building design to clients, medical reports—almost every profession has its own **scopic regime,** that is, cultural expectations for how to coordinate verbal and visual material for maximum impact.[5]

Undeniably, good visuals enhance both your credibility and your persuasiveness.[6] By satisfying the "show-me" attitude prevalent among listeners who've been raised in the visual-electronic revolution of the twentieth century, visual materials provide a crucial means of meeting listener expectations.

TYPES OF VISUAL SUPPORT

There are many different types of visual materials. Depending on your speech topic and purpose, you may choose one or several types of visual support. We will discuss each type and examine specific approaches to using it to supplement your oral presentations.

Actual Objects or Props

You can often bring to a presentation the actual objects or a prop illustrating something you're discussing. Live animals or plants can, under some circumstances, be used to enhance your speeches. If your speech explores the care and feeding of iguanas, you can reinforce your ideas by bringing to the speech an iguana in a properly equipped cage. Describing the differences between two varieties of soybeans may be easier if you demonstrate the differences with real plants. Or you can bring a prop—short for the theatrical word *property*—to provide an illustration. A woman on the weight loss inspirational speaking circuit used to carry around a football-sized blob of squishy material that she said showed her audience what five pounds of ugly fat looked like.[7]

Using the actual object or a prop should focus audience attention on your speech, not serve as a distraction. A speech about snowboarding is enhanced by a display of the essential equipment. A speech about how to repair holes in a plaster wall is clarified by showing pieces of plasterboard at the various stages. Cooking demonstrations are enlivened with samples prepared before the presentation, since you usually don't have time to perform the actual work during the speech.

Your Own Body

You can use your own body to add concreteness and vitality to your presentation. You might, for example, demonstrate yo-yo tricks, warm-up exercises, swing dance steps, sign language, or tennis strokes during your speech. Remember to control the experience. Make sure that everyone, even people in the back rows, can see you. Demonstrate stretching exercises on a sturdy tabletop rather than on the floor. Slow the tempo of a tennis stroke so that the audience can see any intricate action and subtle movements. One advantage of properly controlled visual action is that with it, you can control the audience's attention to your demonstration. You also should dress appropriately. A physical therapy major might add credibility by wearing a uniform when demonstrating CPR, and an aerobics instructor can wear a leotard and tights. Of course, the clothing should not substitute for a clearly visible demonstration of CPR or aerobics.

If you decide to ask another person to demonstrate a technique while you describe it, plan ahead. Instead of hoping for someone to volunteer from the audience, contact one of your classmates and practice the demonstration before you give your speech. In this way, you'll avoid the embarrassing silence that can

Representations convey information in various ways. For instance, an illustration of the parts of an inline skate *(top)* gives an audience a realistic but complicated view of the object. An action shot *(bottom)* provides a feeling of excitement and stimulates listeners' interest.

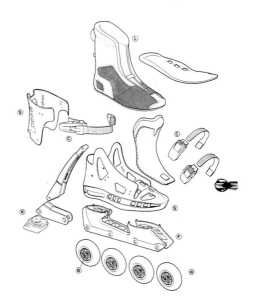

accompany a request for a volunteer, and you'll be certain that your partner can adequately demonstrate the process as you relate it.

Photographs and Slides

Photographs can often be a good substitute for the real thing. Photographs can give the audience a visual sense of your topic. For example, photos can illustrate the damage to fire-ravaged homes or show the beauty of a woods that is threatened by a new shopping mall. Make sure that your audience can see details from a distance. You can enlarge photos or use slides so that people can see them more easily. Avoid passing small photos through the audience, because such activity is disruptive. The purpose of a visual aid is to draw the attention of all members of the audience simultaneously.

Like photographs, slides (35mm transparencies) allow you to depict color, shape, texture, and relationships. It is also easier to show many slides than many photographs. If you're describing the Padre Islands as a good place to vacation, you might use slides to show your audience the buildings and landscape of both islands. If you're giving a speech on the history of locomotives, you can use slides to show various types. If you're speaking against the construction of a river reservoir, you can enhance your persuasiveness by showing slides of the whitewater that will be disrupted by the dam. If you're discussing stylistic differences among famous artists, you might wish to show slides of art works from the neoclassical and baroque periods.

Using slides requires sure practice in handling equipment. It also requires some forethought about the setup of the presentation. Will the correct equipment be available? Have you loaded the slides in the cartridge correctly? Will you speak from the front of the room or from next to the projector? Will your voice carry over the noise of the projector? Do you know how to change the projection lamp? Did you bring along a spare bulb just in case? Will you need an extension cord? Do you know how to remove a jammed slide? Attention to small, seemingly inconsequential details like these will make a major difference in how smoothly the presentation goes. If you operate on the assumption that whatever can go wrong will, you'll be prepared to solve most problems.

One last point: Remember that you can scan photos or 35mm slides unto a disk and then throw them on a computer-projection system (http://www.elmousa.com gives you an introduction to this technology). The ease with which you enhance your images and then, in the actual presentation, can move from image to image makes computer projection systems a great way to bring still images to audiences.

Videotapes and Films

Videotapes and films let you put action into pictures. Videotaped segments from several current sitcoms can dramatically reinforce your claim that minorities are underrepresented in comedy-centered television. Two or three videotaped political ads can help you illustrate methods for savaging opponents. As with all projection equipment, familiarity with the operation of a videocassette recorder or film projector ensures a smooth presentation. Make sure that you can operate the equipment properly and quickly. Forward to the segment you wish to use. Delays increase Your nervousness and detract from your presentation.

Speaking of . . . Skills

Using Visual Aids in Business

It's wise to use visual aids when developing a professional presentation for a client or business meeting. Research has shown that visual aids are effective tools for three reasons. First, visual aids can make your presentation more persuasive. Second, they enhance your audience's estimate of your credibility and appearance of professionalism. Third, presenters using visual aids require less meeting time to achieve their results. Overall, it makes good sense to incorporate visual aids in your presentations. Observe some simple rules:

1. *Prepare a professional look.* The business world by now absolutely expects professional-looking visuals: desktop computer-generated overheads, high-quality slides, folders with eye-catching paper, PowerPoint computer projections, and so on. Sloppy work will kill you.
2. *Always make something to take away.* Large businesses, especially, run on team meetings and project presentation sessions—often, more than one a day. Give the folks coming to your presentation something to take away so that they can remember your work. Summarize the main dimensions of the problem and your proposed solutions; hand out your business card with phone, fax, and e-mail numbers; popular these days is a computer disk with images and important materials on it, given how cheap disks are now.
3. *Know the equipment before you start.* Know how to run the particular VCR or computer projector in the room you're using. Try out the slide projector. Make sure you know where the switch for the power screen is. Fumbling because you don't know which remote runs the VCR and which the sound system will make you look less than professional. These rules apply, with varying degrees of harshness, to your presentations in any other setting as well.

Again, if computer projection is available, you either can load flash graphics or other forms of video streaming or, if you're hooked up to the Internet, can find online streaming images. There's always a danger in trying to go online for materials during a speech, because just about the time you want to head to some URL, the system can go down or a key link on the site will be broken. You can protect yourself by downloading the material onto a CD-ROM and then playing the video/film from that. But be sure to check on the legality of downloading protected material.

Chalkboard or Whiteboard Drawings

Chalkboard (or whiteboard) drawings are especially valuable when you need a quick illustration or want to show something step by step. By drawing each step as you discuss it, you can center the audience's attention on your major points. Coaches often use this approach when showing players how to execute particular plays. Time sequences also can be sketched on a chalkboard. To visually represent the history of the civil rights movement in the United States, you can create a timeline that illustrates key events, such as the arrival of the first slaves in Jamestown, the signing of the Emancipation Proclamation, the passage of the 1965 Voting Rights Act, and the 2001 Patriot Act (which makes room for a curtailing of civil rights).

Whether you use drawings will depend on the formality of the situation. If you're brainstorming ideas for a building renovation with a prospective client, quick sketches might suffice. However, if you're meeting with the client's board of directors, the same rough drawings will be inadequate. The board will expect a polished presentation, complete with a professionally prepared prospectus. Similarly, chalkboard drawings might be sufficient to explain the photovoltaics of solar power to a group of classmates, but when presenting those data as part of a science fair project, you need refined visual support materials. Consider chalkboard or whiteboard drawings for informal presentations.

Transparent and Computerized Overhead Projections

You can use an overhead projector just as you would use a chalkboard: to illustrate points as you talk. However, an overhead projector offers some advantages over a chalkboard. You can turn it off when you've made your point, thus removing a competing image that might distract listeners. Another advantage is that you can uncover one part of the overhead screen at a time, keeping the remainder covered so as to control the flow of information. Finally, you can prepare overheads, including computer-generated graphics, before the speech, giving them a more professional appearance than chalkboard drawings; hence, they dominate corporate talks.

The world of computer-generated graphics is changing almost monthly; being able to work in this medium will be important to you in many kinds of jobs. Just consider the technology that was rolling into the market in mid-2002: portable multimedia computers, large-screen and projection displays, data/video projectors, flat plasma display screens, desktop conference rooms with each seat having its own screen, web conferencing (connecting several sites together into a single electronic meeting), color-display cellular phones that can receive information through handsets with color-active matrix displays. This is the **rich-media** world, that is, a world in which even interpersonal and group communications are handled via technologies. In such a world, you have to know to run the technologies, yes, but even more important, you have to be able to communicate through them. This means that communication technique is everything.

So when you're using an overhead projector, be aware of your technique. First, make your illustrations large enough that the audience can see them. If you are using computer-generated visual materials, you should probably enlarge them. Second, talk to the audience rather than to the screen or the light source. Otherwise, your listeners' attention might drift away from you and your message. Third, be sure to stand so that you don't block the audience's view of your visuals. Fourth, when you're through talking about the illustration, turn off the projector to eliminate the competing message source. Fifth, make sure that your graphics aren't "tired," that is, kinds of items that have been used too, too many times by too, too many speakers.[8]

When you're using other forms of digital access to audiences, make similar adjustments. Even with large-screen displays, hold down the amount of information you put on any single screen, because you don't want to overwhelm listener-viewers by making them scan back and forth across ten feet of numbers and words. If you're in a room with desktop imaging screens at each seat, make sure that you don't push information too hard and too fast. Only a small amount can be seen and understood at a time. And don't expect attenders at a Web conference just to be thrilled to be connected with other sites; adapt your materials to be seen easily on a screen. That means you'll likely want to have one camera on speakers and another devoted to showing material that was videotaped or streamed at an earlier time.

Web Exploration

To practice using and understanding graphs, go to www.ablongman.com/german15e

Graphs

Graphs show relationships among various parts of a whole or between variables across time. Graphs are especially effective for representing numerical data. There are several types of graphs:

1. **Bar graphs** show the relationships between two or more sets of figures (see Figure 11.1). Research has demonstrated that plain bar graphs are the most effective method for displaying statistical comparisons, perhaps because bar graphs represent numbers in a visual form. If you were illustrating the difference between male and female incomes in various fields, you would probably use a bar graph.

2. **Line graphs** show relationships between two or more variables, usually over time (see Figure 11.2). If you were interested in showing popular support for GOP presidential hopefuls Elizabeth Dole, George W. Bush, and John McCain from July through December 1999, you would use a line graph.

3. **Pie graphs** show percentages by dividing a circle into the proportions being represented (see Figure 11.3). A speaker who is raising funds for a local hospice could use a pie graph to show how much of its income was spent on administration, nursing care, drugs, and equipment for terminally ill patients. City managers use pie graphs to show citizens what proportion of their tax dollars go to municipal services, administration, education, recreation, and law enforcement.

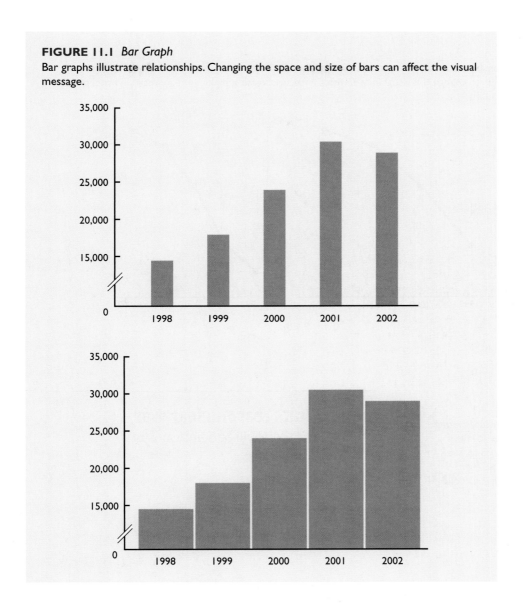

FIGURE 11.1 *Bar Graph*
Bar graphs illustrate relationships. Changing the space and size of bars can affect the visual message.

4. **Pictographs** function like bar graphs but use symbols instead of bars to represent size and numbers (see Figure 11.4). A representation of U.S., Canadian, and Russian grain exports might use a miniature drawing of a wheat shock or an ear of corn to represent 100,000 bushels; this representation would allow a viewer to see at a glance the disparity among the exports of the three countries. You can easily create pictographs with computer clip art.

FIGURE 11.2 *Line Graph*

Line graphs can reveal relationships, but they can also deceive the unwary. These graphs show the same data but use different spacing along the axes to change the visual image, with the second version making the increase in hotel prices seem much greater.

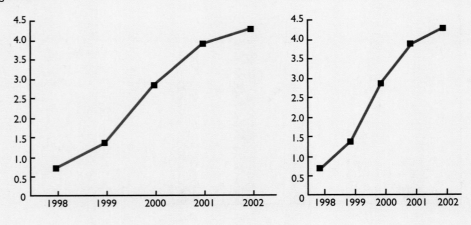

FIGURE 11.3

Pie Graph

Pie graphs dramatize relationships among a limited number of segments. Ideally, a pie graph should have from two to five segments and never more than eight. This one compares three opinions college-age adults have about nuclear war.

Source: USA Today, August 1, 2002, A1.

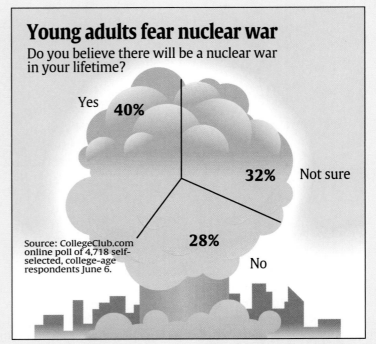

Young adults fear nuclear war

Do you believe there will be a nuclear war in your lifetime?

Yes **40%**

32% Not sure

28%

No

Source: CollegeClub.com online poll of 4,718 self-selected, college-age respondents June 6.

By Lori Joseph and Sam Ward, USA TODAY

All-Star minutes adding up

The Colorado Rapids Carlos Valderrama, the all-time leader in minutes played in Major League Soccer's All-Star Game, will make his sixth appearance Saturday in Washington. MLS All-Star Game minutes leaders:

Minutes

Carlos Valderrama (Colorado) — **435**

Preki (Kansas City) — **366**

Jeff Agoos (San Jose) — **349**

Mauricio Cienfuegos (Los Angeles) — **315**

Marcelo Balboa (New York/New Jersey) — **291**

Source: Major League Soccer

By Matthew James Weeks and Karl Gelles, USA TODAY

FIGURE 11.4
Pictograph
Speakers with artistic or computer skills can create interesting visual aids, such as the graphic representation of minutes soccer players who were elected to the 2002 All-Star Game played in previous all-star games. The pictures really are only horizontal bar graphs, but turning them into a pictograph creates a stronger sense of dynamism and competition.

Source: USA Today, August 1, 2002, C1.

Your choice of bar, line, pie, or pictorial graphs will depend on the subject and the nature of the relationship you wish to convey. A pie graph, for example, can neither easily illustrate discrepancies between two groups nor show change over time. Bar and line graphs don't easily show the total amount being represented.

Regardless of the type of graph you choose, when you're preparing these visual aids, you must be very careful not to distort your information. A bar graph can create a misleading impression of the difference between two items if one bar is short and wide while the other is long and narrow. Line graphs can portray very different trends if the units of measurement are not the same for each time period. You can avoid misrepresenting information by using consistent measurements in your graphs and by using a computer to generate your graphs.

Charts and Tables

Charts and tables condense large blocks of information into a single picture. **Tables** present information in parallel columns, as in the tax tables in the U.S. 1040 tax form. **Charts** can present data in a number of varied forms. The periodic table of elements is a common chart you've probably seen. If they are not too complicated,[9] charts and tables work well in technical speeches. So if you discuss various contributions to the operation of the United Nations, you can break down the contributions of, say, ten countries to five of the major agencies of the U.N. If you want to show why the United States has such trouble establishing a consistent energy policy, your presentation will be much easier to follow if you can show your listeners an organizational chart for the federal government.

There are two special types of charts. **Flipcharts** unveil ideas one at a time on separate sheets; **flowcharts** show relationships among ideas or facts on a single sheet. Both flipcharts and flowcharts may include drawings or photos. If you present successive ideas with a flipchart, you'll focus audience attention on specific parts of your speech. In a speech on fighting in the Operation Enduring Freedom campaign in Afghanistan during the fall of 2001 and spring of 2002, you could use a separate chart for each month of the engagement. If you presented the entire six months on one chart, the chart would become cluttered, and your audience might stray from your explanation to read the entire chart. You could also use separate charts to focus on specific assaults by different military units.

You can use a flowchart to indicate the chronological stages of a process; for example, a flowchart will allow audiences to visualize the stages of a presidential campaign or the process of making cheese. You can also use a flowchart to show relationships among ideas or interdependent actions, such as the competition between conservative and liberal views of "family values." And, of course, you're familiar with organizational flowcharts used by groups to show the relationships among members of the group. In a speech on the passage of a legislative bill, a flowchart would clarify each step of the process. As long as the information is not too complex or lengthy, tables and charts may be used to indicate changes over time and to rank or list items and their costs, frequency of use, or relative importance.

Tables and charts should be designed so that they can be seen and so that they convey data simply and clearly. Too much information will force the audience to concentrate more on the visual support than on your oral explanation. For example, a dense chart, showing all the major and minor offices of your college, might simply overwhelm listeners as they try to follow your explanation. Watch the chartjunk! If the organization is too complex, you might want to develop several charts, each one focusing on a smaller unit of information.

Models

Models can be very attractive to listeners. Like props, **models** are reduced or enlarged scale replicas of real objects. Architects construct models of new projects to show clients. You can use models of genes to accompany your explanation of the genome project. As with other visual aids, models need to be manageable and visible to the audience. You can increase listener interest if you use a model that comes apart so that different pieces can be examined. Be sure to practice removing and replacing the parts before your speech.

STRATEGIES FOR SELECTING AND USING VISUAL AIDS

Your decision about which visual aids will work best for you should be based on three considerations: (1) the characteristics of the audience and occasion, (2) your ability to integrate verbal and visual materials effectively, and (3) the potential of computer-generated visual materials.

Consider the Audience and Occasion

Think about the folks you're talking to when you decide on visuals. Do you need to bring a map of the United States to an audience of college students when discussing the spread of contagious diseases in this country? If you're going to discuss a volleyball team's offensive and defensive formations, should you provide diagrams for your listeners? Can you expect an audience to understand the administrative structure of the federal bureaucracy without providing an organizational chart? Can you really go into a boardroom of a serious corporation without a PowerPoint or Elmo-type computer projection?

How can you answer those questions? It might be quite difficult, for example, to decide what your classmates know about governmental structures or what Rotary Club members know about football plays. Probably the best thing you can do is to do a little firsthand interviewing by speaking with several of your potential listeners ahead of time. In other words, before making any final decisions about visual supporting materials, do as much audience research as you possibly can.

You should also consider the response you would like to achieve with your visual materials. In general, pictorial or photographic visuals can make an audience feel the way you do. For example, you can use slides, movies, sketches, or photographs of your travels in western Colorado to accompany your speech on high plateaus. Such visual aids stimulate your audience to share in the awe and tortured beauty that you experienced. If you show slides of civilian victims in the India-Pakistan conflict, you are likely to gain an emotional response. Such a response can maximize your efforts to persuade your listeners.

Visuals containing descriptive or written materials, on the other hand, can help an audience think the way you do. For example, models, diagrams, charts, and graphs about the population and economy of the Mediterranean area may persuade your listeners to conclude that the United States should send more foreign aid to Turkey. A timeline representing ethnic conflicts in Sri Lanka can help your listeners understand the historical context of contemporary fighting on that island. Such visual aids encourage understanding and thought rather than emotional responses.

As part of your preparation for using visuals, take into account the speaking occasion. Certain occasions demand certain types of visual support materials. The district manager who presents a report of projected future profits to the central office without a printed handout or diagram will probably find his or her credibility questioned. The military adviser who calls for governmental expenditures for new weapons without offering pictures or videos of the proposed weapons and printed technical data on their operation is not likely to be a convincing advocate. A basketball coach without a chalkboard may succeed only in confusing team members at half-time.

Plan ahead to supply the visual media demanded by the situation. If the speaking occasion doesn't appear to require certain visual supports, analyze the occasion further for different visual possibilities. Use your imagination. Be innovative. Don't overlook opportunities to make your speech more meaningful, more exciting, and more interesting for your listeners.

Integrate Verbal and Visual Materials Effectively

To be effective, your visual aids should complement your spoken message. Visuals should save time, enhance the impact of your speech, clarify complex relations, and generally enliven your presentation. Consider the following suggestions for getting the maximum benefit from your visuals:

1. *Use color to create interest.* Use contrasting colors (red on white, black on yellow)[10] to highlight information in an organizational chart or to differentiate segments of a pie graph or bars in a bar graph. As a rule, color commands attention better than black and white.

2. *Keep visual aids clear and simile.* This advice is especially important for charts and other graphic devices. Make essential information stand out clearly from the background. Let simplicity guide your preparation. Many experts recommend that you use 18- to 24-point type for text (36-point type for headings) with no more than two fonts for an effective visual aid.

3. *Make your visuals large enough to be seen easily.* Listeners get frustrated when they must lean forward and squint in order to see detail in a visual aid. Make your figures and lettering large enough so that everyone can see them. Follow the example of John Hancock, who, when signing the Declaration of Independence in 1776, wrote his name large enough to "be seen by the King of England without his glasses."

4. *Make your visuals neat.* Draw neatly, spell correctly, make lines proportional, and make letters symmetrical. Take time to design good looks for digital materials. Such advice might seem unnecessary, but too often, beginning speakers throw together visual materials at the last minute or just type a string of words onto a PowerPoint slide. They forget that their visual aids contribute to audiences' assessment of their credibility. Misspelled words and sloppy graphs will lower listeners' estimation of your competence.

5. *Decide in advance how to handle your visual aids.* Prepare and practice with your visual aids well in advance, especially for demonstration speeches. Sup-

Web Exploration
To learn more about how to integrate verbal and visual materials effectively, go to
www.ablongman.com/german15e

pose you want to show your listeners that anyone can change a tube even on the rear wheel of a bicycle without screwing up the chain and gear-shifting mechanisms. Do you bring in a whole bike? (Probably.) Do you actually change a tube on that bike? (Probably not. It would take too long for the assigned length of the speech.) So do you bring another wheel and change a tube on that? (Yes.) Do you demonstrate how to put the wheel back on the bike? (In part. Unlock the rear wheel on the bike you brought along, take the chain off the sprocket, slacken the cables, then put the chain back on and show your listeners how to adjust the cables. Then show them a chart recording the process step by step.) In thinking through how much of the process you can demonstrate in the available time, you can figure out how to handle actual objects and other visuals.

6. *Compensate orally for any distraction your visual aid might create.* Remember that you're always competing with other message sources for your listeners' attention. Listeners might find the visual aid so intriguing that they miss part of your message. You can partially compensate for any potential distraction by building repetition into your speech. By repeating your main ideas, you give your listeners several chances to follow your thoughts. As added insurance, you also might keep your visual aid out of sight until you need to use it.

7. *Coordinate visual, verbal, and electronic messages.* Mechanical or electronic messages from slides, films, overhead projections, and videotapes can easily distract your listeners. You need to talk louder and move vigorously when using a machine to communicate, or you need to show the film or slides either before or after you comment on their content or draw something on a chalkboard or whiteboard. Whatever strategy you choose, make sure that your visual materials are well integrated into your oral presentation. That is, use transitions that integrate your visual aids with the speech. If you are using a chart, you might say, "This chart shows you what I've been saying about the growing season for different varieties of tomatoes." Also indicate where you obtained the information represented on the chart, and summarize the information before you go on to your next idea.

8. *Hand your listeners a copy of the materials you wish them to reflect on after your speech.* If you're making recommendations to the tenant's association office, provide copies of your proposal for their subsequent action. Or if you're reporting the results of a survey, your listeners will better digest the key statistics if you give each audience member a copy of them. Few people can recall the seven warning signs of cancer, but they might keep a wallet-sized list handy if you order enough for all your listeners from the American Cancer Society. Of course, don't duplicate your entire speech; and for goodness sake, don't just read the handout to your listeners! You and your handouts have different roles in public speaking. For handouts, select only those items that have lasting value or the ability to make your message less complicated.

Speaking of . . . Ethics

Can Pictures Lie?

Can pictures lie? Aren't they each worth a thousand words? Isn't seeing believing? Isn't showing better than telling? Not necessarily, especially in today's visually centered world. Consider the following:

- Hopes of finding American soldiers missing in action in Vietnam (MIAs) were briefly inspired by photos that seemed to show the Americans holding signs that displayed current dates. Those pictures turned out to have been faked.
- During the 1992 presidential campaign, a political action committee (PAC) ran ads that showed Bill Clinton holding hands in victory with Ted Kennedy on the Democratic Convention stage.

What the PAC had done was morphed a picture of Kennedy's head onto Vice President Al Gore's body.

Thanks to digital editing, you now can easily add to or subtract from pictures, printing the altered photos so cleanly that the forgery is almost impossible to detect. Pictures can be altered to show something that isn't true. Or images that transform the meanings of words can be added. The visual dimension can be helpful to both speaker and audience when it is used in morally defensible ways. It can be destructive of the truth when it's not.

These suggestions should enable you to take advantage of visual communication. Good visual aids illustrate and empower your ideas, taking advantage of the visual dimension that your listeners will respond to naturally as they process their feelings and ideas.

Evaluate Computer-Generated Visual Materials

Perhaps we need to say some things in a more focused way about digitized materials. While you might not be able to produce visuals that are similar to the action shots that accompany a televised football game, you can still use readily available computer-generated visual materials. Computers are very effective for processing numerical data and converting them into bar, line, and pie graphs. You can scan in images and even morph them for humorous effects. With a modem and a phone line and in a contemporary electronic classroom, you can put a class online to a Website halfway across the globe. As with other types of visual aids, you should choose the computer graphics that fit your purpose, physical setting, and audience needs. Here are some, suggestions for ways to use such materials:

1. *Use computer graphics to create an atmosphere.* It's easy to make computer banners with block lettering and pictures. Hang a banner in the front of the room to set a mood or establish a theme. For example, a student who wanted to urge her classmates to get involved in a United Way fund-raising drive created a banner with the campaign slogan "Thanks to you, it works for all of us." Initially, the banner captured attention; during the speech, the banner reinforced the

theme. Or if you're going to talk about negative political advertising, get online and go to www.dnc.org to see what the Democratic National Committee is saying about Republican leaders and policies. That certainly will draw your listeners into your topic.

2. *Enlarge small computer-generated diagrams.* Most computer diagrams are too small to be seen easily by an audience. If a computer-projector is not available, you can shoot a 35mm slide right from your screen so that you can project it. Or if you have access to a computer-projection table, images you've stored on a disk can be projected directly.

3. *Enhance the computer-generated image in other ways.* Suppose you printed some images or tables in black and white and don't have computer projectors available in a room. In that case, just work it up by hand. Use markers to color pie graphs or to darken the lines of a line graph. Use press-on letters to make headings for your graphs. Mixing media in such ways can give your presentations a professional look even if you're not working with a color printer or computer projector. If you have access to the right technology, you can create three-dimensional images of buildings, machines, or the human body.

The world of electrified sight and sound offers exciting possibilities for the public speaker. If you learn to integrate personal talk and audiovisual presentation, you'll find that your ability to reach audiences will be enhanced. Working an audience across channels—verbal, visual, and acoustic—allows you to complicate your messages and yet give them a powerful presence that informs and persuades listeners who've been raised on sight and sound.

Compelling computer graphics can draw listeners' attention to your ideas.

Speaking of . . . Skills

Using Visual Aids Effectively

Here are some tips and reminders to assist you in preparing and using visual aids in your presentation:

1. *Good visuals reinforce the spoken message.* They do not convey the entire message.
2. *Have a presentation plan.* Begin with an introduction, and end with a summary or set of conclusions. Identify several major points you want to cover; supporting points reinforce the main points but can be sacrificed if you're running out of time.
3. *Words and graphics should not be complex: remember KISS (Keep it simple stupid).*
   - Complex ideas belong in a handout or paper.
   - Tables generally are not effective. Schematic drawings often are too detailed, but you can modify and simplify the drawing to illustrate only the point you are making, leaving out unnecessary details.
   - Organizational charts cannot be read. Simplify the chart to show only the segments you are discussing.
   - Equations, by themselves, are not an effective visual aid. You can make an equation more visually appealing, however, by adding pictorial elements.
   - Bar, pie, and line charts that are too busy can confuse the audience.
4. *Design visuals to maximize their effectiveness.*
   - The type size of text or characters should be 18 to 24 points.
   - Use bullets and dash lines, but avoid too many subtopics.
   - Use a ragged right margin.
   - Bold text is preferable to underlined text.
   - Avoid overcrowding.
5. *Use—but don't abuse—available technology to produce visuals.*
   - Use your spill check (spell), and then proofread.
   - TEXT IN ALL CAPITALS IS HARD TO READ.
   - Use color carefully: Black backgrounds cause problems. Dark blue works best, but red and blue appear to "jump" when used together.

Source: Adapted from http://omar.llnl.gov/EFCOG/tips.html.

ASSESSING YOUR PROGRESS

Chapter Summary

1. Visual aids can boost listener comprehension and memory and add persuasive impact to a speech.
2. There are many types of visual aids: actual objects or props, your own body, photographs and slides, videotapes and films, chalkboard or whiteboard drawings, transparent and computerized overhead projections, graphs, charts and tables, and models.

3. Types of graphs include bar, line, pie, and pictographs.
4. Flipcharts unveil ideas one at a time; flowcharts show the entire process on a single sheet.
5. In selecting and using visual aids, consider the audience and the occasion, find ways to integrate verbal and visual materials effectively, and work on methods to effectively use computer graphics.

Key Terms

bar graphs (p. 204)
charts (p. 207)
flipcharts (p. 208)
flowcharts (p. 208)
graphs (p. 204)
line graphs (p. 204)
rich-media (p. 203)

models (p. 208)
pictographs (p. 205)
pie graphs (p. 204)
scopic regime (p. 198)
tables (p. 207)
visual aids (p. 198)

Assessment Activities

1. Work in small groups to develop at least three different types of visual aids for the following topics. Appoint a representative from each group to report to the class as a whole, telling about or showing the proposed visual aids.
   a. The procedure for gene sequencing
   b. How to splint a broken arm or leg
   c. How to construct a PowerPoint™ slide
   d. The layout of bird-feeding stations
   e. The procedure for rotating four crops on a piece of farmland
   f. How to replace a washer in a dripping faucet
   g. A method for downloading advertisements from the Internet into your computer
2. Videotape a home shopping or how-to-do-it show, and play the videotape in class. Evaluate the use of visual aids in the show. Were they easily seen? Did they demand attention? Did the speaker use them effectively? What would have made visual aids more effective? Alternatively, write up a one-page description and evaluation for assessment by your class instructor.
3. Without using any visual aids, describe an unusual place you have visited—for example, a cathedral in a foreign city or a historical site. Deliver a four- or five-minute speech to the class in which you describe this place as accurately and vividly as possible. Ask the class to take a moment to envision this place. Now show them a picture of what you have described. How accurately were your listeners able to picture the place? How might you have ensured a more accurate description? What restrictions did you feel without the use of visual aids?

Using the Web

1. As we've seen, http://www.presentersuniversity-com/courses/cs_visualaids. cfm is a most valuable site, containing a series of two- to three-page tip sheets and a thirty-five-page book on visual aids in the electronic age.
2. Doing an exploration via Google or a similar search engine using the phrase "visual aids" will turn up a whole group of general and specific Websites on using visual aids offered by medical and business colleges, consulting firms, and class instructors from around the world.

 Using VideoWorkshop

Watch the speeches in Module 10, "Visual Presentation Aids." As you watch, concentrate on the benefits and many uses of the different visual aids incorporated into these video clips. Then answer Questions 1–21.

References

1. The twentieth century was labeled "ocularcentric": ocular = eye, centric = centered. See Jacques Ellul, *The Humiliation of the Word,* translated by Joyce Main Hanks (Grand Rapids, MI: William B. Eerdmans, 1985); Chris Jenks, ed., *Visual Culture* (New York: Routledge, 1995).

2. A good summary of research into multiple aspects of visual discourse can be found in Paul Messaris, *Visual Literacy, Mind, & Reality* (Boulder, CO: Westview Press, 1994). See also Larry Raymond, *Reinventing Communication: A Guide to Using Visual Language for Planning, Problem Solving, and Reengineering* (Milwaukee: ASQC Quality Press, 1994). For up-to-date advice on physical and electronic visual aids—especially the new technologies—see http://www.presentersuniversity. com/courses/cs_visualaids.cfm.

3. William J. Seiler, "The Effects of Visual Materials on Attitudes, Credibility, and Retention," *Communication Monographs,* 38 (1971): 331–334.

4. Joel R. Levin and Alan M. Lesgold, "On Pictures in Prose," *Educational Communication and Technology Journal,* 26 (1978): 233–244. Cf. Marilyn J. Haring and Maurine A. Fry, "Effect of Pictures on Children's Comprehension of Written Text," *Educational Communication and Technology Journal,* 27 (1979): 185–190.

5. The term *scopic regime* refers to cultural practices that are followed so often that they come to be expected, and without them, a presenter is considered amateurish or unprepared. On the visual and social-cultural theory, see Anthony Woodiwiss, *The Visual in Social Theory* (New York: Athlone Press, 2001).

6. For additional conclusions regarding the effects of various kinds of visual materials, see James Benjamin and Raymie E. McKerrow, *Business and Professional Communication* (New York: Longman, 1994), 175–179. The digital revolution, Robert Lindstrom argues, has only made visualization more important to persuasion. See his *Being Visual,* ch. 1, "The Emerging Visual Enterprise," online at http://www.presentersuniversity.com/courses/cs_visualaids.cfm.

7. See "5 Pounds of Ugly Fat" and "Props as Visuals" on the Presenters University Website (see n. 3).

8. Mary Sandro, "How Visual Aids Undermind Presentations—Three Ways You May Be Boring Your Audience to Tears," http://www.proedgeskills.com/Presentation_Skills_Articles/visual_aids_undermind.htm.

9. *Chartjunk* and *letterjunk* are Denver University's Center for Managerial Communications' words for charts that are overloaded with either too many graphic elements or too many letters, especially decorative ones. See http://www.du.edu/~emuhovic/2021visualaids.html.

10. Margo Halverson, "Choosing the Right Colors for Your Next Presentation," and Marjorie Brody, "Add Pizzazz to Presentations with Multimedia." See the Presenters University Website (n. 3).

Chapter 12

Speeches to Inform

FROM BUSINESS EXECUTIVES to day care providers and parents, speaking to inform is an important part of communication. We are awash in bits and pieces of facts, in the drone of "information radio," in digitized data. As a public speaker, you must compete with the mountain of information that is available to your listeners. You've got to find ways to grab them by the scruff of their psychological necks and the seat of their psychological pants and get them to sit up and take notice. You can do this by packaging facts and ideas in ways that they can understand and remember. That's what informative speaking is all about.

One theme will be sounded again and again in this chapter: Mere information is useless until you put it together in ways that make it clear and relevant to others. Informative speeches clarify facts and ideas for audiences. Without clarification or interpretation, information is meaningless. The informative speaker's job is to adapt data and ideas to human needs. In this chapter, we discuss various types of informative speeches, outline the essential features of informative talks, and then review some ways of structuring each type of informative speech.

FACTS, KNOWLEDGE, AND THE INFORMATION AGE

Web Exploration

To learn more about the difference between information and knowledge, go to www.ablongman.com/ german15e

Our society almost worships facts. A staggering amount of information is available to us, particularly because of such technological developments as electronic media, photostatic printing, miniaturized circuitry, fax machines, and computerized data storage and retrieval systems. Jumping onto the World Wide Web via America Online, CompuServe, or your school's computer network puts you on the information superhighway, which has more lanes than the Santa Monica Freeway. Entire libraries are available online, as are huge collections of words, pictures, and sounds from around the world. Detective Joe Friday from the old (and new) *Dragnet* TV series would never dare say only, "Just the facts, Ma'am" today, for he would immediately drown in data.

By themselves, mere facts tell us nothing. **Information** is but a collection of facts and figures until human beings shape, interpret, and act on it. Public speakers often serve as interpreters of information. They are called on to assemble, package, and present information to other human beings—to turn information into knowledge. To actually create **knowledge**—information that has been given human significance—you have to relate it to people's interests, needs, curiosities, and orientations to the world.

TYPES OF INFORMATIVE SPEECHES

Informative speeches take many forms depending on the situation, the level of knowledge possessed by listeners, and your own abilities as a presenter of data. Three of these forms—explanations or lectures, demonstrations, and oral reports—occur so frequently, however, that they merit special attention. They represent three common ways in which people package information to meet the needs of others.

Explanations or Lectures

"Mommy, what's a 'nerd'?" "Professor Martinez, what's the difference between a 'Website' and a 'home page'?" "Chantel, before I take you on as a realtor, I

Informative speaking can take many forms.

want to know what a 'joint agency' is." You've been asking questions like these all of your life. A speech of explanation doesn't just offer a dictionary definition. Rather, **explanations** define concepts or processes in ways that make them relevant to listeners. Once five-year-old Sarah knows what a nerd is, she'll know she has a human relations problem; once you know what kind of Website a home page is, you'll know whether you want to build one; and once you know that a joint agency can represent both you and the seller or buyer, you'll have the information you need to know whether that's good or bad for your situation.

Lectures, which usually involve more extended explanations and definitions, also increase an audience's understanding of a particular field of knowledge or activity. For instance, a business executive might define "total quality management" and go on to show how such a style can make the company work better; a historian might tell a group of students what sociocultural forces converged to create the American Revolution; and a social worker could lecture an audience of government officials on the local impact the 1996 federal welfare reform package.

Demonstrations

Throughout your life, you've heard classroom instructions, seen job demonstrations, and read instructions for the performance of special tasks. Not only have you gone through many "tell" sessions but you've also had people "show" you how to execute actions—how to sort various kinds of paper for recycling, how to manage a counter at a fast food shop, how to set corner posts for a picket fence. Generally, **demonstrations** explain processes or both explain and illustrate those processes. Demonstrations involve the serial presentation of information, usually in steps or phases, and require clarity because your listeners are expected to learn or reproduce these steps themselves.

Oral Reports

An **oral report** is a speech that arranges and interprets information gathered in response to a request made by a group. Academic reports, committee reports, and executive reports are examples of oral reports. Scientists and other scholars announce their research findings in oral reports at professional conventions. Committees in business, industry, and government carry out special tasks and then present oral reports to their parent organizations or constituencies. Board chairpersons present annual oral reports to the stockholders on the past year's activities. You might have been asked to present a report on possible spring trips for an organization.

Speaking of . . . Skills

Choosing a Topic

If you're searching for informative speech topics, you can develop possible topics by brainstorming (see Chapter 2) or you can develop your ideas from standard subject areas. Consider these subject areas as you generate your own informative speech topics:

1. *People.* We're all curious about the lives of others. Build on this curiosity by focusing on someone you know, someone you admire, or someone unique. You might investigate the lives of the Wright brothers or Blanche Scott, the first American woman to fly. Or what about famous people such as Bill Cosby or Clara Barton? Perhaps villains such as Rasputin or John Dillinger fascinate you.
2. *Places.* This might be an opportunity to talk about a place you've visited or would like to visit—a city, museum, park, or another country. Cities such as Rome or your hometown, museums like the Louvre or the local football hall of fame, parks such as the Everglades or your favorite state park, and countries such as Tanzania or Argentina can be intriguing speech topics.
3. *Things.* The possibilities are endless. Begin with what you already know. You could talk about your baseball card collection, the architectural style of your neighbor's house, or your uncle's antique automobile.
4. *Events.* Famous occurrences make good speech topics. There are recent events such as political elections, the bombing of the World Trade Center, the floods caused by the Mississippi River, or the conflict in Bosnia-Herzegovina. In addition, you might talk

about historical events such as famous battles, unusual discoveries, natural disasters, or memorable celebrations.

5. *Ideas.* Theories, principles, concepts, theologies, and traditions can make excellent informative speeches. You could explain the traditions of Taoism, the theory of relativity, the principles of capitalism, the concept of aging, or the funereal doctrines of Catholicism.

6. *Procedures.* Descriptions of processes can be fascinating. Your listeners may have wondered how watches work, what enables microwave ovens to cook food, or how ballets are choreographed.

ESSENTIAL QUALITIES OF INFORMATIVE SPEECHES

Your goal as an informative speaker is to make it easy for your listeners to retain new information. There are five things you can do to ensure that your listeners remember what you say. You should strive for clarity, associate new ideas with familiar ones, package or cluster ideas, construct strong visualizations, and provide motivational appeal.

Striving for Clarity

Informative speeches achieve maximum clarity when listeners can follow and understand what the speaker is saying. Clarity is largely the result of two factors: effective organization and the careful selection of words.

Achieving Clarity through Effective Organization   The ideas in your speech will be clearer if you limit your points, use effective transitions, and keep your speech moving forward.

1. *Limit your points.* Confine your speech to three or four principal ideas, grouping whatever facts or ideas you wish to consider under these main headings. Even if you know a tremendous amount about the sinking of the ocean liner *Titanic,* you can't make everyone an expert with a single speech. Stick to the basics—the sequence of events and the tragic aftermath. Leave out the discrepancies between the movie depiction and historical facts, the design of the main staircase, and the fate of other White Star ocean liners.

2. *Use transitions to show relationships among ideas.*   Word your transitions carefully. Make sure to indicate the relationship of the upcoming point to the rest of your ideas. You might say, "Second, you must prepare the chair for caning by cleaning out the groove and cane holes"; "The introduction of color to television sports in 1964 was followed by an equally important technology, the slow-motion

Speaking of . . . Apprehension

Information Overload

You're in the library, getting together materials for a speech, when suddenly you're overwhelmed by supporting materials stacking up around you like a vegetable gardener with too much zucchini. What to do? Consider doing the following:

1. *Sample it.* Even if you've found thirteen great examples, pick out only two or three of them. Use the ones you think are most relevant to the audience's needs and desires.
2. *Rotate it.* Use some of the examples this time and some other ones when talking to friends about the topic.
3. *Table it.* If you have too much information to deliver orally, put some of it on a graph or table and either project it or hand it out to your listeners. That way, you won't have to recite all of the numbers, yet they won't go to waste.
4. *Distribute it.* Lots of juicy quotations? Use them not only in the body of the speech as supporting materials, but also in the introduction to set the tone and in the conclusion to wrap up your ideas.

If you do a good job at finding supporting materials, you'll have much too much at your disposal. That's all right. Better than having too little. Be happy in the knowledge that the opposite problem is much, much worse.

Web Exploration

To view examples of informative speeches, go to www.ablongman.com/german15e

camera"; "To test these hypotheses, we set up the following experiment." Such transitions allow listeners to follow you from point to point.

3. *Keep your speech moving forward.* Rather than jumping back and forth between ideas, charging ahead, and then backtracking, develop a positive forward direction. Move from basic ideas to more complex ones, from background data to current research, or from historical incidents to current events. If you are informing your listeners about the triumphs and tragedies of the Kennedy family, you will want to discuss the sinking of PT-109 before the assassination of John F. Kennedy and the death of Michael Kennedy before the airplane crash of John F. Kennedy, Jr.

Achieving Clarity through Word Choice   The second factor in achieving clarity is being understood. You can develop understanding through careful selection of your words. Recall the discussion of the use of language in Chapter 9. For now, think about the following ways to achieve clarity.

1. *Keep your vocabulary precise, accurate—not too technical.* In telling someone how to finish off a basement room, you might be tempted to say, "Next, take one of these long sticks and cut it off in this funny looking gizmo with a saw in it and try to make the corners match." An accurate vocabulary will help your listeners remember what supplies and tools to get when they approach the same project: "This is a ceiling molding; it goes around the room between the wall and the ceiling to cover the seams between the paneling and the ceiling tiles. You make the

corners of the molding match by using a miter box, which has grooves that allow you to cut 45-degree angles. Here's how you do it."

2. *Simplify when possible.* If your speech on the operation of a dimmer switch sounds like it came out of the documentation for computer software, then it's too technical. Listeners can become confused and bored if they are bogged down in unnecessary detail and complex vocabulary. Include only as much technical vocabulary as you need. For a speech on the Heimlich maneuver, you will want to exclude its history and a discussion of the breathing process. Stick to the key ideas—how to detect signs of choking, where to exert pressure, and what to expect if you've completed the procedure correctly.

3. *Use reiteration to clarify complex ideas.* Rephrasing helps solidify ideas for those who didn't get them the first time. You might say, for example, "Unlike a terrestrial telescope, a celestial telescope is used for looking at moons, planets, and stars; that is, its mirrors and lenses are ground and arranged in such a way that it focuses on objects thousands of miles—not hundreds of feet—away from the observer." In this case, the idea is rephrased; the words aren't simply repeated.

Associating New Ideas with Familiar Ones

Audiences grasp new facts and ideas more readily when they can associate them with what they already know. In a speech to inform, try to connect the new with the old. To do this, you need to know enough about your audience to choose relevant experiences, images, analogies, and metaphors to use in your speech.

Sometimes such associations are obvious. A college dean talking to an audience of manufacturers about the problems of higher education presented his ideas under the headings of raw material, casting, machining, polishing, and assembling. He translated his central ideas into an analogy that his listeners, given their vocations, would understand. If you cannot think of any obvious association, you might have to rely on common experiences or images. For instance, you might explain the operation of a department store's pneumatic tube system by comparing it to sucking through a straw, or you could explain a cryogenic storage tank by comparing it to a thermos bottle.

Clustering Ideas

You can help listeners make sense of your speech by providing them with a well-organized package of tightly clustered ideas. Research on memory and organization has demonstrated that the "magic number" of items we can remember is seven, plus or minus two; more recent research has suggested that the number is probably five, again plus or minus two.[1] This research suggests that you ought to group items of information under three, five, or seven headings or in three, five, or seven clusters. You might, for example, organize a lecture on the history of American television around developments in key decades—the 1950s, 1960s, 1970s, 1980s, and 1990s—rather than breaking it down year by year. College registration may be presented to freshmen as a five-step process: (1) secure registration materials, (2) review course offerings, (3) see an adviser, (4) fill out the registration materials, and (5) enter the information into the computer. The American Cancer Society has organized the most common symptoms of cancer into seven categories to help you remember them.

Mnemonic devices in your outline also can provide memory triggers. CPR instructors teach the ABCs of cardiopulmonary resuscitation: (a) clear the *airways,* (b) check the *breathing* and (c) initiate chest *compressions.* A speaker giving a talk on the Great Lakes can show listeners how to remember the names of the lakes by thinking of HOMES: Huron, Ontario, Michigan, Erie, and Superior. These memory devices also help you remember the main points in your outline. Information forgotten is information lost; package your data and ideas in memorable clusters.

Constructing Relevant Visualizations

As we've been emphasizing, relevance is a key to speechmaking success. Using visualizations—recreations of events that people can "see"—can be a powerful technique for engaging listeners; if they can be made to see a process or event, they perhaps can be induced to project themselves mentally into it. So, for example, a student audience might know about the Vietnam War only through the mass media; that's where they had seen it, and thus references to movies and TV programs would be a good way for you to get into the topic. Word pictures help listeners into the world of your informative speech:

> Picture this: You're walking down the Coleman Street in Collegeville, enjoying a sunny afternoon, when you come across a man who looks desperate, and says "Ca-oo-elp-mee-plee-plee-ahm-hafin', ahm-ahm-ahm-hafin'." What do you do? Is this person drunk? Crazy? Sick? In diabetic shock? Having a heart attack? Or maybe just someone participating in a psych experiment? How are you going to handle this situation? Well, in my speech today, I'm going to tell you how to handle it. Today, I want to talk to you about . . .

Notice that the speaker tries to depict a familiar locale and a plausible event in that locale to set up a speech on the new kinds of first aid training currently offered to students at her school. If she's successful in conveying a sense of fear, uncertainty, and mistrust, then she's likely going to have her listeners following the rest of her talk.

Motivating Your Audience

Finally, and perhaps most important, you must be able to motivate your audience to listen. Unfortunately, many people ignore this essential feature of good informative speeches. Many of us blithely assume that because we are interested in something, our audience also will want to hear about it. You may be fascinated

Practice coordinating verbal and visual materials while speaking so that you can do it smoothly and professionally.

by collecting American commemorative stamps, but your listeners may yawn through your entire speech unless you motivate them. You need to give them a reason to listen. To make them enthusiastic, you might explain how stamps reflect our heritage, or you might tell them how competitions are held for stamp art.

Keep in mind what we've said about attention in Chapter 8. You can use the factors of attention to engage the members of your audience and to draw them into your speech.

Thinking through the essential qualities of informative speeches might result in a speaking outline like this one:

SAMPLE OUTLINE FOR A DEMONSTRATION SPEECH

Servicing Your Personal Computer

Introduction

I. It's 2 A.M. and you sit down at your PC, ready to write tomorrow's English composition. There's a flicker of light on the screen and nothing else. Has this ever happened to you?

A typical scenario catches listener attention.

<table>
<tr><td>

Motivation to listen is
provided.

Main topics are previewed.

The structure is repeated in
each of the three sections of
the speech.

First, listeners are given an
overview.

Then, each step of the process
is demonstrated.

</td>
<td>

II. With a little time and patience, you can make sure your personal computer is in tip-top
shape, ready for those last minute assignments. Because these maintenance procedures are
so easy to do, you can save costly repair bills by doing them yourself.

III. There are three basic services that you can complete easily and quickly—changing batteries,
servicing keyboards, and cleaning the mouse. Let's get started with changing your battery:

Body

I. Changing your battery.
  A. Your computer relies on a replaceable battery to keep the date and time chips current
  when your computer is turned off.
    1. You should replace this battery every two years.
    2. Obtain a replacement at your local computer shop.
  B. Here's how to replace the battery.
    1. Unplug the power source.
    2. Remove the cover from the system unit.
    3. Locate the battery on the motherboard.
      a. In some computers, the battery is a cylindrical cell located at the edge of the
      motherboard and covered with a plastic cap.
      b. Another type of battery, found on older PCs, is held in place by wires that must
      also be removed.
      c. Occasionally, batteries are soldered in place and must be replaced at a service
      center.
    4. Replace the battery.

II. Servicing your keyboard.
  A. If your keys begin to stick or you've spilled a soda on your keyboard, it's time to clean
  it.
  B. Here's how to clean your keyboard.
    1. Disconnect the keyboard and turn it upside down.
    2. Remove the assembly screws from the bottom.
    3. Pry apart the keyboard housings.
    4. There are three easy steps to cleaning the keyboard.
      a. Shake out the debris.
      b. Blow out the interior with canned air (don't do this near your computer!).
      c. Use electrical contact cleaner to flush out sticky residue or remove corrosion.
    5. Put your keyboard back together.

III. Cleaning your mouse.
  A. If your cursor moves erratically or if your mouse doesn't slide easily on its pad, it needs
  to be cleaned.
  B. Here's how to service your mouse.
    1. Turn the mouse over.
    2. Remove the housing cover.
    3. Remove the trackball.
    4. Check for lint, dirt particles, or other debris.
    5. Reassemble the mouse.

</td></tr>
</table>

Conclusion

I. With a few simple tools and a little extra time, you can complete the routine maintenance steps to keep your computer running at its best.

II. You can change batteries, service your keyboard, and clean your mouse.

III. All it takes is a few minutes. Do it tonight, so you're ready for that next big English paper.

A final inducement is offered.

The main speech topics are summarized.
Final comments provide closure.

TIPS FOR DEVELOPING INFORMATIVE SPEECHES

Now that we've described the various types and essential features of informative speeches, it's time to examine ways to develop them. Because informative speeches treat large amounts of information, both familiar and unfamiliar, there are some special considerations that you should take into account. One of your primary jobs, whether lecturing, demonstrating, or reporting, is to bring coherence and focus to information. In addition, you must consider your listeners as learners. To that end, you should think about the ways in which people acquire new information most easily.[2] Here are some ways to adapt information to listeners:

1. *Create curiosity.* Often, listeners don't realize the full impact of new information or its potential for improving their lives. You need to pose this possibility for them, creating enough curiosity that they will stick with you through the acquisition of new ideas or concepts. Pretend that you've decided to provide your classmates with information about mole rats. Think about what attracted you to mole rats. Was it the blind, pink, and hairless bodies of the mole rat that first caught your eye in the zoo display? Or was it the intricate patterns of their subterranean tunnels that intrigued you? As you think about what first caught your attention, you may discover the key to creating curiosity in your listeners. You can hook your listeners by starting with the appearance of the mole rat or its tunneling behavior. Once they get a glimpse of the creature or wonder at its maze of tunnels, your job of providing information will be easier.

Apathetic audiences are a special challenge in speeches on unfamiliar concepts, since we're tempted to say, "Well, if I've made it this far in life without knowing anything about quarks or double-entry bookkeeping or knuckleballs, why should I bother now?" You need to make people wonder about the unknown. Use new information to intrigue them. How could you start a speech on knuckleballs? Obviously, most of your listeners will never make it to the major leagues. Most of them will never throw a knuckleball. But some of them will watch baseball, and others can be fascinated by the reason knuckleballs tumble and skitter across home plate. Explain the physics of imbalance—when the stitches on one side of the baseball catch the air while the smooth surface on the other side offers less resistance, you get an erratic flight pattern, otherwise known as a knuckleball. In this way, you can appeal to your listeners' innate curiosity about their world.

2. *Adapt to what your listeners already know.* Most of us approach learning situations, not as blank slates, but with all sorts of preexisting categories of facts, theories of relationships, and attitudes toward learning. We have notions about how the world works, how history happened, and how we fit into all of this. Understanding these predispositions can be critical in developing informative speeches, since all learning involves the merging of new facts and ideas into the framework that already exists in listeners' minds. If your listeners believe that men are better at math, you might disagree, but you'll still have to deal with this predisposition if you want everyone in your audience to think about quadratic equations. If your listeners have "math phobia," then you are dealing with an entirely different predisposition toward your topic. In either case, you should consider what your listeners already think as you construct your speech.

New information is often retained more easily when we know that it can be useful. When we're convinced that we need to know something, we're more likely to learn it. Think about taking your first test for an automobile license. The rules of the road might have seemed somewhat arbitrary, but realizing that you needed to know this information to get a license probably made learning them easier. Besides, it's useful to know who has the right-of-way. As inducement, you might include an explicit statement that indicates how the information can affect your listeners. You could say, "Understanding right-of-way rules at a four-way stop can save you time and trouble. It sure beats ending up in a fender-bender!"

3. *Use Repetition.* Researchers have demonstrated that repetition is critical in increasing recall of ideas and facts. Think about your own experiences. You probably won't learn a new word such as *intrepid* if you repeat it once. But you're more likely to remember *intrepid* with two or three repetitions. Use it in a sentence or repeat it for the fourth time, and research tells us that you're 90 percent more likely to remember it. So what does *intrepid* mean? Courageous or fearless or bold. Try using *intrepid* in a sentence. With all of these repetitions, you're more likely to remember.

It's easy to realize the importance of repetition when you're learning a single fact, but this concept also applies to learning more complex material. People remember more information when it is packaged in a way that emphasizes repetition. During an informative speech, you can reiterate information or embellish it with details. And you can also use the structure of your speech to reinforce learning by building in repetition. That's why you should forecast the main points you'll cover in your speech. Later, those points will be reinforced in the body of your speech. Finally, your summary in your conclusion will give your listeners one more review of the new ideas. If you're going to take your listeners through the steps involved in refinishing a bookcase, for example, give them an overall picture of the process before you start detailing each procedure. Then your listeners will know where you're headed. And they're more likely to go with you. After you've detailed the refinishing process, you should summarize the main ideas in your conclusion. Consider your conclusion a final chance to repeat your main ideas. Your summary will increase the chances that your listeners will retain information much longer. Repeat the main points. You might say "Remember the 4 S's: strip, sand, stain, and seal. . . ." Notice that the main steps in the process are easier to remember because they all begin with "s."

4. *Involve your listeners.* Even though some of your information may be new and difficult, or complex and abstract, you should urge everyone to listen. It might be easiest to start with something familiar. Recall the factors of attention discussed in Chapter 8. Each of them offers a way to capture the attention—and thus the involvement—of your listeners. Although we discussed how you can use the nine factors of attention at the beginning of your speech, you should realize that it shouldn't stop there. Your listeners should be engaged during the entire speech. A process such as tombstone rubbing, for example, looks easier that it is; many people are tempted to quit listening and give up somewhere along the way. If you forewarn them that you'll expect them to try the basic techniques in a few minutes, however, they will be more likely to listen intently because you've appealed to activity and the vital. In another instance, the concept of parallel universes is probably quite foreign to most of your listeners. However, by starting with something familiar—such as the use of time in the film *The Terminator*—you can encourage your listeners to think about parallel universes. You have overcome their initial resistance, so they're receptive to a new idea. In addition, you have linked something new to something familiar. It is more likely that your listeners will remember new material if it is connected with an existing network of information.

Remember, too, that we learn new information in multiple ways. Think about how a young child discovers its world: Any new object is touched, tasted, smelled, and probably thrown. The more ways you can offer your listeners for interacting with a new idea, the more likely it is that they'll retain it. Hands-on experience is great. Or use language to hook their imaginations. Draw vivid examples, and ask compelling questions. Much like the process of childhood discovery, the multifaceted experience of new ideas will generate excitement in your listeners.

5. *Choose an appropriate organization pattern.* Speeches that demonstrate a process or technique often follow a natural chronological or spatial pattern. Consequently, you usually will have little trouble organizing the body of a speech that is primarily a demonstration. For example, it's clear that if you're demonstrating how to make homemade bread, you'll need to show your viewers how to mix the ingredients before showing them how to knead the dough.

Most explanations and lectures use a topical pattern because such speeches usually describe various aspects of an object or idea. It seems natural, for example, to use a topical pattern to structure a speech on careers in television around such topics as careers in broadcast TV, careers in cable TV, and careers in industrial

TV. There are occasions when other patterns might serve your specific purpose better than topical patterns. You might use an effect-cause pattern, for example, when preparing an informative speech on the laws of supply and demand. You could enumerate a series of effects with which people are already familiar—changing prices at the gas pumps—and then discuss the laws of supply and demand that account for such changes.

In many cases, there is competing information and conflicting conclusions about it. The key to packaging this information lies in the way in which the speaker constructs a *viewpoint* or *rationale*. Suppose that you wanted to explain the discovery of the New World. Traditional Eurocentric histories stress the discovery of uncharted lands by men such as Christopher Columbus, Vasco da Gama, or Ponce de Leon. But how would native North Americans see the arrival of Europeans? Clearly, their viewpoint offers a different way to understand historical events.

6. *Use multiple channels.* Many informative speakers take advantage of the power of visual material to capture quantities of information quickly and forcefully. By reinforcing ideas with another channel—the visual, auditory, or kinesthetic—you increase the chances that the information you present will be remembered. Here are some special considerations for incorporating multiple channels:

▶ *Coordinate verbal and visual material.* Demonstrating processes, concepts, or steps often demands that speakers "show" while "telling." Be sure to practice doing while talking, demonstrating your material while explaining aloud what you're doing. Decide where you'll stand when showing a slide so that the audience can see both you and the image; practice talking about your aerobic exercise positions while you're actually doing them; do a Web search for your speech in practice sessions so that you'll be ready to do it for a real audience.

▶ *Adapt your rate.* If you need to let a cream pie cool before adding meringue, what do you do? You can't just wait for the pie to cool. Instead, you should have a cooled pie ready for the next step. You also need to plan some material for filling the time—perhaps additional background or a brief discussion of what problems can arise at this stage. Plan your remarks carefully for those junctures so that you can maintain your audience's attention.

▶ *Adjust the scale.* How can you show various embroidery stitches to an audience of twenty-five? When dealing with minute operations, you often must enlarge them so that everyone can easily see. In this example, you could use a large piece of cloth, an oversized needle, yarn instead of thread, and stitches measured in inches instead of millimeters. You can adapt your techniques to make them visible to all your listeners. At the other extreme, in a speech on how to make a homemade compost frame, you should work with a scaled-down model.

7. *Suggest additional resources.* If you've done your job, your listeners should be excited about what you've told them and eager to learn even more

than you can present in a short speech. Give them the opportunity to continue the discovery of new information on their own. For example, a speaker who is discussing diabetes could conclude by offering listeners the titles of books containing more information, the phone number of the American Diabetes Association, the address of a local clinic, or the meeting time and place of a diabetics' support group. Be sure to include Internet sources as well as electronic and print sources. Screen the material you recommend to be sure that it is both appropriate and of high quality. In an oral report, you can provide the necessary data for further consideration in the form of handouts or a report summary. Your listeners have the specific information they will need to determine future action in front of them as you conclude your report.

Include experts, such as yourself and others, as additional resources. Sometimes what sounds simple in demonstrations may be much more complicated in execution. If possible, make yourself available for assistance: "As you fill out your application form, just raise your hand if you're unsure of anything and I'll be happy to help you." Or point to other sources of further information and assistance: "Here's the address of the U.S. Government Printing Office, whose pamphlet X12344 is available for only three dollars. It will give you more details" or "If you run into a problem retrieving computer files that I haven't covered in this short orientation, just go over to Maria McFerson's desk, right over here. Maria is always willing to share her expertise." Such statements not only offer help but also assure your listeners that they won't be labeled as dimwitted if they actually have to ask for it.

SAMPLE OUTLINE

What Is Diabetes?[3]

Introduction

I. I never knew my grandmother. She was a talented artist; she raised six kids without all the modern conveniences like microwave ovens and electric clothes dryers; and my dad still talks about the time she foiled a would-be burglar by locking him in a broom closet until the police came. My grandmother had diabetes. It finally took her life. Now my sister has it. So do 16 million other Americans.

The speaker uses a vividly developed personal example to gain attention.

II. Diabetes threatens millions of lives, and it's one of nature's stealthiest diseases.

The scope of the problem is explained.

III. It's important to understand this disease because, more than likely, you or someone you know will eventually have to deal with it.

A motivation for listening is provided.

    A. Diabetes is the third leading cause of death behind heart disease and cancer, according to the American Diabetes Association.

Supporting testimony shows the severity of the disease.

Listeners are warned that ignorance of the disease makes the problem worse.

The scope of the problem is expanded by pointing out that other medical conditions are complicated by diabetes.
The three main ideas of the speech are previewed.

The first main point is stated.

Diabetes is defined in medical terms.

The symptoms of diabetes are explained.

The second main point is provided.
Type I diabetes is operationally defined.
Who is affected by Type I is further explained.

The treatment is revealed.

Type II diabetes is operationally defined.

Supporting statistics show the scope of this type.
Who is affected by Type II is further explained.
The treatment is revealed.

The third main point is provided.

The treatments for Type I are explained.

Supporting testimony is offered for new treatments.
Near-infrared beams determine blood sugar levels.
New methods of delivering insulin are outlined.
The treatments for Type II are explained.
Testimony supports the value of weight loss.

B. Over one third of those suffering from the disease don't even know they have it. That simple knowledge could make the difference between a happy productive life and an early death.
C. Furthermore, diabetes is implicated in many other medical problems: it contributes to coronary heart disease; it accounts for 40 percent of all amputations and most cases of new blindness.
D. In the next few minutes, let's look at three things you should know about "the silent killer," diabetes—what it is, how it affects people, and how it can be controlled.

Body

I. What diabetes is.
A. Diabetes is a chronic disease of the endocrine system that affects your body's ability to deliver glucose to its cells.
B. The symptoms of diabetes, according to Dr. Charles Kilo, are weight loss in spite of eating and drinking, constant hunger and thirst, frequent urination, and fatigue.

II. How diabetes affects people.
A. Type I diabetes occurs when your body cannot produce insulin, a substance that delivers glucose to your cells.
1. Only 5 to 10 percent of all diabetics are Type I.
2. This type, also known as *juvenile diabetes,* usually shows up in the first 20 years of life.
3. Type I diabetes can be passed on genetically but is also thought to be triggered by environmental agents such as viruses.
4. Type I diabetics must take insulin injections to treat the disease.
B. Type II diabetes occurs when your body produces insulin but fails to use it effectively.
1. Of all diabetics, 90 to 95 percent have Type II.
2. This type usually shows up after a person turns 40.
3. It often affects people who are overweight; more women are affected than men.
4. Insulin injections are sometimes used to treat the disease, though exercise, proper diet, and oral medications often are enough.

III. How to control diabetes.
A. Type I diabetes cannot be cured, but it can be controlled.
1. Patients must take insulin injections, usually several times a day.
2. Patients need to monitor their blood sugar levels by pricking a finger and testing a drop of blood.
3. According to *Science News,* several new treatments are available.
a. One new device uses near-infrared beams to determine blood sugar level.
b. Insulin can be taken through the nose or in pill form.
c. Pancreatic transplants have been performed with limited success.
B. Type II diabetes can be controlled through life-style modifications.
1. Usually these diabetics are required to lose weight by exercising, according to Dr. JoAnn Manson.
2. Changes in diet are also required.

   3. Some people take oral medications that stimulate the release of insulin, decrease glucose production in the liver, and foster insulin activity.
   4. If these modifications fail, Type II diabetics must take insulin injections.

Conclusion

I. Diabetes is a serious disease in which the body can no longer produce or use insulin effectively.

II. The two types of diabetes occur at different stages in life and require different measures for control of the disease.

III. My grandmother lived with her diabetes for years but eventually lost her life to it. My sister has the advantages of new treatments and future research in her fight with diabetes.

IV. As we age, many of us will be among the 600,000 new diabetics each year. Through awareness, we can cope effectively with this silent killer.

Insulin-stimulating medications are explained.

Insulin injections replace unsuccessful behavior modifications.

Listeners are reminded of the definition of diabetes.

The three main ideas of the speech are reiterated.

The speech reaches closure by referring to the introductory personal example.

Listeners are warned that diabetes could affect them.

SAMPLE SPEECH

The following speech, "The Geisha," was delivered by Joyce Chapman when she was a freshman at Loop College in Chicago. It illustrates most of the virtues of a good informative speech: (1) It provides enough detail and explanations to be clear; (2) it works from familiar images of geishas, adding new ideas and information in such a way as to enlarge listeners' frames of reference; (3) its topical organization pattern is easy to follow; and (4) it gives listeners reasons for listening.

The Geisha[4] *Joyce Chapman*

As you may have already noticed from my facial features, I have Oriental blood in me and, as such, I am greatly interested in my Japanese heritage. One aspect of my heritage that fascinates me the most is the beautiful and adoring Geisha. / I

I recently asked some of my friends what they thought a Geisha was, and the comments I received were quite astonishing. For example, one friend said, "She is a woman who walks around in a hut." A second friend was certain that a Geisha was, "A woman who massages men for money and it involves her in other physical activities." Finally, I received this response, "She gives baths to men and walks on their backs." Well, needless to say, I was rather surprised and offended by their comments. I soon discovered that the majority of my friends perceived the Geisha with similar attitudes. One of them argued, "It's not my fault, because that is the way I've seen them on TV." In many ways my friend was correct. His misconception of the Geisha was not his fault, for she is often portrayed by American film producers and directors as: a prostitute, as in the movie, *The Barbarian and the Geisha,* a streetwalker, as seen

A personal reference establishes an immediate tie between Ms. Chapman and her topic.

Ms. Chapman works hard to bring the listeners—with their stereotyped views of geishas—into the speech through comments many might have made and references to familiar films.

in the TV series, *Kung Fu,* or as a showgirl with a gimmick, as performed in the play, *Flower Drum Song.*/2

The central idea is stated clearly.

A Geisha is neither a prostitute, streetwalker, nor showgirl with a gimmick. She is a lovely Japanese woman who is a professional entertainer and hostess. She is cultivated with exquisite manners, truly a bird of a very different plumage./3

A transition moves the listeners easily from the introduction to the body of the speech via a forecast.
The first section of the body of the speech is devoted to an orienting history that cleverly wipes away most of the negative stereotypes of the geisha.

I would like to provide you with some insight to the Geisha, and, in the process perhaps, correct any misconception you may have. I will do this by discussing her history, training, and development./4

The Geisha has been in existence since A.D. 600, during the archaic time of the Yakamoto period. At that time the Japanese ruling class was very powerful and economically rich. The impoverished majority, however, had to struggle to survive. Starving fathers and their families had to sell their young daughters to the teahouses in order to get a few yen. The families hoped that the girls would have a better life in the teahouse than they would have had in their own miserable homes./5

During ancient times only high society could utilize the Geisha's talents because she was regarded as a status symbol, exclusively for the elite. As the Geisha became more popular, the common people developed their own imitations. These imitations were often crude and base, lacking sophistication and taste. When American GIs came home from World War II, they related descriptive accounts of their wild escapades with the Japanese Geisha. In essence, the GIs were only soliciting with common prostitutes. These bizarre stories helped create the wrong image of the Geisha./6

Today, it is extremely difficult to become a Geisha. A Japanese woman couldn't wake up one morning and decide, "I think I'll become a Geisha today." It's not that simple. It takes sixteen years to qualify./7

A nice transition moves Chapman to her second point on the rigors of geisha training. She discusses the training in language technical enough to make listeners feel that they're learning interesting information but not so detailed as to be suffocating.

At the age of six a young girl would enter the Geisha training school and become a Jo-chu, which means housekeeper. The Jo-chu does not have any specific type of clothing, hairstyle, or make-up. Her duties basically consist of keeping the teahouse immaculately clean (for cleanliness is like a religion to the Japanese). She would also be responsible for making certain that the more advanced women would have everything available at their fingertips. It is not until the girl is sixteen and enters the Maiko stage that she concentrates less on domestic duties and channels more of her energies on creative and artistic endeavors./8

The Maiko girl, for example, is taught the classical Japanese dance, Kabuki. At first, the dance consists of tiny, timid steps to the left, to the right, backward and forward. As the years progress, she is taught the more difficult steps requiring syncopated movements to a fan./9

The Maiko is also introduced to the highly regarded art of floral arrangement. The Japanese take full advantage of the simplicity and gracefulness that can be achieved with a few flowers in a vase, or with a single flowering twig. There are three main styles: Seika, Moribana, and Nagerie. It takes at least three years to master this beautiful art./10

During the same three years, the Maiko is taught the ceremonious art of serving tea. The roots of these rituals go back to the thirteenth century, when Zen Buddhist monks in China drank tea during their devotions. These rituals were raised to a fine art by the Japanese tea masters, who set the standards for patterns of behavior throughout Japanese society. The tea ceremony is so intricate that it often takes four hours to perform and requires the use of over seventeen different utensils. The tea ceremony is far more than the social occasion it appears to be. To the Japanese, it serves as an island of serenity where one can refresh the senses and nourish the soul./11

One of the most important arts taught to the Geisha is that of conversation. She must master an elegant circuitous vocabulary flavored in Karyuki, the world of flowers and willows, of which she will be a part. Consequently, she must be capable of stimulating her client's mind as well as his esthetic pleasures./12

Having completed her sixteen years of thorough training, at the age of twenty-two, she becomes a full-fledged Geisha. She can now serve her clients with duty, loyalty, and most important, a sense of dignity./13

The Geisha would be dressed in the ceremonial kimono, made of brocade and silk thread. It would be fastened with an obi, which is a sash around the waist and hung down the back. The length of the obi would indicate the girl's degree of development. For instance, in the Maiko stage the obi is longer and is shortened when she becomes a Geisha. Unlike the Maiko, who wears a gay, bright, and cheerful kimono, the Geisha is dressed in more subdued colors. Her makeup is the traditional white base, which gives her the look of white porcelain. The hair is shortened and adorned with beautiful, delicate ornaments./14

As a full-fledged Geisha, she would probably acquire a rich patron who would assume her sizable debt to the Okiya, or training residence. This patron would help pay for her wardrobe, for each kimono can cost up to $12,000. The patron would generally provide her with financial security./15

The Geisha serves as a combination entertainer and companion. She may dance, sing, recite poetry, play musical instruments, or draw pictures for her guest. She might converse with them or listen sympathetically to their troubles. Amorous advances, however, are against the rules./16

So, as you can see the Geisha is a far cry from the back-rubbing, streetwalking, slick entertainer that was described by my friends. She is a beautiful, cultivated, sensitive, and refined woman./17

The third point of the speech—how a geisha develops her skills in her actual work—is clearly introduced and then developed with specific instances and explanations.

The conclusion is short and quick. Little more is needed in a speech that has offered clear explanations, though some speakers might want to refer back to the initial overview of negative stereotypes to remind the listeners how wrong such views are.

ASSESSING YOUR PROGRESS

Chapter Summary

1. Speeches to inform seek to package information or ideas so as to create knowledge in listeners.
2. Three types of informative speeches are explanations or lectures, demonstrations, and oral reports.
3. No matter what type of informative speech you're preparing, you should strive for five qualities: ensuring clarity; associating new ideas with familiar ones; clustering ideas to aid memory and comprehension; constructing relevant visualizations to aid in audience comprehension; and motivating your audience.
4. To maximize your ability to reach your audiences, you should create curiosity, adapt to what listeners already know, use repetition, involve listeners, choose an appropriate organizational pattern, use multiple channels, and suggest additional resources.

Key Terms

demonstrations (p. 222)   knowledge (p. 220)
explanations (p. 221)   lectures (p. 221)
information (p. 220)   oral report (p. 222)

Assessment Activities

1. Indicate and defend the type of arrangement (chronological sequence, spatial sequence, cause-effect, and so on) you think would be most suitable for an informative speech on the following subjects:
   a. The status of minority studies on campus
   b. Recent developments in genetic engineering
   c. Mayan excavations in Central America
   d. Tax-free savings for retirement
   e. How a chat room works
   f. Censorship of video games
   g. Diet fads of the 1980s and 1990s
   h. Residential colleges and universities
   i. Buying your first house
   j. What life will be like in the year 2500
2. Ask each member of the class to reflect on an example from the past where they have had to demonstrate a procedure to another person. Share the experiences, commenting on the effectiveness of the demonstration. You might, for example, have shown a new employee how to assemble a hamburger or how to close out a cash register.

Using the Web

1. There are a wide range of reference materials available online, including encyclopedias, dictionaries, yearbooks, historical documents, biographies, magazines, and newspapers. Choose a topic and then conduct a search using online resources to discover facts about your topic. Conclude the exercise by discussing ways to organize and present the facts you've discovered.
2. Consult the Library of Congress Web page. It offers an in-depth discussion of how historians manage overwhelming mountains of data to develop coherent explanations of the past. Apply these strategies as you conduct research and uncover information for your next speech.

 ## Using Video Workshop

Watch the speeches in Module 4, "Topic Selection." As you watch, think about how to select an effective topic for a sample speech of demonstration or explanation. Then answer Questions 1–9.

References

1. For background on information packaging, see G. Mandler, "Organization and Memory," in *Human Memory: Basic Processes,* edited by Gordon Bower (New York: Academic Press, 1977), 310–354; Mandler's articles in C. R. Puff, ed., *Memory Organization and Structure* (New York: Academic Press, 1976); and the classic G. A. Miller, "The Magic Number Seven Plus or Minus Two: Some Limits on Our Capacity for Processing Information," *Psychological Review,* 63 (1956): 81–97.

2. For additional research on learning, see National Research Council, *How People Learn: Brain, Mind, Experience, and School.* Washington, DC: National Academy Press, 2000.

3. Information for this outline is taken from Phyllis Barrier, "Diabetes: It Never Lets Up," *Nation's Business* (November 1992), 77; David Bradley, "Is a Pill on the Way for Diabetes?" *New Scientist* (27 June 1992), 17; C. Ezzell, "New Clues to Diabetes' Cause and Treatment," *Science News* (21 December 1991), 406; Charles Kilo and Joseph R. Williamson, *Diabetes* (New York: John Wiley & Sons, 1987); Mark Schapiro, "A Shock to the System," *Health* (July–August 1991), 75–82: Carrie Smith, "Exercise Reduces Risk of Diabetes," *The Physician and Sportsmedicine* (November 1992), 19; John Travis, "Helping Diabetics Shed Pins and Needles," *Science News* (6 July 1991), 4; Janice A. Drass and Ann Peterson, "Type II Diabetes: Exploring Treatment Options," *American Journal of Nursing,* 96 (November 1996): 45–49; personal experience of one of the authors.

4. Joyce Chapman, "The Geisha," in Roselyn Schiff et al., *Communication Strategy: A Guide to Speech Preparation* (Glenview, IL: Scott, Foresman, 1981). Used with permission of Longman Publishers.

Chapter 13

Speeches to Persuade

N EARLY 2001, *Newsweek* economist Robert Samuelson faced a dilemma: He had opposed large federal tax cuts on the grounds that any extra income the federal government has should be channeled into paying down the debt. Yet he saw many economic indicators—slumping industrial production, miserable Christmas retail sales, declines in auto sales, and the death of Montgomery Ward—that portended trouble for the country. How could he change his position on a tax cut without undermining his own credibility and without making himself appear inconsistent?

He decided on a three-part strategy: (1) Come up with a plan that would work faster than President Bush's plan would. (2) Echo the Democrats' help-the-middle-class appeal. (3) And offer a quick-fix that would seem much narrower than Bush's long-term plan. Thus, he proposed to (1) cut rates across-the-board immediately, not in 2002–2006; (2) distribute more of the rate cuts to the middle tax brackets; and (3) defer the phase out of the estate tax, the so-called marriage penalty, and hold back on new deductions for charitable giving until we can see how the economy does in a few years. Samuelson's persuasive strategies therefore were based on his desire to protect his own credibility, maintain his psychological appeal to more liberal readers, and yet respond to the economic problems the country was facing about the time President Bush was being inaugurated.[1]

Samuelson's persuasive goals were influenced by his knowledge of the public's skeptical attitudes toward both government giveaways and economic projections. He had to make the tax proposal seem both politically and economically reasonable. And he certainly wanted to maintain his own credibility as an understandable, commonsensical analyst. The strategies were useful, as he was asking people to change their ideas or actions in ways that were contrary to directions he'd advocated for the country in earlier articles. He managed to rationalize his change in policy and action.

Web Exploration

To view examples of persuasive appeals go to www.ablongman.com/ german15e

The speaker or writer who persuades makes a very different demand on an audience than the speaker who informs. Informative communicators are satisfied when listeners understand what has been said. Persuaders, however, attempt to influence listeners' thoughts or actions. Whatever the specific purpose, the general purpose of all persuaders is to convince audiences of something. Broadly, persuasion encompasses a wide range of communication activities, including advertising, marketing, sales, political campaigns, and interpersonal relations. *Persuasive speaking is the process of producing oral messages that reorient an audience psychologically or induce it to act in new and different ways.*

At the dawn of the twenty-first century, it is very clear that the world of persuasive speaking has changed radically over the last 100 years. Marketers, especially, began to realize about a quarter-century ago that "throughout the nation, Americans live in distinctive community types, refusing to blend into the mythical melting pot."[2] As a country, the United States has become less and less organized by ideological tenets and ethnic blocs and more and more woven into a variegated web of what we will be calling *lifestyles*. Think of that term as generally vague and subject to many different category systems. It is used to suggest that you probably cannot use idealist value systems (thinking of people as sociologically, economically, or politically motivated generally) or even the old ethnic labels (the characteristics of Irish Americans, Asian Americans, African Americans) when conceptualizing how the country organizes itself routinely. Rather, you're better off seeing where people live, examining what they do and what products they buy, and asking them concrete preference questions ("Do you prefer to watch TV or go to a sports event in the evenings?"). What you'll find are pockets of people in different parts of the country who are more like people living in similar neighborhoods elsewhere than they are like their neighbors in another part of their own town.

We're a fragmented society in many ways, as books such as Robert Putnam's *Bowling Alone* or Joseph Turow's *Breaking Up America* tell us.[3] This means that you have to think of audiences as *segmented,* with the different segments—clusters or cultures—often requiring their own motivational appeals and prods to act. That is why we'll begin this chapter with various approaches to understanding and thinking about groups or clusters of people before talking about *persuasive* and *actuative* speechmaking. Before trying to build speeches to persuade and actuate, you have to be sensitive to at least three analytical concerns:

1. Adapting to listeners' behavioral patterns
2. Enhancing your credibility when selling ideas to audiences
3. Selecting motivational appeals that engage different segments of audiences

ANALYZING THE AUDIENCES OF YOUR PERSUASIVE SPEECHES

PRIZM: Adapting Messages to Listeners' Behavioral Patterns

A popular marketing technique that you can adapt to the process of selecting persuasive strategies is **PRIZM,** which is a so-called lifestyle segmentation system. Its special appeal is that it is geography-sensitive. Constructed out of data from the 1990 census (it will change soon), it defines every neighborhood in the United States behaviorally and demographically. Once the census was tabulated by zip codes, it made possible precise demographic descriptions, and then, when marketing (purchasing or consumption) data were added to those descriptions, sixty-two types of areas or neighborhoods were defined. The distribution of those areas or neighborhoods could be charted by zip code.[4]

Consider the working habitat of one of this book's authors: 52240 is the zip code for Iowa City, Iowa, a smallish town in which the highest percentage of residents come from PRIZM cluster 36, "Towns & Gowns: College Town Singles." These are described as half local (towns) and half student (gowns) populations with "thousands of penniless 18- to 24-year-olds and highly educated professionals, all with a penchant for prestige products that are beyond their evident means." This cluster is dominated by lower-middle-income people, large numbers of whom are under 24, largely white but with a strong Asian population. The zip code of this author's residence, however, is 52361, the countryside around Williamsburg, Iowa. The dominant cluster here is 57, "Grain Belt: Owners & Tenants," with strong ties to farming and the land, "mostly self-sufficient, family- and home-centered." These likewise are lower-middle-income people (who make somewhat more than the Towns & Gowns group), but much older—55–64 and over 65—and intermixed with a population that is Hispanic rather than Asian, largely because of Latino migrant workers. Persuasive speeches delivered in most parts of Iowa City will have a very, very different audience from those given in Williamburg, even though they're only twenty miles apart.[5]

We live in a world that runs on promotions and pitches— persuasion, in other words. What are some examples of persuasive advertising that are evident in this photo?

For the persuader, PRIZM and other consumption-oriented methods for identifying particular segments of audiences is a corrective device. What PRIZM does is recognize that motives aren't always easy to chart in clear ways and that motivational appeals must be understood as operating within environmentally defined situations. One will find Iowans representing almost all of the PRIZM categories, and of course the populations of cities vary markedly as one moves from neighborhood to neighborhood. Trying to convince the citizens of even a 70,000-person city to vote for a bond issue to construct a new sewer system will demand considerable adjustment of motivational appeals as you move from one part of town to another.

Return to Iowa City, Iowa, for a moment. There are five prominent PRIZM clusters there, each of which will have to be approached on the question of a bond issue for a new sewer system in a somewhat different way:

Seeking Votes through PRIZM for a New Sewer System in Iowa City, Iowa

1. *Towns & Gowns:* Little money and no enduring place in the community. Will not be faced with the tax burden. Easy to persuade to vote for a sewer system, though hard to get them to actually get out and vote.

2. *Starter Families.* The "townies" of Iowa City who opted for early marriage and children. Less prosperous neighborhoods, less expensive housing. Probably

can be convinced to vote for the increased taxes by emphasizing swimming pools and other recreational areas made possible by increasing water supply and control.

3. *Boomtown Singles.* Somewhat older and more affluent than Starter Families, more likely single and in technical/technology-centered jobs and living in newer rental units or condos. Harder to get them to understand a long-term commitment to community development in Iowa City. Must have the cost minimized for them.

4. *Middleburg Managers.* Here are the doctors, lawyers, younger faculty members, and local politicians and government service people, about half age 55 and over and about half age 35 and younger. These are likely voters who must be convinced to part with additional cash that they're probably spending on clubs, sports, and exotic travel.

5. *Upward Bound.* Here are the top managers, professors, and company middle- and upper-level executives living in new, single-family homes. While this population is smaller than some of the others in Iowa City, it will be bear the brunt of the cost of the sewer system. The more liberal professoriate can be sold the system with humanitarian appeals to providing for others; the more conservative business community will have to be convinced that better water supplies and control of waste water will help with future community investment, growth, and hence economic potential.

So where are we left when talking about the bond issue in Iowa City? Thinking about motivational appeals (discussed later in this chapter), pleas to vote for civic improvement and environmental improvement (a social obligation in the affiliation cluster) should be aimed at Towns & Gowns and Boomtown Singles. Starter Families should be told about the improved recreational services to tap the achievement cluster of motivational appeals (especially adventure and personal enjoyment). Affiliation appeals to loyalty and tradition can form the bases for arguments aimed at Middleburg Managers, while power-cluster appeals, especially dominance—the responsibilities of leadership—should be manufactured for the Upward Bound neighborhoods.

We leave the rest to you. Think about how to frame the specific appeals, all of which will require serious attention to what you'll see in the visualization step in the motivated sequence. Sewer and water systems take a long time to build, so benefits have to be projected in visionary terms. The point of all this, however, is to demonstrate that using PRIZM-like analysis of audience segments can provide a rationale for particular approaches to motivational appeals and hence for reason-giving in support of persuasive and actuative claims.

Enhancing Your Credibility

Now consider the second essential dimension affecting the persuasive process: credibility, or *ethos.* This issue brings the analysis of segments home—to you and your relationship to the various targeted clusters of listeners. In Chapter 1, we outlined several factors that can determine listeners' perceptions of your credibility—their sense of your expertise, trustworthiness, competency, sincerity or honesty, friendliness and concern for others, and personal dynamism. You should work to maximize the potential impact of all these factors whenever speaking, regardless of purpose, but they are especially important when you seek to change someone's mind or behavior. The following guidelines can assist you in making decisions about the use of credibility as an effective tool in persuasion.

First, when speaking to people who are relatively unmotivated and do not have enough background information to critically assess what they hear, *the higher your credibility, the better are your chances of being a successful persuader.* Conversely, if your credibility is low, even strong arguments will not overcome your initial handicap.[6] Sure, this is obvious, but it's amazing how many speakers think that if they know what they're talking about or have power over a group of listeners, they needn't worry about how they're seen by those to whom they're talking.

Second, *you can increase the likelihood of being judged credible when seeking to persuade an audience by taking steps to enhance your image of competence and sincerity.* People are unlikely to change their beliefs and values if they think you've done a poor job of researching the issues or are insincere; they are less likely to judge you as trustworthy. So (1) carefully set forth all of the competing positions, ideas, and proposals relevant to a topic before you come to your own judgment; (2) review various criteria for judgment—criteria that different segments can apply—to show that your recommendations or positions flow from accepted measures; and (3) show that the recommendations you offer actually will solve the problems you identified in the need step of your speech.

You can increase the audience's sense of your sincerity by (1) opening yourself to correction and criticism (a calmly delivered, relevant response does more to defuse hecklers than does responding in kind), (2) talking directly and warmly with various audience clusters, (3) maintaining direct eye contact, and (4) modestly thanking anyone who has helped you understand and work on the issue.

Third, *heighten audience members' sense of our expertise, friendliness, and dynamism, especially when seeking to move them to action.* People will more likely follow your lead if they believe you know what you're talking about, have their best interests in mind, and are excited about your own proposal. Expertise can be demonstrated by (1) documenting your sources of information; (2) using a variety of sources as cross-checks on each other, especially sources that are recognized as authoritative by various segments; (3) presenting your information and need analyses in well-organized ways; (4) using clear, simple visual aids when they are appropriate or necessary; (5) providing adequate background information on controversial issues; (6) competently separating causes from effects, short-term from long-term effects, hard facts from wishes or dreams, and one proposal from others; and (7) delivering your speeches in a calm and forthright manner.

A sense of friendliness and concern for others can be created by doing the following:

1. Recognizing their human concerns and condition
2. Handling disagreements without personal animosity

3. Depersonalizing the issues
4. Offering solutions geared to the specific situations in which they live or work

An audience's sense of your dynamism can be enhanced by speaking vividly, drawing clear images of the events you describe; using sharp, fresh metaphors and active rather than passive verbs; and expressing your ideas with a short, hard-hitting oral style rather than a long, cumbersome written style and with varied conversational-vocal patterns, an animated body, direct eye contact rather than reliance on your notes, and a firm, upright stance.[7]

A public speaker's principal communicative virtue is the presence of a living, active human being behind the lectern—a person who embodies a message and whose own values are expressed in and through the message. People command more attention and interest than written words, and unlike films and videotapes, people can feel, react to audience members, and create a sense of urgency and directness. Hence, personal credibility is an extremely valuable asset for the persuader and actuator.

A public speaker's principal communicative virtue is the presence of a living, active human being behind the lectern.

Selecting Motivational Appeals That Reflect Listener Lifestyles

We come now to the third key to audience analysis for persuaders: needs and desires. Needs and desires, of course, are psychological constructs—perceptions people have of themselves, their plight in life, their fantasies, their nightmares. Insofar as these perceptions drive people to think and act in particular ways, they are usefully thought of as motive needs. A **motive need** is an impulse to satisfy a psychological-social want or a biological urge. Such needs may arise from physiological considerations—pain, lack of food, or surroundings that are too hot or cold—or they may come about for sociocultural reasons, such as when you feel left out of a group. If you feel the need deeply, your feelings may compel you to do something about your situation. You might eat, adjust the thermostat, or join a group—you're motivated.

Once you recognize the power of motive needs to propel human action, you may ask, "How can I identify and satisfy these needs in a speech? How can I use these basic needs, wants, and desires as the basis for effective public speaking?" The answer to both of these questions is "With the use of motivational appeals." A **motivational appeal** is either a visualization of a desire and a method for satisfying it or an assertion that an entity, idea, or course of action holds the key to fulfilling a particular motive need.

Speaking of . . . Skills

Persuading the Diverse Audience

As we noted in the opening to Chapter 4, one of the most difficult tasks a speaker faces is trying to convince a diversified audience to act together. How can you get racially diversified, bi-gendered, class-stratified audiences of young and old people to work in harmony?

The advice offered in that chapter bears repeating (and rereading if necessary):

- Recognize diversity even while calling for unity.
- Show that particular values are held in common even if they're operationalized differently by various groups of people.
- Encourage different paths to a goal they all can share.
- Exhort people to adjust some of their own lifestyle choices for the greater good of all.
- Assure people that they can maintain their self-identity even when working with people of different values, lifestyles, and cultures.

All of this is good advice, *but can you actually execute it? How?* Well, the bottom line is courage: the courage to recognize differences in explicit ways, to force people to confront and deal with their differences, and to make joint progress on problems caused by those very differences. If you are willing to tackle diversity problems in public speech, the following sorts of topics could be brought up:

1. *Gender differences:* Males as well as females should be talking about solutions to date rape.
2. *Racial differences:* Whites as well as blacks should be reading Malcolm X and Louis Farrahkan and using them as authorities in speeches.
3. *Age differences:* The young as well as the old should be challenging the existence of deplorable living conditions in state mental institutions.
4. *Class issues:* Rich as well as poor need to know how ghettoization has developed across Europe and the United States, examining both its positive and negative cultural effects.

Without the courage to bridge cultural gaps in public talk, we'll remain divided from each other, eternally suspicious and uninformed, silently perpetuating divisions, incapable of working across our cultural gaps when the situation demands it.

Some Common Motivational Appeals If you attempted to list the potential motivational appeals for every audience, you might never finish. The task is endless. Rather than trying to list each individual appeal, consider the general thrust of each motive cluster. A **motive cluster** is a group of individual appeals that are grounded in the same fundamental human motivation. Table 13.1 shows the three motive clusters—affiliation, achievement, and power—as well as some motivational appeals within each cluster.[8] **Affiliation motives** include the desire to belong to a group or to be well liked or accepted. This cluster also includes love, conformity, dependence on others, sympathy toward others, and loyalty. **Achievement motives** are related to the intrinsic or extrinsic desire for success, adventure, creativity, and

Web Exploration
To further analyze motive clusters go to
www.ablongman.com/
german15e

TABLE 13.1 *Motive Clusters*

Individual motivational appeals fall into clusters that share a common theme. Think of a current television advertisement and identify the motive clusters in it.		
Affiliation	**Achievement**	**Power**
Companionship	Acquisition/saving	Aggression
Conformity	Success/display	Authority/dominance
Deference/dependence	Prestige	Defense
Sympathy/generosity	Pride	Fear
Loyalty	Adventure/change	Autonomy/independence
Tradition	Perseverance	
Reverence/worship	Creativity	
Sexual attraction	Curiosity	
	Personal enjoyment	

personal enjoyment. **Power motives** concern primarily the desire to exert influence over others.

If you begin with this list, you'll be in a better position to choose the motivational appeals that have the greatest relevance to your topic and audience. Remember this guideline as you make your choices: *Motivational appeals work best when they are associated with the needs and desires of your listeners.* Analyze your audience, and then choose your motivation appeals on the basis of what you've learned about it.

The Affiliation Cluster.   Affiliation motives are dominated by a desire for acceptance or approval. They're more focused on the social or interpersonal bonds attributed to people than with personal success or power over others. A social desire to be part of a group is an affiliation motive. What follows are some examples of appeals to listeners' affiliation desires:

1. *Companionship and affiliation.* "A friend in need is a friend indeed." "Birds of a feather flock together." The fear of loneliness or separation from others is strong.
2. *Conformity.* "AARP—It's for People Like You." "To get along, you need to go along." We fear not only isolation, but also being too different from others.
3. *Deference/dependence.* "Nine out of ten doctors recommend . . . " "America's deepest thinking president, Abraham Lincoln, has said . . . " You can be made to feel dependent on either majority-rule or extraordinary individuals.
4. *Sympathy/generosity.* "You could be the parent this child has never known for a dollar a day." "Give that others might live," and "Contribute today to help us 'Take Back the Night.' "
5. *Loyalty.* "The camaraderie becomes something that you carry the rest of your life with those individuals. Sometimes you never get a chance to see those individuals again, but in your heart you know you'd do anything for them because they did that for you in a situation which could have gotten them killed."[9] That's how Vietnam vet Ron Mitscher described loyalty in combat conditions.
6. *Tradition.* "It is through our sacred rituals and ceremonies that we are known as a people." The call to collective celebration or worship is a strong affiliative appeal especially in times of crisis and stress.
7. *Reverence/worship.* "But in a larger sense we cannot dedicate, we cannot consecrate, we cannot hallow this ground. The brave men, living and dead, who struggled here, have consecrated it far above our power to add or detract."[10]
8. *Sexual attraction.* "Don't Be Such a Good Boy" (ad for the men's cologne Drakkar Noir). "Nothing gets between me and my Calvins" (ad for Calvin Klein jeans).

The Achievement Cluster.   Achievement motives are focused on individual urges, desires, and goals—an explicit concern for self and for personal excellence, prestige, and success. The following appeals to achievement motives are aimed at audience members as individuals:

1. *Acquisition/saving.* "Earn good money now in our new Checking-Plus accounts!" "Buy U.S. savings bonds where you work—invest in America!" Both of these are blatant appeals to personal accumulation of wealth, but the second makes the act seem more generous by tying it to patriotic motives (see "Tradition" above).

2. *Success/display.* "Hear the Radio That Woke Up an Entire Industry [Bose—Better Sound through Research]." "Successful executives carry the Connerton electronic organizer." These ads play off two kinds of success—corporate (a kind of appeal to majority opinion) and personal (it will make you stand out from the rest).

3. *Prestige.* "L'Oreal—Because You're Worth It!" "The U.S. Marines—Looking for a Few Good Men." Prestige appeals can be focused on either self-reward (L'Oreal) or exceptionalness (the Marines).

4. *Pride.* "Be Proud of America. Support the Troops" (Gulf War slogan). "Lose weight through our diet plan and feel great about your body." Motivational appeals to pride can center on the collective (here, one's country) or on individual characteristics (here, your body, so often a source of anxiety, not pride).

5. *Adventure/change.* "The Polo Sport Arena: A place to test yourself and your environment." "Join the Navy and See the World." Again, appeals to adventure can be personal or collective—but are always centered on self-aggrandizement.

6. *Perseverance.* "It's not the size of the dog in the fight but the size of the fight in the dog." "If at first you don't succeed, try, try again." We want to believe that continual effort will be rewarded, so this appeal can be strong.

7. *Creativity.* "Dare to be different: design your own major." Appeals to creativity are almost always appeals to an inborn talent that separates you in a good way from everyone else—strongly related to pride.

8. *Curiosity.* "Will the Internet bring an end to business computing as we know it?" asks the Microsoft Corporation in one of its ads designed to engage corporate executives. "Curiosity killed the cat; satisfaction brought him back," says conventional wisdom, suggesting that curiosity is dangerous but rewarding.

9. *Personal enjoyment.* "Let the good times roll!" There's often a hedonistic element to this appeal.

The Power Cluster.   All appeals in the power cluster focus on influence or control over others or the environment. All motives in this group feature appeals to one's place in the social hierarchy—a dominant place. People with power motives seek to manipulate or control others, but not all uses of power are negative. With power can (and should) come social responsibility, the demand that power be used in socially approved ways to benefit the group, community, and society. Appeals to power also depend heavily on appeals to affiliation, because power is most constructively used when people see it as being in their own best interest to grant it to others. So motivational appeals from the power cluster are often accompanied by appeals to affiliation. We won't illustrate that in the examples that follow, but you should think how to do it in your speeches.

1. *Aggression.* "We must fight for our rights—if we are to be heard, we dare not let others silence us." Here, the appeal to power is specifically turned into an affiliative "we."

2. *Authority/dominance.* "If the FDA [Food and Drug Administration] will not protect us, we must protect ourselves." "By the power invested in me, I now pronounce you man and wife." Authority for oneself arises from the need for a leader; institutional authority usually comes from an external source, whether divine as in the marriage ceremony or secular, as when the president of the United States begins, "As commander-in-chief, I . . . "

3. *Defense.* "We fight not for our own glory and prestige, but to protect ourselves from ruthless enemies." If one's aggressive actions are viewed as defensive rather than offensive, they're usually thought to be more ethically justified.

4. *Fear.* "Friends don't let friends drive drunk." Here, the appeal to the fear of neglecting one's social responsibility is strong. Use fear appeals cautiously (see the "Speaking of . . . Ethics: Using Fear Appeals" box).

5. *Autonomy/independence.* "Just do it." For a decade, Nike has played on your sense of independent, autonomous action to sell you shoes.

You might have noticed that some of the appeals we've just described seem to contradict each other. For example, fear seems to oppose adventure; sympathy and conformity seem to work against independence. Remember that human beings are changeable creatures, who at different times might pursue quite

Advertisers change motivational appeals when aiming at different segments of society.

different goals and thus who can be reached through many different kinds of verbalizations of their wants and desires. The clusters we've described aren't all-inclusive; but this discussion is enough to get you started in your work on persuasion.

Using Motivational Appeals   In practice, motivational appeals are seldom used alone; speakers usually combine them. Suppose you were selecting a mountain bike. What factors would influence your decision? One would be price (*saving*); a second certainly would be performance (*adventure*); another might be comfort and appearance (*personal enjoyment*); a fourth probably would be the reputation of the manufacturer (*prestige*) or its uniqueness (*independence*). These factors combined would add up to *pride* of ownership. Some of these influences, of course, would be stronger than others; some might conflict. But all of them probably would affect your choice. You would base your decision to buy the bike on the strongest of the appeals.

Because motivational appeals are interdependent, it's a good idea to coordinate them. You should select three or four appeals that are related and that target segments of your audience. When you work from cluster appeals, you tap multiple dimensions of your listeners' lives. Consider the following appeal to your classmates to join in a demonstration against a proposed tuition hike when the Board of Regents meets next month. Most students are very unhappy about tuition increases, yet most think nothing can be done about them. So can you reach them? You can try, perhaps through combining motivational appeals with visualization (see "Visualization" later in this chapter):

> Just think of what we can accomplish. If we all (*affiliation*) gather in front of the administration building, we can show the regents that this is a serious matter. We can show the regents that we're as much a part of the decision-making process as they are (*authority*) and that our individual voices (*independence*) deserve to be heard as much as theirs. When we present our petition to the president of the Board, even after he's tried to ignore us (*perseverance*), he'll see that we're committed and standing on principle, and he'll have to admit that we've got a right to be heard (*success/display*). There's no need to be afraid (*fear*) when you're among friends (*companionship*). It's a cause that's right (*pride*). On that day we'll demonstrate our solidarity (*loyalty*) and force the Board of Regents (*aggression*) to listen to our side of the story!

Notice the interweaving of affiliative and power motivational appeals, with even a couple of appeals to achievement (the prestige of independent action, success/display). Casting the appeals in a vision of success, the speaker hoped, would make them even more vivid and compelling to the listeners.

One final piece of general advice: Inconspicuous appeals work best. Avoid saying, "I want you to *imitate* Jones, the successful honors student" or "If you give to the Russian democracy fund, we'll print your name in the newspapers so that your *reputation* as a caring person will be known to everybody." People rarely admit, even to themselves, that they act on the basis of self-centered motivations—greed, imitation, personal pride, and fear. Be subtle when using these appeals. For example, you might encourage listeners to imitate the

Web Exploration

For examples of motivational appeals, go to

www.ablongman.com/ german15e

actions of well-known people by saying, "Habitat for Humanity counts among its volunteers the former president and first lady, Jimmy and Rosalynn Carter."

ORGANIZING PERSUASIVE SPEECHES: THE MOTIVATED SEQUENCE

Now it's time to think about organizing your appeals into a whole speech. As we've suggested, an important consideration in structuring appeals is your listeners' psychological tendencies—ways in which individuals' own motivations and circumstances favor certain ways of structuring ideas. You must learn to sequence supporting materials and motivational appeals to form a useful organizational pattern for speeches as a whole. Since 1935, the most popular such pattern has been called **Monroe's motivated sequence** (see Figure 13.1).[11] We will devote the rest of this chapter to it.

The motivated sequence ties problems and solutions to human motives. The motivated sequence for the presentation of verbal materials is composed of five basic steps:

1. *Attention.* Create interest and desire.
2. *Need.* Develop the problem by analyzing wrongs in the world and by relating them to the individual's interests, wants, or desires.
3. *Satisfaction.* Propose a plan of action that will alleviate the problem and satisfy the individual's interests, wants, or desires.
4. *Visualization.* Depict the world as it will look if the plan is put into action or if it's not.
5. *Action.* Call for personal commitments and deeds.

Structuring Actuative Speeches

The motivated sequence provides an ideal blueprint for urging an audience to take action. That's what it was designed for, since it was used originally as the basis for sales presentations. Let's look first at some ways in which you might use Monroe's sequence to structure actuating speeches.

Step 1: Getting Attention   You must wake up and engage your listeners at the very beginning of your speech if you hope to get them to move. Remember that startling statements, illustrations, questions, and other factors focus attention on your message. You can't persuade people without their attention.

Step 2: Showing the Need: Describing the Problem   Once you've captured the attention of your listeners, you're ready to explain why change is needed. To do this, you must show that a definite problem exists. You must point out, through facts and figures, just how bad the present situation is: "Last month our fund-raising drive to support the campus radio station fell $3,500 short of its goal. If we can't gain those dollars in this week's emergency drive, we'll have to

FIGURE 13.1 *The Motivated Sequence*
Notice how the audience should respond to each step of the motivated sequence.

Steps	Audience Response

1 Attention

Getting attention

I want to listen.

2 Need

Showing
the need:
describing the
problem

Something needs to be done.

3 Satisfaction

Satisfying
the need:
presenting the
solution

This is what to do to satisfy the need.

4 Visualization

Visualizing
the results

I can see myself enjoying
the benefits of such an action.

5 Action

Requesting
action or
approval

I will do this.

close down two work-study positions. That will not only make it difficult for those students to stay in school but also we'll have to shut down our Friday night live coverage of local music."

In its full form, a need or problem step has four parts:

1. *Statement.* Give a definite, concise statement of the problem.
2. *Illustration.* Give one or more examples explaining and clarifying the problem.
3. *Ramification.* Offer additional examples, statistical data, testimony, and other forms of support showing the extent and seriousness of the problem.
4. *Pointing.* Offer an explanation of how the problem directly affects the listener.

Statement and *pointing* should always be present, but the inclusion of *illustration* and *ramification* will depend on the amount of detail required to convince the audience. Whether you use the complete development or only part of it, the *need* step is critical in your speech. Here your subject is first tied to the needs and desires of your listeners.

Step 3: Satisfying the Need: Presenting the Solution   The solution or satisfaction step urges the adoption of a policy. Its goal is to get your listeners to agree that the program you propose is the correct one. Therefore, this step consists of presenting your proposed solution to the problem and proving that this solution is practical and desirable.

Five items are usually contained in a fully developed satisfaction step:

1. *Statement.* State the attitude, belief, or action you wish the audience to adopt. This is a statement of action: "We need to adopt an incentive system for our Littleton carburetor plant."

2. *Explanation.* Make sure that your proposal is understood. Visual aids such as charts and diagrams can be very useful here. In our example, you would define the incentive system: "By *incentive system,* I mean that workers at the Littleton plant should be paid by the actual number of carburetors completed rather than the hours worked."

3. *Theoretical demonstration.* Show how your proposed solution meets the need. For example, you could say, "Worker productivity will rise because workers are paid not just for putting in time but for completing carburetors."

4. *Reference to practical experience.* Supply examples to prove that the proposal has worked effectively where it has been tried. Facts, figures, and the testimony of experts support your contention: "Production at our New Albany plant increased by 42 percent after we instituted this compensation schedule."

5. *Meeting objections.* Forestall opposition by answering any objections that might be raised against the proposal. You might counter the objections of the labor union by arguing, "Increased plant productivity will allow us to expand the medical benefits for plant workers."

Just as certain phases can sometimes be omitted from the need step, one or more of these phases can be left out of the satisfaction step. Also, the foregoing order does not always have to be followed exactly. Occasionally, you can best meet objections by answering them as they arise. In other situations, the theoretical demonstration and reference to practical experience can be combined. If the satisfaction step is developed properly, at its conclusion the audience will say, "Yes, you're right; this is a practical and desirable solution to the problem you identified."

Step 4: Visualizing the Results   The function of the visualization step is to intensify desire. It should picture for the audience future conditions if your proposal is or is not adopted. In the visualization step, you ask your listeners to project themselves into the future. This projection can be accomplished in one of three ways: by the *positive method*, the *negative method,* or the *method of contrast.*

1. *The positive method.* Describe how conditions will improve under your proposal. Make such a description vivid and concrete. Select a situation that you are quite sure will arise. Then picture your listeners actually enjoying the conditions your proposal will produce. For example, if plant productivity allows better medical benefits, describe the advantages for everyone—lower deductibles, dental care, free eye examinations, and hospice services.

2. *The negative method.* Describe conditions as they will be in the future if your proposal is *not* carried out. Picture for your audience the evils that will arise from failure to follow your advice. Select the most undesirable conditions and show how they will be aggravated if your proposal is rejected. Describe plant employees being laid off, losing their pension plan, and experiencing the trauma of finding new jobs in a tight market.

3. *The method of contrast.* Combine the two preceding methods. Use the negative approach first and then use the positive approach. In this way, the benefits of the proposal are contrasted with the disadvantages of the present system. The following illustration shows how a speaker, urging an audience to get regular blood pressure checkups before problems are apparent, used visual contrasts:

> So what happens when you don't take that simple little step of getting your blood pressure checked regularly? You know what happens. Given how badly Americans eat, how little most of them exercise, and how tense the world of work becomes for too many of us, arteries begin a buildup of fatty deposits, openings narrow, blood flow becomes constricted, breathing becomes more difficult, and sooner or later—boom! You're on the ground in terrifying pain, hoping against hope that the person next to you can call 911 and knows some CPR well enough to sustain your life until professional help arrives.
>
> With proper and periodic blood pressure checks, however, you needn't face the prospect of open heart surgery. When Drs. Andrea Foote and John Erfurt established a worker health program, 92 percent of the hypertensive workers at four different industrial sites controlled their blood pressure. When the Hypertensive Education Program in Michigan and in Connecticut went into effect, insurance rates were cut in both states. Back in 1970, Savannah, Georgia, had the infamous title of "Stroke Capital of the World." But today, with fourteen permanent blood pressure reading stations and special clinics, its stroke rate's been cut in half. And,

of course, if you take advantage of the blood pressure monitoring program at Student Health or even at the Walgreen's drug store downtown, you'll be secure in the knowledge that you're not one of America's 11 million people who have high blood pressure and don't even know it.[12]

Whichever method you use—positive, negative, or contrast—remember that the visualization step must stand the test of reality. The conditions that you picture must be vivid and reflective of the world as listeners know it. Let your listeners actually see themselves enjoying the advantages or suffering the evils you describe. The more realistically you depict the situation, the more strongly your listeners will react.

Step 5: Requesting Action   The function of the action step is to call for explicit action. You can do this by offering a challenge or appeal, a special inducement, or a statement of personal intention. For examples, review the conclusions discussed in Chapter 8. Your request for action should be short and intense enough to set your listeners' resolve to act. Finish your speech firmly and sit down.

The motivated sequence is flexible. You can adapt it to various situations once you are familiar with its basic pattern. Like cooks who alter good recipes to their personal tastes, you can adjust the formula for particular occasions—changing the number of main points from section to section, sometimes omitting restatement from the attention step, sometimes omitting the positive or negative projections from the visualization step. *Like any recipe, the motivated sequence is designed to give you a formula that fits many different situations.* It gives you an excellent pattern but does not remove the human element; you still must think about your choices. Consider the choices made in the following outline of an actuative speech using the motivated sequence.

SAMPLE OUTLINE OF A PERSUASIVE SPEECH

To see how the motivated sequence can work for you, examine the following outline. Notice that the speaker is concerned with accurately reflecting the usual behavioral patterns of people living in retirement communities, making sure that listeners know he or she is a credible Internet user, and seeking motivational appeals that will get at least a significant segment of this group to try out computer-based distance learning.

You're Never Too Old to Learn—Virtually!

The Situation.   As a project for a community education class, you decide to work with the recreation and education center at a local elderly housing project. The center is woefully short of educational materials, and the only teachers who show up are offering crafts classes. You figure out that here's a group of less-mobile people who are ripe for Internet educational experiences.
Specific Purpose.   To persuade people attending the education center to take seriously Web-based classes from around the country.

Attention Step

I. It's too easy to assume that older adults only want to play checkers and make Christmas presents out of plastic milk jugs.

II. In fact, retirees haven't given up living and learning. They're still curious, and now they have time for a broad range of educational experiences.

Work against stereotypes of the elderly's lifestyles. Engage them and improve your credibility (trustworthiness).

Need Step

I. Cognitive psychology has shown us that exercising the brain keeps it alive and active longer.
   A. Mental activity—especially structured activity, such as formal learning—helps to prevent cognitive deterioration.
   B. Yet the elderly often have trouble traveling to three-times-a-week classes at a local college to get that stimulation.

II. Today's retirees are going to live longer than ever and so must keep learning to keep from falling significantly far behind the rest of society.

Work with power cluster motives (especially defense and fear) to make them want to hear more.

Satisfaction Step

I. The Internet and the growing number of high-quality World Wide Web–based classes—more than 500,000 now available online—create great opportunities for people living at this housing project.
   A. You have plenty of computer terminals with browsers.
   B. Because Internet courses often cost much less than bricks-and-mortar classes—most classes run $300–500—you can afford college-level schooling.
   C. You're chatters—good conversationalists—which is just what makes a good Web-based class into a rewarding experience.

II. I will spend this semester as a resource person and tutor for you.
   A. I'll provide technical help for any of you who're new to computer work.
   B. I'll help you surf the Internet to find a course that is to your liking.
   C. I'll be your tutor as well, even setting up some study groups for people who are studying similar kinds of things.

Tie your proposal to environmental elements in the center as well as to achievement motives (pride, success, adventure).

Visualization Step

I. Think of what you have available on the Internet.
   A. The California Virtual Campus has over 2000 courses available online.
   B. Indiana University will let you earn a bachelor's degree in General Studies electronically.
   C. The Rochester Institute of Technology has serious science and technology courses available to those of you who come out of technical backgrounds.
   D. The University of California at Berkeley lets you start courses anytime.
   E. Western Governors University will even give you credit for life experience.

II. While virtual connections with faculty and fellow students are not as good as face-to-face contact in most people's opinions, they can be very rewarding.
   A. Think of the pleasure you can have in chatting about Charles Dickens' *Oliver Twist* in an Introduction to Victorian Literature course offered by an urban Eastern university.

Blend appeals to achievement (prestige, creativity, curiosity, personal enjoyment) and to power (autonomy/ independence), using lifestyle characterizers sensitive to some of the usual interests of active elderly people.

B. Just consider what your life will be like when you can tune into a lecture by a professor working in Cairo while you stay home but are listening alongside a fellow classmate living in Tokyo.

C. Because you no longer have to worry about everything you learn being practical, you can take a course in World Politics from the New School for Social Research in New York, a basic course in midwifery from the University of Pennsylvania, and a course in drawing and design from the University of Washington.

Action Step

I. You all know the value of education; otherwise, you wouldn't have come to this meeting.

> Final appeals to self-achievement and the credibility of the speaker.

A. You all know the value of thinking and understanding and evaluating for your own enjoyment and mental health.

B. You all know that these computers would be doing a lot more good around here if they were being used more productively.

III. And you all know, I hope, that my commitment to your personal and collective development means that today's the day to sign up for the virtual ride of your lifetime down the Information Highway![13]

SAMPLE OUTLINE OF AN ACTUATIVE SPEECH

The motivated sequence works even better on actuative speeches because of the action step. Demands for action can be issued and defended very efficiently by using the motivated sequence. In fact, the desire to structure speeches that move people to action (e.g., to buy a product or engage in another specified behavior) was the impetus behind Alan Monroe's development of this organizational scheme. Read the outline here to get a clear sense of how the motivated sequence can be used in developing an actuative speech. Notice the adaptation of national statistics and information to the local situation in which students find themselves and the use of motivational appeals aimed particularly at a student population (service, yes, but also use of academic knowledge and ways of gaining academic credit while performing that service).

The Chain Never Stops

The Situation.   You are attending college at Buena Vista University in Storm Lake, Iowa. The town is home to a large meat-processing plant run by IBP (Iowa Beef Producers, Inc.). The plant has diversified the community, becoming home to a significant Hispanic population who were brought in to work the plant. Yet you know that wages are low in comparison to those at other U.S. industrial plants, and you know that meat-processing plants are notorious for accidents and lack of support for workers who have had accidents. You want your classmates to help do something about the problems you see.

Specific Purpose. To convince at least five classmates to join you in finding IBP workers who have suffered serious work-related injuries and in helping them get fair compensation for their injuries.

Attention Step

I. "In the beginning he had been fresh and strong, and he had gotten a job the first day; but now he was second-hand, a damaged article, so to speak, and they did not want him....They had worn him out, with their speeding-up and their carelessness, and now they had thrown him away!"
   A. These are words from Sinclair Lewis's 1906 novel *The Jungle.*
   B. Though written a 100 years ago, they still apply to the same place they were written about: slaughterhouses.

II. The meat-processing industry in the United States has grown into a wondrous mixture of industrial technology and human labor, yet Sinclair Lewis could have been writing about an Iowa Beef Processing, Inc., plant in South Dakota, Texas, or even Storm Lake, Iowa.
   A. I'm not singling out IBP or even the local plant.
   B. But I am saying that the meat-processing industry does not have a track record of care for labor that is enviable.
   C. It's the kind of record, as a matter of fact, that some of you might be willing to help correct.

III. Today, I want to review the safety and labor relations record of meat-packing plants and suggest some steps we can take toward bettering that record right here in Storm Lake, Iowa, as part of our education at Buena Vista University.

Need Step

I. First, you need to understand something about the history of meat processing in this country and the role of IBP in modernizing it.
   A. Begun as Iowa Beef Packers, Inc., in 1961, IBP revolutionized the meat-packing industry.
      1. It moved slaughterhouses out of the cities and into the countryside, nearer supplies, to save money.
      2. It automated the process through division of labor, meaning that it could use less-skilled workers who could be paid less than traditional, unionized butchers.
      3. It quit shipping carcasses to grocery outlets but instead packed in smaller, more specialized boxes that were vacuum-sealed and distributed directly to stores, which in turn did not need to hire such experienced meat cutters, saving still more money.
   B. The rest of the meat-processing industry could compete with IBP only by imitating its plant locations, meat-cutting processes, and distribution system—like IBP, economizing the production of consumable meat products that most of you enjoy at extraordinarily low cost.

II. Along with these great innovations, however, came other changes.
   A. While the top four meat packers in 1970 controlled just 21 percent of the beef market, today the top four—IBP, ConAgra, Excel, and National Beef—control about 85 percent of the market.
   B. Wages in the meat-packing industry fell by as much as 50 percent over the last 3 decades, making it one of the lowest-paying industrial jobs in the United States.

Use authoritative imagery to create a sad, even fearful illustration, followed by orienting statements about the meat industry.

Historical background, organized chronologically.

C. Lower wages were possible because new workers were recruited heavily from Mexico.
   1. A wage of $9.50 an hour is a great boon to a Mexican who was making $7.00 a day at home.
   2. The power of unions in the meat-packing industry could be broken when labor was afraid that bosses would send them back to Mexico.

III. All of these changes have adversely affected workers in the industry.

Detailing of current needs.

A. In 1999, more than one quarter of the 150,000 meat packers—40,000 workers—suffered a job-related industry or illness.
   1. Because the chain never stops—the chain on which meat carcasses are moving down the assembly line—up to 400 animals an hour must be processed by workers cutting meat a lightning speeds. (Twenty-five years ago, about 175 cattle went through per hour.)
   2. Workers are regularly cut, hit, hooked, caught in meat tenderizers, burned by beef tallow and other hot solutions, and even decapitated or killed by stun guns. *[Be very careful about how graphic you let your descriptions become.]*
B. Those who are hurt are encouraged to sign a waiver when they're treated, meaning that they give up their right to sue for damages in exchange for medical treatment.
   1. If workers want treatment by the company, they must sign the waiver.
   2. The waiver allows companies to get around the workmen's compensation laws in states like Texas, where a quarter of the U.S. beef supply is processed.
C. Workers who are seriously injured are encouraged to quit or are forced to take menial jobs that they find humiliating.
   1. If you quit, you lose health benefits and have to go on welfare.
   2. If you stay, you might get a job like Michael Grover did. IBP had him picking up dropped dirty towels and toilet paper from the restroom floor all day, every day.
D. Furthermore, some states are seeking to reduce workmen's compensation levels, being lobbied by politicians with connections to the meat processing industry.
   1. Texas Senator Phil Gramm's wife Wendy Lee sits on the board of IBP.
   2. Colorado state Senate Tom Norton, sponsor of a bill to limit compensation, has a wife Kathy who was vice president of ConAgra Red Meat the year he sponsored that bill.

Satisfaction Step

I. What can a class of college students in northern Iowa do about any of this?

Tie solutions to specific skills groups of students have, appealing especially to pride and creativity.

A. We can volunteer at the local meat cutters' union hall and the recreation center downtown, where most of the workers' families come for daytime crafts and activities.
   1. We don't want to go off half-cocked. We need information on injuries, their seriousness, their treatment, and workers' compensation from the company.
   2. We need to establish a level of trust with those families before helping them with work-related and injury- or health-related problems they have.
B. Those of you who are pre-law majors can get a little practice, reading up on Iowa's workmen's compensation laws and the conformity requirements for meat processors.
   1. You can't give advice until you know what you're talking about.
   2. Anyone who has taken "Introduction to Business Law" will be especially valuable as a resource.

C. Someone can get hooked up with ICAN—the Iowa Citizens Action Network—to check on the status of workmen's compensation law reform (proposed limitations) in Iowa.
D. Then, once you know the situation of workers here in Storm Lake and what you need to know about Iowa law more generally, you can become a family counselor.
  1. Working a few hours per week in the counseling desk we're setting up at the recreation center will be easy to work into your schedule.
  2. You even can earn research practicum credit in the Department of Communication, thereby helping yourself move toward graduation.

Visualization Step

I. If the meat-processing industry as a whole does not become more worker-conscious, horror stories will continue to pour out of gigantic plants across the country.
A. Kenny Dobbins's story about his life with Monfort Beef Company. *[Tell his story with good taste, including details about the falling ninety-pound box of meat, his blown disk and back surgery, chlorine inhalation, damaged rotator cuff, broken leg, shattered ankle, and innumerable lacerations.]*
B. Albertina Rios's story about her life with IBP in Lexington, Nebraska.
C. Rual Lopez's story about being hung on a chain and crushed in Greeley, Colorado, while working for ConAgra.

II. If the industry even just lets workers get compensated under the usual state laws, a great stride forward will have been taken.
A. Workers who have been injured will not be so easily fired.
B. They'll be able to go to arbitration for compensation in cases of debilitating injury.
C. And they'll be able to get proper financial help while recovering and state-mandated payments for nondebilitating yet bodily harm.

III. If unions are reinstituted in all meat-packing plants, negotiations for health care, treatment, time off, and necessary retirement will be carried on by the people who count: the local managers and their own labor force.

Action Step

I. "The chain never stops"—that's the cry of workers who kill, skin, clean, cut up, box, and finally ship the meat that appears on American tables every morning, noon, and evening.
A. If the chain doesn't stop, someone—many someones—are going to get hurt.
B. Those of us who enjoy the products of their labor—bacon, burgers, a nice steak—have a moral obligation, it seems to me, to make their life in service to us as good as we can.

II. Come join me tonight at 7:30 in Room 123 down the hall to talk about the kinds of help you can provide, given your interests and schedule.
A. I'll tell you how you can volunteer to meet with families.
B. I'll show you some research projects we need to pursue if you'd rather do that.
C. I'll give you a list of Buena Vista University instructors who will give you academic credit for your work of various kinds.

III. It's time for all of us—at least five of us if you'll join me—to make sure that Sinclair Lewis's *The Jungle* no longer reflects factory life in Storm Lake, Iowa, and all of the other packer towns of this country.[14]

Use personal anecdotes to make the needs more vivid, with mostly positive visualization.

Summarize, call for personal commitment and action.

Speaking of . . . Skills

Inoculating Audiences against Counterpersuasion

In this chapter, we've concentrated on the issue of persuading—increasing or otherwise changing people's acceptance of certain beliefs, attitudes, and values. We have not, however, focused on the ways in which you can increase your listeners' resistance to ideas that run counter to your own. Besides persuading them to accept your beliefs or attitudes, you also might need to protect them against counerpersuasion—attempts by others to influence your audience away from your position.

As in taking a vaccine to ward off a disease, you may inoculate your audience against your opponents' arguments. Studies by Michael Pfau and others of political advertising have found that voters who received previous messages that an opponent would attack the candidate and voters who also received additional refutative arguments against the purported attack were far more resistant to the opponent's message. This offers practical support for the view that forewarning an audience may be helpful. As Benoit's analysis of the research on inoculation has suggested, it does not appear to matter whether the type of forewarning—letting audience members know in advance they'll be exposed to a counterpersuasive attempt—is general, as in "an attack on me is imminent from my opponent" or more precise with respect to the topic and position to be taken by the attacker. Nor does it appear to matter whether the attack really is imminent or comes later.

Another strategy that increases resistance involves the amount of knowledge that people bring to a situation. For example, Hirt and Sherman found that individuals who have greater knowledge are more resistant to refutational arguments. Thus, you can increase potential resistance to messages that are contrary to your own by adding to the audience's knowledge about the issues involved.

For further reading: William L. Benoit, "Forewarning and Persuasion," *Forewarning and Persuasion: Advances through Meta-Analysis,* eds. Mike Allen and Roy W. Preiss (Dubuque, IA: Brown and Benchmark, 1994), 159–184. E. R. Hirt, and S. J. Sherman, "The Role of Prior Knowledge in Explaining Hypothetical Events," *Journal of Experimental Social Psychology,* 21 (1985): 591–643. Michael Pfau, "The Potential of Inoculation in Promoting Resistance to the Effectiveness of Comparative Advertising Messages," *Communication Quarterly,* 40 (1992): 26–44. Michael Pfau, and Michael Burgoon, "Inoculation in Political Communication," *Communication Monographs,* 15 (1988): 91–111.

ASSESSING YOUR PROGRESS

Chapter Summary

1. Speeches to persuade and actuate have psychological and behavioral changes as their primary goals.
2. As you prepare your speech to persuade or actuate, you should consider adapting to your listener's behavioral patterns, enhancing your credibility, and selecting effective motivational appeals.
3. Analysis of audience segments can provide speakers with motivational appeals to use in persuading listeners. PRIZM, a popular marketing technique, is one example of how information about people can be generated.

Speaking of . . . . Ethics

Using Fear Appeals

Common sense tells you that fear appeals are among the most potent appeals to audiences. After all, if you can make your audience feel afraid for the future if a problem is not resolved, your proposal will be just the antidote. Unfortunately, a comprehensive review of decades of research on fear appeals suggests that this common-sense notion is not that well grounded, as "existing explanations of the effects of fear arousing persuasive messages are inadequate."[15] We are not able to offer clear advice about whether the use of fear appeals to gain acceptance of a message outweighs any harms caused by frightening people—perhaps needlessly. The inability to offer such advice raises an ethical question about the use—and potential misuse—of fear appeals. Consider the following scenarios:

1. You give a speech on the increase of date rape on college campuses. To convince your audience that date rape is wrong and extremely common, you create scenarios that appeal to the fears of your listeners. Your scenarios are so vivid that several of your listeners, who are rape survivors, are visibly overcome with emotion. One of the listeners is so upset that she leaves the classroom during

your speech; everyone in the audience sees her leave.

2. You feel very strongly that the college president is wrong to continue investing college money in countries where torture and imprisonment without trial are legal. You present a very persuasive speech about your feelings. In your speech, you appeal to your audience's fears by suggesting that the college president actually is propagating torture and corrupting the values of U.S. citizens to the point that, someday, torture and imprisonment without trial might be legal in the United States. Your listeners become so incensed as a result of your speech that they march to the president's house and set his car on fire.

3. You're preparing to give a speech on hate crimes in the United States. You want to make sure you have your audience's attention before you begin, so you decide to present the details of a series of grisly murders committed in your town by a psychopath, even though these murders were not motivated by hate but by mental illness (and so are not examples of hate crimes).

4. Listeners are more likely to respond to your persuasive message if you are credible. You should demonstrate expertise, friendliness, and dynamism.
5. Motivational appeals visualize human desires and offer ways to satisfy those desires.
6. Commonly used motivational appeals can be grouped into three clusters: affiliation, achievement, and power.
7. Monroe's motivated sequence is an organizational pattern for actuative and persuasive speeches based on people's natural psychological tendencies.
8. The five steps in Monroe's motivated sequence are attention, need, satisfaction, visualization, and action. Each step can be developed by using appropriate rhetorical devices.

Key Terms

achievement motives (p. 249)
affiliation motives (p. 249)
Monroe's motivated
  sequence (p. 254)
motivational appeal (p. 248)

motive cluster (p. 249)
motive need (p. 248)
power motives (p. 249)
PRIZM (p. 243)

Assessment Activities

1. Do a PRIZM-type analysis of your class. Download a copy of the PRIZM questionnaire available from Claritas (see note 4). Reproduce the questionnaire, distribute it, and appoint a small committee to tabulate it (or ask your instructor to do it if your classmates don't want others seeing their individual questionnaires). Distribute the tabulation, and discuss the results as class. As you think about yourselves as an audience, can you find some specific clusters with three to five or more people in each of them? What are lifestyle characteristics or behavioral patterns that most centrally define each cluster? What are some of the important differences between clusters—differences that will require speakers on certain kinds of topics to adjust their motivational appeals? Take notes, and use the PRIZM analysis in planning your future speeches.
2. Develop and present to the class a five- to seven-minute speech. Follow the steps in the motivated sequence. As you construct your speech, remember the strategies discussed in this chapter. Adapt to the audience as you deem appropriate from your analysis of the different segments or clusters of people in your class.

Using the Web

1. Go to http://www.AdCritic.com, sign in, and find an ad to analyze. What motivational appeals make it go? How would you characterize the audience (demographically, by lifestyle) that it's aimed at? Does it work or not? Why or why not?
2. Look at http://usingyourspeechpower.com/motive_appeals_sol.shtml, and compare its list of motivational appeals with the one in this book. Using either or both lists, write down five that you think will work especially well in your classroom. Be ready to suggest what segment of your class is likely to respond well to which of those appeals. (Just don't embarrass anyone!)

 ### Using Video Workshop

Watch the speeches in Module 12, "Persuasive Speeches." As you watch, concentrate on how to identify effective persuasive techniques being used in speeches. Then answer Questions 1–12.

References

1. Information taken from Robert J. Samuelson, "It's Now Time for a Tax Cut," *Newsweek,* 15 January 2001, 25.

2. Michael J. Weiss, *The Clustering of America* (New York: Harper and Row, 1988), 2, quoted in Joseph Turow, *Breaking Up America: Advertisers and the New Media World* (Chicago: University of Chicago Pres, 1997), 45.

3. Robert D. Putnam, *Bowling Alone: The Collapse and Revival of American Community* (New York: Simon and Schuster, 2000). Turow (n. 3).

4. The PRIZM "neighborhood lifestyle segmentation" system was developed by Claritas Inc., a market research firm from San Diego, CA. It is built

around five-digit zip codes, which typically means 2,500–7,500 households per cluster. Those wanting—and willing to pay for—more precise breakdowns, say, by nine-digit zip codes, can get demographic/consumption data on groups as small as 6 to 12 households. See http://www.velocity.Caritas.com/YAYL/yawyfaq.wjsp#where. A full discussion of the uses to which such segmenting systems can be put socially, economically, and politically is available in Joseph Turow, *Breaking Up America: Advertisers and the New Media World* (Chicago: University of Chicago Press, 1997).

5. The information and quotations are taken from http://www.qmsoft.com/solutions/prizm.htm. The Claritas Website (see n. 4) provides more concrete data by zip code.

6. Robert B. Cialdini, *Influence: The Psychology of Persuasion* (New York: Quill, 1993), 205.

7. The most complete summary of credibility research is still found in Stephen Littlejohn, "A Bibliography of Studies Related to Variables of Source Credibility," *Bibliographical Annual in Speech Communication: 1971,* ed. Ned Shearer (Washington, DC: National Communication Association, 1972), 1–40.

8. The clusters that we're using are developed from the work of David McClelland. See Katharine Blick Hoyenga and Hemit T. Hoyenga, *Motivational Explanations of Behavior: Psychological and Cognitive Ideas* (Monterey, CA: Brooks/Cole Pub., 1984), ch. 1; Abigail J. Stewart, ed., *Motivation and Society: A Volume in Honor of David C. McClelland* (San Francisco: Jossey-Bass, 1982); and Janet T. Spence, ed., *Achievement and Achievement Motives* (San Francisco: W. H. Freeman, 1983).

9. From an interview with Ron Mitscher, Vietnam veteran, for *Parallels: The Soldiers' Knowledge and the Oral History of Contemporary Warfare,* edited by J. T. Hansen, A. Susan Owen, and Michael Patrick Madden (New York: Aldine de Gruyter, 1992), 137.

10. Abraham Lincoln, "Gettysburg Address," speech delivered in 1863, reprinted in *Lincoln at Gettysburg: The Words That Remade America,* edited by Garry Wills (New York: Simon and Schuster, 1992), 261.

11. To see how Alan Monroe originally conceived of the motivated sequence—as much, then, a psychological theory as an organizational pattern—see especially the Foreword to Alan H. Monroe, *Principles and Types of Speech* (Chicago: Scott, Foresman, 1935), vii–x.

12. These paragraphs draw their material from Todd Ames, "The Silent Killer," *Winning Orations.* His materials were used by special arrangement with Larry Schnoor, Director, Interstate Oratorical Association, Mankato, MN.

13. Information for this outline gathered from Eyal Press and Jennifer Washburn, "Digital Diplomas," *Mother Jones,* January–February 2001, 34–39, 82–85; and Jon Spayde, "College @ home," *Modern Maturity,* July–August 2001, 60–62, as well as Don Steinberg, "The Lowdown on Online: Everything You Need to Get Plugged In," 63.

14. Information from this outline taken from Eric Schlosser, "The Chain Never Stops," *Mother Jones.* July–August 2001, 38–47, 86–87; and http://www.ibpinc.com/index.htm and http://www.ibpinc.com/about/IBPNewHistory.stm.

15. Frank J. Boster and Paul Mongeau, "Fear-Arousing Persuasive Messages," *Communication Yearbook 8,* ed. Robert N. Bostrom (Thousand Oaks, CA: Sage, 1984), 371.

Chapter 14

Argumentation and Critical Thinking

THE ABILITY TO THINK CRITICALLY is central to your survival in our complex world. You're constantly bombarded with requests, appeals, and pleas to change your beliefs or behaviors. Sorting through all those appeals to determine which are justified and whether you should alter your thoughts or actions requires a cool head, not emotional responses. Before committing yourself, you've got to be able to analyze appeals, to determine if the reasons fit the claim being made. Skilled speakers, too, must be able not only to construct motivational appeals but also to work from facts to logical conclusions. You've got to use your head in reasonable ways, as Mario found out:

"Boy," said Mario, "I'm really bummed out. My best friend and I had a big fight last night. He yelled at me for not taking him seriously. I told him he was crazy for never eating meat. He got even angrier, and then I got scared and told him I'd think about vegetarianism if it would make him feel better, and then he got even more mad. It was a bad argument." "No, it wasn't," another friend Romano replied. "You had a fight, not an argument." "So what's the difference?" queried Mario. "A lot," said Romano. "Arguments depend on your head. Fights depend on your volume."

Mario needs to develop what's called a critical spirit—the ability to analyze others' ideas and requests.[1] *Criticism* is a process of careful assessment, and judgment of ideas. It's also a matter of supporting your evaluation with reasons. As you engage in evaluation—assessing reasons or offering counter-reasons—you become a critical thinker. You also employ critical skills when you advance a claim and then offer reasons why others ought to accept it. Finally, a critical spirit requires fair-mindedness, an important dimension of a person's credibility.[2] Both speakers and listeners need to cultivate the critical spirit.

Argumentation is a process of advancing claims supported by good reasons and allowing others to test those claims and reasons or to offer counterarguments. Through argumentation, people hope to come to reasonable conclusions about matters of fact, value, and policy. The act of arguing does not consist merely of offering an opinion or stating information and certainly not of screaming. An act of arguing is an act one step beyond the act of persuading by appealing to motives.

Different sorts of arguments appeal to different segments of your audience.

Both persuasion and argumentation seek to convince audiences. Persuasion works largely through emotion, while argumentation acts on reasoning. Argumentation commits you to communicating by using good reasons. Consider the differences between televised political spot advertisements for two candidates and a debate between those same candidates. Usually, an advertisement relies most heavily on appeals to listeners' emotions such as patriotism or outrage, while a debate requires candidates to develop reasons for their positions.

You probably engage in argument in many ways. In public forums such as city council meetings, you might provide reasons your community should preserve a marshland rather than allow condos to be built, or you might advocate better community regulation of local day care facilities. You might write a letter to the editor of a newspaper proposing a downtown pedestrian mall. In conversations with friends, you probably argue over sports teams and players. In each of these cases, you'll be more effective if your arguments are sound, with clearly identifiable reasons given for each claim you make. In this chapter, we'll examine the structure of arguments, then offer ways for you to critically evaluate the arguments of others. We'll finish with some tips to help you argue effectively.

RATIONAL THINKING AND TALKING: ARGUMENTATION

To tap the power of rational thought, you've got to learn how to construct an argument. An **argument** is built out of three essential elements that must work together: (a) the claim or proposition you are defending, (b) the relevant evidence that you provide in support of that claim, and (c) the reasoning pattern that you use to connect the evidence with the claim. (See Figure 14.1.)

Types of Claims

Most argumentative speeches assert that (a) something is or is not the case, (b) something is desirable or undesirable, or (c) something should or should not be done. Such judgments or assessments are the speaker's **claims** or propositions. Your first task as an arguer or listener is to determine the type of claim being argued.

Claims of Fact   A **claim of fact** asserts that something is or is not the case. If you're trying to convince listeners that "Using compact fluorescent lightbulbs will reduce your utilities cost significantly," you're presenting a factual claim asserting that a given state of affairs exists. When confronted with this sort of claim, two questions can occur to the critically aware listener:

1. *How can the truth or accuracy of the claim be measured?* If you're asked to determine someone's height, you immediately look for a yardstick or other measuring

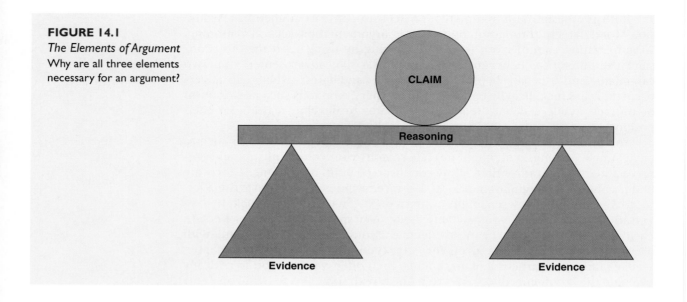

FIGURE 14.1
The Elements of Argument
Why are all three elements
necessary for an argument?

Companion Website

Web Exploration

To compare claims of fact with claims of value go to www.ablongman.com/german15e

tool. Similarly, listeners look for a standard by which to measure the accuracy of a factual claim. Before agreeing with your claim, the critical thinker asks what you mean by "reduce your utilities costs significantly." What percentage reduction in your electrical bill is being considered significant? Against what standard, precisely, is the accuracy of the claim to be judged? As a speaker, you need to build those judgments into your speeches.

2. *Do the facts of the situation fit the criteria?* Now then, to the replacement of lightbulbs: how many have to be replaced to achieve the utility bill reduction you're after? First, get listeners to agree to certain standards of judgment, and then present evidence that a given state of affairs meets those standards. In these ways, you work to gain the assent of listeners to your factual claims.

Claims of Value   When your claim asserts that something is good or bad, desirable or undesirable, justified or unjustified, you're advancing a **claim of value**—a claim about the intrinsic worth of the belief or action in question. Here, too, it is important to ask the following questions:

1. *By what standards is something to be judged?* For example, you can measure the quality of a college by the distinction of its faculty (intellectual value), the excellence of its building program (material value), the success of its graduates (practical value), the size of its endowment (monetary value), or the reputation that it enjoys according to surveys of education excellence (educational value).

2. *How well does the item in question measure up to the standards specified?* Suppose you were considering attending either Apple Valley Community College or State University. You can assess the worth of each institution by the standards you have identified—intellectual, material, practical, monetary or educational.

Your rating is not merely an assertion of personal preference ("I like Apple Valley Community College best.") but can be argued for on the basis of established standards.

Claims of Policy   A **claim of policy** recommends a course of action that you want the audience to approve. Typical examples are "State standards for welfare eligibility should be tightened" or "A test for English competency should be instituted as a graduation requirement." In both instances, you're asking your audience to endorse a proposed policy or course of action. Four questions are relevant to the judgments your listeners are being asked to make when analyzing a policy claim:

Web Exploration
To evaluate claims of policy, go to
www.ablongman.com/german15e

1. *Is there a need for such a policy or course of action?* If your listeners don't believe that a change is called for, they're not likely to approve your proposal. If, for example, students are already required to pass four English courses before graduation, is a test for English competency necessary?

2. *Is the proposal practical?* Can we afford the expense it would entail? Would it really solve the problem or remove the evil it is designed to correct? Does such a policy stand a reasonable chance of being adopted? If you can't show that your proposal meets these and similar tests, you can hardly expect it to be endorsed.

3. *Are the benefits your proposal will bring greater than its disadvantages?* People are reluctant to approve a proposal that promises to create conditions worse than the ones it is designed to correct. Burning a barn to the ground may be an effective way to get rid of rats, but it's hardly a desirable one. The benefits and disadvantages that will result from a plan of action must always be carefully weighed along with considerations of its basic workability. Would an English proficiency test, for example, be fair for international students?

4. *Is the proposal superior to the alternatives?* Listeners are hesitant to approve a policy if they have reason to believe that another course of action is more practical or more beneficial. A program of job training may be a better way to remove people from the welfare rolls than new qualifications tests.

Different types of claims make varying demands on you as an arguer. (See Table 14.1.) Further, arguers must tell audiences how to assess their claims. Articulating criteria or standards for judgment is essential for the person who tries to win an argument. If you think tuition waivers should be tied to financial need rather than academic performance, you must show your listeners why financial need is a better standard for waiving tuition.

Unless there are sound reasons for delay, you should announce your claim early in your speech. If listeners don't see where you're going in your argument, your strongest arguments may be lost on them. Take time to say something such as, "Today, I want to convince you that increases and decreases in student tuition should be coupled with the Consumer Price Index. If the Board of Regents takes this action, the cost of education will be more fairly distributed between the state and the students."[3]

TABLE 14.1 *Types of Claims*

Notice how each type of claim can be analyzed.		
Claim	**Description**	**Analysis**
Claim of fact	Assertion of truth or that something exists	1. By what criteria is the truth or accuracy of the claim measured? 2. Do the facts of the situation fit the criteria?
Claim of value	Assertion that something is good or bad; desirable or undesirable; justified or unjustified	1. By what standards is something to be judged? 2. How well does the thing measure up?
Claim of policy	Recommendation of a course of action	1. Is there a need for this policy or course of action? 2. Is the proposal practicable? 3. Are the benefits of the proposal greater than its disadvantages? 4. Is the proposal better than other courses of action?

Types of Evidence

As you discovered in Chapter 6, supporting materials clarify, amplify, and strengthen the ideas in your speech. They provide evidence for the acceptance of your central idea and its supporting points. Evidence is the base from which an argument builds. It can be presented in any of the forms of supporting materials with which you are already familiar: comparisons and contrasts, illustrations, examples, statistics, and testimony.

There's no single or easy rule for selecting relevant evidence. Supporting material that's relevant to one claim may be irrelevant to another, or it may provide logical proof but not compelling reasons for action. You should consider both the rational and the motivational characteristics of evidence as you select it: Is it reasonable? Is it convincing?

Rationally Relevant Evidence   The type of evidence you choose should reflect your claim. For example, if you're defending the claim that controls on the content of Internet chat rooms violate the First Amendment guarantee of freedom of speech, you'll probably choose testimony by noted authorities or definitions of terms to advance your claim. On the other hand, examples, illustrations, and statistics work better for showing that a problem exists or a change is needed. For example, if you argue that the speed limit in your state should be lowered by 10 miles per hour on interstate highways and have statistics indicating that lives will be saved, you'll be showing that there is a compelling reason for a change. The claim you present requires rationally relevant type of evidence. As you plan your arguments, you should ask yourself, "What type of evidence is logically relevant in support of my claim?"

Motivationally Relevant Evidence   If you hope to convince listeners to adopt your attitudes or actions, your claim must be supported by more than logically relevant evidence. You must get your listeners emotionally involved, as we saw in Chapter 13. That is, your evidence must be motivationally relevant to them. So you should ask two questions:

1. *What type of evidence will this audience demand?* If you want to argue that your city needs to build a new sewage plant, many people will demand that you demonstrate the problems with the present system, a financial plan that won't bankrupt the city, incentives that the new plant will provide for new jobs, and even a plan for laying the lines that won't paralyze neighborhoods. On the other hand, if you're reviewing a new video release for friends, an example from the plot, an analogy to other videos like this one, or an illustration of dialogue would be more forceful as proof than statistical word counts, box office receipts, or testimony from published movie critics. Careful audience analysis, as we discussed earlier, will help you determine what type of evidence is needed to move your particular group of listeners psychologically.

2. *What specific evidence will generate the best response?* You should pose this question once you've determined the type of evidence required by your argument. For example, if you've decided to use expert testimony to support your argument, whom should you quote? Or if you're using an illustration, should you use a factual example or develop one of your own? Will listeners be more moved by a personalized story or a general illustration?

To answer these and similar questions about your listeners, you need to analyze them. A homogeneous audience of townspeople may be suspicious of outsiders. They might react best to local experts or illustrations from the local community or common range of experience: the mayor, a reference to a particular neighborhood, or the town's experience in the flood of 1993. A heterogeneous audience of college students who do not share experience and background, on the other hand, will not know those local experts and probably will prefer geographically varied examples. Such an audience will probably respond better to a nationally known expert and references to well-known communities across the country. You should consider your listeners' demographic or psychological characteristics to choose the most effective evidence for them.

Forms of Reasoning

Reasoning or inference is a process of connecting something that is known or believed (evidence) to a concept or idea (claim) that you wish others to accept. **Patterns of reasoning** are habitual ways in which a culture or society uses inferences to connect what is accepted to what it is being urged to accept. There are five generally accepted reasoning patterns: from examples, from generalization or axiom, from sign, from parallel case, and from causal relation.

Often called inductive reasoning, **reasoning from examples** involves examining a series of examples of known occurrences (evidence) and drawing a

Both constructive and
refutational arguments are
usually necessary for victory.

general conclusion (claim). The inference of this reasoning pattern is "What is true of particular cases is true of the whole class." This inference represents a kind of mental inductive leap from specifics to generalities. For example, the National Cancer Institute has studied hundreds of individual case histories and discovered that people with high-fiber diets are less prone to develop cancers of the digestive tract. With an inductive leap, the Institute then moved to the factual claim "High-fiber diets help control certain types of cancer." Commuters use a similar pattern of reasoning every time they drive during rush hour. After trial and error, they decide that a residential street is the best route to take home before 5:30 P.M. and the expressway after 5:30 P.M. In other words, after experiencing enough instances, they arrive at a generalization and act on it.

Reasoning from generalization (sometimes called deduction) means applying a general truth to a specific situation. It is essentially the reverse of reasoning from examples or induction. In high school consumer education class, you might have learned that buying goods in large quantities saves money (the generalization). Now you might shop at discount stores because they purchase goods in quantity, thereby saving money and passing those savings on to you (the claim deduced from the evidence). Or you might believe that getting a college education is the key to a better future (the generalization). Therefore, if you get a college degree, you will get a better job (claim). This inference gathers power because of experience (you learned it through observation) or by definition (one of the characteristics of education is self-improvement). You ultimately accept this inference because of the uniformities you believe exist in the world.

Reasoning from sign uses an observable mark, or sign, as proof of the existence of a state of affairs. You reason from sign when you notice the tickle in your throat (the evidence) and decide that you're getting a cold (the claim). The tickle in your throat doesn't cause the condition; rather, it's a sign of the virus that does cause it. Detectives are experts at reasoning from sign. When they discover that a particular suspect had motive, means, and opportunity (the signs), they make the claim that he or she might be the murderer. Your doctor works the same way every time he or she examines your respiration and heart rhythms for signs of ailments. Reasoning from sign works well with natural occurrences (ice on the pond is always a sign that the temperature has been below 32°F). However, reasoning from sign can be troublesome in the world of human beings (as when some people take body weight as a sign of laziness or skin color as a sign of dishonesty). Signs, of course, are circumstantial evidence—and could be wrong. Just ask detectives and doctors. Yet we often must use signs as indicators; otherwise, we couldn't project our economy, predict our weather, or forecast the success of political candidates.

Another common reasoning pattern, **reasoning from parallel case,** involves thinking solely in terms of similar things and events. You probably designed your first homecoming float by looking at others; they served as models of what people expect of homecoming floats in your area. Those floats functioned as evidence; the claim was that you should make a similar mark of pride and identification. The inference that linked the evidence and the claim was probably something such as, "What was acceptable as a homecoming float last year will be acceptable/expected this year." Your instructors might use parallel reasoning every time they tell you, "Study hard for this exam. The last exam was difficult; this one will be, too." Obviously this is not a generalization, since every exam will probably not be exactly the same. However, your instructors are asserting that the upcoming examinations and past examinations are similar cases—they have enough features in common to increase the likelihood that careful study habits will benefit you.

Finally, **reasoning from cause** is an important vehicle for reaching conclusions. The underlying assumption of causal reasoning is that events occur in a predictable, routine manner, with causes that account for occurrences. Reasoning from cause involves associating events that come before with events that follow (see Table 14.2). When substance abuse appears to be increasing across the country, people scramble to identify causes: the existence of international drug cartels, corrupt foreign governments, organized crime inside our own borders, lower moral standards, the breakup of the nuclear family, and lax school discipline. What the arguer must do is assert causes that might reasonably be expected to produce the effects—to point to material connections between, for

TABLE 14.2 *Kinds of Reasoning*

Try to think of additional examples of each kind of reasoning.		
Reasoning	**Description**	**Examples**
Reasoning from examples (inductive reasoning)	Drawing a general conclusion from instances or examples	I enjoy the music of Bach, Beethoven, and Brahms. I like classical music.
Reasoning from generalization or axiom (deductive reasoning)	Applying a general conclusion to a specific example	Irish Setters are friendly dogs. I think I'll get an Irish Setter puppy for my niece.
Reasoning from sign	Using an observable mark or symptom as proof of a state of affairs	The petunias are all dead. Someone forgot to water them.
Reasoning from parallel case	Asserting that two things or events share similar characteristics or patterns	North Korea is developing nuclear technology; South Korea won't be far behind.
Reasoning from causal relation.	Concluding that an event that occurs first is responsible for a later event	The engine won't start because the carburetor is flooded with gasoline.

example, foreign governments' actual policies and the presence of drugs in Los Angeles or other American cities. Overall, the inference in causal reasoning is simple and constant: Every effect has a cause.

EVALUATING ARGUMENTS

The reasoning process is the fulcrum on which argument pivots. You must test reasoning in order to protect yourself, both as a speaker and as a critical listener, from embarrassment when you're arguing and from faulty decisions when you're listening to others. For each kind of reasoning, there are special tests or questions that help you determine the soundness of arguments. Consider the following questions as you construct arguments and evaluate those of others:

Reasoning from Examples

1. *Have you looked at enough instances to warrant generalizing?* If you live in Idaho, you don't assume that spring has arrived after experiencing one warm day in February.

2. *Are the instances fairly chosen?* You certainly hope that a teacher doesn't judge your speech skills by listening only to your first speech, when you were

confused and nervous. You want to be judged only after being observed in several speaking situations.

3. *Are there important exceptions to the generalization or claim that must be considered?* While presidential elections show that, generally, "As Maine goes, so goes the nation," there have been enough exceptions to this rule to keep presidential candidates who lose in Maine campaigning hard.

Reasoning from Generalization

1. *Is the generalization true?* Women are more emotional than men; woolly caterpillars come out when winter's about to arrive; private universities provide better education than public universities. Each of these statements is a generalization. You need to determine whether sufficient evidence exists to support the truth of the statement.

2. *Does the generalization apply to this particular case?* Usually, discount stores have lower prices, but if a small neighborhood store has a sale, it might offer better prices than a discount house. While the old saying "Birds of a feather flock together" certainly applies to birds, it might not apply to human beings.

Reasoning from Sign

1. *Is the sign fallible?* As we've noted, many signs are merely circumstantial. Be extremely careful not to confuse reasoning from sign with causal reasoning. If sign reasoning were infallible, the weather forecaster would never be wrong.

2. *Is the observation accurate?* Some of us see what we want to see, not what's there; children see ghosts at night, and jealous lovers can interpret each other's acts in erroneous ways. Be sure that the observation is reliable.

Reasoning from Parallel Case

1. *Are there more similarities than differences between the two cases?* College A and College B may have many features in common—size, location, programs, and so on—yet they probably also have many different features, perhaps in the subgroups that make up their populations, the backgrounds of their faculty, and their historical development. Too many differences between two cases rationally destroy the parallel.

2. *Are the similarities you have pointed out the relevant and important ones?* There are two children in your neighborhood who are the same age, go to the same school, and wear the same kinds of clothes; are you therefore able to assume that one is well-behaved simply because the other is? Probably not, because more relevant similarities than their clothing and age would include their home lives,

their relationships with siblings, and so forth. Comparisons must be based on relevant and important similarities.

Reasoning from Cause

1. *Can you separate causes and effects?* We often have a difficult time doing this. Does stress lead to a propensity to drink too much, or does excessive alcohol consumption lead to stress? Does a strained home life make a child misbehave, or is it the other way around?

2. *Are the causes strong enough to have produced the effect?* Did George Bush's appearance on *Oprah* really win the 2000 election for him, or was that an insufficient cause? There probably were much stronger and more important causes.

3. *Did intervening events or persons prevent a cause from having its normal effect?* If a gun is not loaded, you can't shoot anything, no matter how hard you pull the trigger. Even if Iraq cuts off the United States' oil supply, prices may not go up if enough oil's been stockpiled, if other producers offer competitive rates, or if U.S. consumer gas consumption drops.

4. *Could any other cause have produced the effect?* Although crime often increases when neighborhoods deteriorate, increased crime rates can be caused by any number of other changes—alterations in definitions of crime, increased reporting of crimes that have been going on for years, or closings of major industries. We rationally must sort through all of the possible causes before championing one.

The heart of critical thinking is idea testing. You must learn to use what you have available—the evidence others have presented, your own experience, your wits, and sometimes a trip to the library when the decision's particularly important—to test the rationality and force of others' arguments.

Speaking of . . . Skills

Evaluating Arguments

Undoubtedly you'll participate in disputes or arguments many times as an advocate or a bystander. Often, you'll have to determine if your arguments or those of others were effective. Here are four questions you can ask to help discover the effectiveness of an argument:

1. *What was its effect?* Did the argument convince people to vote? to boycott? to donate canned goods? Clearly, if your argument results in a desired response, it was effective.

However, this is only one way of judging the effectiveness of arguments. You must also ask the next three questions.

2. *Was the argument valid?* Did the arguer follow a logical order of development? Did he or she use supporting materials to prove the points? Were those supporting materials relevant to the claim advanced? If the argument was sound, it can be judged valid.

3. *Was the argument truthful?* Did it meet the test of reality? If an argument doesn't correspond to the way things really are, then it fails the truthfulness test.

4. *Was the argument ethical?* Did it advocate what is morally good? Did the arguer use ethical means to achieve results? This is an especially important test in this age of ethical malaise.

SAMPLE OUTLINE FOR AN ARGUMENTATIVE SPEECH

The Dangers of Chewing Tobacco[4]

Introduction

I. When he was 12 years old, Ricky Bender tried his first plug of chewing tobacco. After all, he was a Little Leaguer and all his heroes in the major leagues chewed tobacco. Fourteen years later, Ricky found out he had oral cancer. The cancer cost him most of his tongue, half of his jaw, and the use of his right arm.

The speaker uses motivationally relevant evidence to gain attention.

II. Little Ricky Bender's case isn't an isolated one. Every day children like little Ricky Bender start using "spit tobacco." It's estimated that 10 percent of teenage males are regular users.

The growing scope of the problem is explained with rationally relevant evidence.

III. It's important that we recognize the dangers of this addictive drug because health problems related to its use are rising dramatically in this country.

Listeners' motivation to listen is developed.

IV. Let's examine the addictive nature of spit tobacco, the health problems it causes, and the myths that surround it.

The speech structure is previewed.

Body

I. The addictive nature of spit tobacco.
   A. Spit tobacco is leaf tobacco that comes in two forms:
      1. Chewing tobacco comes in a pouch in a coarsely shredded form.
      2. More finely shredded snuff is packaged in a tin and is sometimes flavored.
      3. Both forms are put between the cheek and the gum. Nicotine is absorbed through the tissues of the mouth.

   The uses of spit tobacco are explained.

   B. Nicotine dependency results from the use of spit tobacco.
      1. Studies reveal that nicotine blood levels for smokers and spit tobacco users are identical.
      2. Psychological dependency on tobacco results in both users.

   Reasoning from parallel case establishes the similarities between cigarette and spit tobacco use.

3. The only difference between the two forms is that nicotine enters the bloodstream more slowly when it is absorbed through the skin.

II. The health problems caused by spit tobacco.
   A. Dental problems are rampant among spit tobacco users.

Causal reasoning is supported with statistical evidence.

   1. Habitual users injure the linings of their mouths where the tobacco is held.
      a. The first signs of deterioration are halitosis or bad breath and tooth discoloration.
      b. Then teeth begin to decay and gingivitis sets in.
      c. Finally, users begin to lose their teeth prematurely.
   2. Statistics reveal the toll spit tobacco takes on dental health.
   B. The risk of oral cancer increases.

Causal reasoning links nitrosamines to oral cancer.

   1. Nitrosamines, known carcinogenic agents, are formed when spit tobacco is manufactured.
   2. These carcinogens enter the user's bloodstream along with nicotine.
      a. The risk of oral cancer is four to six times higher than for nonusers.
      b. The risk of oral cancer is higher than for cigarette and pipe smokers.
      c. There is also a risk from the expelled tobacco when it comes into contact with skin.

Nicotine is identified as a cause of heart disease.

   C. Heart disease increases with the use of spit tobacco.
   1. Systemic problems result from spit tobacco use.
      a. Within minutes, nicotine causes blood pressure to increase.
      b. The heart is required to pump harder, increasing the heart rate.
   2. The strain on the cardiovascular system over a period of time leads to coronary problems and heart disease.

III. The myths surrounding spit tobacco.

Reasoning from generalization applies overall rates of cancer to spit tobacco users.

   A. It's often called "smokeless tobacco," fostering the perception that it is less harmful than smoking.
   1. The fact is that spit tobacco is just as likely to cause cancer as cigarette smoking.
      a. Oral cancer rates are higher among spit tobacco users.
      b. Other cancers exceed the rates of nonusers.
   2. Heart disease is another result of using spit tobacco.

Reasoning from sign uses advertising and peer pressure to explain spit tobacco use among teenagers.

   B. Some people argue that there is less pressure among teens to use spit tobacco. The opposite is true, peer pressure spirals during the adolescent years.
   1. Companies spend millions of dollars advertising spit tobacco at sponsored rodeos, NASCAR, and other popular events.
   2. Potential users frequent these events.
   3. Studies reveal that peer pressure induced by pervasive advertising is the chief reason for the initial use of spit tobacco.

Conclusion

I. Remember little Ricky Bender? What started as an innocent attempt to emulate his major league heroes cost him most of his face and threatened to take his life.

Return to introductory example reaches closure by reminding listeners of motivationally relevant example.

II. The threat to young people, especially teenaged males, is on an upward spiral.

Listeners are warned about the lethal nature of spit tobacco.

III. It's important for us to recognize that spit tobacco is addictive—not only that, it kills.

DETECTING FALLACIES IN REASONING

Your primary job as a critical listener and arguer is to evaluate the claims, evidence, and reasoning of others. On one level, you're looking for ways that the ideas and reasoning of others are important to your own thinking; and, on another level, you're examining the logical soundness of others' thinking. A **fallacy** is a flaw in the rational properties of an argument or inference. There are many different fallacies. Let's look at eight common ones.

1. *Hasty generalization.* A **hasty generalization** is a claim made on the basis of too little evidence. You should ask, "Has the arguer really examined enough typical cases to make a claim?" If the answer is no, then a flaw in reasoning has occurred. Urging a ban on ibuprofen because some people have had liver problems with it and the closure of a pedestrian mall because of an armed robbery are examples of hasty generalization.

2. *Genetic fallacy.* A **genetic fallacy** occurs when someone assumes that the only "true" understanding of some idea, practice, or event is to be found in its origins—in its "genes," literally or metaphorically. People sometimes assume that if an idea has been around for a long time, it must be true. Many people who defended slavery in the nineteenth century referred to the biblical practices of slavery to support their claim. Studies of origins can help us understand a concept, but they're hardly proof of present correctness or justice.

3. *Appeal to ignorance.* People sometimes appeal to ignorance by arguing with double negatives: "You can't prove it won't work!" They may even attack an idea because information about it is incomplete. "We can't cure all varieties of AIDS so let's just stop therapies until we learn more." Both of these illogical claims **appeal to ignorance** because they depend on what we don't know. Sometimes we must simply act on the basis of the knowledge we have, despite the gaps in it. In countering such claims, you can cite parallel cases and examples. So you might say,

> OK, so we don't have all of the answers to the AIDS puzzle. That doesn't mean we don't work with what we know. Consider the case of tuberculosis. The vaccines against it weren't developed until the 1950s, and yet thousands of lives were saved earlier in the century because TB sanitariums used the physical and pharmacological regimens they had available. Of course, they couldn't save everyone, but they relieved suffering and even prevented the deaths of many with the partial knowledge they had. Give HIV-positive people the same chance—to use what we have now even while we're waiting for the miracle cure.

4. *Bandwagon fallacy.* A frequent strategy is to appeal to popular opinion or to urge people to jump on the bandwagon. The **bandwagon fallacy** assumes that if everyone else is doing something, you should, too: "African Americans don't belong to the Republican Party!" or "But Dad, everyone else is going!" While these appeals may be useful in stating valuative claims, they're not the basis for factual claims. The world has witnessed hundreds of widely believed but

Web Exploration

To practice identifying different types of fallacies, go to

www.ablongman.com/german15e

Speaking of . . . Ethics

Name-Calling

Arguments often threaten to degenerate into fights, not always physical clawing and punching, but certainly into symbolic assaults: attacks on an opponent's intelligence, parentage (or lack thereof), associations, motives, or appearance. Is that ethical? Where do you draw the line?

1. You're having a class argument about ways to control hate speech. You know that your opponent is gay. Do you reveal that information in the debate?

2. Both Michael Dukakis in 1988 and Bill Clinton in 1992 were accused by the National Conservative Political Action Committee of being "card-carrying members of the American Civil Liberties Union." Is that a relevant issue in presidential politics?

3. "Well, you're over thirty, so how would you understand?" "You're a girl, so of course. . . ." "Now, you're black, and so I'd expect you to. . . ." "When you lived in the ghetto, didn't you . . . ?" Is it ethical to make statements like these when arguing with someone?

Name-calling—*argumentum ad hominem* (arguments to the person)—has been used since Homer wrote *The Iliad.* But is it ethical? Anytime? Sometimes? When?

---

false ideas, from the belief that night air causes tuberculosis to panic over an invasion by Martians.

5. *Sequential fallacy.* Often present in arguments based on evidence from causal relations, the **sequential fallacy** arises from the assumption that if one event follows another, the first event must cause the second. Thunder and lightning do not cause rain, although the phenomena often occur sequentially. Even if you usually catch colds in the spring, the two occurrences are not causally related. The season of the year does not cause your cold—a virus does.

6. *Begging the question.* **Begging the question** is rephrasing an idea and then offering it as its own reason. This kind of reasoning is circular thought. If someone asserts, "Abortion is murder because it is taking the life of the unborn," he or she has committed a fallacy by rephrasing the claim (it is murder) to constitute the reason (it is taking life). Sometimes questions can be fallacious, such as "Have you quit smoking on weekends?" The claim, phrased as a question, assumes that you smoke during the week. Whatever your answer to the question, therefore, you're guilty. Claims of value are especially prone to begging the question.

7. *Appeal to authority.* **Appeal to authority** occurs when someone who is popular but not an expert urges the acceptance of an idea or a product. Television advertisers frequently ask consumers to purchase products because movie stars or sports heroes endorse them. Michael Jordan promotes everything from underwear to telephone services. The familiar figure provides name recognition

but not expertise. You can detect this fallacy by asking, "Is he or she an expert on this topic?"

8. *Name-calling.* **Name-calling** is the general label for attacks on people instead of on their arguments. Name-calling may take the form of an attack on the special interests of a person: "Of course, you're voting for O'Casey, you're Irish." Or it may be an attack on a personal characteristic rather than on ideas: "You're just a dweeb (or nerd or retrograde male)." Even dweebs, nerds, and retrograde males sometimes offer solid claims. Claims ought to be judged on their own features, preferably their objective features, not on the characteristics of the person who makes them.

These are some of the fallacies that creep into argumentation. A good basic logic book can point out additional fallacies.[5] Armed with knowledge of such fallacies, you should be able to protect yourself against unscrupulous demagogues, sales personnel, and advertisers. The Latin phrase *Caveat emptor*—"let the buyer beware"—should be a part of your thinking as an audience member. You share with speakers the responsibility of cultivating the sort of critical spirit discussed in the opening of this chapter.

TIPS FOR DEVELOPING ARGUMENTATIVE SPEECHES

As you get ready to pull all of your claims, kinds of evidence, and reasoning patterns together into coherent argumentative speeches, consider the following pieces of advice:

1. *Place your strongest arguments first or last.* This strategy takes advantage of the **primacy-recency effects.** Arguments presented first set the agenda for what is to follow, and a strong opening argument often impresses an audience with its power, thereby heightening the credibility of the arguer (the primacy effect). We also know that listeners tend to retain the most recently presented idea (the recency effect), so you might put your strongest argument at the end of your speech so that listeners will remember your best shot.[6] Decide which position will best help you with the particular audience you face, and then place your best argument there (but then, of course, summarize all of the arguments in your conclusion).

2. *Vary your evidence.* Different listeners are likely to prefer different kinds of evidence, and most listeners want supporting materials that are both logically relevant and psychologically motivating. For example, if you're arguing that more Americans must invest in solar power units for their home electrical needs, general statistics on energy savings and average reduction in costs of utilities are good, but a good, clear illustration with details on what it's like to live in a solar-assisted environment will more likely clinch the argument.

3. *Avoid personal attacks on opponents.* Maintain arguments on an appropriate intellectual level. This tactic enhances your credibility. If you can argue well without becoming vicious, you'll earn the respect—and perhaps the agreement—of your listeners; most know that the more someone screams, the weaker his or her arguments are. Hold your opponent accountable for arguments and reasoning, yes, but without name-calling and smear tactics (see "Speaking of . . . Ethics: Name-Calling").

4. *Know the potential arguments of your opponents.* The best advocates know their opponents' arguments as well as their opponents do; they have thought about those arguments and ways of responding to them ahead of time. Having thought through opposing positions early allows you to prepare a response and feel confident about your own position. Notice how presidential candidates are able to anticipate each other's positions in their debates.

5. *Practice constructing logical arguments and detecting fallacious ones.* Ultimately, successful argument demands skill in performing the techniques of public reasoning. You need to practice routinely constructing arguments with solid relationships between and among claims, evidence, and reasoning patterns; and you need to practice regularly detecting the fallacies in other people's proposals. Critically examine product advertisements, political claims, and arguments that your neighbors make in order to improve your communication skills—as both a sender and a receiver of argumentative messages.

Speaking of . . . Skills

Responding to Counterarguments

Constructing an argument is often not enough. You might have to respond to the objections of others who oppose your ideas. Here are some suggestions for developing an effective response:

1. Listen and take notes. You need to understand your opponent's position before you can refute it.
2. Decide whether to answer the objection. Many times, people just want to vent frustration or be heard by others. Their comments may not be relevant to your argument.
3. Organize your response. Here's a four-step process to help:
   Restate your opponent's claim. "Mary said learning a foreign language is useless."
   Explain your objection to it. "I think learning a foreign language can be beneficial in your career and in your personal life."
   Offer evidence to support your position. "Studies show that . . . "
   Indicate the significance of your rebuttal. "If you want faster career advancement and more satisfying international travel experiences, take a foreign language."
4. Keep the exchange on an intellectual level. Name-calling or emotionally charged ranting harms your credibility.

ASSESSING YOUR PROGRESS

Chapter Summary

1. Argumentation is a process of advancing propositions or claims supported by good reasons.
2. Criticism is a process of careful assessment, evaluation, and judgment of ideas and motives.
3. Arguments are built from three elements: the claim, the evidence, and the reasoning pattern.
4. The types of claims common to arguments are claims of fact, claims of value, and claims of policy.
5. Evidence for arguments can be chosen to reflect the rational quality of the claim (rationally relevant evidence) or to stimulate audience involvement (motivationally relevant evidence).
6. Five forms of reasoning connect evidence and claims: reasoning from examples, reasoning from generalization, reasoning from sign, reasoning from parallel case, and reasoning from cause.
7. A fallacy is a flaw in the rational properties of an argument or inference.
8. Common fallacies are hasty generalization, genetic fallacy, appeal to ignorance, bandwagon fallacy, sequential fallacy, begging the question, appeal to authority, and name-calling.
9. In developing argumentative speeches, (a) organize your arguments by putting the strongest first or last, (b) vary the evidence, (c) avoid personal attacks on opponents, (d) know the potential arguments of your opponents, and (e) practice constructing logical arguments and detecting fallacious ones.

Key Terms

appeal to authority (p. 284)
appeal to ignorance (p. 283)
argument (p. 271)
argumentation (p. 270)
bandwagon fallacy (p. 283)
begging the question (p. 284)
claims (p. 271)
claim of fact (p. 271)
claim of policy (p. 273)
claim of value (p. 272)
fallacy (p. 283)
genetic fallacy (p. 283)

hasty generalization (p. 283)
name-calling (p. 285)
patterns of reasoning (p. 275)
primacy-recency effects (p. 285)
reasoning (p. 275)
reasoning from cause (p. 277)
reasoning from examples (p. 275)
reasoning from generalization (p. 276)
reasoning from parallel case (p. 277)
reasoning from sign (p. 277)
sequential fallacy (p. 284)

Assessment Activities

1. Choose a controversial topic, and phrase it as a question of policy, such as "Should the federal government privatize Social Security?" or "Should all

18-year-olds be required to complete two years of military or domestic service?" As a class, think of arguments for and against the policy. Then determine what rationally and motivationally relevant evidence would be required to develop each argument.

2. Fallacies are often present in assertions made by advertisers. Think of as many assertions made in current television and print advertisements as you can. Choose a member of the class to list them on the chalkboard and then assess the claims. What kinds of fallacies can you detect? Explain why the reasoning in the advertisement is flawed.

Using the Web

1. Individuals and organizations often post their views on the Internet. Locate a Web page that develops an argument. Assess the argument. Is the claim clearly stated? Is supporting material provided to substantiate the claim? Is the supporting material rationally or motivationally relevant? What reasoning patterns are present in the argument? Are they logical?

2. Many argumentative exchanges are available through the Internet. Among other sites, the home page for the White House is a good place to locate practical uses of argument.

Using VideoWorkshop

Watch the speeches in Module 11, "Informative Speeches." As you watch, take note of the strategies speakers use to motivate and interest their audiences. Then answer Questions 1–10.

References

1. Harvey Siegel, *Educating Reason: Rationality, Critical Thinking, and Education* (New York: Routledge, 1988), 1–47. The importance of critical thinking has been underscored in two national reports on higher education: The National Institute of Education, *Involvement in Learning: Realizing the Potential of American Higher Education,* 1984; and the Association of American Colleges, *Integrity in the College Curriculum: A Report to the Academic Community,* 1985. For a summary of research on critical thinking in the college setting, see James H. McMillan, "Enhancing College Students' Critical Thinking: A Review of Studies," *Research in Higher Education,* 26 (1987): 3–29.

2. Fairness or fair-mindedness is one dimension of a primary factor underlying positive source credibility, trustworthiness. See James B. Stiff, *Persuasive Communication* (New York: Guilford Press, 1994), esp. 90–92.

3. A full discussion of the logical grounding of claims in evidence and reasoning is presented in the classic book on argumentation: Douglas Ehninger and Wayne Brockriede, *Decision by Debate,* 2nd ed. (New York: Harper and Row, 1978).

4. Information for this sample outline was drawn from the Johns Hopkins Health Information Website (http://www.intelihealth.com/IH/ihtlH) and Marjike

Rowland, "Man Without a Face to Talk on Dangers of Chewing Tobacco," *Modesto Bee* (2 February 1999).

5. See lrving M. Copi and Keith Cohen, *Informal Logic,* 10th ed. (Englewood Cliffs, NJ: Prentice Hall, 1998); and Frans H. VanEemeren and Rob Grooten-dorst, *Argumentation, Communication, and Fallacies* (Hillsdale, NJ: Lawrence Erlbaum Associates, 1992).

6. The debate over primacy-recency effects continues. For the position that primacy and recency are equally potent, see Stephen W. Littlejohn and David M. Jabusch, *Persuasive Transactions* (Glenview, IL: Scott, Foresman, 1987), 235–236; for the arguments championing the primacy position, see Robert E. Denton, Jr., *Persuasion and Influence in American Life* (Prospect Heights, IL: Waveland Press, 1988), 299–300.

Chapter 15

Speaking at Community- and Group-Centered Events

MUCH HAS BEEN MADE throughout this book about public speaking as both grounded in and governed by cultural understandings of public behavior. There are culturally based understandings at work in every society governing the ways in which people talk and listen publicly. Those understandings also form expectations. People come to expect speakers to talk, move, and even think in ways that are comprehensible and acceptable in the circumstances they find themselves. To be sure, speakers ought not to cave in to the temptation of simply saying what everyone wants or expects them to say. When that happens, public speakers are abandoning the service element of public talk; if you bring audiences nothing new, different, or useful, you're wasting their time.

Some situations—often called **special occasions**—do, however, call for speeches that are particularly sensitive to community or group needs and expectations. Such special occasions have a ritualistic air to them. Members of societies learn that there are generally acceptable—almost required—ways to speak at funerals, weddings, Veterans' Day ceremonies, academic conferences, or breakfasts honoring community leaders. A **community** is a group of people who think of themselves as bonded together—whether by blood, locale, nationality, race, occupation, gender, or other shared experiences or attributes. The phrase *who think of themselves* is the key here. Communities are bonded by shared characteristics or commitments, and those shared characteristics and commitments, often, are recognized—celebrated, probed, redefined—on "special occasions."

In this chapter, we will review some of the special occasions upon which various communities explore those characteristics or common beliefs that bind them together. Often, that exploration occurs through the examination of exemplary members of the community or even the introduction of someone new to the community. At other times, it occurs through the humorous exploration of the group's beliefs or actions; humor can be a gentle but effective way to offer criticism of groups. Not only do groups explore their communities generally and particularly, however. They also seek to bring new knowledge to their members, through public discussions of issues or ideas, through problem-solving interactions, or through panel presentations at meetings such as conventions or monthly assemblies.

We will divide our discussion of such special occasions into two parts. **Community-based special occasion speeches** occur at times set aside to honor community membership or members themselves. We'll look in particular at speeches of introduction, speeches of courtesy (welcomes, responses, acceptances, toasts), and speeches to entertain (because the humorous exploration of group beliefs or attitudes often becomes the basis for changing member behavior). **Group-based special occasion speeches** are given at gatherings where groups want to learn more, solve problems, or explore each other's understandings. So, under this heading we'll examine group discussions, team presentations, and responding to questions and objections as some of the usual ways of getting group work done publicly.

COMMUNITY-BASED SPECIAL OCCASION SPEECHES

Let's now look at three types of special occasion talk: speeches of introduction, speeches of courtesy, and speeches to entertain. How do we live out *E pluribus unum* (Out of many, one)?

Speeches of Introduction

Speeches of introduction are usually given by members of the group that will hear the speech. They're designed to prepare the community (the audience) to accept the featured speaker and his or her message. In a way, a speech of introduction asks permission for an outsider to speak. The decision to grant that permission is based on what the nonmember can contribute to the group: the group must *want* to hear the outsider before the featured speaker can be successful. Or if the speaker is a member of the group, the introduction may serve as a reminder of his or her role and accomplishments within the community or organization.

Purpose   If you're invited to give a speech of introduction, remember that your main objective is to create in others a desire to hear the speaker you're introducing. Everything else should be subordinate to this aim. Don't bore your audience with a long recital of the speaker's biography or with a series of anecdotes about your acquaintance with the person. Above all, don't air your own views on the subject of the speaker's message. You're only the speaker's advance agent; your job is to sell that person to the audience. Your goals should be (1) to arouse curiosity about the speaker and the subject in the minds of the listeners so that it will be easy to capture their attention and (2) to motivate the audience to like and respect the speaker so they'll tend to respond favorably to the forthcoming information or proposal.

Formulating the Content   Usually, the better-known or more respected a speaker is, the shorter your introduction needs to be; the less well-known the person is, the more you'll need to arouse interest in the speaker's subject and to build up the person's prestige. When presenting a speech of introduction, do the following:

1. *Be brief.* To say too much is often worse than to say nothing at all. For example, if you were to introduce the president, you might simply say, "Ladies and gentlemen, the president of the United States." The prestige of the person you introduce won't always be great enough for you to be so brief, but it's always better to say too little than to speak too long.

2. *Talk about the speaker.* Anticipate the audience's questions: "Who are you? What's your position in business, education, sports, or government? What experiences have you had that qualify you to speak on the announced subject?" Build up speakers' identities, tell what they know or have done, but do not praise their abilities as speakers. Let them demonstrate their own skills.

3. *Emphasize the importance of the speaker's subject.* For example, in introducing a speaker who'll talk about the oil industry, you might say, "In one way or another, the oil industry is in the news every day—Middle East concerns, the ups and downs of the cost of heating oil, gasohol research, tanker spills, our energy needs for the twenty-first century. To help us make sense of the industry and the ways it impacts our daily lives, today's speaker. . . ."

4. *Stress the appropriateness of the subject or the speaker.* If your town is considering a program to rebuild its Main Street area, a speech by a city planner is likely to be timely and appreciated. References to relevant aspects of a speaker's background or the topic can tie speaker and speech to the audience's interests.

5. *Use humor if it suits the occasion.* Nothing puts an audience at ease better than laughter. Take care, however, that the humor is in good taste and doesn't

negatively affect the speaker's credibility. The best stories are usually those shared by the introducer and speaker and told to illustrate a positive character trait of the speaker.

SAMPLE INTRODUCTION

The four primary virtues of a speech of introduction are tact, brevity, sincerity, and enthusiasm. These virtues are illustrated in the following introduction.

Introducing a Classmate   *Randolf Brown*

A popular sport in the student union cafeteria is reading through lists of ingredients in prepared foods and candies, especially the chemical additives. One of the best players of this sport I've seen is our next speaker, Angela Vangelisti. Angela is amazing. Even with products like coffee whitener, which contains only one or two things I've even heard of, Angela can identify most of the emulsifiers, stabilizers, and flavor enhancers that make up fake food./1

While identifying chemical food additives passes the time in the cafeteria, there's also a serious side to the game. As Angela knows, there's a difference between blue dye nos. 1 and 2, and between good old yellow no. 5 and yellow no. 6; the cancer risk varies from one to the other. For example, the red dye no. 3 that you'll find in maraschino cherries is related to thyroid tumors. These are some of the reasons I was gratified to learn that Angela would share some of her technical knowledge as a nutrition major in a speech entitled, "How to Read Labels and Live Longer."/2

Speeches of Courtesy: Welcomes, Responses, Acceptances, and Toasts

Speeches of courtesy explicitly acknowledge the presence or qualities of the audience or of a member of the audience. When you extend a welcome to a political candidate who's visiting your class or when you accept an award, for example, you are giving speeches of courtesy.

Typical Situations   Speeches of courtesy fulfill social obligations such as welcoming visitors, responding to welcomes or greetings, accepting awards from groups, and toasting individuals with short speeches recognizing achievements.

Welcoming Visitors.   When guests or visiting groups are present, someone extends a public greeting to them. For example, your basketball announcer might greet the opposing team or a fraternity chapter president might greet the representative from the national office who's visiting your campus. The speech of welcome is a way of introducing strangers into a group or organization, giving them group approval, and making them feel more comfortable.

Responding to a Welcome or Greeting.   Responses are ways for outsiders to recognize their status as visitors and to express appreciation for acceptance by the group or organization. Thus, the representative from the national office who's visiting a fraternity might respond to a greeting, in turn, by thanking the group for its welcome or by recognizing its importance and accomplishments.

Accepting Awards.   An individual who has received an award usually acknowledges the honor. Sometimes the award is made to an organization rather than to an individual, in which case someone is selected to respond for the group. In all cases, the acceptance of awards via a speech is a way of thanking the group and acknowledging the importance of the activity being recognized; for example, people who receive Academy Awards (if they do more than blubber) thank the American Academy of Motion Picture Arts and Sciences for the Oscar and often recognize the importance of making serious films on significant subjects.

Offering Toasts.   While toasts offered to bridegrooms or others can become silly, the act of toasting is usually an important ritual. Toasts are acts of tribute: through them, a group recognizes the achievements of an individual and expresses the hope that the person will continue to achieve distinction. After negotiations, heads of state usually toast each other's positive personal qualities, accomplishments, and desire for future good relations. Ceremonially, toasts can unite fragmented peoples.

Purpose   The speech of courtesy has a double purpose. The speaker not only expresses a sentiment of gratitude or hospitality, but also tries to create an aura of good feeling in the audience. Usually, the success of such a speech depends on satisfying the listeners that the appropriate thing has been said.

Formulating the Content   The scope and content of a speech of courtesy should by guided by the following principles:

1. *Indicate for whom you're speaking.* When you act on behalf of a group, make clear that the greeting or acknowledgment comes from everyone and not from you alone.

2. *Present complimentary facts about the person or persons to whom you are extending the courtesy.* Review the accomplishments or qualities of the person or group you're greeting or whose gift or welcome you're acknowledging.

3. *Illustrate; don't argue.* Present incidents and facts that make clear the importance of the occasions, but don't be contentious. Avoid areas of disagreement. Don't use a speech for courtesy as an opportunity to air your own views on controversial subjects or to advance your own policies. Express concretely and vividly the thoughts that are already in the minds of your listeners.

These virtues are illustrated in William Faulkner's "On Accepting the Nobel Prize for Literature," reprinted in Chapter 9, page 170. Faulkner clearly indicates he's speaking *as* a writer *to* future writers. He honors those young writers by taking their compositional problems seriously; his own difficulties as a writer, which come out in a flood of metaphors and images that make up the bulk of his speech, stand not as arguments but as illustrations of the struggle he finds at the core of all good writing.

Speeches of courtesy are more than merely polite talk. The courtesies extended in welcoming someone into your midst or in thanking someone for work done are statements of your group's rules for living—its guiding principles. In extending courtesies to others, you're acknowledging the culture you share with them.

What follows is a short toast offered to a retiring professor by those attending a spring dinner in his honor. Notice its conciseness, the qualities of the person that form the basis for the tribute, and the use of illustrations (the honoree's values) not only to celebrate the person, but also to suggest to those assembled the nature of the community standards for accomplishment.

A Toast to Leo Brecker

As we prepare to leave the dinner table, I'd like to offer a toast to the man we honor this evening—retiring Professor Leo Brecker./1

Leo, you've been a part of this university for 50 years: as an undergraduate student before and after World War II; as a graduate student; and as a professor of speech education, broadcasting, and mass communication. Your life is indistinguishable from the life of this university. You embody the values everyone else reaches for. You constantly pose what you call the "interesting questions" that are the essence of the scholar's life. You often say that no matter how crazy our students are, they're still the reason we come to work every day. You remind us weekly that we are not only *in* the world but are *of* the world; just as the world gives us the opportunity to study and teach, so do we owe it not only our thanks but our attention and good works./2

In living out the values that justify the very existence of the state university, Leo, you've been the flesh-and-blood example of all that is good in higher education. For that, I toast you—your vision, your daily life, and your ideals that will guide our future. In you, Professor Brecker, we see the best that we can be. I toast you in the hope that the best is indeed yet to come for all of us./3

Speeches to Entertain

Speeches to entertain present special challenges to speakers. As you may recall, in Chapter 2, we identified the speech to entertain as one of the three types embodying an independent general purpose. Discounting slapstick of the slipping-on-a-banana-peel type, most humor depends primarily on a listener's sensitivities to the routines and morals of his or her own society. This is obvious if you've ever listened to someone tell jokes from a foreign country. Often, humor cannot be translated, in part because of language differences (puns, for example, don't translate well) and, in larger measure, because of cultural differences.

Purpose   Like most humor in general, speeches to entertain usually work within the cultural frameworks of a particular group or society. Such speeches may be "merely funny," as in comic monologues, but most are serious in their force or demand on audiences. After-dinner speeches, for example, are usually more than dessert; their topics are normally relevant to the group at hand, and the anecdotes they contain usually are offered to make a point. That point may be as simple as deflecting an audience's antipathy toward the speaker or making the people in the audience feel more like a group, or it may be as serious as offering a critique of society.

Speakers seeking to deflect an audience's antipathy often use humor to ingratiate themselves. For example, Henry W. Grady, editor of the *Atlanta Constitution*, expected a good deal of distrust and hostility when he journeyed to New York City in 1886 to tell the New England Society about "The New South." He opened the speech not only by thanking the society for the invitation, but also by telling stories about farmers, husbands and wives, and preachers. He praised Abraham Lincoln, a northerner, as "the first typical American" of the new age; told another humorous story about shopkeepers and their advertising; poked fun at the great Union General Sherman—"who is considered an able man in our hearts, though some people think he is a kind of careless man about fire"; and assured his audience that a New South, one very much like the old North, was arising from the ashes.[1] Through the use of humor, Henry Grady had his audience cheering every point he made about the New South that evening.

Group cohesiveness can also be created through humor. Especially when campaigning, politicians spend much time telling humorous stories about their opponents, hitting them with stinging remarks. In part, of course, biting political humor detracts from the opposition candidates and party; however, such humor also can make one's own party feel more cohesive. For example, Democrats collected Richard Nixon's 1972 bumper stickers that said, "Nixon Now," cut off the *w*, and put them on their own autos. Democrats did endless turns on the names Bush and Quayle in 1988. Similarly, Republicans poked fun at Michael Dukakis, laughing at a picture of him awkwardly driving a tank. Such zingers allow political party members to laugh at their opponents and to celebrate their membership in the "better" party.

Finally, speeches to entertain can be used not merely to poke fun at outsiders and to celebrate membership but even to critique one's society. Humor can be used to urge general changes and reform of social practices.

Formulating the Content   When arranging materials for speeches to entertain, develop a series of illustrations, short quotations or quips, and stories, each following another in fairly rapid succession. Most important, make sure that each touches on a central theme or point. An entertaining speech must be more than a comic monologue; it must be cohesive and pointed. The following sequence works well for speeches to entertain:

1. Relate a story or anecdote, present an illustration, or quote an appropriate passage.
2. State the main idea or point of view implied by your opening.
3. Follow with a series of additional stories, anecdotes, quips, or illustrations that amplify or illuminate your central idea; arrange those supporting materials so they're thematically connected.
4. Close with restatement of the central point you have developed; as in Step 1, you can use a quotation or one final story that clinches and epitomizes your speech as a whole.

SAMPLE SPEECH TO ENTERTAIN

By organizing your speech materials in the pattern just suggested, you'll not only provide your listeners with entertainment but help them remember your central idea. The speech that follows illustrates the four steps.

A Case for Optimism[2] *Douglas Martini*

Most of you probably have heard some version of this poem:

> Twixt the optimist and pessimist
> The difference is droll:
> The optimist sees the doughnut,
> The pessimist, the hole.

The longer I live, the more I'm convinced of the truth of that poem. Like a doughnut, life may seem full, rich, and enjoyable, or it can seem as empty as that hole in the middle. To the pessimist, the optimist seems foolish. But I'm here today to tell you it's the pessimist who's the foolish one./1

Another way of seeing the difference between an optimist and a pessimist is this way: An optimist looks at an oyster and expects a pearl; a pessimist looks at an oyster and expects ptomaine poisoning. Even if the pessimist is right—which is not very often—he probably won't enjoy himself either before or after he proves it. But the optimist is happy because he always has that expectation of a future reward./2

Pessimists are easy to recognize. They're the ones who go around asking, "What's good about it?" when someone says, "Good morning." If they looked around, they undoubtedly could find *something* good, as did the storekeeper after she was robbed. The day after the robbery she was asked about the loss. "Lose much?" her friend wanted to know. "Some," she said, "but then it would have been worse if the robbers had got in the night before. You see, yesterday I just finished marking everything down 20 percent."/3

There's another story about a happy-go-lucky shoemaker who left the gas heater in his shop turned on overnight, and on arriving in the morning he struck a match to light it. There was a terrific explosion, and the shoemaker was blown out through the door to the middle of the street. A passerby rushed to help and asked if he were injured. The shoemaker got up slowly, jiggled his arms and legs, looked back at the burning shop, and said, "No, I'm not hurt, but I sure got out just in time, didn't I?"/4

Some writers have ridiculed this kind of outlook. The great French writer Voltaire made fun of optimism in *Candide*. "Optimism," he said, "is a mania for maintaining that all is well when things are going badly." A later writer, James Branch Cabell, did a turn on one of Voltaire's phrases when he quipped, "The optimist proclaims that we live in the best of all possible worlds; the pessimist fears this is true."/5

A lot of college professors, too, can't resist the urge to jab a little at optimists. But I, for one, refuse to take them seriously. I like the remark made by literary critic and journalist Keith Preston: "There's as much bunk among the busters as among the boosters."/6

Some may like the cynicism of Voltaire or *Doonesbury* cartoonist Gary Trudeau. But optimism is the philosophy I like to hear preached. There was a grandmother who complained about the weather. "But, Melissa," said her friend, "awful weather is better than no weather at all." So quit complaining. Change the bad things in the world that you can, to be sure, but then work within the rest. And stop expecting the worst. Be the optimist who cleans his glasses *before* he eats his grapefruit!/7

When you're tempted to grumble about your rotten future, remember the doughnut. And, as Elbert Hubbard advised:

As you travel through life, brother,
Whatever be your goal,
Keep your eye upon the doughnut
And not upon the hole.

GROUP-BASED SPECIAL OCCASION SPEECHES

There are many public speaking situations in which you'll be participating in a different role—as part of a group rather than as a single speaker addressing an audience. As a team member, you might present proposals to your employer, you might join a group filing a grievance against a city council, or you might be asked to justify your actions as part of an executive committee.

As a member of a group, you will participate in the discussion of ideas; you may also address an audience as a representative of the group. In either case, your role as a speaker will be changed by your relationship to others in your group. You will need to understand the functions of public group communication. To help you in this role, we will examine the responsibilities of participants in group discussions, panels, and symposia; provide guidelines for developing a discussion plan; and suggest ways to respond to audiences' questions and objections.

Group Discussions

Business people and professionals depend heavily on oral communication for their success. Businesses and professional organizations rely on committees, task forces, and more informal groups to formulate ideas, evaluate courses of action, and put proposals into effect. These exchanges are generally termed group discussions. A **group discussion** is a communication transaction in which a small group of people exchanges and evaluates ideas and information in order to solve a problem. Usually group discussions involve four to six people. As many as twelve people can join the discussion, but as the number of participants increases, the efficiency of the group normally declines.

There can be many different goals for small groups—amateurs gather to discuss art, literature, or coin collecting, for example. Book clubs, genealogical societies, and religious instruction classes function to educate their members. While these are important goals, we will focus on decision-making discussions.

In **decision-making discussions,** participants seek agreement on what the group should believe or do. These groups may also discuss ways of implementing their decisions. In discussions of this kind, participants examine conflicting facts and values, evaluate differences of opinion, and explore proposed courses of action for their practicality. The goal is to arrive at a consensus. A neighborhood homeowners' association might gather to evaluate a local sewer improvement project. A city council might plan for rezoning to control future growth. A subcommittee of a business can discuss how to expand markets. Once decisions are made, these groups might explore ways to implement their plans.

Responsibilities of Participants When you participate in group communication, the most important requirement is that you be knowledgeable about the subject at hand. If you know what you're talking about, you're better prepared to contribute to the group process. For example, before you attend a discussion on locating a minimum-security prison in your neighborhood, you need to research the issue. You should find out how other neighborhoods have been affected by minimum-security prisons. You should investigate what measures will be taken to ensure the safety of neighborhood residents. You also will need to know what economic, environmental, and social impacts such a facility will have in your neighborhood. This information will help you contribute to the discussion.

It's equally important for you to practice good listening behavior as the discussion progresses. Unless you listen to what's going on, you'll forget what's already been said or lose track of the direction in which the group is moving. As a result, you might make redundant or irrelevant comments, require the restatement of points already settled, or misunderstand the positions taken by other participants. In any case, you won't be adding to the progress of the discussion. If you've seen a recent TV talk show, you've probably seen exactly how frustrated and angry people can become when they are ignored or misunderstood. Many times, this frustration can be prevented if everyone listens carefully to the discussion.

You also should be aware of the dynamics of the group and its members. To the extent that you can acquaint yourself with group members' values and interests, you'll be able to judge more accurately the importance of their remarks. You'll also be able to determine the role you must play to make the group discussion profitable. If group members want to chat about the party last weekend instead of tackling the task at hand, you can remind them of the group's purpose; or if the atmosphere becomes tense or members show antagonism, you can relieve the strain by reminding everyone that the whole group will benefit from consensus or by redirecting the discussion until tempers have cooled.

The key to successful group communication experiences is interdependence. Even though discussions are sometimes competitive or hostile, they are ultimately a cooperative activity. You share with others; they share with you. Your ideas are deflected, reshaped, or accepted by others. In the end, they belong to everybody in the group. All group members leave parts of themselves in the final outcome. You are changed, even if just a little, by having worked as part of a team. When group members promote a sense of interdependence, the result is positive and productive.

Responsibilities of Leaders   Effective group leadership requires at least three basic talents. First, the leader of the group must keep the discussion moving. To do this, a leader should call attention to basic issues, remind members of what's on the floor, note common elements in diverse points of view, and strip controversial matters of their unnecessary complexity. It is important for a discussion leader periodically to summarize the results of the discussion. When the group has reached consensus, the leader might say, "Before we move on, let me summarize what I think we've decided." Such restatements will ensure that group members are in agreement and will reinforce the group decision for everyone.

Second, a discussion leader must be impartial. The leader needs to ensure that unpopular viewpoints are allowed expression. The leader must make sure that participants phrase questions and comments in neutral terms. Through the example of the leader, a spirit of cooperation and conciliation will be promoted among participants who may disagree. The leader may ask for opinions from individuals who have not yet contributed to the discussion or may remind the group there are several different interpretations of an idea.

Third and finally, a discussion leader should encourage active participation. At the beginning of a discussion, the leader may be required to present background information to frame the issues. If individuals are hesitant to state their opinions, the leader may stimulate them to participate by asking questions such as "Mary, do you agree with John's position?" or "John, will you give us reasons to consider your viewpoint?" A leader whose manner conveys confidence in participants may encourage group members who have ideas to contribute.

Developing a Discussion Plan   A carefully developed discussion plan will prevent wasted time and effort. Ideally, the entire group will cooperate in determining the discussion plan, but sometimes a leader must take the responsibility for formulating it. The plan can be used in most situations or modified to meet special needs.

Decision-making discussions characteristically raise claims of policy: "What voice should students have in decision making in our department?" "How can our company meet competition from foreign imports?" "What should be done to control the escalating violence among American teenagers?" Answering such questions of policy requires answering secondary questions of fact and value.

The five steps in the following plan for decision-making discussions are adapted from John Dewey's analysis of reflective thinking.[3] This plan is one of several possible ways of deciding on a course of action and is intended to be suggestive rather than prescriptive. Any plan that's developed, however, probably should follow a problem-solution order.

Step 1: Defining the Problem.   After the leader makes introductory remarks stating the general purpose of the discussion and its importance, the group should consider the following questions:

1. How can the problem for discussion be phrased as a question?
2. What terms or concepts should be defined?

If the question has not been phrased before the discussion begins, group members should start by developing it. The question should be specific yet allow for a variety of approaches. For example, it's better to phrase your discussion question as "What should be done to control the escalating violence among American teenagers?" than to phrase it as "Should we control violence among teenagers?" Clearly, you are encouraging many viewpoints when you ask, "What should be done?" Phrasing the question to require a yes or no answer limits the discussion.

To make the discussion flow smoothly, you will need to define the key terms in the discussion question. If your group is considering violence among teenagers, you will probably need to define *violence*. Will you consider vandalism as well as murder to be violence? Are you discussing both misdemeanors and felonies? Should you narrow your discussion to focus on assault with deadly weapons? Another term that probably requires definition is *teenager*. Will you focus on high school students, or will you expand your discussion to include 19-year-olds? As you define your terms, you might discover that the discussion question becomes clearer or even changes. It is easier to conduct a discussion if every group member understands what is meant by each of the key terms in the discussion question.

Step 2: Analyzing the Problem.   This step involves evaluating the problem's scope and importance, discovering its causes, and setting up the basic requirements of an effective solution. The following questions are suggested for this step:

1. What evidence is there that a problem exists?
2. What are the causes of the problem?
3. What do we want a solution to accomplish?

First, your group must look closely at the problem to determine whether it is real. Many factors could account for what seems to be an escalation of violent crime among teenagers. More careful record keeping, an expanded definition of violent crime, or computer access to violent material could all account for a bulge in the statistics.

If your group determines that a problem does exist, then you must identify its causes. Through research and discussion, you might decide that social and economic factors contribute to the problem. The increasing instability of the family, greater access to dangerous weapons, financially strapped schools, and computerization of violent entertainment among the young may all be identified as causes.

At this point in the discussion, it is obvious that teenage violence has many roots. Your group will want to narrow the discussion by limiting the scope of the solution. It isn't feasible to control all of the factors contributing to the problem with one solution. You should decide how much of the problem to solve. For example, you might want to consider only solutions involving the school system, such as confiscation of handguns or stress on teaching moral principles. You might set up budget limitations or focus on one aspect of the problem, such as control of neighborhood gangs. Whatever your group decides, it should develop parameters for evaluating the solution.

Step 3: Suggesting Solutions. In Step 3, group members suggest a wide range of possible solutions and ask the following questions:

1. What are the various ways in which the problem could be solved?
2. What is the exact nature of each proposed solution? That is, what cost, actions, or changes does it entail?

At this stage, it is helpful to list all solutions, preferably on a chalkboard. Group members should volunteer ideas, withholding criticism or judgment until all the possibilities have been listed. Some suggestions might trigger alternatives or other creative proposals. Other suggestions might come from policies or plans proposed by politicians, civic leaders, or friends.

After the proposed solutions have been listed, the group considers each in turn. Members expand on each proposed solution, alter it, or investigate its ramifications. For example, bullet rationing might be suggested as a solution to teenage violence involving handguns. As this solution is considered, group members ask for development of the plan. How will bullets be rationed? How many bullets are now in circulation? How long will it take before bullet rationing makes handguns useless? Will the federal government control all bullet manufacturing? Can people manufacture their own bullets? Will some groups have unrestricted access to bullets? Will this create a black market in bullets? How will the armed services be treated? As you can see, there are a lot of questions to be answered about bullet rationing. The group proceeds through all the proposed solutions in this manner, asking questions and seeking full understanding of each proposal.

Step 4: Evaluating the Proposed Solutions. After your group has fully explored each solution, compare solutions and try to agree on a mutually satisfactory plan. Your group might consider the following questions:

1. What are the similarities and differences among the proposed solutions?
2. How well do the various solutions meet the criteria set up by the group?
3. Which solutions should be eliminated and which ones retained for further consideration?
4. Which solution or combination of solutions finally should be approved?

A group begins selecting its solution by finding the common elements among all of the suggested solutions. For example, your group might discover that each solution focuses on controlling violence through limiting access to handguns. In addition, you might realize that many of the solutions involve creating zones of safety for teenagers, such as schools or recreation centers. Finally, your group has called for stiffer penalties than teenagers currently receive for serious crimes such as murder.

Since cost is an important criterion for adopting a solution, your group can eliminate some solutions immediately. Training a national police force for patrolling schools is costly. As a result, your group will cross this idea off its list of realistic solutions. On the other hand, establishing a uniform code for sentencing teenagers is less expensive. It also meets your group's endorsement of stiffer penalties for teenage crime.

The group might choose its final solution from among the ones proposed by group members, or it might combine several ideas to form a desirable answer to teenage crime. For example, your group might decide to prohibit teenagers from possessing handguns, to install metal detectors in all high-crime areas frequented by teenagers, and to enforce stiffer penalties for crimes teenagers commit with handguns. This solution meets your group's criteria, and it uses the best features of several proposed solutions.

As soon as your group reaches an agreement, the leader sums up the principal features of the accepted plan. If your group has no authority to act, this statement normally concludes the discussion.

Step 5: Deciding How to Put the Solution into Operation. When a group has the power to puts its solution into operation, the following additional questions are pertinent:

1. What is necessary to put the plan into effect? Does it require an official law, an appropriation of money, the formation of a committee, or other action?
2. When and where should the solution go into effect?

In this step, your group will discuss the procedures for implementing its solution. Sometimes your group will meet with other groups to iron out the details of the plan. For example, if you plan to place metal detectors in schools, you will need to estimate costs. You might require contractors to submit bids for the project. You must also arrange to start training school personnel to operate the equipment. When these matters have been decided, your group has finished its task.

Presentations in Teams: Panels and Symposia

When a group is too large for an effective discussion or when its members are not well informed on the topic, a **panel** of individuals may be selected to discuss the topic for the benefit of others, who then become an audience. Members of a panel might be particularly well informed on the subject or might represent divergent views. For example, your group might be interested in UFOs (unidentified flying objects) and hold a discussion for your classmates. Or your group might tackle the problems of tenants and landlords. Whatever your topic, the audience should learn the basic issues from your discussion.

Another type of audience-oriented discussion is the **symposium.** In a symposium format, usually three to five speakers present short speeches on different facets of a subject or offer different solutions to a problem. This format is especially valuable when the speakers are recognized experts. The symposium is commonly used at large conferences and conventions. For example, if you attend a conference on education, you might learn from symposium speakers about careers for the next century or new technologies for teaching.

Various modifications of the panel and symposium formats are possible. Sometimes the two can be successfully combined. Frequently, the speeches of the symposium are followed by an informal exchange among the speakers. Then the meeting might be opened up for audience questions, comments, and reactions.

The essential characteristic of both the panel and symposium is that a few people discuss a subject or problem for the benefit of a large audience.

Preparing for Panels and Symposia When you are part of a panel or symposium team, it's important that you take others into account as you plan your remarks. The team approach involves several constraints that you don't face in other speaking situations. First, you have to fit your comments into a general theme. Suppose the theme of your panel is "Improving Health Care on Campus." This topic imposes certain substantial and stylistic limits on you. You'll be expected to talk about the current state of health care, requirements for good health care, personal responsibilities for improved health, and high-risk health practices.

Second, remember that you might be responsible for covering only a portion of a topic or theme. In most panels and symposia, speakers divide the topic into parts to avoid duplication. Doing so provides the audience with a variety of viewpoints. You might divide the responsibilities of a five-member panel as follows:

Speaker 1: The current status of health care on campus
Speaker 2: Standards for effective health care
Speaker 3: Changes needed in our campus health care system
Speaker 4: Changing high-risk health behaviors among students
Speaker 5: Paying for a campus health care system

Third, the more you know about the subject under discussion, the better. You should be ready to discuss many facets of the topic in addition to the part of

Panels and symposia combine the expertise and viewpoints of several speakers.

the discussion for which you are responsible. Analyze each aspect of the subject or implication of the problem you think may be discussed by following these four steps.

1. *Review the facts you already know.*   Go over the information you've acquired through previous reading or personal experience, and organize it in your mind. Prepare as if you were going to present a speech on every phase of the topic. You'll then be better qualified to discuss any part of it.

2. *Bring your knowledge up to date.*   Find out whether recent changes have affected the situation. Fit the newly acquired information into what you already know.

3. *Determine a tentative point of view on each of the important issues.*   Decide what your attitude will be. Is health care on campus currently adequate? What changes are necessary? How will changes affect most students? What responsibilities can students take for their own health? Stake out a tentative position on each issue that is likely to come before the group. Have the facts and reasons that support your view clearly in mind. Be ready to contribute to the group whenever it's most appropriate.

4. *Anticipate the effect of your ideas or proposals on the other members of the group or the organization.*   Will your proposal require people to change their personal habits? What are the economic repercussions of changes in the health care system? Some forethought may enable you to adjust to possible opposition. The more thoroughly you relate your facts to the subject and to listeners, the more effective your contributions to the discussion will be.

Participating in Panels and Symposia   Present your point of view clearly and succinctly. Participation in a panel or symposium should always be guided by one underlying aim: to help group members think objectively and creatively so that they can analyze the subject or solve the problem at hand. To this end, present and organize your contributions in a way that will best stimulate people to think for themselves.

Your delivery will, of course, vary according to the nature and purpose of the discussion and the degree of formality being observed. In general, however, speak in a direct, friendly, conversational style. As the discussion proceeds, differences of opinion may arise, tensions may increase, and some conflict may surface. You should be sensitive to the evolution of the discussion and adjust the way you voice your ideas and reactions. You might calm participants by using humor or by suggesting a compromise on a difficult issue, for example.

Clearly organized ideas are easiest to understand and should stimulate group members to think for themselves. Inquiry order or elimination order work well. Begin by stating the nature of the problem as you see it; next, outline the various hypotheses or solutions that occurred to you; then tell why you rejected certain solutions; finally, state your own opinion, and explain the reasons for it. In this way, you give other group members a chance to examine your thinking and to add other ideas. At the same time, you'll be making your contribution in the most objective and rational manner possible.

Remain sincere, open-minded, and objective. Above all, remember that a serious discussion is not a stage for prima donnas or an arena for settling personal problems. When you have something to say, say it modestly and sincerely. Always maintain an open, objective attitude. Accept criticism with dignity, and treat disagreement with an open mind. Your primary purpose is not to get your own view accepted but to work out the best group decision. The best result is a team effort.

Responding to Questions and Objections

Direct feedback from listeners is often a part of public group communication. In meetings, listeners are usually given a chance to ask questions. Panelists frequently direct questions to each other; professors ask students to clarify points made in classroom reports; club treasurers are often asked to justify particular expenditures; and spokespersons usually field questions about statements they've made.

Sometimes, questions require only a short response—a bit of factual material, a yes or no, or a reference to an authoritative source. But at other times, questions from listeners require more detailed responses. For example, some questions call for elaboration and explanation. After an oral report, you might be asked to elaborate on some statistical information you've presented. Other questions call for justification and defense. Politicians often must defend positions they've taken. In open hearings, school boards seeking to cut expenditures must justify their selection of school programs to be eliminated. University officials might be asked to defend specific campus policies. In these special cases, the response to questions and objections calls for a brief speech.

Techniques for Responding to Questions   Responses to questions that call for elaboration and explanation are, in many ways, equivalent to informative speeches. Think of your responses as short informative speeches in which you offer listeners ideas and information in response to their needs and interests. Consider the following points on how to turn your responses into effective informative speeches:

1. *Give a whole speech.* Your responses should include an introduction, a body, and a conclusion. Even though a response is an impromptu speech, you're still expected to structure ideas and to present information clearly. An elaborated remark might take the following form:
   a. *Introduction:* A rephrasing of the question to clarify it for the other audience members; an indication of why the question is a good one; a forecast of the steps you will take in answering it.
   b. *Body:* First point—often a brief historical review; second point—the information or explanation requested.
   c. *Conclusion:* A very brief summary (unless the answer was extraordinarily long); a direct reference to the questioner to see if further elaboration or explanation is required.

2. *Directly address the question as it has been asked.* Nothing is more frustrating to a questioner than an answer that misses the point or drifts from the query. Suppose that after you have advocated a pass-fail grading system for all colleges, you are asked how graduate schools can evaluate potential candidates for advanced degrees. The questioner is calling for information and an explanation. If your response is a tirade against the inequities of letter grades or the cowardice of professors who refuse to give failing grades, you probably won't satisfy the questioner. A better response would include all of the factors— letters of recommendation, standardized tests, number of advanced courses taken, and so on—that graduate schools can use to evaluate candidates. If you're unsure what the point of the question is, ask before you attempt an answer.

3. *Be succinct.* While you certainly don't want to give a terse yes or no in response to a question calling for detail, neither should you talk for eight minutes when two minutes will suffice. If you really think that a long, complex answer is needed, you can say, "To understand why we should institute a summer orientation program at this school, you should know more about recruitment, student fears, problems with placement testing, and so on. I can go into these topics if you'd like, but for now, in response to the particular question I was asked, I'd say that. . . ." In this way, you're able to offer a short answer, leaving other listeners an opportunity to ask additional questions.

4. *Be courteous.* During question periods, you might be amazed to hear a person ask a question that you answered during your talk. Or another person might ask for information so basic that you realize that your whole presentation was probably too complex. In these situations, it's easy to become flip or overly patronizing. Avoid those temptations. Don't embarrass a questioner by pointing out that you've already answered the question; don't insult your listeners. If you really think it would be a waste of the audience's time for you to review fundamental details, simply say that you're willing to answer questions after the meeting.

Techniques for Responding to Objections   A full response to an objection has two parts: (a) It answers the objection *(rebuttal),* and (b) it rebuilds the original ideas *(reestablishment).* Suppose that at an office meeting, you propose that your division institute a management-by-objectives system of employee evaluation. With this approach, supervisors and employees plan goals together. You contend that this approach increases productivity, gives employees a voice in determining their own futures, and makes company expectations more concrete. During a question period, someone objects, saying that the approach means more busywork, that supervisors aren't really interested in involving employees in work decisions, and that job frustration rather than job satisfaction is the more likely result.

Your rebuttal rests on effective arguments. You can cite the results of studies at other companies similar to your own (reasoning from parallel case). You say that those studies conclude that paperwork doesn't increase, that supervisors like having concrete commitments from employees on paper, and that employee satisfaction probably increases because job turnover rates usually go down (reasoning from sign). Following your rebuttal, you reestablish your original arguments by reporting on the results of interviews with selected employees in your own company. They think the system would be a good one.

Responding successfully to objections involves the following communication techniques:

1. *Be constructive as well as destructive when responding to objections.* Don't simply tear down the other person's counterarguments; constructively bolster your original statements as well. Reestablishment rationally shores up your position and, consequently, increases your credibility.

2. *Answer objections in an orderly fashion.* If several objections are raised by a single questioner, answer them one at a time. You might need to jot down the objections as they are stated. This approach lets you respond to each objection and helps listeners sort out the issues raised.

3. *Attack each objection in a systematic fashion.* Refutation usually proceeds in a series of four steps:

   a. State the claim that you seek to rebut: "Joe has said that a management-by-objectives system won't work because supervisors don't want input from their subordinates."
   b. State your objection to it: "I don't agree with Joe because I know of three studies done at businesses much like ours, and these studies support my position."
   c. Offer evidence for your rebuttal: "The first study that reinforces my point was done at the XYZ Insurance Company in 1991. This study was duplicated by subsequent studies at several other companies in 1993 and 1994."
   d. Indicate the significance of your rebuttal: "If our company is similar to the three I've mentioned—and I think it is—then I believe our supervisors will likewise appreciate specific commitments from their subordinates, quarter by quarter. I think we will have to agree that my position is most feasible."

4. *Keep the exchange on an intellectual level.* Counterarguments and rebuttals can degenerate into name-calling exchanges. Little is settled in verbal battles. Effective decision making is more likely to occur when the calm voice of reason dominates than when group members squabble.

Answering questions and responding to objections are vital parts of the group communication process because they allow us to interact directly with others. We are made accountable for what we say by questioners and counterarguers. Through verbal exchanges we can discover flaws in logic, insufficient evidence, prejudices, and unfeasible plans of action. By testing our ideas in the give-and-take of the public forum, we ultimately contribute to the group process and its sense of community.

ASSESSING YOUR PROGRESS

Chapter Summary

1. Special occasions often call for speeches that reflect community or group interests.
2. Speeches of introduction prepare an audience by arousing their curiosity and motivating listeners to respond positively to the speaker and the message.
3. Speeches of courtesy acknowledge the presence or qualities of special individuals or audiences such as welcoming visitors, responding to greetings, accepting awards, or offering toasts.
4. While challenging, speeches to entertain can range from merely funny to speeches that deflect audience antipathy to speeches that generate greater audience cohesion.
5. Group decision-making discussions usually seek agreement on a solution to a problem or a plan of action.
6. A plan for a decision-making group discussion should define the problem, analyze the problem, suggest solutions, evaluate the proposed solutions, and decide how to put the desired solution into operation.
7. Team presentations may take the form of panels or symposia. Panels consist of a group of individuals who discuss a topic for the benefit of listeners. In a symposium, three to five speakers present short speeches on a topic.
8. A response to a question is much like a short informative speech in which a speaker offers ideas and information to meet the needs and interests of questioners.
9. A response to an objection should answer the objection (rebuttal) and rebuild the original ideas (reestablishment).

Key Terms

community (p. 292)
community-based special
   occasion speeches (p. 292)
decision-making
   discussions (p. 299)
group discussion (p. 299)
group-based special
   occasion speeches (p. 292)

panel (p. 304)
special occasions (p. 292)
speeches of courtesy (p. 294)
speeches of introduction (p. 292)
speeches to entertain (p. 296)
symposium (p. 304)

Assessment Activities

1. Imagine that your class is the committee that invites outside speakers to campus. Develop a list of prominent individuals you would like to ask to campus to speak. Then assign each member of class to develop and present a speech of introduction for an individual from the list.
2. Review the qualities of speeches of courtesy. Develop an award for everyone in your class, and ask each person to accept their award with a speech.

3. Divide your class into small decision-making groups of three to six members. Follow the steps in developing a discussion plan and seeking a solution to a problem identified by the group. Ask each group to present its findings in either a panel or symposium.

Using the Web

1. Many collections of speeches can be located by using the Internet. Use this resource to discover speeches to entertain. What kinds of speeches did you find? What was the purpose of each speech? How did the speaker use humor to achieve the purpose?
2. Find the latest presidential press conference by using the Internet. Examine the questions and responses. Identify the techniques for responding to questions or objections. How effectively did the speaker use techniques for responding to questions or objections to address members of the press? Can you think of ways to improve the responses?

Using VideoWorkshop

Review Module 3, "Audiences," as you think about adapting your special occasion speech to your listeners.

As you prepare for decision-making group discussion, review Module 5, "Research," to investigate problems and discover solutions.

References

1. Henry W. Grady, "The New South," *American Public Addresses: 1740–1952,* edited by A. Craig Baird (New York: McGraw-Hill, 1956), 181–185.

2. Based in part on material taken from *Friendly Speeches* (Cleveland: National Reference Library, n.d.) and on material developed for earlier editions of this book.

3. See John Dewey, "Analysis of Reflective Thinking," *How We Think* (Boston: D. C. Heath, 1993), Chapter 7.

Index

Credits

TEXT—60: Excerpt from "Strength through Cultural Diversity" by Henri Mann Morton from *Native American Reader: Stories, Speeches and Poems.* Copyright © 1989. Reprinted by permission of The Denali Press; 63: Excerpt from speech at the Republican National Convention by Mary Fisher. Copyright © 1996 by Mary Fisher. Reprinted by permission of Mary Fisher, Clinical AIDS Research and Education (CARE) Fund at the University of Alabama/Birmingham; 93: Excerpt from Esther Grassian, "Thinking Critically about World Wide Web Resources." From http://www.library.ucla.edu. Reprinted by permission of Esther Grassian, UCLA College Library; 103: Excerpt from speech at the Republican National Convention by Mary Fisher. Copyright © 1996 by Mary Fisher. Reprinted by permission of Mary Fisher, Clinical AIDS Research and Education (CARE) Fund at the University of Alabama/Birmingham; 140: Excerpt from Nicholas Fynn, "The Free Burn Fallacy," *Winning Orations* 1989. Reprinted with permission of the Interstate Oratorical Association, *Winning Orations,* Larry Schnoor, Editor; 143: Excerpt from "Have You Checked Lately?" by Deanna Sellnow from *Winning Orations.* Reprinted with permission of the Interstate Oratorical Association, *Winning Orations,* Larry Schnoor, Editor; 147: Excerpt from "The Flood Gates of the Mind" by Michael Twitchell from *Winning Orations.* Reprinted with permission of the Interstate Oratorical Association, *Winning Orations,* Larry Schnoor, Editor; 159: Excerpt from Daniel Pedersen, Vern E. Smith, and Jerry Adler, "Sprawling, Sprawling," 23–27. From *Newsweek,* 19 July 1999. Copyright 1999 Newsweek, Inc. All rights reserved. Reprinted by permission; 168: Excerpt from "The Strangler" by Charles Schaillol from *Winning Orations.* Reprinted with permission of the Interstate Oratorical Association, *Winning Orations,* Larry Schnoor, Editor; 169: Reprinted by arrangement with the Estate of Martin Luther King Jr., c/o Writers House as agent for the proprietor New York, NY. Copyright 1961 Dr. Martin Luther King Jr., copyright renewed 1989 Coretta Scott King; 170: William Faulkner's speech on accepting the Nobel Prize for Literature, December 10, 1950. Copyright The Nobel Foundation; 186: Figure from *The Hidden Dimension* by Edward T. Hall, copyright 1966, 1982 by Edward T. Hall. Used by permission of Doubleday, a division of Random House, Inc; 206: Adaptation of "Line Graphs" from Smith Travel Research, as reported in *USA Today,* October 27, 1995, B1. Copyright © 1995, *USA Today.* Reprinted with permission; 206: Pie Graph taken from *USA Today,* August 1, 2002, A1. Copyright © 2002, *USA Today.* Reprinted with permission; 207: Pictograph taken from *USA Today,* August 1, 2002, C1. Copyright © 2002, *USA Today.* Reprinted with permission; 235: From Joyce Chapman, In Roselyn Schiff, et al., "The Geisha," in *Communication Strategy: A Guide to Speech Preparation.* Published by Allyn & Bacon, Boston, MA. Copyright © 1982 Pearson Education. Reprinted by permission of the publisher; 257: Excerpt from Todd Ames, "The Silent Killer," *Winning Orations.* Reprinted with permission of the Interstate Oratorical Association, *Winning Orations,* Larry Schnoor, Editor.

PHOTOS—xx: Bob Daemmrich/Bob Daemmrich Photography, Inc.; 3: AP/Wide World Photos; 5: CORBIS; 8: Sonda Dawes/The Image Works; 11: AP/Wide World Photos; 16: Steve Rubin/The Image Works; 21: Robert Ullmann; 28: Getty Images Inc.—Stone Allstock; 34: Jeff Greenberg/PhotoEdit; 37: EyeWire Collection/Getty Images/EyeWire, Inc.; 41: Culver Pictures, Inc.; 48: Jeff Greenberg/PhotoEdit; 51: Roger Dollarhide; 56: Mark Richards/PhotoEdit; 59: Bruce Ayres/Getty Images Inc.—Stone Allstock; 71: Stephen Ferry/Getty Images, Inc.—Liaison; 77: CORBIS; 79: Bob Daemmrich/Bob Daemmrich Photography, Inc.; 90: Bob Daemmrich/Bob Daemmrich Photography, Inc.; 95: Michael Keller/CORBIS; 105: Getty Images Inc.—Stone Allstock; 114: Olympia/PhotoEdit; 124: Dunwell Photography, Steve/Getty Images Inc.—Image Bank; 132: CORBIS; 148: Carol Halebian/Getty Images, Inc.—Liaison; 154: Bob Daemmrich/Bob Daemmrich Photography, Inc.; 156: Starr/Stock Boston; 166: Getty Images Inc.—Stone Allstock; 168: Mark A. Johnson/CORBIS; 174: Michael Newman/PhotoEdit; 187: Rhoda Sidney/Stock Boston; 188: Kathy Ferguson/PhotoEdit; 189: Mark Richards/PhotoEdit; 196: Carl J. Single/The Image Works; 200: Roller Blade, Inc; 213: Jon Feingersh/CORBIS; 218: Steve Rubin/The Image Works; 221: Jeff Greenberg/The Image Works; 227: Paul Conklin/PhotoEdit; 240: Getty Images Inc.—Stone Allstock; 244: Robert Brenner/PhotoEdit; 247: Cleve Bryant/PhotoEdit; 252: Levi Strauss & Co.; 268: AP/Wide World Photos; 270: P. F. Gero/Corbis/Sygma; 276: Andrew Yates PR/Getty Images Inc.—Image Bank; 290: David Young-Wolff/PhotoEdit; 305: CORBIS.